Financial Governance in East Asia

The focus of international financial reform in recent years has largely been on a global level, in terms of improving the international financial architecture, and on a national level, in terms of getting domestic economic and structural policies right. But there is also a growing appetite for addressing issues on a regional level. In East Asia, for example, governments have sought deeper regional policy dialogue with the creation of the ASEAN+3 forum and enhanced financial cooperation by setting up the Chiang Mai Initiative. In order to maintain strong and effective regional institutions, *Financial Governance in East Asia* argues, regional policy dialogue and surveillance processes will have to be improved. In addition, further development of regional mechanisms is needed to provide financial support to prevent and resolve financial crises.

These developments raise many questions including:

- What is 'best-practice' regional policy dialogue?
- How is a regional financial architecture complementary to the global architecture?
- What sorts of institutions work well at a regional level?
- Do regions need a regional monetary fund?
- What is going on in East Asia and how is it different to other regions?

By outlining the importance of a well designed regional architecture alongside global mechanisms and sound domestic policies, the contributors argue that although there is no single track to reduce the risks of financial crises, there is certainly a place for regional institutions and cooperation. This book will interest all those concerned with the financial future of East Asia whether from an Asian Studies, economics, international relations or business studies background.

Gordon de Brouwer is Professor of Economics in the Asia Pacific School of Economics and Government at the Australian National University.

Yunjong Wang is Senior Research Fellow and Director of Center for Regional Economic Studies at the Korea Institute for International Economic Policy.

Routledge Studies in the Growth Economies of Asia

Financial Governance in East Asia

Policy dialogue, surveillance and cooperation

**Edited by Gordon de Brouwer
and Yunjong Wang**

LONDON AND NEW YORK

First published 2004 by RoutledgeCurzon

Published 2013 by Routledge
2 Park Square, Milton Park, Abingdon, Oxon, OX14 4RN

Simultaneously published in the USA and Canada by
Roudedge
711 Third Ave, New York NY 10017

Routledge is an imprint of the Taylor & Francis Group, an informa business

Typeset in Garamond by Australia-Japan Research Centre, Canberra, Australia

British Library Cataloguing in Publication Data
A catalogue record for this book is available from the British Library

Library of Congress Cataloging in Publication Data
Financial governance in East Asia: policy dialogue, surveillance and
cooperation *I* edited by Gordon de Brouwer and Yunjong Wang.
    p.cm. -(RoudedgeCurzon studies in the growth economies of Asia) Includes
    bibliographical references and index.
        1. Financial Institutions--East Asia. 2. Financial institutions--East
Asia-Management. 3. Financial Institutions--East Asia-State supervision.
4. Corporate governance-East Asia. 5. Finance-East Asia. 6. Financial crises--East Asia.
I. De Brouwer, Gordon. II. Wang, Yun-jong. III. Series

HG187.E37F549 2004
332.1'5'095-dc22   2003016220

ISBN 978-0-415-32282-9 (hbk)

Contents

Figures

Tables and boxes

Contributors

Gordon de Brouwer is Professor of Economics in the Asia Pacific School of Economics and Government and Executive Director of the Australia–Japan Research Centre, at the Australian National University. <gordon.debrouwer@anu.edu.au>

Menzie D. Chinn is Professor of Economics in the Economics Department at The University of California Santa Cruz and Research Associate of the National Bureau of Economic Research. <chinn@ucsc.edu>

Ian Dickson is an analyst at the Department of Treasury in Australia. <idickson@treasury.gov.au>

Prasanna Gai is a Fellow in the Economics Division of the Research School of Pacific and Asian Studies at The Australian National University. <prasanna.gai@anu.edu.au>

Phil Garton is the Specialist Adviser in the International Economy Division of the Department of the Treasury, Australia. <pgarton@treasury.gov.au>

Stephen Grenville is Adjunct Professor of the Asia Pacific School of Economics and Government at the Australian National University, formerly Deputy Governor at the Reserve bank of Australia. <stephen.grenville@anu.edu.au>

C. Randall Henning is Associate Professor of the School of International Service at The American University and Visiting Fellow at The Institute for International Economics in Washington D.C. <henning@iie.com>.

Takatoshi Ito is Professor at the Research Centre for Advanced Science and Technology and Faculty of Economics at The University of Tokyo. <tito@rcast.u-tokyo.ac.jp>

Masahiro Kawai is President of the Policy Research Institute in the Ministry of Finance, Japan. <masahiro.kawai@mof.go.jp>

Andrew Kilpatrick is Head of Country Economics and Policy at Her Majesty's Treasury in London. <andrew.kilpatrick@htm-treasury.gsi.gov.uk>

Haruhiko Kuroda is Special Advisor to the Cabinet, Official Residence of the Prime Minister, Japan. <hkuroda@kantei.go.jp>

Koji Narita is Deputy Director of the General Coordination Division of the Planning and Coordination Bureau in The Financial Services Agency, Japan. <k-narita@fsa.go.jp>

Martin Parkinson is Executive Director of the Macroeconomics Group in the Department of the Treasury, Australia. <mparkinson@treasury.gov.au>

Ramkishen S. Rajan is Senior Lecturer in the School of Economics at The University of Adelaide, and Visiting Researcher at the Institute of Southeast Asian Studies, Singapore. <ramkishen.rajan@adealaide.edu.au>

Yunjong Wang is Senior Research Fellow in the Department of International Macroeconomics and Finance at the Korea Institute for International Economic Policy. <yjwng@kiep.go.kr>

Shinichi Yoshikuni is Chief Representative for the Hong Kong and Pacific Office of the Bank for International Settlements. <shinichi.yoshikuni@bis.com>

Preface

The papers from this volume are the product of a three-year cooperative policy research program on Future Financial Arrangements to Support Development in East Asia. The aim of the program of research is to bring senior policymakers, academics and business people from East Asia together in an informal setting to think creatively about ways to improve financial arrangements in the region. The research has focused on policy dialogue and surveillance, deepening financial cooperation in East Asia, and analysis of the scope for possible common currency arrangements in the region. The papers in this volume are inputs into that process.

The research program is currently chaired by Peter Drysdale and Gordon de Brouwer (Australia–Japan Research Centre, Asia Pacific School of Economics and Government, Australian National University), Masahiro Kawai (Ministry of Finance, Japan, and University of Tokyo) and Eiji Ogawa (Hitotsubashi University). Professor Takatoshi Ito (University of Tokyo) was actively involved at the start of the program.

The papers in this volume were presented at a series of policy research workshops organised jointly by the Australia National University and other institutions in East Asia. These include joint policy research workshops with the Australian Treasury in Canberra in November 2001, the China Center for Economic Research (CCER) at Peking University in Beijing in March 2002, and the Korea Institute for International Economic Policy (KIEP) in Seoul in November 2002.

The success of this work, evident in the quality of the papers published in this volume, has been due to the strong support of many institutions and individuals. First and foremost, we would like to thank the primary funding agencies, the Ministry of Finance (Japan), AusAID and Axiss Australia, for providing sustainable funding and valuable intellectual input and support. We would also like to thank the Australian Treasury, CCER, and KIEP for their strong support and excellent assistance in co-hosting the research policy workshops with the ANU.

Many people have provided support, input and encouragement in putting these papers together. For fear of missing out on someone, we would like to thank these people collectively and in general. But two people stand out for their extraordinary contribution in making this volume possible. We are especially grateful to Mr Haruhiku Kuroda and Professor Peter Drysdale for their deep foresight and leadership in developing the Project.

We would also like to thank the people who helped put the papers together in an accessible volume. In particular, we thank Sue Mathews, Marilyn Popp and Minni Reis for their hard work and great effort. We are also grateful to RoutledgeCurzon for excellent editorial guidance and support. All shortcomings remain ours alone.

Gordon de Brouwer and Yunjong Wang
Canberra and Seoul
June 2003

Abbreviations

AAB	Asian Arrangements to Borrow
AAD	Arab accounting dinar
ACC	Asian Consultative Council (of the BIS)
ACU	Asian currency unit
ADB	Asian Development Bank
AFMM	ASEAN finance ministers meeting
AFTA	ASEAN free trade arrangement
ALADI	Latin American Integration Association [Asociación Latinoamericana de Integración]
AMF	Asian Monetary Fund
APEC	Asia Pacific Economic Cooperation
ARIC	Asia Recovery Information Center ASA
ASA	ASEAN Swap Arrangement
ASEAN	Association of Southeast Asian Nations
ASEAN+3	ASEAN plus China, Japan and South Korea
ASCU	ASEAN Surveillance Coordinating Unit
ASEM	Asia-Europe Meeting
ASP	ASEAN Surveillance Process
BCBS	Basel Committee on Banking Supervision
BIS	Bank for International Settlements
BEPGs	Broad economic policy guidelines
BOJ	Bank of Japan
BSA	bilateral swap arrangement
CCL	contingent credit line
CFA	cooperative financing arrangement
CGFS	Committee on the Global Financial System
CLM	community loan mechanism
CMI	Chiang Mai Initiative
CPSS	Committee on Payment and Settlement Systems
EAEG	East Asian Economic Grouping
EAVG	East Asian Vision Group
EC	European Community
ECB	European Central Bank

ECOFIN	European Economics and Finance Ministers Council
ECSC	European Coal and Steel Community
ECU	European currency unit
EDP	excessive deficits procedure
EDRC	Economic and Development Review Committee
EEC	European Economic Community
EFC	Economic and Financial Committee
EFTA	European Free Trade Association
EMCF	European Monetary Cooperation Fund
EMEAP	Executives Meeting of East Asia and Pacific (Central Banks)
EMS	European Monetary System
EMU	economic and monetary union
EMUA	European monetary unit of account
EPA	economic partnership arrangement
EPC	Economic Policy Committee
EPU	European Payments Union
ERI	exchange rate index
ERM	exchange rate mechanism
ERPD	Economic Review and Policy Dialogue
EU	European Union
EUA	European unit of account
FDI	foreign direct investment
FLAR	Latin American Reserve Fund [Fondo Latinoamericano de Reservas]
FLOD	first line of defence
FRMS	Framework for Regional Monetary Stability
FSAP	Financial Sector Assessment Program
FSF	Financial Stability Forum
FTA	free trade agreement
G-7 etc.	Group of Seven etc.
GAB	General Arrangements to Borrow
GCC	Gulf Cooperation Council
GDP	gross domestic product
IAIS	International Association of Insurance Supervisors
IAPM	international arbitrage pricing model
IASC	International Accounting Standards Committee
ICAPM	international capital asset pricing model
IFC	International Finance Corporation
IMF	International Monetary Fund
IMFC	International Monetary and Financial Committee
IOSCO	International Organization of Securities Commissions
KIEP	Korean Institute for International Economic Policy
LIBOR	London interbank offered rate
LTCM	long-term capital management

MERCOSUR	Mercado Común del Sur
MFG	Manila Framework Group
MPC	Monetary Policy Committee
MTFA	medium-term financial assistance
MTFS	medium-term financial support
NAB	New Arrangements to Borrow
NAFTA	North American Free Trade Agreement
NATO	North Atlantic Treaty Organization
NBSA	network of bilateral swap arrangements
OECD	Organisation for Economic Co-operation and Development
OEEC	Organization for European Economic Cooperation
PAFTA	Pan-Arab Free Trade Agreement
PAFTAD	Pacific Trade and Development Conference
PBEC	Pacific Basin Economic Council
PECC	Pacific Economic Cooperation Conference
PPP	purchasing power parity
PSI	private sector involvement
RBA	Reserve Bank of Australia
REMS	regional economic monitoring and surveillance
REMU	Regional Economic Monitoring Unit
RFA	Regional Financing Arrangement
RMFC	regional monetary and financial cooperation
ROSCs	Reports on the Observance of Standards and Codes
RTA	regional trade agreement
SCP	stability or convergence program
SDDS	Special Data Dissemination Standards
SDR	Special Drawing Right
SDRM	sovereign debt restructuring mechanism
SEACEN	South East Asian Central Banks
SEANZA	South East Asia New Zealand Australia (Central Banks)
SCP	stability or convergence program
SGP	Stability and Growth Pact
SLOD	second line of defence
SRF	Supplemental Reserve Facility
STMF	short-term monetary support facility
STMS	short-term monetary support
UIP	uncovered interest parity
UK	United Kingdom
UN	United Nations
US	United States
VSTF	very short-term financing
WP-3	Working Group 3 (of the OECD)
WTO	World Trade Organization

1 Policy dialogue, surveillance and financial cooperation in East Asia

Gordon de Brouwer and Yunjong Wang

East Asia has a growing desire to strengthen its regional identity and forge effective and robust regional frameworks and institutions. This is the outcome of three main forces. One is the financial crises of 1997 and 1998, which revealed internal structural instabilities in some countries and the risk of relying too heavily on the uncertain goodwill of outsiders, notably the United States and the International Monetary Fund (IMF). Another is the internal economic and growth dynamic of East Asia, where intra-regional trade and investment and economic interdependence are rising. The third is the economic development and increasing openness of China, which represents an unprecedented opportunity to engage constructively and inclusively with a country that may be the world's next economic superpower.

Satisfying this desire is not an easy task. It requires change and commitment. If it is done on the cheap, the result will be insubstantial. Strong and effective financial governance is essential if strong and effective regional institutions are to be built. At this point in time, policy dialogue, surveillance and financial cooperation lie at the core of financial governance in East Asia.

The three elements are separate, but they build on each other. Policy dialogue refers to the framework by which policymakers from different countries come together to discuss issues. Surveillance is one set of issues by which policymakers not only share information and views on the events and problems of the day, but also can seek collegial advice, insights and support in dealing with domestic and international policy issues. Financial cooperation relates to the mechanisms by which countries can provide financial support to each other, regionally or globally, in the event of financial crisis. Financial cooperation is effective only if it is built on a solid foundation of policy dialogue and surveillance.

This volume brings together a range of expert views and assessments about the state of financial governance in East Asia and how this structure can be deepened and strengthened. We have grouped these views into four sets. The first presents some East Asian perspectives on the nature of policy dialogue and surveillance in the region. The second draws on the insights of other countries and regions in policy dialogue and surveillance. The third looks at prospects for deeper financial cooperation in East Asia. The final set outlines a range of views on unilateral, regional and multilateral approaches to crisis prevention, minimisation and resolution.

POLICY DIALOGUE AND SURVEILLANCE IN EAST ASIA

The next two chapters in this volume examine a range of issues concerning official policy dialogue and surveillance on macroeconomic and financial issues in East Asia.

In 'Policy dialogue in East Asia: principles for success', Stephen Grenville looks at what East Asia can expect to gain from regional policy dialogue and how it can go about realising these gains. Much of the talk on improving policy dialogue in East Asia focuses on the gains from policy coordination. While not disparaging this, Grenville believes that one of the primary gains from regional policy dialogue is in fact the coalescing of common interests and views in the region and projecting these in global rules setting.

Grenville argues that there are three elements to this. First, behaviour within nation states is fairly highly regulated, even in market-based economies, but international cross-border activity is not. East Asia may be able to help fill in these regulatory gaps. Second, cross-border rules are set by other regional country groupings, notably Europe and the United States, with their interests in mind. East Asia should be a part of the rules setting process to ensure that its interests are protected and projected. Third, East Asia is poorly represented in many global institutions, and regional groupings may be a mechanism to address this 'democratic deficit'. Altogether, Grenville views regional and global policy dialogue and surveillance as complements.

Grenville sets out some desirable characteristics for regional groupings. The region should be comfortable with some overlap in policy groupings because it draws in different interested parties and helps build consensus. Groupings should be based on countries with common interests. If they are set up for the purpose of promoting frank conversations between policymakers, the number of participants is better kept to a manageable size. They also need the support of experts and a well-functioning physical secretariat to provide intellectual and logistical support. As a model, Grenville prefers the Bank for International Settlements over the IMF. He thinks that in the region the Manila Framework Group (MFG) and ASEAN+3 have the most potential as tools for effective surveillance, macroeconomic policy discussion, crisis management and reserves pooling, technical cooperation, and projecting the region's interests globally.

In Chapter 3, 'IMF and ADB perspectives on regional surveillance in East Asia', Gordon de Brouwer draws together views on regional surveillance expressed by IMF and Asian Development Bank (ADB) officials. Both the IMF and the ADB take surveillance seriously and have increased resources allocated to supporting it. Both institutions are deeply engaged in East Asian surveillance processes and have particular views on, and interests in, these processes. But they differ in aspects of emphasis.

The IMF lives and breathes surveillance. As economies have become more complex and interdependent, the need to understand the links and limit the vulnerabilities that they create has become paramount. The IMF is actively involved in surveillance in many ways, and has sought to improve and expand surveillance over time. It puts primary emphasis on global surveillance mechanisms and, within the context of regional processes, on ensuring that the insights from experiences of all countries, including those from outside the region, are brought to help inform the regional debate. With respect to East Asia, the IMF sees a range of particular challenges in improving surveillance, including clearly defining the goals, focus and structure of regional surveillance, ensuring that global links are not weakened, and using the regional process to meet the region's own needs (rather than imitate the European process).

The ADB is more of a newcomer to surveillance and has set up an infrastructure to support regional surveillance, especially for the ASEAN and ASEAN+3 processes. It is more overtly committed to the notion of a regional financial architecture, including cooperative regional financing and exchange rate arrangements, in which it would like to have a core function. The ADB puts the emphasis on regional surveillance as a device to garner better ownership of policy dialogue and reform, and to balance global and outside assessments with well-articulated and sound regional views and assessments.

The IMF and ADB share common ground in terms of their commitment to robust and effective surveillance mechanisms, although they differ in their enthusiasm for regional processes. Both institutions have particular strengths: the IMF's is its unrivalled experience and frankness in policy analysis and surveillance; the ADB's is its strong on-the-ground presence in East Asia. But they also have weaknesses. The IMF is seen as too aloof from the region. It is seen as not active enough in East Asia, not particularly interested in regional institution building, and sometimes too arrogant in its manner. The ADB is seen as too adventurous. It is pushing the boundaries of its role as a regional development bank into a role of regional monetary fund, potentially diverting resources from its core function of supporting development in the whole Asia Pacific region. As a development bank, its policy remit does not cover the region's industrialised economies. And it is inadequately staffed for the job. This creates challenges for the two institutions themselves and for regional policymakers in how they might use them.

INSIGHTS FROM OTHERS' EXPERIENCE WITH POLICY DIALOGUE AND SURVEILLANCE

The search for viable mechanisms for policy dialogue, surveillance and financial cooperation are, of course, not isolated to East Asia. Many countries in other regions have been, and still are, grappling with the same sorts of issues and problems. The next three chapters in this volume draw on the experience of other countries and regions in setting up surveillance processes and structures to support regional economic and financial cooperation.

In Chapter 4, 'Structures to support stability and growth: some observations based on UK experience', Andrew Kilpatrick draws on insights from the UK Treasury to discuss how the United Kingdom has used the regional policy dialogue and surveillance processes of the European Union in the post-war period to support the domestic economy. He makes two basic points.

The first is that the only way to secure domestic economic stability and growth is to get the country's basic macroeconomic framework right. This means having flexible, transparent and market-based economic systems, supported by responsible and robust monetary, fiscal and financial frameworks. This is all the more important in the contemporary globalised domestic economy, where external shocks are relatively frequent, large, and quickly transmitted. Countries are responsible for themselves; the burden of making good policy lies at home.

Kilpatrick also sees a clear and important role for regional policy dialogue and surveillance in this process. Embedded in regional institutions for policy dialogue, rigorous multilateral surveillance can support domestic policymaking, and hence domestic stability and growth, by providing mechanisms for frank and useful discussion of economic issues and problems in a constructive and supportive environment, and by creating peer pressure for policymakers in less well-performing countries to pursue corrective stabilising policies.

Developing the sort of policy dialogue infrastructure that promotes effective surveillance is not an easy task. In the first place, it takes a lot of time. Kilpatrick highlights the many steps involved in creating, running and maintaining institutions for regional policy dialogue in Europe. The process started with cooperation in simple areas of common interest and progressed unevenly. On occasion, the steps were big, led by politicians with a vision for a united integrated Europe. At times, they were small, just holding ground or under enormous internal pressure (such as in 1992 when the European exchange rate mechanism fell apart); in these cases, the sheer inertia of the bureaucratic and institutional process helped keep regional cooperation going.

Policy dialogue in Europe proceeded on the basis of functional cooperation: from its genesis in the European Coal and Steel Community to the focus on regional monetary cooperation to reduce financial uncertainty. It is still present in the current structure of European policy dialogue, with special dialogue forums for pressing European macroeconomic issues, like the budgetary surveillance program built into the Stability and Growth Pact to deal with Europe's chronic tendency to fiscal deficits, the policy dialogue program built into the Employment Guidelines to deal with Europe's relatively inflexible labour markets, and the Cardiff process for economic reform to engineer a regional mechanism and constituency for domestic structural reform. The implication for East Asia of the success of functional policy dialogue in Europe is clear: institutions for policy dialogue should be created, and they should focus on the economic issues that are important to East Asia.

The next chapter, 'The complex political economy of cooperation and integration', draws on some insights from European experience more generally.

Randy Henning uses the various models that political economists have used to explain European institution building to explain past and likely future cooperation and integration in East Asia. He critically assesses a range of theories of integration, including the role of the market and institutions in driving integration, cooperation in one area 'spilling over' to other areas, converging national political interests, and the pattern of global influence and control.

Henning reckons that East Asian integration looks relatively deep in terms of market interaction but is superficial in terms of institutions, particularly because these have been dominated by East Asian countries' bilateral relationships with the United States. As East Asia moves into more regionally oriented trade and investment integration, it is likely that this will spill over into deeper financial and monetary cooperation. National political interests are still very diverse in the region, but the financial crisis and the imperative of stable development in China and its integration into the world economy may be changing this.

Stability or otherwise in the global system – and particularly economic and political stability in the United States – can be a key driver of forces towards regional integration. Henning argues that, contrary to perceptions, a desire for political integration was not the primary driving force of economic integration in Europe. Systemic shocks, especially from the United States (including the collapse of Bretton Woods), were critical in the formation of a European currency union. It took repeated shocks over several decades to get Europe to focus on monetary integration at the regional level.

There was nothing inevitable in this. The integration of markets in goods and services and in capital and labour were important in constructing a foundation for monetary integration to take place. But it was how this basis was used, and how political support was garnered in response to global instability, that ultimately created a consensus for monetary union. Indeed, the consensus about conditions for entry and which countries would enter monetary union were only made at the last moment. For East Asia, the prospects for deeper monetary integration depend on two factors. The first is that the endogenous preconditions for integration – namely, that the region be deeply economically integrated by trade and investment – need to be sufficiently in place. The second is that global conditions are such that monetary integration is a feasible (and the 'right') response to systemic instability and imbalance.

In Chapter 6, 'A stocktake of institutions for regional cooperation', Takatoshi Ito and Koji Narita focus on possible frameworks to implement financial cooperation. These include surveillance, crisis financing, and monetary integration. To put discussion into perspective, they start with a look at multilateral organisations and forums and at how particular regions elsewhere in the world have approached regional cooperation. They provide substantial detail about European, Arab and Latin American policy dialogue and cooperation. They highlight that Europe has been the most successful of these regions. But even there, progress in regional financial and monetary cooperation has been far from smooth and elements of cooperation have been subject occasionally to stress and collapse. Success has in large part been due to persistence by key parties involved.

Ito and Narita argue that deep integration in East Asia will require effective surveillance mechanisms as a first step. They reckon that one of the most successful surveillance processes is that of the Working Group 3 subgroup of the OECD's Economic Policy Committee, which holds a one-day private meeting four times a year attended by deputies from largely G-10 finance ministries and central banks. Discussions are chaired by the IMF, are detailed and frank, and cover key macroeconomic issues in industrialised and emerging market economies. The region would do well to try to emulate its success. Ito and Narita critically discuss experience with the MFG, APEC finance ministers meetings, ASEAN finance ministers meetings, ASEAN+3 finance ministers meetings and the Executives Meeting of East Asia and Pacific Central Banks (EMEAP). While the region has made some progress with surveillance, it can make further improvements.

Ito and Narita also look at financial cooperation processes. A similar story emerges with respect to financial cooperation. Europe again stands out as a region that has cooperated in an effective manner to manage systemic risks. East Asia has made some progress with the Chiang Mai Initiative (CMI) but it is only a first step forward.

The five chapters on policy dialogue and surveillance discussed above cover a lot of ground. The main follow-up issue that emerged in discussions on these papers was balancing the value of insights from Europe's experience with integration with the danger of seeing its path as the only one or 'the right one' for East Asia. Discussion focused on three elements of Europe's experience.

The first element is that integration in Europe has been supported by a long history of dialogue over a wide-ranging set of policy issues in a wide-ranging set of institutions. These policy issues have changed over time in response to the vicissitudes and problems of the day. The issues have ranged from the collapse of the gold standard, managing post-World War I reparations, post-World War II reconstruction, payments imbalances, different economic cycles, movement of capital, exchange rates, structural imbalances and rigidities, and financial market supervision. The institutions used as the vehicles for discussion have existed at political and bureaucratic levels, ranging from the Council of Economic and Finance Ministers and their myriad committees to the BIS and the European Commission. Maintaining strong bilateral relations have remained important in this process.

This system of institutions and meetings was flexible enough to bring new issues to the table and was robust enough to provide an apparatus to maintain dialogue and contact even when there had been political setbacks and major economic and financial disturbances. There was nothing automatic or necessary about the system's capacity to deliver this. Most crucially, it depended on policymakers being able to trust and respect each other and develop constructive working relationships. This could happen because key senior people were committed to a process of engagement and openness and the structures allowed the same people to stay in regular contact with each other over long periods in the formative years of European institution building.

Looking at the implications for East Asia, there was uniformity in discussions on policy dialogue that the region needs stronger frameworks and institutions for surveillance. There is wariness about the excessive legalism and formalism that seem characteristic of European integration, but there is a general view that regional policy dialogue needs a stronger institutional underpinning, such as a secretariat to provide logistical support and think-tanks to provide ideas and technocratic support. Sending the same senior people to meetings, having a regular, independent and authoritative chair, and using specialists to provide background material, could be useful in improving surveillance in East Asia. The rotation system that is characteristic of many East Asian bureaucracies – by which staff change positions every two years and have strong policy-process skills but weak specialist knowledge and connections – is a constraint on policymakers developing expertise and professional relationships with their counterparts.

The main challenge in strengthening dialogue and surveillance in East Asia is securing political commitment to engage in frank discussion about domestic policy issues and problems. This is more of a problem in some countries than in others. Some countries appear to be inclined to see discussion on economic and financial issues as a challenge to the domestic policymaking authorities and a form of interference in internal affairs. But hectoring and invasiveness are certainly not the intention of those in the region who advocate more substantive surveillance, as the papers in this volume show. As policymakers build up a set of constructive experiences with experiments in surveillance, East Asian policy dialogue and cooperation will, hopefully, develop and mature. Without widespread political commitment, regional surveillance and policy dialogue in East Asia will lack substance.

The second element discussed in relation to the European experience was that monetary integration in Europe was substantially influenced by that region's relationship with the United States. This was not just a reaction to the collapse of Bretton Woods and Europe's various experiences in dealing with external shocks in an environment of open capital markets, although events such as these had a profound impact since the common market had been predicated on the fixed exchange system underpinned by Bretton Woods and capital controls. It was also an attempt to give Europe a bigger voice in world affairs to advance its interests and balance those of the United States. There are loud echoes of this in post-crisis East Asia.

For East Asia, the rise of regionalism poses new challenges. East Asian regionalism is partly based on dissatisfaction with economic and financial instability in the world's major economies, especially due to big movements of the US dollar against the yen and euro. And it is partly based on deep dissatisfaction with how the United States responded to the crisis and exercised its power. Europe responded to these sorts of issues by looking inwards, constructing external trade barriers and expensive schemes to protect segments of its economy and constraining the product and input markets, especially labour markets. This reduced the welfare gains to Europeans and outsiders. East Asia is in a position to respond more constructively than Europe. East Asia's interests are fundamentally global; a retreat to 'fortress Asia' would weaken economic growth, development, stability and welfare.

Europe also had the advantage of a clear economic leader in monetary management, Germany. East Asia does not. Japan is the region's biggest economy, but weak growth, deflation and a dysfunctional financial system also make it one of the region's more vulnerable economies. This means that the costs in achieving consensus about policy aims and frameworks are likely to be higher in Asia than Europe.

There is a desire to create an East Asian Community as a strong statement of the region's identity and a framework to project its interests. But what is East Asian? Is it just ASEAN+3? The East Asian region also includes Hong Kong and Taiwan, on the one hand, and Australia and New Zealand on the other. There is a strong argument that the first two of these economies are implicitly included because they are part of China, although they do not have a direct voice in dialogue and ideas-setting. Some more explicit form of inclusion would be valuable, especially in discussions on financial markets and institutions.

The second set of countries is sometimes referred to as a separate bloc, Oceania, but in fact these are developed economies which are highly integrated with the rest of East Asia. They are not big economies in the scheme of things, but excluding them is not a trivial issue. In the first place, including them in regional forums expands the set of developed economies with well-functioning economic and financial systems and markets. Including them also means that the East Asian community and identity are not defined by ethnicity ('no blue eyes, blond hair'). This matters strategically because it constrains the pursuit of regionalism as an exercise in demagogy and populism.

A third element discussed was whether European monetary integration remains unfinished business. People are inclined to see their point in time as the endpoint or even the culmination of history. It would be misleading to think that the status quo is forever. European monetary union is in the process of being expanded because of the expansion of the European Union to Eastern Europe. This represents a shift in the balance of power within Europe from big to small countries, and potentially a realignment from Western European dominance. Regimes do not last forever, as the history of exchange and monetary regimes and composition of regional blocs over the past century show. For East Asia, the point to keep in mind is that the endpoint of European monetary union is itself a moving feast.

FINANCIAL COOPERATION

The next three chapters in this volume look at regional financial cooperation in East Asia for the prevention and resolution of financial crises. Two of these chapters set the context for regional financial cooperation, looking at the political economy and theoretical motivations for enhanced regional financial cooperation. The third chapter sets out possible instruments for cooperation and possible institutional vehicles to implement them.

In Chapter 7, 'Strengthening regional financial cooperation in East Asia', Haruhiko Kuroda and Masahiro Kawai discuss the need for stronger financial cooperation in East Asia. They believe that the 1997–98 financial crisis prompted East Asian economies to realise the potential benefits of having stronger cooperative institutions for crisis prevention, management and resolution. They argue that the regional financial architecture needs to be improved. They outline recent developments in financial cooperation in the region and examine possible directions for the future.

Kuroda and Kawai recommend that the regional surveillance process be made more effective. They canvass the option of creating a common pool of foreign exchange reserves to allow more flexible financial support at times of crises and contagion while minimising the problem of moral hazard. The arrangement must be consistent with the global framework. In particular, it must ensure private sector involvement for crisis management and resolution. They also argue that the choice about exchange rate regimes should be coordinated at the regional level, with a long-term vision of regional monetary integration. There is no presumption that the 'region' for financial cooperation is the same as the 'region' for monetary union.

In the next chapter, 'The management of financial crises: theory and policy', Prasanna Gai outlines an analytical framework for thinking about the relative benefits of international policy cooperation in dealing with financial crises. He starts at the general level, critically examining the theoretical literature on the causes and welfare effects of financial crises and ways to deal with them, including country clubs, swap arrangements, national liquidity management and payment standstills. He then sets out a useful and accessible model to analyse the incentives and tradeoffs in the design of sovereign debt contracts and the way the official sector can influence them. He shows that the benefits of a coherent crisis resolution framework are most likely to accrue if the official sector can identify the source of the financial problems and apply emergency financing effectively.

Gai's analysis highlights the importance of both effective monitoring, surveillance and policy dialogue and well-functioning institutions that perform or facilitate these functions. He discusses first the role of IMF programs in catalysing private finance. He argues that, to leverage private sector involvement effectively, official sector finance must improve the incentives of debtors to voluntarily engage in policy adjustment and willingly maintain credit lines to the crisis country. One element of this is tightly focused conditionality aligned to actual outcomes relevant to the financial problems at hand.

Gai also sees two implications for regional policy dialogue in East Asia. The first is that there is a potential role for greater regional dialogue and coordination with creditors. He suggests expanding the MFG to also act as a 'country club' for ensuring full communication between policymakers and private sector participants. Increased transparency is not a panacea against crisis, but it adds additional scrutiny and discipline which may bring significant welfare benefits. The second is that there is an underlying logic for developing an 'Asian Arrangements to Borrow' (AAB), as argued by Wang in the next chapter, because it brings additional firefighting power to crisis management, and home-country ownership of reform in such management.

In Chapter 9, 'Instruments and techniques for financial cooperation', Yunjong Wang opens up discussion of the various devices through which the region can deliver financial support. He sets the context by outlining the rationale for regional financial cooperation and critically assessing existing multilateral financial arrangements. He also appraises existing arrangements for support in East Asia, including the ASEAN swap arrangement and the network of bilateral swap arrangements set up under the CMI by the ASEAN+3 countries.

Wang canvasses a number of options for regional liquidity facilities beyond the CMI. These include an AAB and an Asian Monetary Fund. The proposals envisage multilateral cooperation, and so go beyond the NBSA, but they have different modalities. The AAB, modelled on the New Arrangements to Borrow, would allocate credit to countries on the basis of need, subject to an overall constraint set by benchmark economic criteria, a penalty rate of interest, and effective monitoring and surveillance. The AMF would be an institutional arrangement to pool and allocate funds to regional countries in crisis. There is concern about the costs associated with a large bureaucratic institution.

UNILATERAL, REGIONAL AND GLOBAL RESPONSES TO CRISES

The next four papers in this volume look at some of the issues about how countries might deal with financial crises: should they go it alone, should they seek regional support, or should they rely on global mechanisms?

In Chapter 10, 'The compatibility of capital controls with the development of financial markets', Menzie Chinn looks at one aspect of unilateral action by countries. Countries can impose capital controls to prevent or deal with a financial crisis. Chinn explores empirically whether capital controls affect a country's financial development. Financial development is important because it is expected to improve the efficiency of the allocation of financial resources and the monitoring of capital projects. Chinn investigates a substantially broader set of proxy measures of financial development than the standard measures, such as the volume of bank intermediation and an increasing role for equity capital. He also uses a variety of measures of capital controls, including the

IMF's measures of exchange restrictions and Quinn's index of financial openness.

Chinn reports some interesting outcomes. The econometric results suggest that the rate of financial development, as measured by private credit creation and stock market activity, is negatively related to the existence of capital controls. However, the strength of this relationship varies with the empirical measure used and with the level of development. The negative relationship between capital controls and financial development is most robust with respect to the equity market. Equity market activity appears to be linked to capital controls in both the full sample and a restricted sample of developing countries. The results pertaining to equity market development are of particular importance, as recent work suggests that equity markets are more important than bank-directed finance for the transfer of new technology.

In Chapter 11, 'Unilateral, regional and multilateral options for East Asia', Ramkishen Rajan looks at the array of options available for policymakers to deal with financial crises. He starts by observing that in a world where policymakers face the risk of financial crises on the capital account of the balance of payments, countries also face the risk of contagion and so need to have an array of policy responses at hand. Because these crises present themselves as a shortage of liquidity, it is important that countries have sufficient access to liquidity to deal with them.

Countries can act unilaterally to safeguard against capital account crises, through capital controls and the accumulation of foreign exchange reserves. They can also use foreign banks and private contingent credit lines (CCLs). There are limitations associated with all these. For example, capital controls can affect investor confidence. The carry cost of large foreign exchange reserves can be substantial because the interest paid on domestic liabilities is typically greater than the interest received on foreign assets. And private CCLs are likely to be small and hard to actually use in a crisis. This is because the providers of the lines do not like them being used, and because financial institutions are likely to reduce exposures to the countries, or others like it, to minimise the risks created by the facility and the signal it gives that the country has problems (that is, dynamic hedging).

Rajan argues that there is a need for cooperation to deal with these risks. One solution has been the development of the IMF's CCL facility. Rajan argues that this is ineffective since the loss of control and sovereignty entailed in using the facility outweighs the gain from the option value of access to a CCL facility. Moreover, countries will not use the facility because to do so would signal weakness and may itself cause a loss of market confidence. Multilateral solutions might not be the best way to deal with contagion. Rather, given that contagion and spillovers tend to be regional rather than global, it might be better to design mechanisms at the regional level.

Rajan argues that regional arrangements may indeed be superior to multilateral arrangements because countries' vested interests in a regional facility might be higher, either in terms of the likelihood of them being used (because crises are regional) or because countries have closer ties and relations with other countries in the region. For these reasons, he supports a quick-dispersing regional credit facility which would act basically as a lender of last resort in a financial crisis. It would act independently of the IMF, at least in the preliminary stages, so long as the crisis remains relatively small and localised.

Martin Parkinson, Phil Garton and Ian Dickson follow up analysis of some of these issues in Chapter 12, 'The role of regional financial arrangements in the international financial architecture'. They focus on some key issues and challenges that need to be considered in thinking about how regional arrangements might evolve.

They start by looking at the factors that have led to increased pressures on IMF resources, particularly in the past decade, and that have given rise to large-scale financing from sources outside the IMF in the midst of crises. The changing nature of balance of payments crises associated with increasing capital mobility, and the uncertainties surrounding the effectiveness of official financing, are crucial issues in constructing mechanisms and institutions for crisis financing.

Regional financing arrangements can relate to those provided by the IMF in different ways. One approach – which they call 'complementary financing' – involves both the IMF and a regional facility in an explicitly coordinated approach from the beginning of any crisis. Either the IMF or the regional facility could take the role as lead crisis manager, supplemented by funds from the other in either a first or second line of defence role (that is, funds that are either firmly or else provisionally dedicated by countries in support of an IMF package). Looking back on the experience in the East Asian crisis, Parkinson, Garton and Dickson judge that second lines of defence are ineffective and counterproductive; Ito and Narita reach the same conclusion in Chapter 6. Parkinson, Garton and Dickson also examine an alternative model – 'concentric lines of defence' – which entails the lead manager initially acting alone, with only implicit back-up from the 'lender of second resort' should the approach of the lead manager fail. Both models have supporters in East Asia, but the latter has garnered most attention.

While recognising the rationale for advocating a 'concentric lines of defence' approach, Parkinson, Garton and Dickson outline a number of challenges that need to be addressed to ensure that such proposal is feasible. The challenges include issues of appropriate crisis diagnosis; the relationship to current moves to develop effective mechanisms for private sector involvement (PSI); the credibility of lending conditions; and possible coordination failures if the IMF is the 'lender of second resort'.

In the final chapter in this volume, 'The Basel process and regional harmonisation in an Asian context', Shinichi Yoshikuni provides some insights into how the BIS sees the interactions between regional and global developments. He notes that the globalisation of financial markets has produced seemingly conflicting results. On the one hand, central banks and regulatory authorities have cooperated to come up with a set of standards to be applied globally, with the so-called Basel Process serving as one of the central vehicles. On the other hand, repeated episodes of financial crises with volatile market activities have led to calls for regional cooperation between such institutions. Yoshikuni suggests that there are two pressing issues.

The first issue is whether – and how – global standards can be reconciled with regional interests. Yoshikuni describes how regional sentiment in East Asia pressured the BIS to become less Europe-centric and to focus on developments in East Asia. He also argues that globalism and regionalism are not mutually incompatible, even if tensions exist at times. He says that they can be complementary forces that condition each other: sustainable globalism will bend to accommodate regional elements, and sustainable regionalism will be open enough to avoid insularity and loss of economic opportunity. In a fundamental sense, the dichotomy between global and regional interests is false.

The second issue – rethinking bank regulation – is whether it is possible to incorporate regional elements in the Basel Process, and indeed whether independent regional bodies are needed in addition to the Basel Process. Yoshikuni argues that regulatory harmonisation embedded in the Basel Process is a key element in the international regulatory infrastructure. This process has been influenced by market participants and regional developments. Moreover, globalisation – which creates new interdependencies between markets and institutions – has forced it to interact and be consistent with other regulatory bodies. Regional interaction is a part of this because markets and institutions operate in both a global and regional framework. While there is limited scope to create institutions to regulate matters that have fundamental global reach, there is a clear role for cooperation at the regional level to influence global developments and ensure that they meet regional needs.

These four papers cover much of the regional debate about how to ensure that unilateral, regional and multilateral approaches to crisis prevention and resolution are successful and complementary. They evoked considerable debate. Discussion mainly focused on regional financing facilities. Discussants identified three issues to be kept in mind in working out the details for a regional facility.

The first is having the right infrastructure in place to understand what is going on. Rajan's proposal for a regional CCL, for example, was read by some as implying that qualifying countries are more or less automatically entitled to financial support; that is, because they are fundamentally sound, any financing difficulty they face is basically an illiquidity problem, due, for example, to a self-fulfilling panic. This assumes that policymakers and markets can readily distinguish between liquidity difficulties and structural 'solvency' problems. The reality is that this is hard to do, especially because capital account crises tend to occur when there is some existing policy or financial weakness, ranging from a macroeconomic policy imbalance to a policy vulnerability such as an inappropriate exchange rate, poor transparency, weak governance or inadequate prudential regulation. Understanding what is going on is important to ensuring stability.

The risk of thinking that a crisis is due to liquidity when it is really due to structural imbalance is insufficient conditionality; the result is that the crisis will probably continue or re-emerge and that market confidence will be lost. The risk from thinking that a crisis is structural when in fact it is not is that the country is forced into more policy adjustment than is required. These risks are hard to balance.

The IMF's revealed preference would seem to be that it regards the first type of risk as more serious: too much conditionality is better than too little. The view that a country cannot have too much good policy has some obvious intuitive appeal. But there is a risk that pushing too hard on conditionality can unleash new political uncertainties and cause a program to unravel and confidence to be lost. The experience of Indonesia in 1997 and 1998 is a case in point.

For a regional facility, the main issue is whether it would bend in the opposite way to the IMF and be more likely to err in provide financing without sufficient conditionality, which would exacerbate the crisis. This is not a necessary outcome from a regional facility. Nor is it a likely outcome. Likely creditor countries in East Asia – for example, Japan, China, South Korea, Singapore and Australia – have no desire to put public funds at risk. The region has runs on the board in this respect. For example, in 1997 Japan declined requests from Thailand and South Korea for unconditional bilateral funding to boost their reserves.

A related issue for policymakers is how to coordinate regional and global initiatives. Supporters of a regional facility support a role for the IMF if the regional facility does not initially succeed. This basically makes the IMF the underwriter of the regional facility, but it is unlikely to be a role that the IMF itself will seek to play, all else given. If the regional round of financial stabilisation is completely independent of the global round, then coordination failures and greater uncertainty are more likely. Embedding the regional architecture in global processes, at least through clear dialogue and communication between the various channels, looks important.

Finally, there is a tendency to classify the spread of crises as being largely regional. This is true to a degree, but there are also many cases where financial crises spread to other regions. Global contagion was evident in 1998 with the spread of the Russian and Brazilian crises. For example, concern about Russian default in mid-1998 severely affected the currencies of Australia and South Africa at the time, well beyond the Russian region. Global risk management and portfolio repositioning can themselves be the vehicles for global contagion. A regional arrangement may still be an appropriate mechanism to provide financial support even in a cross-regional or global crisis. The rationale is marshalling regional resources to support regional partners.

END PIECE

East Asia is undergoing change and there is momentum to create a stronger regional economic and financial community. One dimension of the region's aspirations is the creation of strong robust mechanisms for financial governance, namely policy dialogue, surveillance and financial cooperation. We hope that this volume provides insight into the way this debate has emerged, what issues are facing the region, and how the debate might evolve in the future.

2 Policy dialogue in East Asia: principles for success

Stephen Grenville

INTRODUCTION

A key rationale for policy dialogue within an East Asian regional grouping is to make globalisation work better for the region. We have a commonality of interest because geography and contiguity still matter, even in a world of globalisation (perhaps even more than before). We are not alone. We can learn much from the experience of those around us, and the gaining of this experience is the often nebulous and formless process of talking issues through with people with common interests. We may meet to discuss a specific topic, but we end up with wider knowledge, and better general understanding, of each other.

The sort of regionalism which I hope will develop over time in East Asia goes well beyond policy dialogue. Indeed, I do not think policy dialogue in its narrow sense is the most pressing need. Policy dialogue, as it evolved in the post-war period, was largely about macroeconomic policy coordination, and this was really relevant only for the largest countries – essentially the G-3. For the rest of us, this was not a case of policy dialogue, but of policy monologue: the G-3 did what they could in terms of international coordination, and we wore the results, principally in the form of often inconvenient, substantial fluctuation in G-3 exchange rates. International macroeconomic policy coordination is still a major issue, and perhaps we might hope to have some input to it from the periphery, but this will not be central to our East Asian regional arrangements.

Policy dialogue is important for trade and (less certainly) exchange rate arrangements, because regional arrangements have the potential to be very important for the development of policy in these areas. However, I do not discuss these issues here: the first is beyond the scope of the paper; the second is discussed elsewhere (see de Brouwer and Kawai 2003).

This still leaves important regional policy issues, including the possibility of policy coordination in the face of a repeat – or variation – of the 1997–98 Asian crisis. I will certainly discuss this. But the much more general, wider and perhaps more important issue relates to globalisation: how to maintain the momentum which has brought so much benefit (particularly to this region);

how to make it work better with better rules; and how to get proper representation for our interests in the forums which determine the parameters – the 'rules of the game' – for globalisation. This, in my view, should be a central focus of regional policy dialogue.

The paper is set out as follows. First, I discuss some functions of regional cooperation as it relates to policy coordination and globalisation and outline some characteristics of regional arrangements. Next, I describe some international models for regional cooperation and explore some features of the existing relevant regional groupings in East Asia. I then analyse the effectiveness of existing institutions and models for specific functions, before setting out some conclusions.

FUNCTIONS OF REGIONAL COOPERATION

Policy coordination

Having downplayed the centrality of macroeconomic policy coordination in my introduction, let me be more specific about where a degree of policy coordination will still be important. I have left aside trade and exchange rates, acknowledging the importance of each of these. But beyond these, I do not see a compelling reason why, say, the countries of Asia should be running similar monetary or fiscal policies, or even why they should coordinate their different macroeconomic policies. The real work of macroeconomic policymaking is, broadly speaking, a domestic matter.[1] Getting domestic economic policy settings right is the core issue.

Surveillance, however, is one aspect of policymaking where regional cooperation might make a real and substantial contribution. The term 'surveillance' is an unfortunate way of describing the process, because it has connotations of checking up and looking over the shoulder of policymaking in individual countries; in other words, it is something more intrusive than is generally acceptable in this region. It is a question of when 'peer pressure' becomes interference. The principal objective of surveillance should be not to 'catch out' and expose any policymakers who are doing the wrong thing, but rather to act as an advocate of good policies and as a catalyst for reform: the context has to be positive and supportive, not negative, proselytising and adversarial.[2] Reluctance to be too assertive is, to some degree, the current characteristic, but policymakers need to be actively involved in the process if surveillance is to have a beneficial effect.

How have other countries dealt with this problem? Perhaps I can explain the point more clearly by referring to the surveillance process of the Organisation for Economic Co-operation and Development (OECD), particularly in relation to Australia. Each year during the 1980s, we faced the interrogation of our peers (the OECD secretariat and two 'examining' countries), who quizzed us on both macroeconomic and microeconomic policies, invariably from the viewpoint of hard-edged economic analysis. They were not always right, but they always approached the process from the viewpoint of best-practice economics. Why was this so valuable to the policymaking process? It made it easier for the national bureaucrats (who, by and large, agreed with these policies) to get these policies implemented within a diverse decision-making framework in which less economically rational views might well have prevailed. The examinations received quite wide publicity and added spice and fire to the policy debate. This was often inconvenient but it required the bureaucrats to defend the (imperfect) policies of the time, and helped us move to better policies.

Policy coordination may also be relevant in crisis response. In this case, cooperation will occur mainly in the pooling of foreign exchange reserves. For lack of something better, building up large foreign exchange reserves allows international capital flow volatility to be handled through substantial reserve holdings. This is inefficient, but pooling makes it less so. Moreover, regional groups share enough self-interest to help each other for reasons beyond simple altruism: we are all going to be more ready to help our neighbours than to participate in some kind of collective action for a more distant region. One consequence of this is that regional arrangements could be used to supplement the International Monetary Fund (IMF) arrangements, rather than adopting the more universal approach of the New Arrangements to Borrow (NAB).

Let me quote, with approval, Yung Chul Park (2000), who has spoken about the relationship between regional cooperation and the slow progress of reform of the international financial system. He said:

> One development that has encouraged regional cooperation in East Asia has been the slow progress of the reform of the international financial system. The urgency of reform in the G-7 countries has receded considerably with the rapid recovery of East Asia ... As long as the structural problems on the supply side of capital are not addressed, East Asian countries will remain as vulnerable to future crises as they were before. Instead of waiting until the G-7 creates a new architecture, whose effectiveness is at best questionable, it would be in the interest of East Asia to work together to create its own system of defence.

Globalisation

Globalisation is even more important than policy coordination to regional cooperation. Policy must be attuned to the needs of the new globalised world, in order to foster globalisation and, at the same time, ensure that we all get maximum benefit from it. Here, I would like to discuss some characteristics of globalisation and examine the rules required for successful globalisation. First, let me make a point which is close to tautology, but full of policy implication nevertheless: globalisation means that an increasing part of our economic relations are with external parties. Indeed, for many East Asian economies, foreign trade (exports and imports taken together) far exceeds GDP, as shown in Table 2.1).

Table 2.1 Foreign trade as a percentage of GDP

Australia	36
China	42
Hong Kong	255
Indonesia	79
Japan	18
Korea	84
Malaysia	202
New Zealand	54
Philippines	99
Singapore	296
Thailand	108
United States	20

Domestic trade and investment are subject to myriad controls and regulations, even in the most 'free market' economies. In contrast, international relations are lightly regulated. Rodrik[3] has stated:

> The dilemma we face as we enter the 21st century is that markets are striving to become global while the institutions needed to support them remain by and large national.

Does this disparity in regulatory density reflect some innate characteristic – for example, that international relationships are simpler – or does it reflect the greater difficulty of regulating across sovereign borders? It seems to me to be the latter, and we should address this deficiency.

Rules

The need for 'rules of the game' seems, if anything, to be greater in a globalised world than in a less integrated world. There are two defining characteristics of globalisation. One is the importance of scale, as optimal business units tend to become larger and larger as technology improves. The other is 'winner takes all', and the related concept of 'first mover advantage'. Together, these characteristics produce areas where monopoly or quasi-monopoly will be important. The old response to monopoly was to break it up and force competition, but this will be precluded or restricted in a globalised world because it would result in inefficiencies. An alternative would be to establish a network of rules which addresses the issues raised by these imperfectly competitive firms. Such rules would not be specific to any one country, but would be developed in a uniform way and acceptable to all. They would address issues such as monopoly, intellectual property rights and legal issues, and perhaps prudential supervision, capital flows, taxes and 'industry policy' as well. In short, closer relations between countries lead to a greater need for uniformity in, for example, tax or investment regimes. Tom Friedman (1999) has called such rules the 'golden straitjacket', a concept which captures two important characteristics of the process – the degree of uniformity which globalisation will impose and the generally beneficial nature of these rules.[4]

Rules to govern global relationships will generally need to be uniform and multinational. However, regional input will also be required, to ensure that the universal rules apply to all countries. A good set of rules requires recognition of the great diversity of circumstances and institutions between countries. A specific example is the rules on prudential supervision. The rules relevant to banks in East Asia are likely to be somewhat different from those for other areas, reflecting the different degree of complexity and make-up of banks. We would not want a set of international rules which unfairly penalised banks in East Asia simply on the grounds that they were not the same as banks in London or New York.

Representation

At the general level, the collective wisdom of worldwide experience needs to be incorporated into the 'golden straitjacket' more effectively than it has been to date. It is now part of the conventional wisdom that there were various deficiencies of perception and analysis in the international response to the Asian financial crisis. The 'one size fits all' approach came out of earlier Latin American experience, and was a poor fit for East Asia in 1997. To some extent these deficiencies were driven by a 'democratic deficit' – inadequate representation or the inability to have our voice heard above the confident assertions of those whose policy prescription was driven by doctrinal interests, vested interests or, sometimes, simple ignorance.

Regional groupings are the main way to address this democratic deficit. This region is inadequately represented in many of the forums which determine the important issues surrounding globalisation. East Asia has an IMF quota of less than 15 per cent, but accounts for more than 20 per cent of world GDP, almost a quarter of world trade, and almost half of world foreign exchange reserves. The region pays a price for inadequate representation. Prominent American economist David Hale (2001: 8) has observed:

> In the past, the U.S. government has only supported major (IMF) interventions for countries in which the U.S. had a military base. During the Asia crisis, for example, the U.S. acted aggressively to support Korea, but played a much less significant role in Thailand and Indonesia.

Much of our effort in regional groups should be directed towards correcting this.

There have been very important improvements in international financial architecture since the crisis. The IMF has added new lending facilities that should be better able to handle the demands of capital account crises. It has also started to pay greater attention to financial markets and financial systems and has critically examined its policy prescriptions and its general approach to conditionality. Representation has greatly improved, with an additional eight Asian countries gaining membership of the Bank for International Settlements (BIS). The creation of the G-20 (with six Asian members) is a good breakthrough. At a more detailed level, the negotiation of the Basel II Capital Accord involved a degree of consultation entirely missing from Basel I (which had been tailored specifically for the G-10).[5] The Financial Stability Forum (FSF), the IMF and the G-20 have tried to improve countries' resilience to crises by promoting adherence to standards and codes and there has been much discussion about how the private sector could help to prevent and resolve crises.

Within central banking circles, there was some support for the formation of an Asian BIS, given the Eurocentric focus of the existing organisation. This was satisfied by the setting up of a BIS office in Hong Kong and the creation of the Asian Consultative Council (ACC) of the BIS, which gives Asian central banks a greater say in the operation of the organisation. Some Asian countries have also been invited to attend some of the Basel and G-10 committees associated with the BIS, although, sadly, not as permanent full members.

But the issue of ensuring that our voice is heard remains unresolved. The IMF still pays inadequate attention to this region, and other more representative groups (such as the G-20) are still trying to find a role for themselves in a world which is crowded with competing and overlapping institutions, none ready to diminish their own status and power, and many governed by inadequately representative views. Who should be represented in the councils of the world? Representation should not simply depend on GDP, though this is important. It should also depend on what contribution each participant can make to the debate and to the production of a universally acceptable set of rules. To be more specific, the G-10 representation is deficient not just because of its limited numbers, but because of the uniformity of view of its European-dominated membership.[6]

International dialogue takes place at the multilateral, regional and bilateral levels. We should not be surprised or concerned at this 'layering'. Nor should we be overly concerned if there is a fair degree of overlap between groups and meetings. If an issue is important, then it probably needs to be discussed in a variety of forums, each of which will bring different insights to bear. Checks and balances are important. Groups are not simply about getting together to make decisions; they are often about getting together in order to learn about decisions or discussions which have taken place elsewhere. We should not be surprised to see finance ministers meeting separately from central bankers, with the two groups subsequently meeting together.

CHARACTERISTICS OF REGIONAL ARRANGEMENTS

Avoiding territorial exclusivity

We should not allow some ill-defined principle of 'territorial exclusivity' to constrain dialogue which would otherwise be useful. When the Asian Monetary Fund (AMF) was proposed after the onset of the Asian crisis, some people argued that it would overlap with the IMF. This no doubt coloured the views not only of the IMF itself, but also of those who had a more prominent position within the IMF than they would have had within an AMF. Similarly, many countries have three levels of government, each with its own contribution to make, and each interacting with the others in ways that should be fruitful. Regional issues on which there is a degree of consensus can be passed up to the higher global level, and broad nation-wide views can be passed down to the regional level. Petty territorial jealousies have no place in discussions about the proper number of organisations and their relationships.

Commonality of interest

Regional arrangements should focus on bringing together groups with common interests and ensuring that they are linked, both upwards and downwards, in useful ways. Commonality of interest is the most important criterion for useful interaction. It does not mean that all participants must be at the same stage of development, but it probably does mean that they should be travelling along much the same path, albeit at different distances and speeds. Commonality of interest makes an effective consensus possible, which can be passed to the next level of international dialogue.

Determining the numbers

What are the right numbers for a group? If the issues revolved around trade or currency unions, then economic analysis can offer useful guidance on which countries should be included. Who are (or potentially could be) good trade partners? What countries meet the criteria for an optimal currency area? The original APEC membership, for example, makes economic sense as a trading group because of established trading ties.[7] But some fruitful dialogue is more general and nebulous.

At one level, one might ask whether it matters. For example, it was not until the last minute that the membership of the European single currency system was known. Far more countries joined than most people had expected, and eventually there will probably be even more participants than the original proponents envisaged. That said, there seems to be a lot to be said for keeping numbers down to manageable levels. For practical purposes, this might be defined in terms of how many people can comfortably sit around the same table and who can speak to each other without microphones. When we get to the size of universal 'one country, one vote' type of representation (as seen in the UN), effective decision-making becomes extraordinarily difficult and 'lowest common denominator' outcomes often prevail.

Let me give a concrete example of a response to the vexed issue of numbers. The G-20 was, at one stage in its evolution, rather larger than it is today. It was recognised that it needed to be contracted. Size is particularly important for surveillance: smaller groups can have much more candid (and therefore useful) discussion than can larger groups. Small may well be beautiful. If, over time, the various participants develop knowledge, empathy and understanding of the practical policy constraints, then so much the better.

Developing the rules

Globalisation rules should be developed in a two-way process: regional groups should provide input into rule-making; they should then act to put these rules in place in their individual countries (or at least adapt their own rules to fit the straitjacket). Regional groups should 'spread the word' in order to improve policy. Policy improvement can result not only from the surveillance process, but also from swapping ideas and simply observing the way other countries go about doing things. Globalisation is leading to a degree of policy uniformity or similarity, and to the extent that this is 'best practice', the quicker we all adapt to it the better.

The rules should be developed by experts or technicians – those who know the nuts and bolts of a particular issue rather than the arm-waving generalists. If the degree of detail in domestic rules and regulations is any indication of what it takes to ensure good and efficient commerce within countries, why should international dealings require less complexity? These international rules may well be the same ones which apply in domestic jurisdictions, but only the technicians can accurately assess whether this is appropriate. Any compromise will be on the basis of technical and expert issues, not on the basis of voting power at the table.

Secretariat

If 'bricks and mortar' institutions with permanent staff are an important part of regional dialogue, the mindset and style of the secretariat need careful consideration. How big should it be? How assertive should it be? These are tricky questions which require answers tailored to regional conditions, but it is not necessary to take the existing conditions as immutable. For example, present dialogue suffers from not having a sufficiently assertive secretariat presence. The reluctance to allow a more intrusive presence may need to be respected, but equally it needs to be sensitively changed over time. These things do not happen by themselves: they need a view on what should be done and a degree of leadership to achieve this.

MODELS FOR COOPERATIVE ARRANGEMENTS

Europe

The obvious model for policy coordination in the broad sense is Europe. Over four decades, European countries have progressed to economic union despite a history of hostile relations. Europe's success can be attributed to two main factors. The first was an economic dynamic: the exploitation of the obvious economic advantages of geographic proximity. The second was an underlying political imperative: a number of politicians were firmly of the view that greater integration would reduce the prospects of future conflict. This was actively supported by the United States.

The G-10 had a much more specific genesis, having been formed from the countries that agreed to provide a loan facility to back up the IMF's resources in 1962. These resources were to be made available in the event of potential impairment of the international financial system, and therefore only to the G-10 countries themselves. The G-10 subsequently became central to the world financial system, in the context of both the IMF and the BIS. The enormously influential Basel Rules for Prudential Supervision were developed by (and initially for) the restricted club of the G-10.

Groups which form for one purpose can metamorphose into groups with new functions – in the case of the G-10, far more important than the initial function. The G-10 example also illustrates why it is important to gain a seat at the table from the outset, since the incumbent members – particularly the smaller ones – will try to avoid dilution of their power. The group's effectiveness over an extended period probably reflects a relatively small and focused membership. However, as the world has developed, the G-10 has looked increasingly unrepresentative of the global economy, giving a disproportionate say to small European economies and no say to the rapidly developing countries of Asia and Latin America.

Three lessons can be learned from the example of the G-10. First, groups need specific tasks to weld them together; 'frank and fruitful exchanges of views' are good, but not enough. The Europeans started with such a specific project – the Coal and Steel Community, something of real substance. Second, patience is not just a virtue; it is a necessity in a world where it takes time to build institutions. Progress is not steady: projects may stall for a time, and the group has to hold together waiting for the tide to turn. Third, there must be a sense of community and common interest stemming from geographic contiguity, which goes beyond simple economic linkages.

If progress towards closer international relations is important, then institution building will be an important element. 'Virtual' secretariats may have their place, but real bricks and mortar institutions, with effective and active secretariats, will be needed. Charles Wyplosz (2001) makes a compelling case that European integration was hugely assisted by the presence of Europe-wide institutions, which could provide some ongoing momentum and, in particular, could 'pull a plan out of the drawer' when the country representatives were ready to discuss the next step. Such plans will be ready – waiting in the 'bottom drawer' to be put on the table when circumstances are propitious – only if there are bureaucrats with an ongoing vested interest in pushing the plan forward.

Bank for International Settlements and International Monetary Fund

There are some noticeable differences between the BIS and the IMF. The BIS has few staff and sees its role as confined to organising meetings and writing catalytic discussion papers to help its members to reach reasonable conclusions or an acceptable consensus. It might have a 'party line' on various issues, and staff members are intellectually high-powered and often hold views strongly, but by and large they keep these views to themselves. Their job is to facilitate the dialogue, not to set the agenda and guide the participants to the 'right' conclusion. The BIS is rather like a club where people meet to thrash out issues, perhaps like the coffee houses of old London.

By contrast, the IMF is like a religious order which has worked out, over the years, what is 'right' and, armed with a view about infallibility, wishes to impose this on the world. Lest this seem unfair to the Fund, let me hasten to add that the BIS and the IMF serve different purposes; the Fund's role may well require it to be more assertive and confident of the righteousness of its cause than the BIS. In the present context, I want merely to point out that there are different styles of policy coordination, and that regional organisations will need to develop a style and mindset appropriate to the task at hand.

My own view is that the BIS model fits the regional task best, with its emphasis on the facilitation of discussion rather than the imposition of doctrine. These sorts of 'style' or 'mindset' issues might seem to be arrived at almost by accident, but in fact it is the opposite: good administrators of such organisations can set style and mindset or even, at a pinch, change it once it has been set.

OECD

The OECD is also worth mentioning. Lean in its staffing but wide in the scope of its work, it has done much to emphasise 'good economics' (even though this sometimes turned out to be wrong), and proselytised for the powerfully attractive idea that good economics would also be good politics. The OECD carries out its debate in public (at least to the extent that its country studies are always made public), even if the most strident criticisms are muted because of country sensitivity. For Australia, my assessment is that the OECD had a far greater influence on policymaking than the IMF, and that it was generally in the right direction.

East Asian regional institutions

APEC

APEC is the broadest grouping in the region. It bridges East Asia and North America, but also incorporates Chile, Mexico and Russia. APEC focuses on trade, which has seen its fortunes wax and wane with developments in global trade, although the addition of finance ministers meetings and leaders meetings have broadened its coverage. Its principal achievement to date has been the Bogor Declaration, under which developed countries agreed to strive for free trade and investment by 2010 and developing countries by 2020. However, even this has shown the tensions inherent in a relatively disparate group: initial calls by some countries for a binding and measurable process have been significantly watered down. The finance ministers process has focused on encouraging regional dialogue and promoting capacity building and may not be suited to a more substantive agenda, particularly given political tensions between China and Taiwan.

Manila Framework Group

Like APEC, the Manila Framework Group (MFG) bridges East Asia and North America. It had its genesis in the push for the AMF in the midst of the Asian crisis. It is regarded as one of the better surveillance mechanisms among the regional groups; it also takes an interest in global architecture issues. It could be (but is not yet) the forum for developing regional positions which are then taken to world forums such as the International Monetary and Financial Committee (IMFC) and G-20. One of the MFG's main initial functions was to provide a cooperative financing arrangement to supplement IMF resources. This was reflected in the second line of defence facilities offered to Indonesia and South Korea. Member countries have discussed the possibility of a more formal ongoing arrangement, but most members would prefer to pursue this through ASEAN+3.

EMEAP

The Executives Meeting of East Asia and Pacific Central Banks (EMEAP) is narrower than APEC or the MFG. It is a purely central bank forum, drawn from the East Asian core of APEC and the MFG. Its goal is to strengthen cooperation among the central banks of the region, but some members would like it to become a more substantial organisation, along the lines of the BIS. To this end, EMEAP has established a system of bilateral repurchase agreements over US Treasuries, to provide short-term foreign currency liquidity support. EMEAP's strength is its specialist working groups, which promote good practices and better understanding at a technical level. This is, potentially, the forum for developing regional consensus on such issues as capital flows (for example, Chilean-style inflow taxes and dealing with *in extremis* crisis resolution). The value of the forum at the highest level is now being tested by the formation of the BIS ACC, which has drawn Asian countries more into the mainstream of BIS activities. EMEAP is already the forum for developing regional positions on financial issues, so the close link with the BIS is natural and logical.

SEACEN

The South East Asian Central Banks group (SEACEN) is a longstanding grouping of central bankers, focused on Southeast Asia, but with membership spread as wide as Sri Lanka, Korea and Mongolia. One of the initial aims of SEACEN was to establish an ASEAN voting group for the IMF and the International Bank for Reconstruction and Development. The voting group still exists and SEACEN governors continue to meet annually, although SEACEN's significant outward contribution appears to be its training and research efforts through the SEACEN Centre.

ASEAN and ASEAN+3

ASEAN is the oldest regional group and has relatively uniform interests and views. It has some runs on the board with the ASEAN Free Trade Area (which has been strengthened since the crisis) and a multilateral foreign currency swap arrangement. More recently, it has set up a surveillance mechanism, with the assistance of the Asian Development Bank (ADB), in an effort to foresee and forestall crises.

ASEAN+3 comprises ASEAN plus China, Japan and the Republic of Korea. Its broad agenda covers economic, social and political fields. However, its most important achievement has been the Chiang Mai Initiative (CMI), which incorporates a regional financing arrangement (building on the ASEAN arrangements) to supplement existing international facilities.

The significant momentum in ASEAN+3 may reflect East Asia's equivalent to Europe's 'integrate to avoid further conflict' imperative. There is also a strong belief that the international institutions are not set up to work in Asia's favour and that Asia must therefore look after itself – particularly given the large proportion of world reserves held in Asia. This has been felt very strongly since the Asian crisis and it is no coincidence that the CMI grew around those countries that felt most aggrieved. Countries in ASEAN+3 have more in common than the groups that bridge the Pacific, and the smaller size of ASEAN+3 may have made it a more workable decision-making entity, although it is difficult to determine whether this reflects physical numbers or simply the greater uniformity of country interests embodied in the group.

Reserve pooling arrangements could have occurred within the MFG or EMEAP, but ASEAN+3 seems to be where the action is at present. Just as G-10 gravitated from its original narrow specific purpose to become the centre of prudential supervision, ASEAN+3 might be where the more general foreign exchange rate discussions occur. Australia supports these moves, regardless of the forum in which they evolve. Obviously, we would like to have a seat at the table, since we believe Australia has much to offer from its own experience and resources. We also feel our own policymaking has been enriched through our engagement with Asia and we have certainly appreciated the input of like-minded countries from the region in the difficult international debates of recent years.

Should the CMI continue to develop towards an ultimate goal of becoming a regional monetary fund, my view is that we should support it. If there were major developments in this regard, participants presumably would want to assess whether the MFG, the APEC finance ministers meetings, EMEAP and SEACEN are still playing a unique role.

It is probably too early to assess which groups will continue to play a useful role, given uncertainty over a future world trade round, the G-20's unformed mandate, and the future directions of ASEAN+3. We should, nonetheless, critically watch developments among the regional groupings over the next two to three years with a view to making tough decisions when the time is right.

DEVELOPING THE BEST FORUMS FOR THE REGION

Surveillance

I argued above that surveillance should act as advocacy for good policies and a catalyst for reform. We are still looking for a regional institution which can do this with the appropriate degree of rigour, finesse and intrusiveness. The MFG is probably still the best candidate, but it has not yet found the right formula. The members have to be more ready to accept a greater degree of intrusion into their domestic policymaking domain if it is to be effective. The OECD has shown how it can be done – with a secretariat and two 'examining countries' providing the lead on the inquisitorial process. Each country knows that it will have its turn in the hot seat, so its vigour in inquisition is tempered by this knowledge. But countries also know that they have been given the function of the 'tough cop', so they feel under pressure to ask the difficult questions.

In the MFG the IMF has the secretariat role, but in my view it has not found the right 'voice' for the part. It is either too clinical in its written material (giving rote standard aggregations and forecasts which come out of 'winding the handle' on models) or too proselytising in its oral interventions on sensitive issues (usually with the active and vocal support of the United States). In my experience, it has spent too much time defending policies it advocated during the Asian crisis, when most participants have already made up their minds about the issues and find it tiresome to have to sit through another round of self-justification.

Could the ADB do the job? Not without putting in a much greater effort on its economic analysis. It would need to decide more clearly whether it is the dispenser of projects or of economic advice: these are very different subjects, and need a different mix of staff and probably a different managerial outlook. The ADB made a good start with some work on specific aspects of the recovery (particularly on the region's dependence on electronics exports) but would need to go further if it was to take on this role effectively.

Could there be an entirely different approach to surveillance modalities? One way would be to get specialised international agencies – such as the BIS, universities, the Toronto Centre or even private sector bodies such as the Institute for International Finance – to provide 'one-off' discussions on specific topics. Such an approach would need stronger chairmanship than is usually provided.

Could the surveillance be better done in a different group such as ASEAN (which already has a surveillance process) or the more intimate groupings such as Four Markets or Six Markets?[8] It is hard for me, as an outsider, to judge the ASEAN surveillance. The small groups (Four and Six Markets) provide useful opportunities for dialogue at a different level and on more specialised topics; they should not be seen either as the main forum for surveillance or as rivals for such a forum.

In short, more 'zip and zing' is needed so that participants go away with the feeling that they have learned something from the experience of other countries, have been taxed in their defence of their own policies, and are under some pressure to implement better policies when they return home. All this is a big ask, but more needs to be done to move the MFG meeting on from the rut into which it has fallen. The MFG is still the best bet, but it needs a lot more work. It might help if the chair country felt the degree of responsibility for a fruitful meeting that, for example, the Canadians have felt with the G-20.

Macro policy

One of the major pieces of unfinished business from the Asian crisis relates to exchange rates. Countries in the region are generally floating, but doing so with a degree of discomfort. So far so good, but everyone knows that exchange rate systems are only 'tested to destruction' occasionally, and no one is sure how these systems will behave under pressure. There will be a tendency to link this debate with the reserve pooling discussions in ASEAN+3. There is an obvious relationship here, but it would be a pity if that were the only (or even the main) forum for debate about exchange rate regimes. The discussions within the G-20 vigorously explored the case for the 'ends of the spectrum' view before ultimately pulling back from this view to the current consensus that other parts of the spectrum are legitimate possibilities.

We should not forget the obvious point that, while an issue might be discussed in one forum (for example, the G-20), this does not preclude a more country-focused discussion in regional groups (for example, ASEAN+3). The wider debate is needed to ensure that all available experience has been taken into account (for example, the Argentine experience with a currency board) and to ensure that the current policy vogue is not simply a reaction to the particular circumstances of recent specific experience. The regional discussion is needed to ensure a good fit for the particular circumstances, and to give the quieter participants in the debate room to explore their ideas in a sympathetic setting.

The other big unresolved macro issue which should find a central place in the regional debate is capital flows. Various factors contributed to the Asian crisis, but the size of the inflows and their ultimate volatility was a central issue. Will it happen again? 'Not soon' is the probable answer, but when it does there is still no accepted best-practice response. An ongoing discussion of the issue in a regional forum might give individual countries the courage to do what none (except China) was able to do before 1997 – say to the financial markets of the world that they would accept these funds, but only on the terms (and at the pace) that could be safely absorbed.

What is the right forum for these macro policy debates? I have already implied an answer: they can and should take place in a variety of forums. The task is to make sure that discussion in one place is not precluded just because it has been discussed in another. Again, within the East Asian region, the MFG provides an obvious place, but with rather different agendas from the present ones. And again what seems to be needed is a BIS-style secretariat which could produce high-quality papers designed to stimulate discussion. Another way to help tie the regional framework together would be to use a specialised forum such as EMEAP to work up and 'predigest' controversial and difficult macro topics such as capital flow, and then discuss them more generally at a bigger forum. There is a precedent for this: work done by EMEAP received further consideration in the wider forum of the MFG in Melbourne in 1999.

Crisis management and reserve pooling

The AMF remains unfinished business. A regional fund can supplement multilateral funds because countries will be more ready to dip into their pockets for a neighbour than for a distant mendicant. A regional fund with a secretariat would be able to interpret events and advocate appropriate action (including appropriate conditionality) or, at the very least, be in a position to act as 'honest broker' in disputes between a country and an international financial institution.

This is about dialogue, channels of communication and supplementary efforts, not about replacing the IMF. Those of us who have criticised aspects of the Fund's work do so because we accept how important and central it is to our objectives. We want it to do things a bit differently, but we certainly want it, and we know that a regional body is not a replacement. That said, if the Fund is readier to help countries far from our shores and our interests (see Hale 2001), the supplementary funds which some countries (Australia included) have contributed to the New Arrangements to Borrow (successor to the General Arrangements to Borrow) in providing supplementary funds for use by the IMF might be better allocated closer to home, perhaps to an AMF.

The action on reserve pooling is in ASEAN+3. We watch with interest to see how the ASEAN efforts in pooling reserves are going, and hope the day might come when this dialogue can be opened to a wider audience (including Australia). There is a lot to be said for any pooling arrangements to work very closely with the surveillance process; if the MFG turns out to be the most effective forum for surveillance, there would be an unfortunate disconnect between the two closely related elements.

Technical cooperation

I want to use EMEAP to illustrate how the current dialogue could be given more substance by emphasising specialised technical areas of cooperation.

This suggestion starts from the idea that technical exchanges were important in the process of European integration.[9] When specialists from different countries get together to discuss quite technical issues – not the arm-waving issues of foreign relations – they find that they have a lot in common with their counterparts.

To illustrate the point, I need to go into a degree of detail. I focus on central banks because that is where my personal experience lies. However, a whole range of technical subjects lend themselves to the sort of cooperation under discussion here. Two areas in particular (prudential supervision and payments systems) have been the focus of very useful work in EMEAP, and we could take this to a significantly higher degree of regional integration. I have already argued for a stepping up of the level of debate within the MFG; now, I am putting the case for more substance in the dialogue than at present.

Let me start with an inventory of the international cooperation in prudential supervision and then see whether I have got the multilateral–regional split about right and, more important, whether the pieces need to be tied together more effectively. The relevant international body here is the BIS or, more properly, the Basel Committee, which is a G-10 committee serviced by the BIS. It makes the rules (designs the golden straitjacket) in this particular area.

First, I will explain how the BIS – which is not particularly representative of the world – got this powerful role. The original Basel Agreement was designed by and for the G-10, who very explicitly disavowed any intention to force it on a wider group of countries. But once the G-10 banks had signed up to this set of rules, they formed a quorum in world banking. Therefore, any bank which considered itself to have even a remote connection to the international world was more or less forced to sign up, or agree to meet the rules.

The Basel Committee recognised this. When it came to revise the rules a few years back, it began a comprehensive consultation process with non-G-10 countries, facilitated by the BIS. So far, these rules have been made only with the G-10 countries in mind. These are the countries with sophisticated financial systems that are highly integrated internationally. Some of the countries in our region may face a different set of challenges in this area, challenges that might argue strongly in favour of simple banks, perhaps with a lesser degree of integration with non-bank financial enterprises. Perhaps, too, the legal framework might be less powerful and the information available for credit analysis may be quite scanty.

In short, the full complexities of Basel II (the new rules) might not be relevant. At the same time, the deficiencies in the local legal and informational environments might suggest that the prudential regulator has a larger, more intrusive, role to play in some countries. Did the consultation process allow a full harmonisation (in a competitive neutrality sense) between the sophisticated approaches and the simpler ones that are likely to prevail in much of this region? Will the world banking system understand that 'simpler' does not necessarily mean more risky? In short, was the region able to effectively present its unique needs in the process of revising the rules?

In asking this, the question is directed at the central banks of the region, not the Basel Committee. It was up to the region to put its case. But its institutional infrastructure for doing this was not up to the task. The Basel Committee consulted, primarily, the South East Asia, New Zealand and Australia (SEANZA) Forum of Banking Supervisors. SEANZA is in many ways a moribund remnant of an earlier era of cooperation, based around a subset of the old British Commonwealth. The BIS may well have seen this as a convenient group, because it meant that the world could be neatly divided into three – G-10, Americas and Asia – for the purpose of consultation. It should be said in their defence that they also asked for the views of EMEAP supervisors. But, at the end of the day, the interaction between the region and the rule-makers was less than satisfactory; it seems doubtful whether a set of rules has been achieved which takes into account the special characteristics of the region, or prepares the banks of the region to work well in the Basel II world. A strong regional body covering this specialisation would have done a better job.[10]

This is an area that lends itself to the sort of technical cooperation through regional institutions that was the glue which held the European integration process together during the long gestation period of European unity. The next stage of cooperation might include the formation of a bricks-and-mortar, permanently staffed institution to foster cooperation in specific nuts-and-bolts areas such as prudential supervision. The basis of such an institution already exists, in the form of the SEACEN Centre in Kuala Lumpur. This has done sterling work over a number of years, particularly in training prudential supervisors. But its existence has not inhibited all sorts of other efforts in this field from going ahead without much coordination. APEC has an initiative to train supervisors, based in Manila; the IMF has its institute in Singapore and various individual projects in the field of supervision; and just about all the G-10 countries run various stand-alone technical assistance projects in the region. The BIS Financial Stability Institute and the Toronto Centre wing into the region from time to time, but they are not an integral part of the ongoing work in any substantive sense.

What about a concerted effort to bring all this together in one place, with full support from within and outside the region? Such a body could become the centre of excellence in this field. It would become the mouthpiece of the region in talking to Basel. Its discussions would heighten awareness not only of the rules, but also of the way problems were handled in the region. There could be a beneficial form of contagion as supervisors saw things being done in a useful way in one country. The proposal would force on providers of technical assistance a degree of coordination and consistency which is sometimes lacking at present.

The message is a general one: the next stage of regional cooperation should aim at building a variety of specialised, technically oriented forums of cooperation with enough common interest and common objectives to support a permanent secretariat. If such common interest can not be identified and built on, the overall endeavour of closer regional ties will fall apart. The existing groupings (I can speak in particular about the technical working groups spawned by EMEAP) have found enough common ground to make me think that it is time for the next stage: detailed cooperation at a technical level.

Globalisation

Regional groupings have two roles in the globalised world: to ensure that we are properly represented when the rules are being written; and to give us a louder, clearer voice in the multilateral forums.

The sort of technical cooperation I discuss here provides the building blocks of the major issue of globalisation. To the extent that this is about writing the rules of the golden straitjacket, these rules in most cases are technical ones, best formulated by experts in the field rather than by diplomats. Strong regional technical bodies will give us a voice in setting these rules.

To the extent that globalisation is about getting a louder voice in the councils of the world (especially places like the IMF), all these regional forums have a role to play: what is needed for the louder voice is a well-formulated and well-founded opinion which can be articulated so confidently, and on behalf of so many people, that it cannot be ignored.

APEC has one outstanding characteristic which makes it unique and gives it a special role to play in globalisation: the Leaders Meeting. Obviously, this is about much more than outlandish shirts and photo opportunities. Political leaders want results, but if their travels widen their horizons and remind them of our global interdependencies, then APEC has a valued place in the regional dialogue. The issue is whether it could do better still. Each time it meets, bureaucrats in each member country search for 'initiatives' and 'deliverables'; the danger is that they will take on issues which might be more appropriately handled elsewhere. They might better see themselves as promoters, urgers and facilitators, and worry less about attaching the APEC label to specific proposals.

Leadership is about getting other people to do things you want done, not about doing them yourself. Will this be enough to keep APEC going? It will, provided the American President attends, and whether he does or not will have much more to do with the political agenda in America than with the concrete achievements of the meeting. All other leaders can come back from the meeting and say, 'I told the President ...' That should be enough to convince the voters at home that it was worth while.

So we should not force too much into the APEC framework. It has had a strong specialisation in trade issues, and there is much to be said for it not taking on too much. It should be the guardian of virtue when it comes to trade, but if there is not much to be done in this area at a particular time, then APEC should just bide its time and its leaders admire each other's shirts. It should also guard against becoming too large. It was already a bit too big before Russia joined, and it is a real pity that big-power politics triumphed over sensible regional membership criteria in bringing about this enlargement.

CONCLUSIONS

What then are the principles for success for policy dialogue in East Asia?

First, regional dialogue is not inimical to globalisation; it is its handmaiden and ally.

Second, we should not worry too much about overlaps and layering of forums. This is inevitable and perhaps even desirable. We have to accept that the process of international dialogue is, like many good things in life, rather inefficient if evaluated from a narrow perspective, with a fair bit of wasted time and effort. We may recall what they say about advertising: 'Half is wasted; we just don't know which half.' Even more importantly, much of the effort is a very long-term investment, and such long-term projects are hard to evaluate on an ongoing, narrow cost–benefit basis.

Third, the dichotomy between regional and multilateral dialogues is a false one if the objective is to show one to be superior to the other. The clear need is for both; the issue is how to find the right balance between the two and, more importantly, how to make sure they work together to reap the potential synergies available. They are complementary and mutually reinforcing, not rival. It is easy for them to become rival, and for stronger institutions to attempt to stake out exclusive territory (the international financial institutions may sometimes have been guilty of this) but whenever one tries to claim exclusivity, this should be resisted on principle. The 'model' is one of institutions at different levels and different coverage, passing information and ideas in both directions – learning and providing value at the same time. This mindset or *modus operandi* is, unfortunately, far from universal.

Fourth, the central criterion in determining the groupings should be commonality of interest. If this can be established, the necessary energy and internal dynamic follows.

Fifth, the specific tasks or topics of dialogue can be grouped in various ways. I distinguish two main groups: a set of issues relating to macroeconomic policy (surveillance; crisis management, including the pooling of reserves; and exchange rate issues) and a set of issues relating to the broad topic of globalisation (where the most important function of dialogue is to help in the formation of the set of global rules that form Friedman's golden straitjacket).[11]

Sixth, we need patience. We should remember how long it took for Europe to succeed, and how this degree of success was not assured until the last moment.

Finally, European experience reminds us how important it is to have specific regional institutions, where there are permanent bureaucrats always keeping the flame of cooperation burning, even when interest is flagging elsewhere, so that the flame can be stoked into a real fire when the climate is right or when the need arises.

As for the institutions themselves, we can learn something from the European experience but there is no universal model for all regions of the world. When we look at the European experience and see how it might be related to Asia, the obvious difference is the lack of the kind of driving and determined leadership which took Germany and France from being enemies to being close allies in this endeavour. The unlikely historical basis of this allegiance might give hope for Asia. But where will the leadership come from? Japan has its own domestic preoccupations and, even before these became so dominant, showed no great capacity to seize the leadership opportunity. It might be understandably hurt that its initiative during the crisis – the AMF – was so promptly and definitively dismissed out of hand. Can China do it? It would be on the basis of potential and promise, rather than as a model to emulate, and it is not clear how Japan would react. Would it be too much to hope that, just as Europe was pushed and promoted by two unlikely allies (France and Germany), Japan and China might be able to find, here, some important common interests?

America has an ambivalent role in all this. The success of its market-based economy is a model for all, but some will want to take their own paths at their own pace. America hates to be excluded from any of the action, but it has such a large presence that it is hard for it not to be the elephant in the canoe. It showed during the Asian crisis that it is quicker to help strategic partners than those not so close to the perceived centre of its interests. It would help if it were less strident, a better listener, more tolerant of diversity, and more conscious of the various stages of historical evolution. For these reasons, it might accept, with resignation and even grace, that there will be some forums where participants will be more comfortable without it.

In the short term, all this will be hard and frustrating work. The Asian crisis has set back these cooperative efforts hugely and created a divide between Northeast and Southeast Asia which may inhibit the sort of East Asian cooperation which seemed so natural before 1997. The set of regional institutions which now exist are a reasonable basis, but they need an injection of energy, enthusiasm and dynamism.

NOTES

1   I have argued that there is only a minor role for international macro policy coordination (and this largely confined to the G-3). But as international interdependence increases, the need to know and understand what is happening

in the world economy increases. The current international conjuncture is perhaps more coincident in its cyclical shape than would be imposed on it by globalisation as such – the coincidence of downturns in the G-3 is, to a large extent, idiosyncratic. But there can be little doubt that the international linkages are much stronger than 10 years ago, and in all probability will be much stronger still in 10 years time. For all of us, an ability to forecast how the rest of the world is moving will be critical to our own policymaking.

2   As Dobson (2001: 26) observes, 'Peers must be willing to supply constructive criticism and those in potential or actual difficulty must be willing to accept objective analysis. Unless governments are willing to enter into this kind of give and take, the regional mechanism will simply become another overlay of officialdom.'

3   Dani Rodrik, quoted in *The Economist*, 29 September 2001, p. 19 of 'Survey: globalisation'.

4   It would be easy to exaggerate just how universal and all-encompassing the golden straitjacket may be. It does not seem true, for example, that tax rates will have to become uniform across countries.

5   The draft capital accord of the Basel Committee on Banking Supervision to commence in 2004, replacing the current capital accord (Basel I).

6   For more discussion of the role and rationale for regional arrangements, see Grenville (1998).

7   See Garnaut (1993: 308).

8   'Four Markets' includes finance officials and central bankers from Japan, Hong Kong, Singapore and Australia. 'Six Markets' also include China and South Korea.

9   For example, the role of the European Coal and Steel Community in initiating the European Union.

10 Two strong supporters of the need for a more country-specific and institution-responsive approach to prudential supervision and regulatory rules are Kane (2001) and Ball (2001)

11 Friedman (1999).

REFERENCES

Ball, R. (2001) *Infrastructure Requirements for an Economically Efficient System of Public Finance Reporting and Disclosure*, Washington DC: Brookings–Wharton Papers on Financial Services.

de Brouwer, G. and M. Kawai (2003 forthcoming) 'Economic linkages and implications for exchange rate regimes', in *Exchange Rate Regimes in East Asia*, London: Routledge.

Dobson, W.K. (2001) 'Deeper integration in East Asia: implications for the international economic system', in *East Asia and the International System: Report of a Special Study Group to The Trilateral Commission*, The Triangle Papers, No. 55, New York: The Trilateral Commission, pp. 11–35.

Friedman, T.L. (1999) *The Lexus and the Olive Tree*, New York: Farrar, Straus and Giroux.

Garnaut, R. (1993) Discussion of 'Is there a currency bloc in the Pacific?' by Jeffrey A. Frankel, in A. Blundell-Wignall (ed.), *The Exchange Rate, International Trade and the Balance of Payments*, Sydney: Reserve Bank of Australia, pp. 308–310.

Grenville, S.A. (1998) 'The Asian crisis and regional cooperation', address to the International Seminar on East Asia Financial Crisis, Beijing, 21 April (http://www.rba.gov.au).

Hale, D. (2001) 'Can broadband investment revive the U.S. technology sector in 2002?', *The Global Economic Observer, Zurich Research* 27, 7 September.

Kane, E. (2001) *Relevance and Need for International Regulatory Standards*, Washington DC: Brookings and Wharton Papers on Financial Services.

Park Y.C. (2000) 'Beyond the Chiang Mai Initiative: Rationale and Need for a Regional Monetary Arrangement in East Asia', paper presented to the seminar on 'Regional Cooperation: The Way Forward' at the annual Asian Development Bank meetings, Honolulu, 8 May.

Wyplosz, C. (2001) 'A monetary union in Asia? Some European lessons', in D.W. Gruen and J. Simon (eds), *Future Directions for Monetary Policies in East Asia*, Sydney: Reserve Bank of Australia, 124–155.

3 IMF and ADB perspectives on regional surveillance in East Asia

Gordon de Brouwer

East Asian policy dialogue on economic and financial developments within the region and beyond it occurs in a range of forums. These include the APEC Finance Ministers' Meeting, the ASEAN+3 Finance Ministers' Meeting, the ASEAN Finance Ministers' and Governors' Meetings, the Manila Framework Group (MFG), the Executives Meeting of the East Asian and Pacific Central Banks (EMEAP), the China-Japan-Korea Finance Ministers' Meeting, and the Four Markets Group. There is consensus in the region that there are now enough forums for policy dialogue. But there is also general agreement that many of them do not fulfil their potential as forums for substantive and effective economic monitoring and surveillance. In this context, there is an appetite to reform and strengthen some of these forums, especially the ASEAN+3, ASEAN and MFG meetings.

This chapter looks at ways to strengthen monitoring and surveillance in regional policy dialogue from the perspective of the International Monetary Fund (IMF) and the Asian Development Bank (ADB). These institutions are the core providers of much of the intellectual and logistic support for many of the meetings. They are involved in many meetings, either as presenters on recent developments or as observers. They also have their own views on, and their own interests in, the processes. The way they perceive regional surveillance may influence the way regional arrangements evolve. And as regional arrangements evolve, the roles they play may also change.

The chapter is structured in the following way. The first section looks at IMF perspectives on regional surveillance. The next section looks at ADB perspectives. The final section critically examines some elements of these different perspectives. Because the regional debate on surveillance is still developing, the chapter also sets out some guidelines for how the region should assess the role of different institutions in regional debate.

IMF PERSPECTIVES

The IMF lives and breathes surveillance. Economic and financial surveillance of member countries is one of its key functions:

One of the core responsibilities of the IMF is to maintain a dialogue with its member countries on the national and international repercussions of their economic and financial policies. This process of monitoring and consultation is normally referred to as 'surveillance', though there is nothing clandestine about it. Indeed, the consultation process has become increasingly open to public scrutiny in recent years. (IMF 2003: 1)

Surveillance has become more important over time, as economies have become more sophisticated and complex and as the connections between economies grow. Interdependencies within each economy and interdependencies between economies are expanding, and so the process of monitoring and debating countries' economic policies will remain important.

In recognition of this, the IMF has its own surveillance processes as well as participating in surveillance processes elsewhere, including in Europe and Asia. Let me consider the IMF's own surveillance processes first. The IMF's mandate to conduct surveillance comes from its Articles of Agreement, using surveillance to assess 'whether a country's economic developments and policies are consistent with the achievement of sustainable growth and domestic and external stability' and, more broadly, international stability (IMF 2003: 1).

The IMF conducts its own surveillance through three main mechanisms. The first is a general process of regular interaction, normally every year, with the key authorities of member countries through the Article IV consultation process, according to which:

These consultations focus on the member's exchange rate, fiscal, and monetary policies; its balance of payments and external debt developments; the influence of its policies on the country's external accounts; the international and regional implications of those policies; and on the identification of potential vulnerabilities. (IMF 2003: 1)

More controversially, they may also cover related policies which have macroeconomic consequences, like labour and environmental policies.

The second mechanism is the IMF's own reporting on economic and financial issues. The IMF's World Economic Outlook and Global Financial Stability reports provide opportunities for discussing developments and policies in key countries.

The third mechanism is through IMF lending programs to support adjustment in member countries, although this is usually referred to as conditionality. When the IMF extends its lending facilities to a country in need, it closely monitors and assesses domestic economic and financial developments. This can involve placing IMF staff on the ground in the country concerned. This is not what is ordinarily meant by surveillance; the debate about the suitability or otherwise of IMF programs is separate.

Following the various national and regional financial crises that have occurred in the past decade, the IMF has worked on ways to improve its surveillance. It regularly reviews its surveillance internally (IMF 2002a, b). Surveillance is also on the work program of the IMF Evaluation Office. The IMF highlights four ways in which it is strengthening surveillance (IMF 2003: 2).

The first is by improving the information provided by countries, especially with regard to timeliness, reliability and comprehensive coverage. The IMF's Special Data Dissemination Standards (SDDS) set out a benchmark for countries with capital market access to release key market information in an open and consistent manner. The information includes data on external reserves, cross-border liabilities, and short-term external debt.

The second is through improving the continuity of IMF surveillance. One East Asian criticism of the Fund in the late 1990s was that one visit one week a year was not sufficient for IMF staff to understand the complexities of the local economy and institutions and how decisions are made and put into effect. To improve continuity, the IMF has supplemented annual consultations, with interim staff visits to the country concerned and frequent informal meetings of the Executive Board to review developments in selected countries.

The third is to widen the focus of surveillance beyond the standard macroeconomic fundamentals to other aspects of vulnerability. These include a closer and more detailed examination of the financial sector, capital account issues, and external vulnerability (including aspects of policy interdependence and risks of contagion).

The fourth area pursued by the IMF has been to clarify basic international standards and enforce their observance. These include monetary and fiscal codes, codes for the financial sector and codes for data transparency. By monitoring countries' observance of international standards, there are increased incentives to adopt and improve adherence to such standards. In this context, the IMF and the World Bank have set up a Financial Sector Assessment Program (FSAP) and adopted a program of Reports on the Observance of Standards and Codes (ROSCs) (IMF 2003:2). Many of these ROSCs are published.[1]

The IMF is also involved in the internal surveillance processes of other countries or regions. Examples are IMF attendance at the G-7, the Organisation for Economic Co-operation and Development (OECD) and the Bank for International Settlements (BIS). In East Asia, the IMF is an active participant and presenter in the meetings of APEC Finance Officials, ASEAN and the MFG.

The involvement of the Fund in regional policy dialogue is motivated by a number of factors. The IMF has established expertise in macroeconomic surveillance, as well as the staff and financial resources to support it. Being able to draw on the experience of a big pool of countries over time enables the IMF to speak with authority about macroeconomic and financial issues. The IMF also has responsibilities for global financial stability; being involved in regional surveillance dialogue enables it to better assess vulnerabilities in systemically important economies and regions.

The IMF is active in promoting effective monitoring and surveillance in East Asia. It also closely follows the way a regional financial architecture in East Asia is developing and how it is likely to evolve over time. The ASEAN+3 process is of most interest in this respect. The ASEAN+3 work program includes developing a regional cooperative financing arrangement, improving regional surveillance mechanisms, and exploring options for stronger monetary cooperation in the region. These cut across some of the core functions of the IMF. So far, they have not done so in a way which undermines the IMF. For example, the Chiang Mai Initiative (CMI) requires IMF conditionality (or the likelihood of such conditionality) before 90 per cent of available funds can be disbursed.

But it is possible that other aspects, especially with respect to surveillance, may develop in ways that give less prominence to the IMF. The IMF has played a central role in the MFG surveillance process. Given the regionalist motivations of ASEAN+3 and its aspirations for an effective regional architecture, it is unlikely that the IMF would be the central agency for surveillance in the ASEAN+3 process. The IMF thinks that five conditions must be met if the regional policy process is to be effective.

First, the objectives and purpose of a regional mechanism must be well defined. A regional mechanism is not an end in itself but is a means to the end of stable and strong economies. The ASEAN+3 grouping is intent on avoiding crises. That is a worthy aim but policymakers need to be clear about what they have to do to achieve it. Policymakers need to define what regional surveillance should do. It is not enough for ASEAN+3 to just be a BIS-style coffee house in which people can talk issues over gently.

Second, the focus of regional surveillance must be clearly defined. Surveillance can include sharing information, dialogue on key issues, and even giving policy advice. What does ASEAN+3 want its surveillance to include? The approach taken to dealing with these issues varies, depending on the content. Surveillance on macroeconomic issues is different from that on financial sector vulnerabilities, requiring different sets of expertise and knowledge, as well as different degrees of intrusiveness.

Third, the guidelines for regional policy dialogue on surveillance must be clearly understood and set out. These guidelines can either be general and outline broad policy objectives or be more specific, rules based and legalistic, like targets for fiscal policy. This is a choice that is up to the countries involved. The IMF has a mix of these in its surveillance process: ROSCs and FSAPs are more rules oriented than the more general Article IV process, which covers broader trends, developments and issues. In terms of its internal surveillance processes, East Asia has to work out whether it wants a general or specific form of surveillance.

Fourth, the relationship between regional and global surveillance must be clearly determined. To put this at its most provocative, one might ask why the region needs its own surveillance process when a global process already exists in the form of IMF surveillance. One needs to consider the advantages of regional surveillance. The IMF does not subscribe to the view that the regional surveillance and financial cooperation will lead to Gresham's law of conditionality, with weak surveillance and conditionality pushing out strong surveillance and conditionality.

But the IMF does think that the advantages of global processes should not be ignored in the rush to find regional solutions. For example, proponents of regional dialogue argue that a regional mechanism boosts country ownership of policy and enables local institutional knowledge to be brought to the analysis and solutions of domestic economic and financial problems. But being local may also make it difficult to be completely frank about the problems a country is facing or to say no when it is right to say no. It can be useful to pass this pressure on to outsiders. Having outsiders with global experience involved in regional debate is also useful because it brings a wider set of insights to bear on problems. It is important not to be too dogmatic about the rights of regional surveillance and the wrongs of global (that is, IMF) surveillance. Ideally, the two can complement each other.

Fifth, effective surveillance mechanisms take time to develop, so speed is not of the essence. There is a lot to lay out in developing an effective regional surveillance mechanism. This means being prepared to be modest about what can be achieved in the short term. East Asia clearly wishes to move fast in developing regional processes. One should not, however, look at established cases, especially Europe, and just import their approach and techniques. Europe is relatively legalistic in its approach; it may be more useful for East Asia to adopt a practical approach tailored to its own circumstances.

ADB PERSPECTIVES

The ADB is also active in promoting and supporting economic surveillance in East Asia. It has pursued this through its Regional Economic Monitoring Unit (REMU), which was established in early 1999. REMU was established at the request of the ASEAN finance ministers to support the ASEAN Surveillance Process. The ADB sees REMU as part of the larger issue of regional monetary and financial cooperation (RMFC) in East Asia, encompassing information exchange and surveillance systems, regional resource and reserve pooling, exchange rate coordination, and domestic financial sector restructuring and reform.

The ADB's policy and research focus on the RMFC agenda was stimulated by the East Asian financial crisis. The ADB sees RMFC as not just a 'naive shift to regionalism and desire to mimic Europe'. Rather, RMFC is motivated by at least four economic factors.

First, there is a desire to put in place an effective architecture to deal with the problem of cross-country contagion that occurred in the region in 1997 and 1998. The mainstream view in East Asia is that regional mechanisms to provide funds in a financial crisis can be an important complement to global mechanisms.

Second, there is a view that international liquidity is insufficient to deal with future crises, so the region needs to build up its own resources. An element of this debate is that the region's access to international liquidity has not always been fair, especially in the terms and conditions of the IMF support packages. In this view of the world, a regional mechanism is not just desirable but necessary.

Third, taken as a whole across East Asia, financial markets are not deep and sophisticated, financial institutions are not strong and robust, and financial governance is not well developed or fully effective. The region shares a common vulnerability in finance.[2] For a development bank like the ADB, this means that there is a big regional work program.

Fourth, exchange rate developments in one country affect other countries, especially those with close economic ties in the region: exchange rate spillovers matter. The ADB sees value in exploring whether there are economic gains from cooperation in exchange rate management in East Asia and how these gains, if they exist, can be realised.

Work on regional financial and monetary cooperation is still in its early stages. The ADB sees four areas in which this work will advance: strengthening regional surveillance; developing the cooperative financing framework set up in the CMI, including multilateralising the framework by, for example, the centralised pooling of reserves in the region; developing proposals for regional cooperation in financial sector restructuring; and exploring various ideas for cooperative exchange rate regimes in East Asia.

These issues are being debated and are not yet resolved. It is difficult to prejudge how they will evolve. In the short to medium term (out four to five years), the ADB thinks that there is a need for stronger regional monitoring and surveillance, increased regional coordination in financial sector restructuring and development, and cooperation in reserve pooling. However, immediate exchange rate coordination at the regional level through any type of tying in of intra-regional exchange rates is considered not only not desirable but also not feasible. Hence, it recommends that exchange rate coordination should be approached more cautiously and gradually than coordination in surveillance and reserves pooling, perhaps after significant progress has been made in these two other areas of cooperation and substantial trust-building and political consensus has been mustered.

The ADB sees substantial value-added to regional economic monitoring and surveillance (REMS) over and above what is already done by global-level institutions. Merits of REMS are many, but at least four of them deserve special mention.

First, it is conceivable that East Asian countries may be more willing to engage in a frank exchange of information with a regional body over which they exercise substantial direct control than with a global institution where they may exert relatively much less influence.

Second, a regionally specialised unit may also have the advantage that the producer and user of the information share a common analytical framework. Greater scope for specialisation in regional economic situations and development issues has been acknowledged by the international community in the broader area of economic development, for example, through the formation of regional development banks.

Third, countries in East Asia may simply find it useful to pass information about each other's economies through a different analytical filter from that of the global institutions. Regional differences in analytical perspectives and in the diagnosis on economic problems have always been important.

Fourth, because a specifically regional monitoring mechanism would provide a device for analysing developments within the region on the basis of an analytical perspective that Asian countries find congenial, the credibility and perceived usefulness of this information may be enhanced.

Overall, the ADB sees a role for 'properly structured and well managed' surveillance activities at the national, regional and global levels. They can complement each other. This leads to considering the actual and potential role of the ADB in regional economic monitoring and surveillance. Consider, first, its current role. Within the framework of advancing regional monetary and financial cooperation, the ADB (2003) defines the role of regional economic monitoring and surveillance to be to:

> ... assist the developing member countries of ADB – both individually and collectively – to harness the full benefits of global financial integration and international capital flows while at the same time minimizing any disruptive effects.

The REMU was set up to perform this monitoring within the ADB. It has three functions. The first is to monitor economic policies and financial architecture issues from a regional and subregional perspective and disseminate the results to promote prudential economic management. The second is to strengthen the capacity for economic monitoring at the regional and subregional levels by providing technical assistance and advisory services. The third is to strengthen the ADB's relations with other international financial institutions, as well as regional and subregional bodies, by providing monitoring inputs to various meetings and discussions.

The REMU seeks to achieve these functions by providing analytical and capacity building support to the ASEAN Surveillance Process and housing the Asia Recovery Information Center (ARIC).[3]

The ASEAN finance ministers signed a terms of understanding in October 1998 establishing the ASEAN Surveillance Process. Ministers requested ADB support. Based on the principles of peer review and mutual interest among ASEAN member countries, the ASEAN Surveillance Process is intended to strengthen policymaking within the ASEAN grouping. The process monitors sectoral and social policies as well as the usual parameters of exchange rates and macroeconomic aggregates. It also includes provisions for capacity building, institutional strengthening, and sharing of information. The ASEAN finance ministers meet twice a year for policy coordination under the ASEAN Surveillance Process.

The ASEAN Surveillance Process is the first concrete attempt by a group of developing countries to exchange information on economic developments and policies, and to consider individual and collective responses to events that could negatively impact on subregional economic wellbeing. The ADB has set up a number of regional technical assistance projects to be implemented by REMU in support of the ASEAN Surveillance Process. These projects are to provide inputs to the ASEAN surveillance reports, conduct studies on specific topics, and strengthen the capacity of ASEAN officials and institutions on surveillance-related matters. Several of these technical assistance projects are already being implemented, one with co-financing from AusAID, the Australian Agency for International Development.

The ARIC concept first emerged at a meeting on development cooperation, 'Responding to the Asia Crisis', held in Sydney on 5 March 1999.[4] This meeting gave high priority to the need for accurate and timely information on the economic and social impacts of the Asian crisis and how recovery was progressing. Such information was seen as being vital to decision-makers in making informed choices on how best to respond to the crisis and to sustain the recovery's momentum.

Acting on a proposal by the Australian Government, the meeting agreed that an Internet-based facility would provide the most efficient means of gathering, collating and disseminating this information. The Australian Government subsequently invited the ADB to house the ARIC at its headquarters in Manila, which ultimately resulted in the ADB approving a regional technical assistance project for this purpose that is funded entirely through a grant from AusAID.

The ARIC web site has three objectives.[5] The first is to monitor the social and economic impacts of the Asian crisis and the recovery process with a view to making it easier to identify the remaining policy agenda for a sustained social as well as economic recovery. The second is to provide information on the response to the crisis by the international community, concerned governments, non-government organisations, and civil society at large. The third is to monitor and contribute to ongoing discussions of policy reform in response to the crisis.

I now consider the role that the ADB says it would be willing to play in regional economic monitoring and surveillance. There are three key elements.

First, the ADB would be willing to play a greater role in examining key aspects of policy reform in the region. It would be willing, for example, to manage a regional arrangement to coordinate financial sector reform in East Asia, such as an East Asian Banking Advisory Committee or an Asian Financial Institute.

Second, the ADB would be keen to extend its technical support for regional surveillance beyond ASEAN to the ASEAN+3 – a process that is already under way.

Finally, as East Asia extends and deepens its cooperative financing arrangements, the ADB would like to play a formal role in these regional financial arrangements. In particular, it volunteers to manage the pooling of regional foreign exchange reserves, including the disbursement of those reserves and the identification and enforcement of associated conditionalities for lending.

SOME ISSUES

Having looked at IMF and ADB views on surveillance, especially regional surveillance in East Asia, we can see some striking similarities and differences in what they say. At the start, it is worth emphasising the similarities, because they are very important. Both institutions are firmly committed to the view that effective monitoring and surveillance of macroeconomic and financial conditions and policies is an essential element in promoting regional economic stability. Both institutions support open and substantive policy dialogue in the region. Both institutions have many high-quality staff.

The differences are less important than the similarities. The IMF and ADB have different degrees of enthusiasm about regional financial dialogue, with the IMF more guarded and the ADB a more enthusiastic supporter. These are genuinely held beliefs. But what is clear to policymakers in the region is that these institutions' beliefs also reflect their interests. The IMF is the global incumbent with a wealth of experience in surveillance and a big and unrivalled pool of intellectual talent. It is the main game and may see itself this way. The ADB is the younger institution and sees an opportunity to position itself at the core of an East Asian infrastructure. It is the only existing institution in the region that can play this role.

Both institutions have something to offer regional policy dialogue. Both institutions, however, face serious impediments in projecting their views and interests in the region.

The capabilities and resources of the IMF are widely acknowledged in East Asia, and these are the Fund's greatest asset in surveillance. The willingness of the IMF to speak independently and directly on issues is also appreciated, even if regional policymakers at times criticise it for insensitivity. But it is hamstrung. One feature of East Asian regionalism that underpins the ASEAN+3 process is a desire to find Asian solutions to Asian problems. This is itself a product of the tension that arose during the Asian financial crisis between East Asia on the one hand and the IMF (and the United States) on the other.[6] In some quarters, the IMF is seen as part of the problem, not the solution, although this does not seem to be the majority view in East Asia. But the fact that the IMF is so clearly an outsider puts it at a disadvantage in terms of current regionalist sentiment in the region.

One example is the way in which many in the region view the approach of the IMF (and, for that matter, the United States) in MFG meetings. The MFG has been seen in the region as largely a forum for the IMF and the United States to pursue economic reform in East Asian countries, rather than a forum for genuine dialogue between countries in East Asia and North America on key macroeconomic issues of concern. Takahashi (2002: 4) is blunt about the assessment of the MFG by Japan (and others):

> The Manila Framework meeting was once called the 'Asian G-7' and was expected to become an important forum for policy dialogue. However, in reality, discussion at this forum is not lively, partly because of its nature. Namely, the US (and the IMF) unilaterally preach to Asian countries.

Such dissatisfaction led to reform of the MFG in 2003 under the stewardship of South Korea. Responsibility for dialogue has been shifted more to country members and there is a greater focus on research-based discussion of issues that matter to the region, while still welcoming the active participation of the IMF.

The perception in the region is that the IMF is more interested in using regional policy dialogue forums to advance the cause of economic reform rather than facilitate dialogue, create trust and mechanisms for cooperation, and better secure economic stability and prosperity, including the pursuit of economic reform. This perception is probably a caricature of what IMF officials really want for the region. But it creates some distance between regional policymakers and the Fund because there are suspicions that the aims of the two sides are different. To some extent, this would be alleviated by greater involvement of IMF staff, especially at senior levels, in East Asian discussion and dialogue.

The ADB faces a different set of constraints. The ADB could play an important role, not just in regional dialogue, surveillance and reform processes, but also in regional cooperative financing arrangements. But the ADB is a new entrant to the business of regional monitoring and surveillance. REMU, the unit that is responsible for this job within the ADB, is small in size and other resources. A substantial enlargement of both the professional capacity and other resources devoted for regional monitoring and surveillance within the ADB would be required for the institution to effectively perform the duties of regional monitoring and surveillance.

Some in the region also have concerns that the geographic coverage of the ADB is too wide to make it the base for East Asian dialogue and cooperation. Moon et al. (2003: 15) argue that ADB assistance goes to 43 countries. They say:

> … there are limits to … [its] ability to strengthen solidarity among members. It will be very difficult to bring all these [43] countries together for regional cooperation.

The ADB is Asian (as well as Pacific), but some see it as too broad to be *East Asian*. It is more supportive of regional processes than the IMF, but its diverse responsibilities and wide membership mean that it too is seen by some as not sufficiently representing the aspirations of East Asia in financial and monetary cooperation. For an institution which is meant to service the development needs of the Asia Pacific region, there are also concerns that scarce resources are being diverted from otherwise important development projects, especially in countries outside East Asia. And because it is a development bank, its policy responsibilities do not include surveillance of the region's developed economies, notably Japan.

END NOTE

The issue of policy dialogue for monitoring and surveillance of macroeconomic and financial developments and policies is a complicated one. This chapter has looked at the issue from the perspective of the IMF and the ADB, two of the key multilateral institutions involved.

Both institutions think that effective monitoring and surveillance of macroeconomic and financial conditions are an essential element in securing economic and financial stability. Both support regional dialogue for this purpose. Where they differ is in the emphasis. The IMF cautions against regional mechanisms for their own sake; it says they need to be purposeful, substantive, and well managed. The IMF sees the development of surveillance mechanisms as a regionally-based initiative, but believes it can assist because it can bring a global perspective and experience. The ADB has been strongly supportive of regional arrangements, has helped build surveillance capacity in ASEAN and has provided information on developments in particular countries. It would like to play a bigger role.

Both institutions face constraints. The IMF has well-established credentials in surveillance, but it is seen as an outsider to the region; this limits the degree to which the region will want to involve it in regional institutions. The ADB is an Asia Pacific institution and so also has limited appeal as an institution for East Asia. As a regional development bank rather than regional monetary fund, it is not clear that it is the most appropriate vehicle to deliver regional surveillance and financial cooperation.

In the final instance, it will be up to Asia to decide how it wishes to proceed on regional surveillance. In the process, some 'competition' between the IMF and ADB is likely to be healthy and beneficial for all concerned.

NOTES

This chapter is based primarily on presentations made by Charles Adams, Assistant Director, International Monetary Fund Regional Office for Asia and the Pacific, and Srinivasa Madhur, Principal Economist, Regional Economic Monitoring Unit, Asian Development Bank, at the conference on 'Linkages in East Asia: Implications for

Currency Regimes and Policy Dialogue', Seoul, Korea, 23–24 September 2002. The author is grateful to Peter Drysdale and Simon Smiles for comments and suggestions. The views expressed in this paper are the author's, and responsibility for any errors is the author's alone. The analyses and assessments presented here do not necessarily reflect the official views of the International Monetary Fund and the Asian Development Bank, or their Boards of Directors or the governments the directors represent.

1 See <http://www.imf.org/external/np/rosc/rosc.asp>.
2 For example, see de Brouwer (2003a).
3 The next five paragraphs draw heavily on ADB (2003).
4 ARIC can be accessed at <http://aric.adb.org> or through the ADB web site at <http://www.adb.org>.
5 The ARIC web site is designed primarily for use by government agencies, the international assistance community, private sector users, NGOs, economic policy analysts, academic researchers, and journalists. It includes seven sections: Recovery Watch, Social Dimensions, International Assistance, Country Focus, ARIC Indicators, Meetings and Conferences, and Key Hyperlinks. Under the ARIC initiative, REMU staff and consultants also prepare an Asia Recovery Report twice a year.
6 See de Brouwer (2003b).

REFERENCES

ADB (Asian Development Bank) (2003) 'The Regional Economic Monitoring Unit', available at <http://www.adb.org/REMU/default.asp>.

de Brouwer, G.J. (2003a) 'Financial markets, institutions, and integration in East Asia', *Asian Economic Papers*, 2(1).

—— (2003b) 'The IMF and East Asia: A changing regional financial architecture', in Chris Gilbert and David Vines (eds), *The IMF and the International Financial Architecture*, Cambridge: Cambridge University Press.

IMF (International Monetary Fund) (2002a) 'Biennial review of the implementation of the Fund's surveillance and of the 1977 surveillance decision', report prepared by the Policy Review Department, International Capital Markets Department and Research Department, 13 March.

—— (2002b) 'Reforming the IMF: Progress since Prague 2000', available at <http://www.imf.org/external/np/exr/ib/2002/120502.htm>.

—— (2003) 'Fact sheet on surveillance', available at <http://www.imf.org/external/np/exr/facts/surv.htm>.

Moon, W., D.R. Yoon and C.Y. Ahn (2003) 'The role of regional development banks: Financing for development and solidarity in East Asia', paper presented at the International Seminar on 'A New Financial Market Structure for East Asia: How to Promote Regional Financial Market Integration', organised by the Korea Institute for International Economic Policy (KIEP), Hawaii, 7–8 February.

Takahashi, W. (2002) 'Comments at the ASEAN+3 High Level Seminar on Management of Short-term Capital Flows and Capital Account Liberalization', paper presented in Beijing, 11 October, mimeo, Bank of Japan.

4 Structures to support stability and growth: some observations based on UK experience

Andrew Kilpatrick

INTRODUCTION

Britain has a long tradition of being an open trading nation. Even in the latter part of the nineteenth century, external trade was approaching a level equivalent to around one-quarter of GDP, only marginally lower than where it is today.

Trade can play a vital role in growth and development. This has been true both in the United Kingdom (UK) and elsewhere. By opening up new markets and exploiting new resources, by seeking out comparative advantage and increasing specialisation and choice and by allocating capital to activities and regions where rates of return are high, trade has provided numerous economic advantages. But in the nature of their openness, trading nations are also more susceptible to external shocks and events outside their direct control. In particular, exchange rate pressures and their impact on economic conditions can pose awkward problems for the authorities in such countries.

Over its long trading history the UK has been involved in numerous currency and trade regimes – from the gold standard, the sterling area and the Commonwealth preferential tariff regime to Bretton Woods, the European Free Trade Association (EFTA), the European Economic Community (EEC), the exchange rate mechanism (ERM) and now a free-floating system. This paper does not attempt to review the reasons for switches from one regime to the next. Instead it draws on recent UK experience, including in the context of the European Union (EU), to look at economic and institutional structures that appear suitable for stability and growth in the modern context of instant communications and global capital flows. The paper focuses mainly on macroeconomic aspects from a UK–EU perspective but the principles and issues raised seem pertinent elsewhere, including in the East Asia context.

I look first at some lessons from the British experience of policymaking prior to 1997, lessons which have been taken into account in the subsequent redesign of Britain's economic and financial policies. Next, I discuss structures for economic stability in a global context; here I consider macroeconomic frameworks and some underlying principles that seem most conducive to the achievement of economic stability, including exchange rate stability. In the final section of the paper I describe some developments in the EU since the Maastricht Treaty that have broadened and deepened the institutional framework for economic cooperation in a regional context.

I draw no conclusions for appropriate currency regimes. I argue that adoption of clear principles, such as transparency and accountability, and the creation of institutions with clear objectives and focused responsibilities can strengthen credibility and provide room for appropriate, though suitably limited, discretion for policymakers to deal with economic shocks. This provides a strong basis for stability, growth and stable international linkages.

Rigorous multilateral surveillance carried out on a regional basis and consistently applied, and associated peer pressure, can also support stability and growth. Deeper linkages and closer integration can be aided by this route but rely on strong political commitment as much as on effective institutions for economic coordination. The EU experience suggests that intensive cooperation takes time to evolve and requires significant commitment and resources.

MACROECONOMIC INSTABILITY IN THE UNITED KINGDOM BEFORE 1997

After a long period of sustained expansion during the 1950s and 1960s, the breakdown of the Bretton Woods fixed exchange rate regime followed by the oil crisis in 1973 ushered in a new phase of weaker and disruptive growth in the UK. For most of the next two and a half decades UK policymakers pursued unsuccessfully a range of monetary and fiscal policy regimes. The resulting macroeconomic instability was costly to business, hampered growth and investment and exacerbated a growing problem of structural unemployment.

For these reasons the UK has since 1997 undertaken fundamental reforms to create institutional structures designed to achieve much greater economic stability. The changes were informed by lessons learned from previous experience.[1]

Monetary policy

Prior to 1997, the UK adopted several monetary policy regimes, as summarised in Box 4.1. Figure 4.1 illustrates the UK's poor inflation record between 1967 and 1997. During the 1970s annual inflation averaged 13 per cent, peaking at almost 27 per cent in August 1975. In the 1980s inflation fell back to an average of 7 per cent, but it was well above the German inflation rate of 3 per cent, for example. Inflation was not only high but also volatile, increasing uncertainty and the costs from unanticipated inflation.

Although there are many reasons for the UK's poor inflation record, a key contribution arose from poor institutional arrangements. Monetary policy should be a stabilising force for the economy. However, mistakes were made

Box 4.1 Post-war UK monetary policy regimes prior to 1997

In the post-war period there have been significant changes in the prevailing monetary regimes. These arrangements reflected a process of learning and adaptation to the problems generated by previous regimes and changing institutional and external environments.

In the post-war period it is possible to identify five broad monetary policy regimes, each with different institutional constraints and external environments, prior to the introduction of the new monetary framework in 1997. The regimes are as follows.

Fixed exchange rates (Bretton Woods), 1948–71. There were direct controls on domestic credit, strong foreign exchange controls on capital account, and relatively passive monetary policy aiming to raise growth and employment. The current account and exchange rate acted as a discipline on policy. The results were a stop–go policy, balance of payments crises, devaluation and gradually increasing inflation and unemployment.

Floating exchange rate, no monetary anchor, 1971–76. There were credit controls and exchange controls; and monetary policy targeted growth and employment. The results were rapidly accelerating inflation and volatile growth rates.

Monetary targets, 1976–87. From 1979 exchange and credit controls were liberalised. Monetary policy was directed at controlling different monetary aggregates in order to reduce inflation. As a result, the behaviour of monetary aggregates was unpredictable, there were complications due to financial liberalisation, and inflation was reduced at the expense of output volatility and unemployment.

Exchange rate targeting, 1987–92. There were no exchange and capital controls. Markets were increasingly globalised. Monetary policy was constrained by the exchange rate target. The results were inappropriate monetary policy for domestic conditions, an overvalued exchange rate, recession and ejection from the exchange rate mechanism (ERM) due to capital movements and lack of credibility of policy.

Inflation targeting (post-ERM), 1992–97. There was an open economy and a floating exchange rate. Monetary policy was directed mainly at inflation, but was still managed by the Chancellor of the Exchequer. Some transparency was introduced. The results were that inflation fell, but the framework was not fully credible as expectations of inflation remained above official targets.

which meant that inflation was higher and more volatile than it should have been. This fostered economic instability and harmed the long-term performance of the UK economy. Many of these policy mistakes were made because the aims and procedures of monetary policy were not properly defined.

Figure 4.1 Inflation in the United Kingdom, 1967–97, per cent

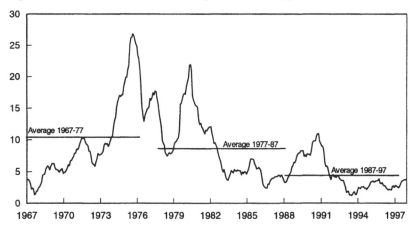

Source: UK Treasury.

Inappropriate objectives

Price stability offers the best contribution monetary policy can make towards meeting the objective of high and stable levels of growth and employment. However, for many years monetary policy was not solely directed at maintaining price stability. Indeed, it was thought that tolerating higher inflation could enhance rather than damage long-term growth and employment. As we now know, and as Figure 4.2 illustrates, attempts to hold down unemployment not only failed in the long term, but also were associated with accelerating inflation and ultimately higher unemployment.

Partly because of high and volatile inflation, sterling's exchange rate was also volatile throughout much of this period, adding to the problems of economic management. Figure 4.3 shows sterling's exchange rate index (ERI) from 1970 on. Sterling declined from DM6.54 (€4.48) to the pound to DM3.89 (€2.66) between 1973 and 1979, reflecting the high relative rate of inflation in the UK. It then fluctuated between DM2.74 (€0.67) and DM5.07 (€3.47) until 1987. At this point policymakers attempted to use monetary policy to target the exchange rate directly. However, for a number of reasons this objective of policy turned out to be inappropriate and could be achieved only at the expense of price and output stability. For example, as a consequence of the UK's ERM membership, interest rates were prevented from being reduced quickly enough in 1991 and 1992 to forestall a move into recession.

Specifying objectives

It is also important to ensure that the goal of monetary policy is specified properly. For example, in the 1980s UK policymakers believed that low

Figure 4.2 Inflation and unemployment in the United Kingdom, 1967–2001, per cent

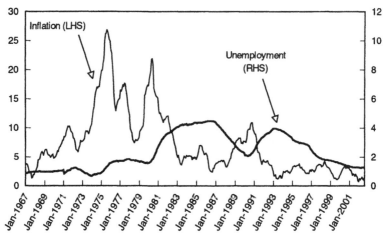

Source: UK Treasury.

Figure 4.3 UK nominal exchange rate (exchange rate index), 1970–2002

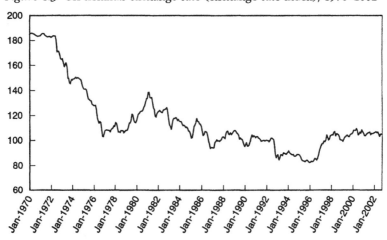

Source: UK Treasury.

inflation could be achieved by rigidly targeting various monetary aggregates. While the attempt to control inflation was laudable, money supply targets reflected a theory of how monetary policy operated which paid insufficient attention to the impact of institutional changes on the relationship between prices and money. The development of global capital markets, financial deregulation and changing technology had led to significant and unanticipated changes in the velocity of circulation of money. As a result, there was no clear and stable relationship between money demand and inflation, making it impossible to rely on fixed monetary rules to deliver price stability.

The experience highlights a key shortcoming of targeting intermediate variables, rather than the inflation rate. Intermediate targets can lead to an excessive focus on the targeted variable at the expense of the wide variety of other important indicators of inflationary pressures. On a number of occasions, it became clear the intermediate targets that had been set were not delivering the results expected. However, rather than abandoning this approach, policymakers tried to modify it by setting different target ranges or by targeting different indicators, including the exchange rate. In the UK this happened on almost an annual basis during the 1980s and early 1990s and undermined the credibility of policy.

Looking forward

A lack of clear, stable objectives was also one of the main reasons why the authorities were sometimes slow to react to changing circumstances. Without well-defined objectives, policymakers find it more difficult to be proactive. Inflationary pressures were thus often allowed to build up before corrective action was taken. Interest rates were eventually higher and more volatile than they otherwise would have been. Moreover, earlier tightening of policy might have forestalled the booms and subsequent recessions or might have made them less severe.

Identifying roles and responsibilities

In monetary policy regimes prior to 1997 the government was responsible both for designing the monetary policy framework and for taking policy decisions to meet the stated target. Moreover, in addition to advising on and implementing the government's monetary policy decisions, the Bank of England was responsible for managing the government's debt, as well as the regulation and supervision of the financial sector.

The specific nature of the government's responsibilities remained less than clear due to the ambiguous specification of its objectives. Moreover, by giving the Bank multiple responsibilities, it was not always obvious which activity was of paramount importance to the Bank.

Until the 1990s, monetary policy was generally conducted on an ad hoc basis. Although a range of informal conventions was in place, no specific guidelines on how decisions should be made were set. There was not even a precise and regular timetable for monetary policy decisions to be made and announced. There was often little consistency in monetary policy over time, and outsiders were unable to examine effectively the process by which decisions were made.

This problem was compounded by the fact that monetary policy decisions were made in the context of a political process where short-term pressures were often paramount. Although politicians had access to the advice of independent experts, they would not always follow that advice, making monetary policy even more difficult to predict.

The mere fact that monetary policy decisions were made by politicians created the suspicion that they would be based on short-term political factors, rather than in the economy's long-term interests. Long-term interest rates contained a risk premium to reflect the possibility that the timing and magnitude of interest changes might reflect political considerations.

Transparency and accountability

Monetary policy also lacked transparency. Policymakers operated behind closed doors, and decisions were often made with little or no explanation to the wider public.

This lack of transparency meant it was not easy to hold policymakers to account for their performance. More importantly, it meant that policymakers were unable to build credibility with markets and with the general public. Because people did not have a clear idea of what policymakers were trying to achieve and how they were operating, they did not have full confidence that policymakers would be able to deliver long-term price stability.

Fiscal policy

In the period to 1997, the UK's fiscal policy experience was also one of instability and lack of clarity. Figures 4.4 and 4.5 show the volatile paths for the overall fiscal deficit, public debt and net worth that the UK experienced from the 1970s on. There were periods of substantial deficit, rapid build-up of debt and declines in net worth. Similar volatile patterns can be found for the output gap and growth. This instability frequently translated into uncomfortable policy choices.

Between 1979 and 1996 the overall deficit averaged more than 3 per cent of GDP. Moreover, there was a substantial decline in public sector net investment, from around 6 per cent of GDP to less than 1 per cent. Compared with other G-7 countries over this period the UK had a more volatile economy, invested less, grew more slowly and had higher inflation.

The purpose and precise objectives of fiscal policy were left unspecified or vague, allowing policymakers an inappropriate degree of discretion. Policy could thus be changed in the light of circumstances, both economic and political, but without great risk of being called to account, at least in the short term.

A notably serious failing during this time was improper coordination of fiscal and monetary policy. This might seem paradoxical, given that the decision to set both the fiscal stance and the interest rate rested in the hands of one person, the Chancellor of the Exchequer. But more often than not short-term interest rates were cut within a few days of the announced budget package. Between 1979 and 1996, interest rates were cut on 14 such occasions, and raised on only two.

Figure 4.4 Public sector net borrowing (per cent of GDP)[a] 1970–99

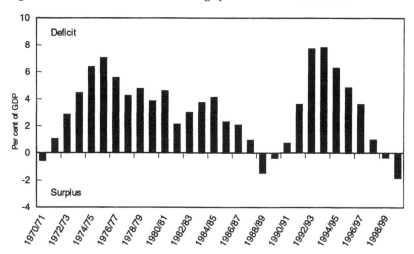

Note
a   Excluding windfall tax and associated spending.
Source: UK Treasury.

It also appears that the stance of fiscal policy did not always work fully in the interests of stability. For example, during the 1980s and early 1990s the underlying stance of policy seems to have been relatively tight when the economy was weak, and loose when the economy was overheating.

Cyclical effects

This problem arose in part because there was insufficient care in taking account of the effects of the economic cycle on public finances. A particularly instructive episode occurred between 1986 and 1996. During this economic cycle output is estimated to have ranged from some 4 per cent above trend in the late 1980s to a similar amount below trend in the recession of the early 1990s. The overall fiscal balance also fluctuated significantly, from a surplus of just over 1 per cent at its peak in 1988 to a deficit approaching 8 per cent of GDP by 1993.

When the fiscal position moved into surplus (1988–89) after a long period in deficit there was a belief that the economy's potential had increased – there were few visible signs of inflation, for example – and that the economy would remain strong and the surplus would last. Commentators and politicians began to talk of 'supply-side' miracles and even in terms of 'repaying the national debt', and policy was loosened.

The underlying position was not so rosy, however. Potential output had not risen as far as thought. When it became clear that output was well above

Figure 4.5 Public sector net debt and net worth (per cent of GDP)

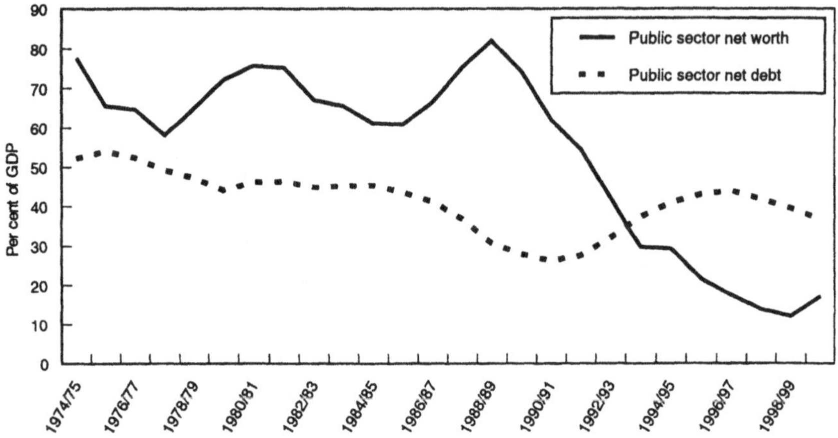

Source: UK Treasury.

potential, it was too late: inflation accelerated, policy was tightened and the economy went into reverse.

One lesson to be drawn from this episode is the importance of trying to take into account the impact of the economic cycle on public finances. Such estimates are necessarily imprecise but it is far better to make some attempt to adjust for the cycle than none at all.

Had such an attempt been made, an unwarranted loosening of fiscal policy at the top of the cycle might not have occurred. In retrospect, the output gap was strongly positive by the late 1980s, and it implied that a large component of the fiscal surplus was due to cyclical (and thus temporary) rather than structural factors. Estimates now show that, rather than being in surplus, the underlying fiscal position was one of deficit of the order of 1 per cent. The loosening of policy merely acted to compound the difficulties of an overheating economy and forced a greater subsequent retrenchment than would otherwise have been necessary.

Trend growth

A further dimension to this experience concerned the assessment of trend growth, rather than the position of the economy in relation to trend. Trend growth was thought to have increased substantially. In fact, throughout the 1980s the economy had confounded the critics and recovered strongly with little evidence of inflation.

Published estimates of the medium-term growth path set out in successive budget reports were thus moved up gradually from an average of 2¼ per cent annual growth (over 4–5 years ahead) in the early part of the period to

3 per cent by 1989. Based on an assumption of a medium-term growth path of 3 per cent, the fiscal projections were duly overestimated, making tax cuts seemingly viable and consistent with a stable fiscal and debt position. It was not long, however, before it became clear that trend growth had been significantly overestimated and had to be revised down.

Consequences for public spending

By creating uncertainty, mistakes about medium-term assumptions also carried important consequences for public spending settings. In parallel with the often short-term and expedient approach to fiscal policy, a ritual of bid, counter-bid, escalation and deadlock characterised much of spending policy during this time. Annual jousting between spending departments and the Treasury would typically continue until time ran out and a special council of ministers or even the Prime Minister was required to declare in favour of department X or Y.

In effect the planning horizon was a year ahead. This led to inefficiencies of various kinds, including, for example, poor value for money spending at year end under a 'use it or lose it' mentality. While indicative plans were set for years 2 and 3, little attention was paid to them, not least because the economic and fiscal projections on which they were based constantly changed. Institutional 'short-termism' prevailed and investment in particular suffered as a result.

Lessons

Some broad conclusions and lessons may be drawn from the experiences of this period. In particular, macroeconomic policy should benefit from clear principles and targets; transparency and accountability; well-defined roles and responsibilities among the key actors; operational independence for the monetary authority in setting interest rates; adequate mutual support between fiscal and monetary policy in promoting stability; caution against over-optimistic and insufficiently forward-looking assessments; taking account of the effects of the cycle on the public finances; and a more stable and long-term framework for public spending decisions. Fiscal and monetary decisions should always be made in the best interests of the economy.

Structures for economic stability in a global context

So far I have examined aspects of the UK's performance and have tried to draw out some lessons for policy. The following section of the paper develops these ideas in a global context. Macroeconomic stability provides the best backdrop to achieving structural reform, trade and growth. It supports stable linkages between countries in a region in a benign way and fosters further integration.

An increasingly integrated regional and global economy clearly offers great benefits to countries if they pursue policies for stability and growth. But it also poses new challenges for macroeconomic policy. Sound policies can allow countries to boost trade and attract international capital more quickly, in greater volumes and at a lower cost than ever before, supporting new investment, regional integration and higher growth. But policies perceived to be unsustainable can lead to volatile capital flows, excessive financing costs and slower and more volatile economic growth. Moreover, this acts as a barrier to regional integration since economic convergence is jeopardised and cooperative arrangements are put under strain.

In this new global environment, and largely irrespective of the particular features of regional economic linkages, it is important that macroeconomic and financial frameworks in countries set clear long-term goals, are able to respond flexibly to shocks and build credibility. This can best be achieved through the pursuit of constrained discretion.

Macroeconomic stability involves low and stable inflation rates, fiscal positions and debt levels which are consistent with long-term solvency and an exchange rate regime that does not distort relative prices. While these factors cannot by themselves ensure strong and sustainable growth, they are a precondition for it. They provide the platform from which structural changes in labour, product and capital markets can be translated into durable improvements in productivity and living standards, and poverty reduction. While macroeconomic frameworks for stability are not sufficient to induce regional integration they are necessary for successful linkages.

However, a key policy question is how best to achieve and sustain macroeconomic stability in the face of exogenous economic shocks. There are five main reasons for this. First, with greater integration into a regional (and world) economy, the potential source of shocks (both positive and negative) is likely to widen. Second, as trade and financial links deepen, external shocks are likely to have bigger effects on the domestic economy and differences between countries are amplified. Third, as capital accounts become more open, and financial markets more sophisticated, so the speed of transmission of shocks is likely to increase. Fourth, greater exposure to international capital markets is likely to increase the importance of perceptions of the strength of fundamentals and expectations of future policy changes. Finally, greater openness may also result in structural changes to underlying economic relationships and economic structures, by changing relative prices.

Discretion versus rules

One approach to dealing with these exogenous shocks would be for policymakers to operate with complete discretion, taking each situation as it comes, and responding in the way that seems most appropriate at the time. However, history suggests such an approach is unlikely to build credibility.

In part, this stems from the 'time inconsistency' problem: governments find it hard to commit to long-term goals if short-term pressures point in another direction (Barro and Gordon 1983). Without a binding commitment to low inflation, for example, governments have a short run incentive to boost inflation, in order to lower unemployment below its natural rate. But rational agents anticipate the government's opportunistic behaviour, and adjust price and wage-setting behaviour accordingly. The end result is higher inflation, but without any output gain.

An alternative approach would be to forgo discretion altogether in favour of fixed rules, such as a money supply growth rule. By 'tying its hands' to a fixed rule, the government forces itself to commit to its long-term policy goal. A credible commitment should reduce inflation expectations and long-term interest rates.

But, as we saw in the UK case, rigid rules-based frameworks can run into a number of difficulties, which are likely to be more acute in a more integrated, global economy. One is that the relationships on which such rules are based – such as stable money demand functions or exchange rate arrangements like the ERM – are prone to break down in the face of asymmetric shocks such as financial deregulation, rapid capital flows, changing technology and tastes and country divergences. Another is that rigid rules do not provide the flexibility needed to respond to economic shocks – leading to substantial costs of adjustment or, at the extreme, to irresistible pressure on the rule itself. If a fixed rule becomes too costly to maintain, it will tend to undermine credibility, rather than support it.[2]

'State-contingent' rules might be an alternative but there will always be a tendency to want to cater for many plausible states of the world. Exceptions may then be drawn too widely, undermining the credibility of the rule; and the room for debate over whether the target is met widens substantially.

Rather than complete discretion or fixed rules, it seems preferable to seek constrained discretion. Here long-term stability requires an overall framework that constrains macroeconomic policy to achieve clear long-term and sustainable goals, but that gives discretion to respond flexibly to shocks. If policymakers have a sufficiently credible commitment to long-term stability, then they will be able to exercise discretion without damaging long-term expectations.

Policy credibility can be enhanced, and therefore be more effective, if the objectives of policy are clear and if the way in which those objectives are to be pursued is transparent.

Three key principles for a framework of credible constrained discretion are clear, sound long-term policy objectives; pre-commitment, through institutional arrangements and procedural rules; and maximum openness and transparency, and clear accountability.

Long-term policy objectives

A first step in shifting the policy focus towards sustainable long-term goals is to set appropriate objectives for macroeconomic policy which are clearly defined, and against which performance can be judged. By themselves, long-term objectives cannot guarantee credibility. Simply announcing a low inflation target, for example, is not sufficient to build a reputation for low inflation. Governments must also demonstrate their commitment over time and eliminate 'time inconsistency' by building a track record of sound performance.

Institutional support and procedural rules

Credibility can be enhanced by designing procedures and institutions which support long-term stability. The higher the cost for a government to break its promises or change its objectives, the more likely the public and investors are to believe that decisions are being taken for sound, long-term reasons.

An important element in this context is the removal of potential conflicts of interest. Monetary policy, fiscal policy, debt management and financial regulation can all benefit from having separately identified objectives, for the achievement of which a particular person or institution is responsible. Situations where a policy instrument is frustrated in achieving its objective because of the need to have regard to another objective are rarely good for credibility. Conflicts of this kind can arise, for example, when interest rates and exchange rates are both seen as instruments of policy, for example, in controlling inflation. Other examples include monetary financing of fiscal deficits, avoiding interest rate rises for fear of the effects on the budget deficit or financial sector and turning a blind eye to bad loan problems to avoid compromising macroeconomic policy settings.

Identifying separate institutions for each policy objective may help improve performance, because the institution can then focus its efforts more directly and strengthen its expertise and knowledge on its area of responsibility. It can also enhance accountability, because it is much easier to see whether or not the objective has been met.

A second aspect of the removal of potential conflicts of interest is the distancing of short-term political influence from day-to-day decision-making. For example, the creation of an independent central bank with a clearly defined remit to achieve low inflation removes an immediate source of inflationary bias, while providing a clear and unambiguous statement of the policy target.

This argument is not so easily applied to fiscal policy since fiscal policy involves economic and social objectives that go beyond macroeconomic stability. Nonetheless, governments can put in place procedures which encourage a long-term focus – for instance, greater use of explicit fiscal rules, legal requirements that commit governments to set long-term objectives and account for their performance, and public expenditure management procedures to ensure that spending plans are consistent with the fiscal objectives of the government as a whole.

Credibility in part also relies on a belief that institutional arrangements will survive political change. That is why stable institutions, strengthened where possible by legislative frameworks, help. Even for those countries where a reputation for sound macroeconomic policy has been built up, there is a risk that credibility may be lost if the institutional framework is not able to support it going forward. This is particularly true if the credibility of the existing policy stance is built on the reputation of an individual, rather than the institution which the individual heads.

Openness, transparency and accountability

Imperfect information – about the true state of the economy and, more importantly, about the true motivations of policymakers – makes it very hard for policymakers to build a reputation quickly. Even if macroeconomic errors begin as mistakes rather than deliberate deception, the more suspicion there is about motivation, and the greater the asymmetry of information between government and the investing public, the higher is the short-term cost that is paid in lost credibility when things go wrong.

Transparency can therefore make it easier for governments to undertake discretionary policy actions without damaging long-term credibility. If actions are clearly explained and if it is shown how expected outcomes are consistent with long-term goals, it is possible to achieve flexibility to deal with real crises and build consensus for difficult decisions.

Greater transparency also means it is easier to hold policymakers to account for their performance. The public are able to examine the arguments and issues that lie behind policy decisions and should be able to find a thorough explanation of key decisions.

Credibility can be further enhanced through formal accountability procedures. For example, in the UK, legislation requires that the minutes of the Monetary Policy Committee (MPC) and the voting record of individual members are published on a regular and timely basis, along with a quarterly inflation report. The non-executive directors of the Bank of England are also required to keep the procedures of the MPC under review and members of the MPC appear regularly before parliamentary committees.

Recent experiences in policy frameworks

In recent years, there has been a substantial shift in policymaking away from pure discretion, and from fixed rules, towards frameworks that aim to build more credibility in less rigid and more institutional ways.

In most industrialised countries, pure discretion has disappeared and monetary policy has been characterised by a move towards independent central banks backed by greater transparency in decision-making. It has taken time for monetary authorities to establish a reputation for delivering price stability. But clearer frameworks, backed by procedures that have enhanced transparency, openness and accountability, have strengthened policy credibility.

Recent experience of exchange rate regimes also shows that the proportion of intermediate exchange rate arrangements has fallen significantly during the last decade, with a rise in the number of countries adopting 'hard' pegs at one extreme and floating rates at the other (Fischer 2001).

A number of fiscal frameworks aimed at building credibility have also emerged. One is the use of fixed fiscal targets or rules such as the EU Stability and Growth Pact (see below). Another is legislative requirements for governments to set long-term objectives, account for their performance, and provide transparent and timely budget reports (e.g. the UK's Code for Fiscal Stability, Australia's Charter of Budget Honesty and New Zealand's Fiscal Responsibility Act). Another is legislative limits on discretionary spending (e.g. the Gramm–Rudman–Hollings Acts, Omnibus Budget Reconciliation Acts and the Balanced Budget Act in the United States). Finally, some emerging markets have introduced (or are introducing) fiscal responsibility laws to enhance the medium-term credibility of fiscal policy. This marks a substantial shift away from pure discretion.

A systematic consideration of policy objectives, the incentives for achieving those objectives, and the means by which policymakers will be held accountable, is increasingly an integral part of the international surveillance agenda. It is also a useful reference point to guide the orientation of International Monetary Fund (IMF) programs, helping to identify policies that might be needed to restore or enhance credibility.

Improved standards and codes fit well with these principles. The Reports on the Observance of Standards and Codes (ROSCs) do not promote specific monetary or fiscal policies, recognising that appropriate policies for countries will differ depending on their individual circumstances. Instead, the standards and codes framework requires countries to set out their own long-term objectives, put in place proper procedures, and promote the openness and transparency needed to keep markets well informed. This process helps to improve understanding and promote best practice in many detailed areas that underpin macroeconomic and financial frameworks.

Structures for monetary policy

Long-term objectives: domestic nominal anchors

Price stability requires an anchor for inflation expectations. The two most frequently adopted domestic anchors are monetary growth targeting and inflation targeting. An external anchor – the exchange rate – is discussed in the next section.

Monetary growth targeting is a 'rules-based' approach to policy credibility. It is useful only if there is a stable and predictable relationship between money supply and inflation. Although common in the 1980s in many industrial countries, it was undermined by the breakdown of money demand functions after financial deregulation and the development of globally integrated capital markets.

Money supply targeting is relatively uncommon in emerging markets. Small open economies, usually pursuing structural reforms, may face unstable velocities of circulation of money (IMF 1997). It may still be possible to make a case for targeting in relatively closed, structurally stable economies. But other approaches are likely to be more credible and more transparent.

An inflation target shifts attention to the final objective, thereby enhancing both the clarity and the discipline of monetary policy, yet providing policymakers with potentially greater scope to respond to shocks. Inflation targets have been adopted in Australia, Brazil, Canada, the UK, South Africa and elsewhere.

In moving towards inflation targeting, three factors need to be considered, including any transitional path to low inflation, particularly in emerging markets and developing countries (Kasa 2001; IMF 2000a). The first is the fiscal position. Inflation targeting may not be credible initially in countries that have historically relied on the inflation tax to finance government deficits. Parallel fiscal reforms may therefore be desirable for such countries. The second is the health of the financial and corporate sectors. There may be an inconsistency in the short term between external and internal stability with implications for the behaviour of the exchange rate. Robust prudential regulation and supervision will be needed to help the financial and corporate sectors to cope. The third is transmission mechanisms from policy instruments to inflation. Successful inflation targeting relies on reasonably well understood transmission channels, and on a sound methodology for devising inflation forecasts. In some countries, the channels through which changes in interest rates affect the economy are often uncertain and unreliable. This partly reflects their small open nature, and also rapid structural change.

The role of the exchange rate is particularly important. In many small, open economies – often subject to large external shocks relative to their size – the exchange rate has a significant effect on monetary policy outcomes. Small countries also import a bigger share of what they consume, and so may be less inclined to pursue an inflation target. This may mean it is necessary to adapt the interest rate setting rules typically used (either explicitly or not) in industrial countries (for example, the Taylor rule) as such rules do not usually take explicit account of the exchange rate. Targeting inflation in small, open economies may therefore be more difficult than in larger industrial countries.

Institutional arrangements

One obvious institutional change to enhance credibility is to grant independence to the central bank. There is a case for distinguishing between target independence and operational, or instrument, independence. The government itself may wish to retain responsibility for setting the objective of monetary policy and designing the framework to ensure that the objective of monetary policy remains accountable to the public through the political system. The central bank would then be responsible for delivering the objective, price stability, through independent use of the instrument, interest rates.

Openness, transparency and accountability

Procedures designed to improve openness and transparency include the publication of the target or its range, any voting records, minutes of decision-making committees and inflation forecasts. Regular publications, press conferences and speeches by monetary policymakers further aid openness and understanding.

In the UK, following bank independence, greater transparency and the symmetric inflation target set by the government have helped to deepen public support for the arrangements and have made clear there is no deflationary bias. Accountability has also been enhanced by parliamentary committees' examination of MPC members.

All economies are vulnerable to external events or temporary difficulties, which can cause inflation to depart from the desired level. Attempts to restore inflation back to target too rapidly in such circumstances might cause undesirable volatility in output. Monetary policy should therefore not overreact to temporary shocks in order to keep inflation at its target level at the expense of instability in output and employment. The flexibility required can be achieved under credible arrangements.

Long-term objectives: exchange rate regimes

An alternative to a domestic nominal anchor for monetary policy is an external anchor based on some form of fixed exchange rate. It is instructive to consider how such an anchor fits with the principles for building credibility: a clear long-term objective, backed up by strong institutions and procedures and in an environment of maximum openness and transparency.

For such a framework to offer a clear long-term objective, the intention must be to keep the fixed exchange rate arrangement over the long run. The circumstances in which such a long run commitment makes sense for a country are familiar (IMF 2000b): the economy is not deeply integrated into world capital markets; the economy is very open, with a high share of trade with the country to which it is pegged; the economy and financial system already extensively rely on its partner's currency; the shocks the economy faces are similar to those facing the country to which it is pegged; the country is willing to give up monetary independence for its partner's monetary credibility; fiscal policy is flexible and sustainable; and labour markets are flexible.

For some countries, pegged exchange rate regimes can work. But countries unable to satisfy these criteria will inevitably find it harder to convince markets of the appropriateness, and hence credibility, of any long run exchange rate commitment. Broken pegs usually represent significant dents to policy credibility.

There may be circumstances in which countries might adopt an exchange rate peg, without intending a long run commitment. For example, countries might use the exchange rate as a disinflationary anchor from very high rates of inflation or before fully liberalising capital account transactions. But in these cases, it should be obvious that no credibility can be gained by pretending that the exchange rate peg will last indefinitely. Indeed, the opposite is more likely to be the case: credibility will be enhanced by setting out in advance an exit strategy to a more appropriate long-term objective.

For many countries, particularly small emerging markets and developing countries, historical, geographical and political considerations will be a factor in choosing the appropriate exchange rate regime. Often, the menu of policy choices available may be more limited than for most industrial countries. Moreover, exchange rate stability may be seen as a key objective in itself (for example, to facilitate trade), suggesting consideration of a wider variety of policy objectives than simply the choice of nominal anchor (IMF 1997).

For countries like the UK, exchange rate stability must be achieved on the basis of sound economic fundamentals – in particular, low and stable inflation, a well-regulated financial sector, steady and sustainable growth and sound public finances. Exchange rate stability therefore may be seen as the outcome of all other economic policies.

Institutional arrangements and procedures

One obvious institutional element is the nature of the exchange rate regime. 'Hard' pegs – currency boards or monetary unions – essentially attempt to bolster credibility by making the institutional commitment as strong as possible, thereby aiming to reduce any devaluation risk premium (or, more generally, any variability premium). 'Soft' pegs are more akin to a fixed monetary rule, with no new institutional backing. This is perhaps one reason why many consider that they are more difficult to maintain than 'hard' pegs.

It is likely that the institutional arrangements for an external anchor – even for a 'hard' peg – could be put in place much more quickly and visibly than an alternative domestic anchor. It is tempting to assume that, as a result, a peg can build credibility more quickly than a domestic anchor, and perhaps at less cost. However, experience suggests that this is not so: pegs are crisis prone and unlikely to be viable over long periods (IMF 2000b). A notable feature of exchange rate stabilisation programs is that the vast majority have ended in balance of payments crises (Calvo and Vegh 1999). Indeed, it is now significantly more demanding to maintain a pegged exchange rate in an environment of more open international capital flows.

One reason is that a fixed exchange rate does not allow any scope for constrained discretion in response to shocks. It is a fixed, rigid rule. Shocks therefore have to be absorbed elsewhere in the economy if stability is to be maintained. The real credibility of any peg thus does not come from the peg itself, but from putting in place the wider institutional arrangements which support the regime and facilitate adjustment. Key areas include wage and price setting behaviour, labour mobility, a strong and well regulated banking and financial system and fiscal position, good debt management and sound macroeconomic policy institutions.

Experience suggests that a peg in itself cannot be relied upon to be the driver for essential, wider-ranging reforms. These rely on political will and commitment. Indeed, while pegging often increases the necessity for reform, it also makes it harder to achieve, because monetary policy can no longer be used to support growth (and growth tends to be the best backdrop for reform). Countries with 'soft' pegs are particularly exposed. While countries may still opt to pursue such arrangements, the domestic policy requirements to sustain these intermediate solutions have become much tougher in today's environment.

Openness and transparency

By its very nature, an exchange rate peg is clear and highly visible. But, as with other fixed rules, the reduced scope to accommodate shocks – for example, compared to an inflation target – means it can be harder to operate.

A peg therefore requires greater transparency, not over the exchange rate itself, but over the policies required to make the peg a success – for example, the nature and scope of labour market reforms, the strength of the banking and financial sectors and the sustainability of the government's fiscal position. Only then will investors be able to make informed decisions as to the sustainability of the exchange rate regime. Regular surveillance, adherence to key standards and codes and use of financial sector assessment programs (FSAPs) can all serve to promote this transparency.

Exit strategies

Countries that do not wish to commit to a fixed exchange rate as a long-term objective may need to consider a suitable exit strategy. Floating exchange rate regimes are the increasingly relevant choice for countries having important and generally expanding involvement with modern financial markets.

While countries are unlikely to want to exit a peg during a period of stability, this can be the best time to do so. Empirical work suggests that exiting is most easily achieved during an appreciation. The chances of success will be enhanced if the exchange rate anchor is replaced with a commitment to low inflation (for example, inflation targeting reinforced by an independent central bank) (IMF 1998).

Countries are unlikely to want to give up a peg voluntarily during a crisis, because of the perceived loss of credibility and because of the potential cost to the economy in terms of possible dislocation and inflation.

Capital account liberalisation

Recent experience, not least the Asian financial crisis, has shown that the sequencing of liberalisation with reform is crucial. There are risks associated with rapid capital account liberalisation in advance of a well-functioning macroeconomy, open and transparent policymaking, deep financial markets and effective regulation.

Experience suggests that countries with pegged exchange rates that have yet to open up their capital account should liberalise capital accounts gradually whilst at the same time pursuing the institutional arrangements that will allow them to operate in a world of increasing capital flows, either with a peg or with a floating exchange rate.

One approach is to use country-specific 'road maps' for the opening up of capital accounts. Such maps should offer guidance on the speed of liberalisation, and on the appropriate reforms – strengthening the financial sector, including through enhanced banking and financial services supervision, stronger bankruptcy laws and property rights – needed to make it a success. Where countries have weak financial sectors and are at the earlier stages of liberalisation, there may be a case for measures to discourage excessive short-term capital inflows whilst encouraging longer-term flows. But such measures should be seen as a temporary means of facilitating the reforms needed to ensure orderly and sustainable liberalisation.

Structures for fiscal policy

Long-term objectives

Fiscal policy has a number of objectives, including ensuring equity and providing public goods. But the pursuit of these objectives is constrained by the need to maintain sustainable public finances over the long term.

Ideally, a sound fiscal position should be compatible with allowing automatic stabilisers to operate over the economic cycle. However, other than in exceptional circumstances, discretionary fiscal policy is an unsuitable tool for active demand management. Tax and spending changes take time, and there is a risk that a counter-cyclical fiscal policy may inadvertently become a pro-cyclical policy. The political and social costs associated with fiscal retrenchment make it hard to reverse tax cuts and spending increases, thereby risking a temporary cyclical increase becoming a structural budgetary change.

The ability to meet the objective will depend on the country's stage of development, available sources of revenue, access to external credit markets, demography, long-term growth prospects, and so on. These factors will act as a further constraint on fiscal policy.

Institutional procedures to support fiscal stability

The institution which sets fiscal policy needs to control the policy mechanisms to deliver the desired outcomes. If individual parts of the public sector are not brought together under a common planning process then the risk is that they may undermine the achievement of the overall fiscal objective. That is, the whole of the public sector (including regional or sectoral bodies) is best included. The framework also needs to be clear as to the short-term objectives and how they are expected to be met, and their consistency with longer-term objectives.

Pre-commitment can be achieved by following fiscal rules which allow some room for flexibility to respond to shocks, backed by legislative and parliamentary redress and independent auditing of key assumptions underpinning fiscal projections.

Transparency and accountability

Governments should give a clear statement of their fiscal objectives and any operating rules they choose to adopt. Where departures are made from those rules, it is appropriate that these should be fully explained and justified. Details of key assumptions, regular updates of data relevant to the objectives and analyses of developments on taxes and spending all form part of a transparent approach that strengthens the credibility and consistency of policy. Such approaches also facilitate cross-country comparisons that may be needed in the context of regional integration.

The IMF's Code for Fiscal Transparency, for example, emphasises four key principles. The first is the clarity of roles and responsibilities, reflecting the importance of establishing clear boundaries between the government's fiscal, monetary and public corporation activities. The second is the public availability of information, to promote the timeliness and comprehensive reporting of budget information. The third is open budget preparation, execution and reporting, to ensure the appropriate levels of coverage, accessibility and integrity of fiscal information, ensuring where possible that such reporting is consistent with international accounting and statistical standards. The fourth is independent assurances of integrity, so that the public can be assured of the credibility of the information presented.

Of particular concern are failures to account for 'quasi-fiscal' activities (for example, when state-owned enterprises are involved in providing social services); the use of 'off-budget' items to conceal the true impact of government on the economy; the degree to which allowances are made for contingent liabilities; and the use of cash rather than accrual accounting to disguise the true magnitude and timing of fiscal operations.

The budgetary process

The budget process must weigh up the competing claims of individual parts of the public sector against the government's overall objectives, including the requirements of longer-term fiscal sustainability. Where sources of revenue are limited, the budget process should be able to reallocate funds towards high-priority areas and, where necessary, identify areas where budgetary savings can be made.

Many countries have adopted multi-year projections as a means of ensuring the consistency of current fiscal projections with the demands of medium-term sustainability. This helps to bring a consolidated approach to budget planning by integrating tax, expenditure and debt plans, and focuses attention on the consistency of the fiscal projections with the government's fiscal objectives.

There is always a risk that such projections become based on an overly optimistic view of the strength of the fiscal position. For example, if the growth potential of the economy is overstated, and future spending pressures understated, this can lead to the illusion that more resources are available than is likely. Ideally, a cautious approach should be taken to the assumptions used, such as the trend growth rate. This helps to avoid the risk of costly policy reversals. There may also be a useful role for an independent audit of the fiscal projections to further boost accountability.

Public debt management

Recent debt market crises have highlighted the importance of sound debt management practices for maintaining overall stability. This is all the more important as debt has been built up. However debt management is often seen as an adjunct to fiscal or monetary policy, rather than an important area of policy in its own right. This leads to problems if short run fiscal or monetary considerations are allowed to override prudent debt management.

Excessive reliance on short-term floating rate and foreign currency debt poses risks. It leaves a country exposed to interest rate and currency fluctuations and hence vulnerable to financing crises. Countries need to trade off minimising the cost of debt over the longer run, subject to risk. If the credibility of macroeconomic settings is in doubt, a debt portfolio too heavily weighted towards these types of debt may imply a substantial increase in the cost of debt servicing and, in the extreme, push an economy into crisis.

Guidelines for public debt management prepared by the IMF and World Bank provide a comprehensive framework for debt management. The draft guidelines emphasise the following key principles. First, the risks in the government's debt management strategy should be carefully monitored and evaluated. Debt managers should be aware of the tradeoffs between cost and risk. Second, there should be sufficient coordination between the fiscal, monetary and debt management authorities. Responsibilities of the respective bodies should be clearly defined and publicly disclosed. Ideally, responsibility for debt management and monetary policy should be separated. Third, the government should publish regularly information on the government's financial position, including the composition of the debt portfolio and any financial assets. Debt management operations should be transparent and predictable. Fourth, the accountability framework for debt management should be publicly disclosed. The integrity of the debt management process needs to be assured, with regular auditing by external auditors, and clear monitoring and reporting procedures. Finally, debt managers should consider fully the impact of contingent liabilities on the government's portfolio.

Coordination of monetary and fiscal policy

One potential concern with central bank independence is that it may lead to less effective coordination of monetary and fiscal policy. By separating responsibility for monetary and fiscal policy, the two sets of policymakers could find it more difficult to have both arms of policy working in the same direction.

However, this view fails to recognise that, even if monetary and fiscal policy decisions are made by the same set of policymakers, they may not be well coordinated. In the case of the UK, the IMF concluded that 'experience before 1997 shows that having both policy instruments under the control of the government provides no guarantee of effective policy coordination' (IMF 1999).

In theory, the mix of monetary and fiscal policy could be used together to manage shocks to the economy. Because they affect different parts of the economy, the two instruments could be used simultaneously to target two different stabilisation objectives (for example, price stability and balance of payments equilibrium).

There are questions over the practicality of this approach. Because tax and budgetary changes take time, it may be more 'efficient' for monetary policy to take on the larger role in demand management, with fiscal policy concentrated on more medium-term goals. If the government holds both policy levers, this may magnify the credibility problem for monetary and fiscal policy. For example, if seignorage is an important source of revenue for the government, the government will be reluctant to lower inflation without endangering fiscal sustainability.

Alternatively, a monetary policy conducted by an independent authority helps to reinforce incentives for prudent fiscal policy. For a given inflation target, a looser fiscal stance will tend to lead to a tightening of monetary policy. Hence the payoff to fiscal loosening is reduced.

Nonetheless, important coordination issues may arise when the responsibilities for monetary and fiscal policy are separated. For example, Blake and Weale (1998) demonstrated that, where the monetary and fiscal authorities must learn each other's policy objective and reaction function, there may be considerable welfare losses, particularly if their initial guesses are some way from the true outcome.

In the UK, the new macroeconomic framework puts in place procedures to ensure that there is appropriate coordination between fiscal and monetary policy. There are three reasons for this. First, the government sets the objectives for both monetary and fiscal policy. Second, the objectives are clear, and the procedures transparent, so both sets of policymakers are aware of what the other is trying to achieve and how the other will react to their policy decisions. Third, the process is aided by the presence at MPC meetings of a (non-voting) representative from HM Treasury who is able, in particular, to provide information on fiscal policy settings.

Monetary policy can be designed symmetrically so that deviations above the inflation target are treated just as seriously as those below it. Fiscal policy on the other hand is asymmetric – given that deadweight costs of distortionary taxes are an increasing function of the tax rate, it is more costly to tighten fiscal policy than to loosen it, which suggests erring on the side of caution in setting fiscal policy. Nonetheless symmetric monetary policy combined with a cautious approach to fiscal policy should not pose a coordination dilemma if policymakers are clear about each other's intentions.

With stable macroeconomic frameworks in place, coordination across national boundaries which respects the subsidiarity principle becomes less complicated. Nonetheless success will depend on factors such as the degree of integration and consistency of targets, as well as on political will and effective institutional mechanisms.

REGIONAL INTEGRATION: STRUCTURES FOR ECONOMIC COOPERATION AFTER THE MAASTRICHT TREATY

Over the past five years, the UK has put in place economic structures and institutions designed to achieve greater economic stability. The results so far have been encouraging, with inflation having remained close to the target of 2½ per cent throughout this time and with growth averaging 2¾ per cent.

The previous section of the paper set out important principles in the design of policy for open trading regimes in a global market. Appropriate macroeconomic and financial frameworks can help achieve economic stability and provide an environment conducive to closer regional linkages. Greater regional integration presents additional opportunities for closer coordination and cooperation over economic policies. This section of the paper turns to the question of whether and how specific regional institutional structures might support this process. I look at this in the context of the EU.

In addition to reforms to the domestic policy framework, the UK has continued to play an active role in the EU. Here, along with the introduction of the euro in 2002 in 12 member states and the issue of the UK's 'five tests' assessment,[3] there have been developments, particularly in extended and intensified mutual surveillance, which have encouraged stable linkages between member states. I turn to these aspects of policy development. First, however, I review briefly some background in the context of the EU, partly to illustrate the depth of cooperation and integration that has evolved in Europe over a long time. This may throw some light on policy questions over regional integration in East Asia.

Patterns of trade

Over time the pattern of UK trade has shifted significantly. For a long period the Commonwealth – as a free trade area – acted as a particular magnet for UK trade. But the members of the Commonwealth stretched across the globe, from Canada to South Africa, from India to Australia and New Zealand. Change was inevitable as tariff barriers came down, competition intensified and geographical proximity to markets became important. By the 1960s it was clear that Europe, rather than the Commonwealth, was the key market for British business.

Nonetheless, while the UK had applied to join the European Community at its inception in 1957, membership of the European Economic Community came only in 1973. Since that time, trade with the EU has expanded considerably. Indeed, the greater part of the UK's trade is now with the EU. In 2001 over 51 per cent of total UK trade (exports and imports of goods and services) was with EU countries; around 15 per cent of the total was with United States and another 15 per cent with Asia.

In some respects the importance of trade for the UK and the increasing pattern of regional concentration are similar to the experience of a number of Asian countries. Figures from the World Trade Organization (WTO) for 2000 show that intra-Asia merchandise trade had risen to a share of 49 per cent in the total, with 26 per cent of Asia's trade going to North America and 17 per cent to Western Europe. This pattern – of a dominant large local market and smaller but significant markets in other parts of the hemisphere – is similar for many countries within the region, such as South Korea, China and Indonesia. For many Asian countries trade as a share of GDP is much higher than in the UK, although only Japan (6 per cent), China (4 per cent) and Korea (3 per cent) have shares of world trade of a similar scale to the UK (over 5 per cent).

Linkages between economies go deeper than trade, however. In particular, incomes per capita between EU member states are not widely dispersed, and economic and financial linkages are already strong, having evolved over many decades. This is an important contrast with East Asia since differences here imply a lower degree of convergence than has been achieved in the EU.

Institutional structures in the European Union

The EU has developed a series of formal and informal structures designed to achieve greater economic convergence and stability among member states. There are four broad dimensions to this: political, legal and institutional frameworks; economic integration through the creation of a single market; decentralised but coordinated financial market regulation and supervision; and macroeconomic convergence based on surveillance and policy coordination.

This paper focuses on the last of these. But it is worth considering the other elements briefly.

Political, legal and institutional frameworks

A central feature of the EU lies in its origin following the devastation of Europe as a result of the Second World War. Six European countries – France, Germany, Belgium, Luxembourg, the Netherlands and Italy – formed the European Coal and Steel Community (ECSC) in 1951 as a first step towards integration and as a way of preventing war in Europe happening again.

The success of the ECSC led to the 1957 Treaty of Rome, which created, among other things, the European Economic Community. Although heavily geared around economic integration, the process had from the start a clear political basis. As a consequence, the institutional and legal framework that underpins the EU has a firm base that now, almost half a century on, is deeply rooted.

In fact, the Community has developed a large number of institutions and decision-making procedures to support a broad range of policy responsibilities. The European Commission plays a key role and wields considerable influence, for example through its unique power of being able to introduce proposals for Community legislation. Moreover, Community law, once adopted, has precedence over national laws and must be respected by member states. As integration has deepened there has been a sharp rise in the number of legal acts adopted, amounting to some 2,000 to 2,500 acts per year over the last 10 years.

Strong political, institutional and legal underpinnings have helped create a sound basis for greater monetary and exchange rate cooperation. Indeed, the Treaty of Rome explicitly stated that there was a need to 'promote co-ordination of the policies of the Member States in the monetary field to the full extent needed for the functioning of the common market'. And increasing cross-border trade and investment flows have independently helped motivate economic cooperation at several levels.

Economic integration through the single market

Although customs duties and quantitative restrictions on imports and exports of goods and services within the Community had been eliminated by 1968, and a common external tariff erected, non-tariff trade barriers continued to exist. Attempts to eliminate these barriers and create a genuine single market took time. Even with favourable interpretations of the law and treatment of cases by the European Court of Justice, and with considerable pressure from the European Commission, it took several years to move from the 'customs union' stage to the single market program.

The Single European Act was agreed in 1986 and led to the adoption of around 300 measures to complete the Community's internal market. The ultimate decision to go ahead with the single market program was helped by the application of qualified majority voting. The intention was to have completed the program by the end of 1992. Considerable progress has been made towards completion of the single market, but there is still work to be done – for example, in financial services and energy.

Decentralised but coordinated financial market regulation and supervision

Along with the development of the single market, financial market regulation and supervision have been strengthened in member states, including through the Financial Services Action Plan. In keeping with the principle of subsidiarity, regulation is conducted by the authorities of the home country. This reflects the need to be close to the market and a model of 'mutual recognition'. But rapid growth of cross-border activities has led to greater coordination and cooperation among financial market supervisors, development of core standards and mutual exchanges of information. These arrangements have helped to ensure markets are well regulated and properly understood, giving them sufficient freedom to grow rapidly without putting at risk the stability of financial systems.

Macroeconomic convergence based on surveillance and policy coordination

For many years macroeconomic coordination between EU member states focused on exchange rate management. Exchange rate coordination was partly motivated by the desire to avoid competitive devaluations. Thus in the aftermath of the collapse of Bretton Woods, the six original members of the EU created the 'snake': a mechanism for the managed float of currencies within narrow bands against the dollar. However, oil crises, the weak dollar and differences in economic policy meant the 'snake' lost most of its members within a couple of years.

In 1979 the European Monetary System (EMS) was created, largely through pressure from France and Germany. The EMS was based on fixed but adjustable exchange rates, and all member states except the UK participated. Exchange rates were based on central rates against the European currency unit (ECU), a weighted average of the participating countries' currencies. Bilateral rates based on these central rates had to be contained within a 2½ per cent band (6 per cent for Italy). The EMS helped to reduce exchange rate variability among its members. But strains arose in 1992 and 1993 following German unification, and a number of countries were not properly converged.

A desire among some member states to move to full economic and monetary union led to another stage of development towards the end of the 1980s which resulted in the Maastricht Treaty. The push towards monetary union motivated greater coordination of economic policies to achieve convergence, the introduction of common rules on budgetary finance and the creation of an independent supranational central bank. Thus the Maastricht Treaty of 1992 ushered in a new era of integrated policymaking.

The UK negotiated an 'opt-out' from monetary union in the Maastricht Treaty but participated fully in the debates underlying the process which led to the creation of the euro. A decision on whether or not to adopt the euro in the UK will be triggered when the Chancellor's 'five tests' are assessed in June 2003. However, whether or not the UK adopts the euro, the mechanisms for economic cooperation and coordination within the EU are of value in their own right. Indeed, institutions and procedures that support economic stability are important for successful economic policymaking and help exchange rates to be more stable.

Coordination became deeper following the Maastricht Treaty. The treaty instituted a number of well-defined convergence criteria, covering inflation rates, long-term interest rates and budgetary positions. As a result, monetary and fiscal policies became a key focus for policymakers rather than simply the position of exchange rates relative to their fluctuation bands.

Moreover, following the ERM crises of 1992 and 1993, fluctuation bands were widened to ±15 per cent. This created a degree of flexibility which enabled policymakers to shift attention to more fundamental policy convergence questions. It could not solve the 'impossible trinity' – free movement of capital, monetary policy independence and a fixed exchange rate – but it allowed room for progress to be made, for example by reducing the scope for speculative attacks.

After 1993, surveillance became more effective. The procedures intensified and became more comprehensive. Member states, including the UK, remained free to set policy appropriate for their own economies and to deal with country-specific shocks. Nonetheless, policy in the EU context came to be conducted within certain agreed parameters.

Four main areas of policy coordination and cooperation involving all member states in the EU have now been put in place. These are very comprehensive, operate on an annual basis and cover both macroeconomic policy and microeconomic/structural reforms. The first is the broad economic policy guidelines (BEPGs), which were strengthened throughout the 1990s and again in recent years. The second is the Stability and Growth Pact (SGP), signed in 1997, which covers budgetary matters. The third is the Luxembourg process (1997), which covers employment guidelines. The fourth is the Cardiff process (1998), which monitors progress on economic reform in product and capital markets.

In addition, twice a year a confidential macroeconomic dialogue (Cologne process) is held between the social partners, European Central Bank, Council and Commission.

By way of illustration of what regional integration can mean in practice I look here at the first of the two items on the list above: the BEPGs and the SGP.

Broad economic policy guidelines

Under the treaty, member states are required to coordinate their policies to achieve the Community objectives of sustained non-inflationary growth and a high level of employment. Article 99(1) states:

> Member States shall regard their economic policies as a matter of common concern and shall co-ordinate them within the Council ...

The BEPGs provide the centrepiece to this requirement. They cover both macroeconomic and structural policies; provide a consistent and coherent overview of policy requirements; and are formulated by consensus, which provides peer pressure for change and successful coordination. The BEPGs are politically binding but are not legally enforceable. Recommendations can be made, and can be addressed specifically to a member state, but no pecuniary sanctions can be imposed. That said, peer pressure in this context can be intense, and failure to comply with a recommendation may make progress on other issues or in other spheres covered by the Community more difficult for a recalcitrant member state.

The annual BEPGs provide a comprehensive framework for economic policy within the EU, and address both monetary and budgetary policies and progress on economic reform. They describe how the EU and its member states will set policies to achieve sustained non-inflationary growth and a high level of employment. The broad approach is in keeping with the principles outlined earlier.

In recent years the BEPGs have provided more concrete and country-specific guidelines. In 2001, a public recommendation was addressed to a member state for the first time for being inconsistent with the BEPGs. The Commission has extended the procedure, and now adopts an implementation report ahead of each year's BEPGs. This adds to the peer pressure on member states.

The annual procedure is intensive and involves both the European Economics and Finance Ministers Council (ECOFIN) and the European Council (heads of state). At the start of the year the Commission prepares papers for an orientation debate at ECOFIN, along with its implementation report on the previous year's BEPGs. Following this debate, again on the basis of Commission work, the Economic and Financial Committee (EFC) considers macroeconomic issues, including budgetary trends, and the Economic Policy Committee (EPC) examines structural reforms. The Spring Economic Council gives the Commission political guidance. The Commission then prepares its recommendation for the BEPGs. ECOFIN holds a political debate on the BEPGs before remitting its advice to the EFC and EPC for the next stage of preparation of the draft BEPGs. The draft returns to ECOFIN for consideration and subsequently is sent by ECOFIN to the June European Council. Finally, subject to any changes by the European Council, the BEPGs are adopted by ECOFIN.

The procedure illustrates the extent of involvement of officials and ministers from all member states in reaching consensus and consistency over the broad shape of economic policy in the EU. There is a good deal of agreement over the appropriate framework for economic policy, helped in part by having covered similar ground over successive years. The macroeconomic framework described earlier is consistent with the BEPGs, allowing EU member states such as the UK to follow procedures that are appropriate for domestic economic conditions and appropriate in the EU context.[4]

Stability and Growth Pact

The Maastricht Treaty gave a clear commitment to sound public finances. In particular, it laid down a procedure, the excessive deficits procedure (EDP), which required member states to avoid excessive deficits, defined by reference values of 3 per cent for the ratio of the general government deficit to GDP and 60 per cent for the ratio of general government gross debt to GDP.

Further clarification of the treaty was required ahead of full monetary union, and because many member states in the mid-1990s had deficits or debt ratios above the reference values. Political agreement to clarify and strengthen the EDP was reached at the Dublin Europe Council in December 1996 and led to the formal adoption of the SGP in Amsterdam in 1997.

The SGP comprises a European Council (political) resolution and two regulations. The resolution provides guidance to member states, the Commission and the Council to adhere to the rules and regulations of the pact and, in particular, to aim for medium-term budgetary positions which are close to balance or in surplus.

The first regulation deals with surveillance and coordination, requiring stability or convergence programs (SCPs) to be submitted by member states, and to be annually updated and examined by the Commission and the Council with a view to giving early warning of potential breaches of the SGP. The SCPs themselves are intended to be comprehensive statements of budgetary policies and macroeconomic conditions and include, for example, sensitivity analyses and assessments of long-term fiscal pressures. The EFC examines each member state's updated stability or convergence program in depth ahead of the ECOFIN examination.

The second regulation focuses on the EDP, speeding up the process, acting as a deterrent to excessive deficits and providing for sanctions – in this case fines of up to 0.5 per cent of GDP – in the event of a member state failing to comply with the SGP. It also defines the circumstances – principally, a severe economic downturn where real GDP falls by at least 2 per cent – under which a budgetary deficit of more than 3 per cent will be accepted.

In 2001, a code of conduct helped to clarify the need to take the impact of the economic cycle into account, the desirability of cautionary margins to allow room for uncertainties, costs of ageing populations, and so on. The procedure now involves standardised tables and other elements to enhance comparability, as well as standard statistical definitions (for example, ESA95).

As with the BEPGs, the annual cycle is intensive and time-consuming, involving the Commission, member states, the EFC and ECOFIN. While fiscal policies remain decentralised and the proper concern of individual member states, the process of examination and debate within a transparent and well-defined framework helps to clarify policy intentions and objectives.

Luxembourg and Cardiff processes

Although they are comparatively recent additions to the process of surveillance and economic coordination, the employment guidelines (Luxembourg process) which are aimed at improving labour market performance (covering employability, entrepreneurship, adaptability and equal opportunities) through national action plans, and product and capital market reform (Cardiff process) which is aimed at improving the functioning of markets and productivity performance, both involve similar procedures and debates to the BEPG and SGP processes.

Surveillance

In the EU, economic surveillance and coordination have the following characteristics. Processes are thorough; information is comprehensive and pooled and is based on common standards and definitions; and assessments are consistent and technically robust. There is benchmarking and learning from others' mistakes and successes, which acts as a catalyst for reform and adoption of best practice. The Commission provides independent analysis and knowledgeable advice, and offers a means of policing and advancing the procedures. There are frequent in-depth discussions of both macroeconomic and structural issues by officials and ministers of member states, in both formal and informal meetings. These foster a deeper understanding of the issues, greater consensus and better diagnosis of problems. They also provide a safety valve when difficulties arise. Peer pressure can be exerted on countries, sometimes intensively, with explanations sought from member states by officials or ministers, and unsatisfactory performances exposed. Political discussions at ECOFIN and European Councils provide leadership and direction for the coordination of economic policies. Recommendations to member states (and the threat of them) are a source of discipline, and in the SGP potentially go beyond peer pressure in that fines can be imposed *in extremis*.

It should be clear by both the scale and nature of the various surveillance and coordination processes described above that the level of activity in some respects goes deeper than through standard surveillance routes such as the OECD Economic and Development Review Committee or IMF Article IV reports. The different routes are nonetheless complementary, particularly if unnecessary duplication is avoided.

It is also the case that the procedures involve significant resources and are highly time-intensive. In part, this reflects the desire to achieve consensus and avoid mistakes or misunderstandings as well as the needs implied by the single currency. It also reflects the continuing desire to maintain a decentralised model of economic coordination rather than a more federalist approach. By coordinating in this way, the principle of subsidiarity is respected while common ground can be found.

CONCLUSION

An increasingly integrated global economy brings new opportunities. But it also poses new challenges for macroeconomic policy. Credibility has become more important, and more quickly rewarded by international capital markets. Conversely, dents to credibility have become more quickly and severely punished.

As economies become more open and more integrated, the sources of economic shocks are likely to widen, and shocks will be transmitted more quickly. Expectations and perceptions matter more. Greater openness is also likely to change underlying economic relationships and structures. Macroeconomic and financial frameworks and the credibility of policies are thus likely to be more severely tested.

Countries that have already built up a track record of credibility over a long period will have more room to respond to shocks in a discretionary way, without undermining that credibility and putting stability at risk. The challenge for all countries is to manage the shocks while enhancing credibility at the same time.

A macroeconomic framework designed to achieve stability provides the best backdrop to structural reform, increasing trade flows and growth. If achieved across the board it supports stable linkages between countries in a region and allows their further integration through both trade and investment and economic reform. Clear objectives, sound institutional arrangements, maximum transparency and full accountability are important principles behind successful macroeconomic frameworks. In this respect I make four points.

First, price stability as the goal of monetary policy may best be served by inflation targeting, supported by central bank independence and transparency in decision-making. This provides scope for policy flexibility, although small open economies may still face pressures from exchange rate volatility.

Second, fixed exchange rate regimes may work under certain circumstances but the policy requirements for their successful operation have become increasingly onerous. The credibility of such regimes ultimately depends on implementing wide-ranging reforms, based on sound institutions.

Third, in fiscal policy a focus on long-run sustainability, backed by institutional procedures to support a stronger commitment to fiscal responsibility, is of benefit. Public debt management might aim to minimise costs over the long term subject to risk.

Fourth, a comprehensive financial supervisory and regulatory regime, and effective corporate governance arrangements, based on clear principles, offer the best scope for maintaining market confidence, promoting public awareness of financial products, protecting consumers and ensuring efficient allocation of resources.

A sound macroeconomic and financial sector regime, combined with an active approach to structural reform, can give scope for dealing with economic shocks. This in itself provides a strong basis for stability, growth and stable international linkages.

Rigorous multilateral surveillance on a regional basis, consistently applied and with associated peer pressure, can also support stability and growth. Deeper linkages and closer integration can progress through cooperation and coordination. But they rely on strong political commitment as well as on effective institutions to bring closer convergence. The EU experience suggests that intensive cooperation takes a long time to evolve and requires significant commitment and resources.

NOTES

1   A detailed description of these changes can be found in HM Treasury (2001).
2   See, for example, Drazen and Masson (1994).
3   See, for example, the HM Treasury paper provided to the Treasury Committee on the Treasury's approach to the preliminary and technical work on the 'five tests', 6 September 2002, and 'UK Membership of the Single Currency: an Assessment of the Five Economic Tests', HM Treasury (1997)
4   A good description of the details of the procedures for the BEPGs and other economic policy coordination mechanisms in the EU can be found in DGECFIN (2002).

REFERENCES

Barro, R.J. and D.B. Gordon (1983) 'Rules, discretion and reputation in a model of monetary policy', *Journal of Monetary Economics* 12 (1) (July): 102–121.

Blake, A.P. and M. Weale (1998) 'Costs of separating budgetary policy from control of inflation: a neglected aspect of central bank independence', *Oxford Economic Papers*, 50 (3) (July): 449–467.

Calvo, G.A. and C.A. Végh (1999) 'Inflation Stabilization and BOP Crises in Developing Countries', Cambridge MA: National Bureau of Economic Research Working Paper No. 6925 (February).

DGECFIN (Economic and Financial Affairs Directorate General) (2002), 'Co-ordination of economic policies in the EU: a presentation of key features of the main procedures', DGECFIN Euro Paper 45 (July). Available at <http://europa.eu.int/comm/economy_finance/publications/euro_papers/2002/eup45en.pdf>.

Drazen, A. and P.R. Masson (1994) 'Credibility of policies vs credibility of policymakers', *Quarterly Journal of Economics* 104: 735–754.

Fischer, S. (2001), 'Exchange Rate Regimes: Is the Bipolar View Correct?', speech delivered to the American Economic Association (January).

HM Treasury (2001) *Reforming Britain's Economic and Financial Policy*, Basingstoke: Palgrave.

—— (1997) 'UK Membership of the Single Currency: An Assessment of the Five Economic Tests', London: HM Treasury.

IMF (International Monetary Fund) (1997) 'Credibility Without Rules? Monetary Frameworks in the Post-Bretton Woods Era', IMF Occasional Paper No. 154.

—— (1998) 'Exit Strategies: Policy Options for Countries Seeking Greater Exchange Rate Flexibility', IMF Occasional Paper No. 168.

—— (1999) 'United Kingdom: Selected Issues', IMF Staff Country Report No. 99/44.

—— (2000a) 'Adopting Inflation Targeting: Practical Issues for Emerging Market Countries', IMF Occasional Paper No. 202.

—— (2000b) 'Exchange Rate Regimes in an Increasingly Integrated World Economy', IMF Occasional Paper No. 193.

Kasa K. (2001) 'Will Inflation Targeting Work in Developing Countries?' San Francisco: Federal Reserve Bank of San Francisco.

5 The complex political economy of cooperation and integration

C. Randall Henning

INTRODUCTION

The international crises of 1997–99 shook the confidence of Asian states in multilateral monetary and financial cooperation. Unsatisfied with the responses of both the United States and the International Monetary Fund (IMF) to their crises, Asian governments have considered regional cooperative arrangements that could help to shield them from future disruptions in international capital flows. The ambitious 1997 proposal for an Asian Monetary Fund (AMF) is one salient example. Although an AMF has not come into being, finance ministries and central banks in the region have implemented more pragmatic forms of cooperation. During 2000–01, in particular, the ASEAN+3 group established a set of bilateral swap arrangements under the framework of the Chiang Mai Initiative (CMI).

To begin building a theory of political economy of Asian monetary and financial cooperation, I draw on the rich body of theory developed to explain European monetary integration. First, I survey several of the most prevalent theoretical approaches to European integration and examine their relevance to East Asia. I ask whether each approach explains the relatively modest degree of Asian monetary cooperation that has occurred compared to Europe, sorting the successful from unsuccessful, and also what each successful approach predicts for the future of Asian cooperation. By establishing the markers for such explanations, I aim to contribute to a more general theory of regional monetary and financial integration.

Moravcsik (1998) advocates generalising theories of European integration by testing them against cases outside Europe. Doing so would help to further reconnect the study of European integration and international political economy, the separation of which Anderson (1995) laments. Gamble and Payne (1996), Katzenstein (1996), Frankel (1997) and Mattli (1999), among several others, examine regionalism with an emphasis on trade integration. Cohen (1993, 1997) examines historical cases of monetary integration and the dynamics of currency regions. There is a lack of comparisons of contemporary regional monetary projects and a general explanation for successes and failures. Mansfield and Milner (1999) advocate greater study of financial regionalism and the links between financial and trade integration.

MARKET INTEGRATION

A prominent approach to European integration revolves around the integration of regional markets in goods and capital. Growth of intra-regional trade confers on private actors and governments an interest not only in the reduction of trade barriers but also in currency and monetary stability. Regional market integration thus fosters commitments among states to monetary cooperation, as currency fluctuations can disrupt trade and investment.

Let me compare present degrees of market integration in Europe and Asia. In 1997, intra-regional exports of the 15 members of the European Union (EU15) were 59.4 per cent of their total exports, while the intra-regional imports of the EU15 were 64.0 per cent of their total imports. Intra-regional exports of the 11 members of the Economic and Monetary Union were 46.9 per cent of total Euro-11 exports, while intra-regional imports were 51.8 per cent of total Euro-11 imports.[1] Among the countries of East Asia, intra-regional exports reached more than 47 per cent of total exports in the mid-1990s, before the financial crisis (Table 5.1). Exports to the region reached 43.2 per cent of Japan's total exports, 56.8 per cent of China's total exports, and higher percentages of many other countries' total exports in 1997 (Table 5.2).

Next, let me compare the present levels of market integration in Asia to those that obtained in Europe at the advent of regional monetary cooperation there. Interestingly, intra-regional exports of the six members of the European Community were 48.6 per cent of their total exports in 1970, while intra-regional imports were 48 per cent of EC6 total imports – roughly comparable to the recent Asian ratios.[2] In 1970, notably, the EC6 committed themselves to forming an economic and monetary union by 1980. Although that plan proved to be wildly ambitious, the European states floated their currencies jointly against the dollar after the dissolution of the Bretton Woods regime, and in 1979 created the European Monetary System (EMS).

As a percentage of regional GDP, intra-Asian trade flows are comparable with intra-European trade at the beginning of monetary cooperation but, again, less significant than present European trade. For the region as a whole, intra-Asian exports represent about 9 per cent of regional GDP. Although exports to East Asia are less than 4 per cent of GDP for Japan, they represent almost 9 per cent of GDP for Australia and between 10 and 15 per cent of GDP for China, Hong Kong, South Korea, Indonesia, the Philippines and New Zealand. The ratios for Thailand and Vietnam are larger and those for Malaysia and Singapore much larger (see Table 5.3). In Europe, intra-regional exports comprised 8.7 per cent of the combined GDP of the six members in 1970 and 12.9 per cent of EU15 GDP and 15.9 per cent of euro-11 GDP in 1997.

Table 5.1 Direction of East Asian exports, 1980–97

	1980	1981	1982	1983	1984	1985	1986	1987	1988	1989	1990	1991	1992	1993	1994	1995	1996	1997
Intra-regional exports as % of total EA-17 exports	38.4	37.8	38.3	37.3	36.5	35.7	32.7	34.4	37.2	38.1	40.3	41.7	42.0	42.5	45.0	47.1	47.4	45.4
Regional exports to Japan as % of total regional exports (minus Japan)	22.6	21.7	21.1	19.5	19.3	19.0	16.6	16.6	17.0	16.9	15.8	14.7	13.4	13.1	13.2	13.7	13.7	12.5
Regional exports to China as % of total regional exports (minus China)	2.8	2.7	2.4	2.7	3.7	6.0	4.9	4.6	5.5	4.9	4.9	5.9	7.1	9.3	9.3	9.3	9.9	10.4
Regional exports to US as % of total regional exports	18.8	19.6	19.8	22.5	25.8	27.3	28.7	26.6	24.0	24.2	22.1	20.3	20.1	21.0	20.9	19.2	18.6	19.0

Note: EA = East Asia. East Asia includes ASEAN-10 (Brunei, Cambodia, Indonesia, Laos, Malaysia, Myanmar, Philippines, Singapore, Thailand and Vietnam), plus China (Mainland and Hong Kong), Japan, Korea, Taiwan, Australia, and New Zealand.

Source: International Trade Division, Statistics Canada, World Trade Analyzer.

Table 5.2 Exports to East Asia as percentage of total exports, 1980–97

	1980	1981	1982	1983	1984	1985	1986	1987	1988	1989	1990	1991	1992	1993	1994	1995	1996	1997
China	56.3	58.2	55.6	57.5	61.8	59.8	55.3	58.8	63.2	61.4	67.7	70.2	68.4	54.2	58.0	59.1	57.8	56.8
Hong Kong	18.3	18.7	20.1	18.2	16.1	13.2	13.4	13.3	13.2	13.9	14.1	13.1	12.9	11.8	12.1	12.5	12.3	11.9
Korea	31.4	30.6	29.0	25.8	27.7	27.5	27.5	29.9	34.3	37.7	37.7	39.7	43.1	45.5	46.6	48.8	50.0	46.1
Japan	29.5	28.4	27.7	28.7	28.3	28.3	26.2	28.2	30.6	31.9	32.8	34.9	35.9	39.0	41.6	44.8	45.2	43.2
Brunei	86.8	83.7	85.6	91.3	92.3	92.9	90.6	95.4	83.0	79.4	95.9	98.1	84.5	96.5	95.3	89.9	81.9	69.7
Cambodia	37.8	17.3	12.4	34.0	63.7	36.2	6.2	12.7	56.4	76.1	83.6	48.4	66.2	76.8	75.7	64.0	40.8	15.3
Indonesia	66.2	64.8	72.8	66.3	64.8	64.3	61.8	63.0	63.9	64.2	65.8	65.3	62.1	60.5	59.7	59.7	59.6	59.4
Laos	61.0	37.7	57.0	64.1	15.3	61.4	40.6	11.4	48.1	74.6	85.7	11.8	52.7	45.4	22.7	33.3	25.1	33.3
Malaysia	54.5	59.2	62.7	60.1	60.5	62.2	58.4	58.8	57.8	56.7	59.4	59.6	57.8	56.6	55.6	56.1	59.2	57.9
Myanmar	62.0	55.6	41.4	48.7	54.5	55.8	61.8	59.1	72.9	80.6	80.3	77.6	64.5	67.0	67.2	68.6	63.3	51.0
Philippines	45.2	42.7	42.4	37.9	39.7	41.9	38.5	39.7	40.0	39.6	38.8	39.5	35.5	35.8	38.7	42.2	44.2	43.4
Singapore	47.2	50.3	52.5	48.5	45.6	45.2	44.0	45.5	47.6	48.2	48.6	50.5	49.6	52.7	57.2	58.4	58.7	57.6
Thailand	43.6	42.1	43.5	42.6	40.2	41.5	42.7	41.5	41.0	40.9	39.8	41.7	42.7	46.1	49.5	52.3	53.5	52.0
Vietnam	52.8	48.1	65.7	62.0	74.5	70.6	61.5	66.5	69.5	62.8	76.5	67.8	59.3	59.9	58.3	59.0	57.5	50.8
Taiwan	31.2	31.5	29.5	27.9	27.9	29.7	27.8	30.2	35.5	36.5	41.8	41.9	43.8	48.6	52.1	52.8	52.1	46.6
Australia	47.7	52.2	51.9	54.2	53.6	53.7	53.0	52.9	54.9	56.9	56.4	61.8	61.7	64.2	66.1	69.1	66.7	62.0
New Zealand	38.2	39.7	39.5	40.9	42.4	41.8	43.2	44.4	50.5	51.4	49.3	51.9	54.0	53.4	56.5	58.6	57.3	56.2
EA region	38.4	37.8	38.3	37.3	36.5	35.7	32.7	34.4	37.2	38.1	40.3	41.7	42.0	42.5	45.0	47.1	47.4	45.4

Note: EA = East Asia.

Source: International Trade Division, Statistics Canada, *World Trade Analyzer.*

Table 5.3 Exports to East Asia as percentage of GDP, 1980–97

	1980	1981	1982	1983	1984	1985	1986	1987	1988	1989	1990	1991	1992	1993	1994	1995	1996	1997
China	3.6	4.6	4.7	4.4	4.8	4.7	5.0	6.2	10.0	8.3	11.3	12.9	12.5	8.6	12.9	12.6	11.1	11.8
Hong Kong	13.4	13.7	14.1	14.1	14.1	11.9	12.4	13.4	14.5	15.4	15.7	15.2	15.5	13.9	14.0	15.6	14.6	13.2
Korea	9.3	9.6	9.0	7.9	9.1	9.3	9.3	10.8	11.7	11.0	9.9	9.9	10.7	11.0	11.1	12.5	12.8	12.1
Japan	3.9	3.8	3.8	3.7	3.9	3.9	2.9	2.8	2.8	3.1	3.3	3.3	3.4	3.4	3.5	3.9	4.1	4.4
Cambodia						0.1	0.1	0.7	2.0	5.2	4.5	1.8	3.9	3.2	2.6	2.8	1.3	1.0
Indonesia	18.0	15.7	17.7	16.5	16.3	14.2	12.2	15.1	15.1	15.4	16.1	16.0	16.3	15.0	14.1	14.0	13.9	15.5
Laos	1.6	1.2	2.8	1.7	0.1	0.3	0.2	0.9	8.0	9.8	6.4	5.3	4.9	5.9	7.1	7.6	6.0	8.6
Malaysia	30.7	28.8	30.1	29.1	30.1	32.6	31.0	34.8	36.0	38.9	42.4	43.6	41.6	42.7	45.0	47.6	48.1	7.3
Myanmar	4.9	4.8	3.8	4.5	3.9	3.2	2.6	1.8	2.6	1.7	1.6	1.2	1.3	1.1	0.9	0.9	0.6	0.3
Philippines	8.5	7.0	6.1	5.8	7.0	6.7	6.6	8.2	7.6	8.0	7.4	7.9	6.8	7.7	8.1	9.9	11.3	13.5
Singapore	77.3	74.1	71.2	58.9	56.5	57.6	54.4	63.3	72.1	71.3	69.1	67.2	63.3	67.0	77.0	82.3	81.1	76.0
Thailand	9.2	8.8	8.7	7.0	7.2	8.0	9.2	10.0	10.8	11.7	11.1	12.6	13.0	14.4	15.5	17.7	15.9	20.0
Vietnam	0.3	0.6	0.8	0.6	0.4	1.7	0.7	0.7	1.6	7.9	13.4	14.5	15.7	16.9	17.5	17.1	17.6	17.9
Taiwan	15.9	15.3	14.4	13.8	14.7	15.6	15.5	16.4	17.8	16.6	18.6	19.6	18.8	21.9	22.9	25.6	25.0	22.2
Australia	7.0	6.5	6.5	6.4	6.5	7.6	7.2	7.2	7.1	7.4	7.9	8.8	9.4	9.8	9.6	9.7	9.6	9.5
New Zealand	9.8	9.8	10.0	9.9	10.7	11.3	10.0	9.4	10.4	11.2	11.1	12.4	13.8	13.4	13.5	13.6	13.0	12.4
EA region	6.5	6.5	6.7	6.2	6.5	6.5	5.1	5.4	5.9	6.3	6.9	7.1	7.3	7.0	7.7	8.4	8.9	9.3

Note: EA = East Asia. Data for Cambodia are unavailable before 1993; data for Brunei are unavailable.

Source: International Trade Division, Statistics Canada *World Trade Analyzer*; IMF *World Economic Outlook*.

On the investment side, Japanese foreign direct investment (FDI) flows to the region increased substantially in the mid-1980s but remained less than a quarter of total FDI outflows and roughly half of such investments in the United States during the early and mid-1990s. The financial crisis sharply reduced Japanese FDI in the region after 1997. Similarly, Japanese bank loans comprised about one-half of total international loans to the region during the late 1980s and early 1990s, but declined dramatically as a percentage of total loans during the mid- and late 1990s.

The market integration approach is ambiguous with respect to the absolute intra-regional trade and investment ratios that should trigger regional monetary cooperation. The time lag between the reaching of high ratios and the actualisation of cooperation is not specified. Most importantly, a more complete approach would combine market integration with regional political relations and institutions.

As a partial framework, nonetheless, this approach is consistent with the difference in the level of European and Asian regional monetary cooperation. But this is barely the case, as intra-Asian trade ratios approach those of Europe in the 1970s. The market integration approach must thus predict that, assuming intra-regional trade and investment continue to grow, some of the current proposals for exchange rate and financial cooperation will be implemented.

REGIONAL INSTITUTIONS

Regional institutions and the 'spillover' from one issue area to another are critical features of neofunctionalism. The dense network of Western European regional institutions – its formal governing institutions as well as its more technical and less formal ones – distinguish it from other regions. This institutional network facilitated the exchange of information, striking of agreements, monitoring and enforcement of bargains, and making of side payments among member states. Some of the institutions of the European Union, the European Commission and the European Parliament, in particular, act in their own right to advance integration.[3] Martin (1993) argues that these institutions were critical for smoothing the way to the Maastricht Treaty agreement. Cohen (1993) argues that the presence of robust institutions distinguishes successful from unsuccessful monetary unions in the past.

East Asia has its share of regional institutions. The non-governmental Pacific Basin Economic Council (PBEC) and Pacific Trade and Development Conference (PAFTAD) were created in the late 1960s. The Association of Southeast Asian Nations (ASEAN) was created in 1967. The intergovernmental Pacific Economic Cooperation Conference (PECC) was first convened in 1980 with the political objective of forging an economic community in the Pacific. After the rejection of the East Asian Economic Grouping (EAEG), which would have excluded Australia, New Zealand and the United States, the Asia Pacific Economic Cooperation (APEC) forum was created in 1989 (Crone

1993; Katzenstein 1996). When momentum toward liberalisation within APEC stalled in the mid- and late 1990s, Japan, China and South Korea joined meetings with ASEAN in what has come to be called the ASEAN+3. This new grouping has precisely the same membership as the Mahathir-inspired EAEG of a decade earlier, but did not attract the vehement opposition of the United States and has held constructive meetings, including at summit level. Foremost among the monetary and financial institutions is the Asian Development Bank (ADB), created in 1966. Officials from 11 central banks have met informally since 1991. Since the mid-1990s, APEC has convened a finance ministers meeting. The Manila Framework Group was convened in late 1997 to consider the Asian financial crisis.

With the relatively recent exception of ASEAN+3 and the central bankers meetings, however, these institutions define the region as the Pacific and thus include countries from outside East Asia, notably the United States. Historically, those institutions thus organised, and arguably perpetuated, a Pacific order that was based on American dominance. As Crone (1993: 517) has written:

> The system of relations was an essentially bilateral one, between the U.S. on the one hand and each of the countries the U.S. chose to relate to on the other; each partner, of course, manoeuvered to secure from the U.S. maximum advantage for itself. Clearly most governments preferred to keep their distance from regional economic organisations and thereby avoid being drawn into a forum that would erode their bilateral clout and threaten their values. Neither the hegemon nor its regional subordinates found extensive regime formation to their advantage ...

Accordingly, institutions of the Asian region have been notoriously weak. The strongest, APEC, is essentially a consultative forum operating under consensus with no binding rules and a small secretariat. Katzenstein (1996: 139) compares the organisation not to the European Community but to the second pillar of the Maastricht Treaty, which facilitated negotiations and coordinated foreign and security policy of member states on a purely intergovernmental basis. Haggard (1994) has argued that regional organisations in Asia have facilitated transnational networks but have not developed into policymaking institutions. Kahler (1995: 108) concludes:

> On nearly every dimension of institutional development – strength, scope, centralisation, domestic political linkages – Pacific institutions lie at one end of the international distribution.

The weakness of these institutions would explain why, despite their number, deeper regional integration has not yet taken hold in Asia. In the future, ASEAN+3 could serve as an important institutional building block. But in its present form, this organisation probably cannot make side payments, monitor agreements or enforce bargains – actions that are necessary to underpin robust monetary and financial cooperation. Unlike the European Commission, no present Asian institution could play the roles of initiator, entrepreneur, broker and enforcer. With present institutions, Asian monetary integration will occur through intergovernmentalism or not at all. If Asian institutions were to proliferate and strengthen, on the other hand, the neofunctionalist approach would predict more robust cooperation.

SPILLOVER

As developed by neofunctionalists (Haas 1964), the concept of spillover captures the notion that cooperation in some areas (such as coal and steel) leads to cooperation in others (such as the common market), because the sectors of advanced economies are interdependent. Functional spillover is complemented by political spillover, through which the interests of societal groups coalesce supranationally around expanding cooperation, and institutions created to implement cooperative agreements become active.[4]

The application to European monetary integration is fairly straightforward. The formation of the common agricultural policy and the common market led to the search for currency stability in the form of the 'snake' and then the European Monetary System (McNamara 1993). The common market and the expansion of the membership of the European Community led to the formation of the single market, an important feature of which was the elimination of capital controls and liberalisation of trade in financial services. The free movement of capital within (and beyond) the European Union then forced member states to choose between accepting more flexible exchange rates, which would undermine the single market, or press onward toward monetary union (George 1985; Padoa-Schioppa 1990; Delors Report 1989; European Commission 1990a, b). As developed in the European context, spillover suggests that cooperation on trade and behind-the-border impediments to trade will lead to cooperation on monetary and financial matters.

The spillover approach suggests that the weakness of Asian trade regionalism historically explains the weakness of monetary and financial cooperation compared to Europe. With the stalling of liberalisation under APEC, however, a plethora of new proposals to liberalise trade on a subregional basis have been put forward (Scollay and Gilbert 2000). If these were to advance, the logic of spillover would anticipate further monetary and financial integration as well.

The region continues to show interest in an Asian monetary fund, and ASEAN+3 has in principle endorsed the development of swap facilities. These developments raise the spectre that the European sequence of trade and monetary integration could be reversed in Asia (Bergsten 2000). Spillover would anticipate that close financial cooperation in the form of mutual financial facilities to combat precipitate capital withdrawal would lead to more general monetary cooperation as well. If regional monetary and financial stability led to increased trade, more formal trade integration might then follow. Because the concept of spillover cannot account for the first serious step in regional integration, however, this approach could not explain monetary or financial cooperation that occurs prior to trade or political cooperation.

DOMESTIC POLITICS

Domestic political approaches to European monetary integration stress the economic interests of societal groups and distributional conflicts as manifest in external monetary policymaking. Economic sectors that are harmed by currency volatility, such as traded goods producers and international investors, gain from regional monetary integration. Conversely, firms and workers that are shielded from exchange rate fluctuations prefer to maintain national monetary autonomy (Eichengreen and Frieden 1994; Frieden 1991a, b). Moravcsik (1998) has analysed in detail the convergence of preferences between France and Germany (and the divergence of those of Britain), a necessary precursor to the Maastricht agreement (see also Moravcsik 1991).

Analysis of the domestic determinants of national preferences in Asia would reasonably revolve around development models and market integration. Several countries in the region, though by no means all, adopted critical features of the early Japanese model of developmental statism (Johnson 1987). State intervention was particularly prominent in the financial sector (Loriaux et al. 1997; Haggard et al. 1993; Haggard and Lee 1995). At the same time, East Asian countries were quick to shift to export-oriented trade strategies (Haggard 1990; Bowie and Unger 1997), which proved to be spectacularly successful in stimulating trade and income growth (World Bank 1993). As a result, East Asian countries' exports became intensely competitive with one another. To the extent that exchange rate policy was an instrument of national competition, governments of the region would be reluctant to enter into regional commitments that would constrain the use of this tool. These considerations are thus consistent with the absence of regional monetary cooperation in the past.

Are national preferences regarding monetary and financial cooperation presently converging or diverging? Increases in intra-regional trade and investment over the last 15 years certainly increase the stakes of domestic groups that are exposed to international transactions in regional cooperation. The reduction of barriers to capital flows complicated the use of the exchange rate to achieve commercial advantage and placed a premium on maintenance of market confidence. Were it to spawn reform of national financial systems and government–business relations (analysed in Haggard 2000), the 1997–99 financial crisis could well precipitate a shift in external monetary preferences. China might well perceive advantages to regional cooperation to pre-empt financial instability while moving toward convertibility on the capital account and simultaneously reforming the domestic financial sector.

CREDIBILITY AND COMMITMENT STRATEGIES

In Europe, countries that historically experienced high inflation but later became determined to seek price stability sought to give credibility to that commitment by pegging their currencies to the German mark, thereby reducing the unemployment cost of disinflation. When their central banks were not independent from their governments or were otherwise suspected by the markets, states could 'borrow' credibility from the Bundesbank by using the German currency as a 'nominal anchor.' France, Spain, Italy, Portugal and Greece are among those countries to whom this strategy was attributed (see, for example, Giavazzi and Pagano 1988; Giavazzi and Giovannini 1989).

In East Asia, Japan is not functionally equivalent to Germany in such commitment strategies. First, although Japan's consumer price performance has indeed been quite stable, asset prices have fluctuated greatly, the financial system has been fragile throughout the 1990s, and the yen has been volatile. Moreover, the Bank of Japan was subordinate to the Ministry of Finance until relatively recently. More fundamentally, Japan's broader economic performance was dismal through the 1990s. Second, most of the other countries in the region have not been the macroeconomic miscreants that Britain, France and Italy, for example, were during their periods of double-digit inflation. Japan's regional partners generally followed conservative, orthodox macroeconomic policy (see, for example, World Bank 1993). Rather than using the Japanese yen as the nominal anchor, therefore, they stabilised their currencies against the dollar (McKinnon 2000).

The credibility approach might nonetheless apply to Asia through a different commitment mechanism. The Asian financial crisis drove many of the currencies of the region off their dollar pegs and into a flexible or managed floating regime. These states are thus mindful of the need to maintain market confidence in order to avoid renewed capital panic. The credibility of commitments to stability-oriented policies can be reinforced by central bank independence, by adherence to policy rules (such as inflation or monetary targeting) or through international commitments such as firm exchange rate pegging. Regional commitments could be part of future strategies of countries within the region to maintain market confidence in the presence of potentially volatile capital flows (see Williamson 2000).

STRUCTURAL REALISM

Neorealist scholars have argued that European integration in general and economic and monetary union in particular were made possible by the power structure of the global system that prevailed after World War II. Specifically, bipolarity transformed the nature of interstate relations in Europe. Located between the superpowers and gathered under the protection of the United States and the North Atlantic Treaty Organization (NATO), Western European countries could pursue absolute gains through economic integration and discount relative losses (see, for example, Waltz 1979: 70–71). The passage of the Maastricht Treaty, deepening of the European Union, enlargement of its membership to 15 states, and formation of the monetary union in the 1990s, after the collapse of the Soviet Union, dealt devastating blows to the validity of neorealism in Europe.[5]

East Asia has confronted a more complex security structure than Western Europe, however. Four countries played leading roles historically: the United States, the Soviet Union, Japan and China. Soviet–American rivalry shared the limelight, so to speak, with intra-regional rivalries that were much more intense than those within Europe. Their location between the superpowers was not sufficient to reconcile Japan and China, in contrast to the reconciliation between France and Germany. Although Soviet–American rivalry might have suppressed some of these intra-regional tensions, resentment and suspicion of Japan in Korea and Southeast Asia constrained East Asian regionalism.

A neorealist thus might have expected that the dissolution of the Soviet Union would unleash greater intra-regional conflict in East Asia than had been the case in Western Europe and that it would set regional cooperation back farther. Owing to the persistence of the communist regimes in China and North Korea, the principal sources of security tension come from within rather than outside the region. The North Korean nuclear program, firing of missiles across Japan, Chinese criticism of Japan during the revision of the Japan–US Security Treaty and multiple cross-straits crises keep military matters high on the agenda and sensitise governments to relative losses from economic cooperation.

Substantial advances in APEC integration, pursuit of subregional initiatives or robust cooperation in the monetary and financial arena would thus be inconsistent with the logic of system-based neorealism for East Asia. But regional economic integration has been insufficient to decisively falsify neorealism. To the extent that outside powers are relevant to regional politics, the dissolution of the Soviet Union left the United States in a far more privileged position, arguably rendering East Asia more susceptible to American interests. Once APEC had served the purpose of pre-empting the EAEG and prodding the Europeans to accede to the Uruguay Round, American preferences had been satisfied, the United States withdrew active support for regionalism and APEC momentum stalled.

REGIONAL POLITICS

An alternative structural explanation focuses on the distribution of material capabilities at the regional rather than the systemic level. Specifically, the dominance of a single country within a region can facilitate monetary cooperation by providing inducements for policy adjustment and carrying the costs of enforcement of agreements. In this vein, for example, Dyson (1994) argues that German power, among other factors, explains the Maastricht Treaty agreement. Economists who argued that the success of the EMS during the 1980s was due to countries' willingness to peg to the German mark as a 'nominal anchor' were labelled the 'German dominance' school. Similarly, Cohen (1993) argues that the presence of a regional hegemon explains the durability of historical monetary unions.[6]

In terms of national GDP as a proportion of regional GDP, Germany was less dominant among the EC6 in 1970 and is presently less dominant among the Euro-11 and EU15 than Japan has been and continues to be within East Asia. Germany generated 37.3 per cent of EC6 output in 1970 and about 32 per cent of Euro-11 output and about 25 per cent of EU15 output at the inception of the monetary union in 1999. Measured at market exchange rates, the Japanese economy is seven-and-a-half times larger than the ASEAN-10 economies combined and roughly 10 times larger than the South Korean economy. On this measure, Japan thus represents about 60 per cent of the GDP of East Asia as a whole (Table 5.4). Japan's regional partners appear considerably larger when compared on the basis of purchasing power parity. China even looms larger than Japan on that basis. For assessing the ability of Japan to influence its regional neighbours through international trade and finance, however, the market exchange rate is arguably the more relevant measure.

GDP weight arguably understates Germany's power within Europe on monetary matters. Germany's price stability, role as regional investor, role in trade and credibility in the markets, and the role of the German mark as a regional currency, arguably strengthened German influence beyond what economic size alone would suggest. Conversely, Japan's economic size almost certainly overstates its influence within East Asia. Although it holds massive foreign exchange reserves and is the world's largest international creditor, Japan has a fragile banking system and its economy stagnated through most of the 1990s. Japan became a substantial source of FDI only in the mid-1980s and its capital markets remain less developed than they might be. The Japanese currency thus plays a considerably smaller international role than the country's share in international trade and finance might indicate.

Regional hegemony, as measured by relative economic size, has thus been a poor predictor of monetary cooperation in East Asia. As China continues to grow faster than Japan, and if Japan fails to undertake structural reform, the distribution of economic capabilities within the region is likely to be increasingly bipolar. The ramifications for regional monetary cooperation depend on whether there is a shift in Chinese and Japanese preferences, and structural models can reveal little about this.

SYSTEMIC INSTABILITY

I have argued elsewhere (Henning 1998) that conflict and instability within the international monetary system were closely and causally associated with European monetary integration. The behaviour of the United States was particularly important to the stability of the system. When the United States fostered system-wide stability, European states had little to gain on the margin

Table 5.4   Ratio of GDP to regional hegemons at market exchange rates (per cent), 1970–2000

	US GDP as proportion of NAFTA	German GDP as proportion of EU-15	German GDP as proportion of Euro-11	Japan GDP as proportion of EA-17	China GDP as proportion of EA-17
1970	89.1	24.5	31.8	44.0	18.5
1971	88.8	25.1	32.6	44.8	18.1
1972	88.5	25.3	32.5	57.4	20.3
1973	87.9	26.5	33.2	56.7	19.1
1974	86.3	26.3	32.7	55.6	18.1
1975	85.9	24.6	30.9	55.3	18.8
1976	85.9	25.3	31.5	56.8	16.4
1977	87.3	25.8	32.0	58.9	16.0
1978	87.6	26.1	32.3	62.6	15.1
1979	86.9	25.4	31.7	59.8	16.7
1980	85.5	23.9	30.4	57.2	17.8
1981	84.8	22.7	29.4	59.0	15.8
1982	87.2	22.8	29.4	56.9	16.2
1983	88.0	23.5	30.0	58.3	16.1
1984	88.2	23.0	29.4	58.0	15.7
1985	88.6	22.4	28.8	61.0	15.5
1986	89.9	23.3	29.3	69.1	11.6
1987	89.3	23.6	29.5	70.4	10.8
1988	88.2	22.8	29.0	72.0	9.0
1989	87.5	22.2	28.3	69.4	9.8
1990	87.2	22.7	28.5	67.6	10.5
1991	86.7	24.5	30.7	68.8	10.0
1992	86.9	25.8	31.9	68.6	10.8
1993	87.2	27.6	33.8	69.0	11.6
1994	87.6	27.8	34.2	69.4	10.0
1995	89.3	28.5	34.8	67.6	11.0
1996	89.1	27.2	33.4	62.4	13.2
1997	88.7	25.8	32.7	59.7	15.3
1998	89.3	25.6	32.5	60.2	17.9
1999	89.5	25.4	32.1	61.4	18.3
2000	89.5	25.5	32.0	59.8	19.2

Notes: EA = East Asia; NAFTA = North American Free Trade Agreement.
Source: *World Economic Outlook.*

from regional monetary cooperation. When the United States contributed to international monetary instability – through excessively expansionary or restrictive macroeconomic policies, current account deficits, demands for macroeconomic policy adjustments on the part of European governments, and use of the exchange rate as a weapon to secure those adjustments – European states had compelling incentives to create a regional 'island of monetary stability'. Accordingly, periods of stabilising American behaviour saw few advances in European monetary integration, while periods of destabilising behaviour witnessed advances in regional integration. European monetary union is thus largely a defensive reaction to shifting American preferences and pressure for policy adjustments (Henning 1998; see also Loriaux 1991, Dyson 1994 and Loedel 1997).

Systemic instability alone is not sufficient to produce regional integration: a certain degree of regional market integration (at least) also appears to be necessary. Successive American attempts to extract more expansionary policies from the Japanese government did not lead Japan to seriously consider regional monetary cooperation as a buffer. However, market integration may now have increased to the point where systemically produced disruption to intra-regional trade and investment is disturbingly large relative to GDP. Recently, the primary source of systemic disturbance has been large and volatile capital flows, interacting with domestic banking systems and capital markets, and the contagion transmitted through them. The Asian financial crises of 1997–98 brought very sharp recessions, sent tens of millions of people below the poverty line, and prompted a general review of economic policies in general and regional cooperative arrangements for mutual support in particular.

During the 1990s, in contrast to the previous three decades, US domestic macroeconomic policy and external payments stabilised the international economic system. By accepting the burden of global current account adjustment in the wake of the crisis, the United States almost single-handedly helped to pull Asian and other crisis-stricken states out of severe recessions. Nonetheless, US trade conflict with Japan and complicity in or tolerance of wide swings in the yen–dollar exchange rate rendered unmanageable the policies of many Asian states of pegging their currencies to the dollar or to a basket of currencies in which the dollar was heavily weighted. When the crisis struck, the United States was late to respond, delaying deployment of its Exchange Stabilization Fund (Henning 1999). The contrast to the quick deployment in the case of Mexico in 1995 was not lost on Asian governments. The US Congress refused to approve an increase in IMF quotas and funding for the New Arrangements to Borrow, until the 'flight to liquidity' in autumn 1998, a dramatic worsening of the crisis and a storm of global criticism. These failures to take timely action created strong incentives for East Asian states to create mutual support arrangements. Interest in developing regional arrangements would probably be strongly reinforced by another crisis in the region.

CONCLUSION

This paper has reviewed several prominent theories of European monetary integration and assessed their applicability to East Asia. Two questions were asked of each approach: Does the approach explain why European monetary integration is advanced while Asian monetary and financial cooperation is in its infancy? What does the approach predict for the future of Asian monetary and financial cooperation? Several findings are worth emphasising.

First, several explanations of monetary integration in the European context are not considered here for reasons of space and data availability. McNamara (1998, especially 56–71) argues that European monetary integration was based on a 'consensus of competitive liberalism'. 'Pragmatic orthodoxy' in macroeconomic management and the acceptance of export-oriented strategies (World Bank 1993) might well provide the basis for shared economic ideology in East Asia. Shared diagnosis of the 1997–98 currency crisis as capital account and liquidity problems, and shared prescriptions for treating such crises, could reinforce a common regional economic ideology. The notion that monetary union was principally motivated by a desire to secure political unification, by contrast, while popular among many analysts of the European case, has virtually no applicability in Asia. Similarly, in the politics of Asian regionalism there is no apparent reason why the criteria for an optimum currency area – while relevant to the economic case for integration – would play any more significant a role than the minor role such criteria played in the political discourse over monetary union in Europe.

Second, most of the approaches I have examined were consistent with the formation of monetary union in Europe and the absence of substantial monetary cooperation in Asia. Structural realism and regional hegemony, by contrast, do not explain the greater monetary progress in Europe compared to Asia.

Third, the 'successful' approaches generate somewhat different predictions for the future of monetary cooperation in East Asia. Market integration, systemic instability and commitment approaches predict substantial progress in regional monetary and financial cooperation over the next decade. Domestic political approaches, as construed here, view the convergence of national preferences as probable and the chances for strengthening regional monetary cooperation as fairly good, depending, as in the case of commitment and systemic instability approaches, on continued integration of goods and capital markets.[7] These predictions might not be sufficiently differentiated to clearly falsify some approaches while confirming others as the fate of proposals for enhanced monetary cooperation in Asia unfolds. To further cull these approaches, scholars will have to test them against the experience of other regions, particularly the Western hemisphere.

Fourth, this review demonstrates that all of these approaches are partial explanations. Even the successful explanations are individually insufficient to fully account for European progress relative to Asia. Market integration provides a good example: high ratios of intra-regional trade relative to total trade underpin the rationale for regional exchange rate stabilisation. But such ratios are not sufficient to explain the variation among East Asia, Europe, North America and the Western hemisphere in terms of monetary cooperation. Additional factors, such as domestic politics, regional institutions, regional politics and systemic instability, are also needed. Conversely, these additional approaches would not predict regional monetary cooperation in the absence of market integration at the regional level. A comprehensive theory of regional monetary integration will have to combine these approaches.

NOTES

1   Calculated from United Nations statistics provided by the International Trade Division of Statistics Canada.
2   Calculated from United Nations, Direction of Trade Statistics Yearbook, various years.
3   For a discussion of 'supranationalism,' see, for example, Sandholtz and Zysman (1989), Anderson (1995) and Moravcsik (1991).
4   Recent critical commentary includes Moravcsik (1998) and Mattli (1999).
5   This is effectively conceded by Grieco (1995).
6   Cohen writes that interstate politics matters more than satisfaction of the economic criteria for an optimum currency area. 'Compliance with commitments is greatest in the presence of either a locally dominant state, willing and able to use its influence to sustain monetary cooperation, or a broad network of institutional linkages sufficient to make the loss of monetary autonomy tolerable to each partner.' (Cohen 1993)
7   Only structural realism and regional structure, the unsuccessful approaches, predict clear backsliding on regional cooperation.

REFERENCES

Anderson, J.J. (1995) 'The state of the (European) Union: From the single market to Maastricht, from singular events to general theories', *World Politics* 47: 441–65.
Bergsten, C.F. (2000) 'The New Asian Challenge', *Institute for International Economics Working Paper 00-4*, Washington DC: Institute for International Economics.
Bowie, A. and D. Unger (1997) *The Politics of Open Economics*, Cambridge, UK: Cambridge University Press.
Cohen, B.J. (1993) 'Beyond EMU: the problem of sustainability', *Economics and Politics* 5 (July): 187–202.
—— (1997) 'The political economy of currency regions', in E. D. Mansfield and H. V. Milner (eds) *The Political Economy of Regionalism*, New York NY: Columbia University Press.
—— (1998) *The Geography of Money*, Ithaca, NY: Cornell University Press.
Crone, D. (1993) 'Does hegemony matter? The reorganization of the Pacific political economy', *World Politics* 45: 501–25.
Delors Report [Committee for the Study of Economic and Monetary Union]. (1989) *Report on Economic and Monetary Union in the European Community*. Luxembourg: Office of Official Publications of the European Community.
Dyson, K. (1994) *Elusive Union: the Process of Economic and Monetary Union in Europe*, London and New York: Longman.
Eichengreen, B. and J. Frieden (1994) 'The political economy of European monetary unification: An analytical introduction', in B. Eichengreen and J. Frieden (eds), *The Political Economy of European Monetary Unification*, Boulder CO: Westview Press.
European Commission (1990a) 'Economic and Monetary Union: The Economic Rationale and Design of the System', Brussels: European Commission.

—— (1990b) 'One market, one money: an evaluation of the potential benefits and costs of forming an economic and monetary union', *European Economy* 44 (October).

Frankel, J.A. (1997) *Regional Trading Blocs in the World Economic System*, Washington DC: Institute for International Economics.

Frieden, J.A. (1991a) *Debt, Development, and Democracy: Modern Political Economy and Latin America*, Princeton NJ: Princeton University Press.

—— (1991b) 'National economic policies in a world of global finance', *International Organization* 45 (4): 425–52.

Gamble, A. and A. Payne (eds) (1996) *Regionalism and World Order*, London: MacMillan.

George, S. (1985) *Politics and Policy in the European Community*, Oxford, UK: Clarendon Press.

Giavazzi, F. and M. Pagano (1988) 'The advantage of tying one's hands: EMS discipline and central bank credibility', *European Economic Review* 32 (June): 1055–82.

Giavazzi, F. and A. Giovannini (1989) *Limiting Exchange Rate Flexibility: the European Monetary System*, Cambridge MA: MIT Press.

Grieco, J. M. (1995) 'The Maastricht Treaty, Economic and Monetary Union, and the Neo-realist Research Programme, *Review of International Studies* 21 (1): 21–40.

Haas, E. (1964) *Beyond the Nation State*, Stanford CA: Stanford University Press.

Haggard, S. (1990) *Pathways from the Periphery: The Politics of Growth in the Newly Industrializing Countries*, Ithaca NY: Cornell University Press.

—— (1994) 'Thinking About Regionalism: The Politics of Minilateralism in Asia and the Americas', Paper prepared for the Annual Meetings of the American Political Science Association, New York, 1–4 September.

—— (2000) *The Political Economy of the Asian Financial Crisis*, Washington DC: Institute for International Economics.

Haggard, S., C.H. Lee and S. Maxfield (eds) (1993) *The Politics of Finance in Developing Countries*, Ithaca NY: Cornell University Press.

Haggard, S. and C.H. Lee (eds) (1995) *Financial Systems and Economic Policy in Developing Countries*, Ithaca NY: Cornell University Press.

Henning, C.R. (1998) 'Systemic conflict and regional monetary integration', *International Organization* 52 (3): 537–73.

—— (1999) *The Exchange Stabilization Fund: Slush Money or War Chest?*, Washington DC: Institute for International Economics.

Johnson, C. (1987) 'Political institutions and economic performance: the government–business relationship in Japan, South Korea, and Taiwan', in F. C. Deyo (ed.), *The Political Economy of the New Asian Industrialism*, Ithaca: Cornell University Press.

Kahler, M. (1995) *International Institutions and the Political Economy of Integration*, Washington DC: Brookings Institution.

Katzenstein, P.J. (1996) 'Regionalism in comparative perspective', *Cooperation and Conflict* 31 (2): 123.

Loedel, P.H. (1997) 'Enhancing Europe's international monetary power', in P.-H. Laurent and M. Maresceau (eds), *The State of the European Union, Vol. 4: Deepening and Widening*, Boulder CO: Lynne Rienner.

Loriaux, M. (1991) *France After Hegemony: International Change and Financial Reform*, Ithaca NY: Cornell University Press.

Loriaux, M., M. Woo-Cumings, K.E. Calder, S. Maxfield and S. Perez (eds) (1997) *Capital Ungoverned: Liberalizing Finance in Interventionist States*, Ithaca NY: Cornell University Press.

Mansfield, E.D. and H.V. Milner (eds) (1997) *The Political Economy of Regionalism*, New York NY: Columbia University Press.

—— (1999) 'The new-wave of regionalism', *International Organization* 53 (3): 589.

Martin, L.L. (1993) 'International and domestic Institutions in the EMU process', *Economics and Politics* 5 (July): 125–44.

Mattli, W. (1999) *The Logic of Regional Integration: Europe and Beyond*, Cambridge, UK: Cambridge University Press.

McKinnon, R.I. (2000) 'The East Asian dollar standard, life after death?', *Economic Notes* 29 (1): 31–82.

McNamara, K.R. (1993) 'Common markets, uncommon currencies: system effects and the European Community', in R. Jervis and J. Snyder (eds), *Coping with Complexity in the International System*, Boulder CO: Westview Press.

—— (1998) *The Currency of Ideas: Monetary Politics in the European Union*, Ithaca NY: Cornell University Press.

Moravcsik, A. (1991) 'Negotiating the single European act', in R.O. Keohane and S. Hoffman (eds), *The New European Community: Decision-making and Institutional Change*, Boulder CO: Westview Press.

—— (1998) *The Choice for Europe: Social Purpose and State Power from Messina to Maastricht*, Ithaca NY: Cornell University Press.

Padoa-Schioppa, T. (ed.) (1990) *Efficiency, Stability, and Equity: A Strategy for the Evolution of the Economic System of the EC*, Luxembourg: Office of Official Publications of the European Community.

Root, H.L. (1996) *Small Countries, Big Lessons: Governance and the Rise of East Asia*, Oxford, UK: Oxford University Press.

Sandholtz, W. and J. Zysman (1989) '1992: Recasting the European bargain', *World Politics* 42 (October): 127.

Scollay, R. and J. Gilbert (2000) 'New Sub-Regional Trading Arrangements in the Asia Pacific', unpublished manuscript, APEC Study Centre, University of Auckland.

Waltz, K.N. (1979) *Theory of International Politics*, Reading MA: Addison-Wesley.

Williamson, J. (2000) *Exchange Rate Regimes for Emerging Markets: Reviving the Intermediate Option*, Washington DC: Institute for International Economics.

World Bank (1993) 'The East Asian Miracle: Economic Growth and Public Policy', Washington DC: World Bank.

6 A stocktake of institutions for regional cooperation

Takatoshi Ito and Koji Narita

INTRODUCTION

There is deep interest in East Asia in developing mechanisms and institutions to support policy dialogue, surveillance and financial cooperation. Other regions have also looked at these issues. In this paper, we describe the main global surveillance organisations and assess four regional institutions that have been established to support and promote regional financial cooperation – the European Payments Union (EPU), the European Monetary Cooperation Fund (EMCF), the Arab Monetary Fund and the Latin American Reserve Fund (Fondo Latinoamericano de Reservas, FLAR). Financial cooperation in the broad sense includes policy dialogue and surveillance, as well as mechanisms and institutes to provide financial support for liquidity shortfalls or financial crises. We discuss existing surveillance mechanisms in Asia and suggest how lessons learned from the analysis of the regional institutions can be applied to regional cooperation and future financial arrangements in East Asia.

GLOBAL SURVEILLANCE ORGANISATIONS

Before looking at regional financial arrangements, it is useful to put these in a broader global context. There are three main global surveillance organisations: the International Monetary Fund (IMF), the Organisation for Economic Co-operation and Development (OECD) and the Group of Seven (G-7).

The IMF, the OECD and the G-7

The IMF conducts annual reviews of the performance of all member countries and more frequent reviews of countries that receive IMF assistance. The reviews include macroeconomic assessments of monetary and fiscal conditions and policies, capital and financial market reviews, and reviews of external (export and import) balances. Policy analysis and review under specific programs such as standby arrangements and enhanced structural adjustment facilities also exists, but this is not peer-type policy surveillance. The OECD also conducts annual reviews on its members, which are the economically advanced countries. The IMF and OECD reviews are relatively institutionalised and go through a transparent process of drafting and report approval.

The OECD has another surveillance forum: Working Party 3 (WP3), a subgroup of the Economic Policy Committee, which comprises the chairs of G-7 countries and of the Netherlands (with Belgium), Sweden (with Denmark and Norway) and Switzerland. This grouping is roughly the same as the G-10 – the G-7 countries plus the Netherlands, Belgium, Sweden and Switzerland. Representatives from both the IMF and the European Central Bank (ECB) also attend meetings of both WP3 and the G-10. Representatives from the ministry of finance and the central bank (usually deputy ministers of the ministry of finance and deputy governors, or their deputies) meet for a one-day, closed-door meeting four times a year, without issuing reports or statements. Discussions are very frank and detailed, covering macroeconomic issues in the major economic regions (North America, Japan and Europe) as well as risk in emerging market economies and commodity markets.

The G-7 finance ministers and their deputies also meet and communicate frequently. The G-7 comprises the seven largest economies in the world. The G-7 forum ensures that the seven countries coordinate their policies on matters that are of concern for the global economy. Most meetings are informal, but the ministers meet formally about three times a year and issue a formal communiqué.

The role of emerging market economies

The international community now recognises the importance of involving key emerging market economies in discussions on global finance. This was prompted by recent currency crises in Mexico (1994–95), Asia (1997–98), Russia (1998), Brazil and Turkey (1999–2000) and Argentina (2001–02). When a country of a certain size develops a currency crisis or a banking crisis, it affects the stability of the global financial system. Advanced countries such as those represented by the G-7 became increasingly concerned that crises like those in Mexico and Asia could occur elsewhere, with adverse global effects.

Emerging market economies, on the other hand, felt that they were under increasing scrutiny from the international community, including the G-7, G-10 and IMF, without having their views and voices fairly represented. Many Asian economies believed that the liberalisation of domestic financial markets and external capital flows was a potential risk for the stability of financial markets, although advanced countries were pushing liberalisation strongly in emerging market economies. Many Asian economies also considered that hedge fund speculation on currencies contributed to the difficulties of small open economies during the volatile period of 1997–98.[1] As a result of these considerations, advanced economies, led by the G-7, created two new forums to allow for frank discussions involving emerging market economies: the Financial Stability Forum (FSF) and the G-20.

The FSF was created under the leadership of Andrew Crockett, Chief Manager of the Bank for International Settlements (BIS). It moved quickly to establish three working groups: highly-leveraged institutions, capital flows, and offshore financial centres. The groups included core members of the G-7 and several emerging market economies. The FSF has subsequently expanded its activities to include analysis of banking, deposit insurance, standards and sound financial systems.

The G-20 consists of 19 countries plus the chair of the European Union (EU). The 19 countries include some relatively large and advanced countries, the G-7 countries, and some emerging and developing countries with large populations or incomes that are systemically important for the stability of the global financial system. Like the G-7, the G-20 has no legal mandate, international treaty or permanent secretariat. However, it has the potential to develop into an important international forum able to conduct surveillance on global financial issues.

The Asian crises of the late 1990s led to consideration of how to strengthen international financial institutions. Efforts to reform such institutions were commonly referred to as building a new international financial architecture.[2] Many academics put forward radical reform plans, from abolishing the IMF to transforming the IMF into an international bankruptcy court. There were also discussions about streamlining IMF roles and lending facilities. In the end, only minor changes were made and actual institutional changes were modest.

One institutional change was to convert the interim committee of the IMF into a permanent body called the International Monetary and Financial Committee (IMFC), with regular 'deputies meetings'. The IMFC structure parallels the IMF board chairs; the committee can discuss both IMF institutional issues and current global economic and financial issues. The IMF also created a new department that is dedicated to capital market surveillance.

On the financing side, there were two important developments for the IMF. First, there was a quota increase, as a result of which the IMF is better endowed to deal with large-scale financial support packages for emerging market economies. Second, arrangements were put in place to allow the IMF to borrow from rich countries if it develops a short-term liquidity problem. This will allow it to support many crisis-hit countries simultaneously. This arrangement builds on the General Arrangements to Borrow (GAB), which has been in place since the inception of the IMF but which, after the Asian crises, was thought to be insufficient for future crises. The GAB membership is the same as the G-10 membership. The expansion of the G-10 was discussed but rejected for an alternative solution, the New Arrangements to Borrow (NAB), which involves 25 members, including richer developing and emerging market economies. Box 6.1 shows the membership of the different groups and forums.

All in all, there has been some progress in creating new forums and carrying out some internal reorganisation in the international financial institutions to strengthen surveillance on financial issues. However, the existing international financial institutions have not been radically or seriously reorganised.

Box 6.1   Membership of different groups and forums

G-7   US, Japan, Germany, France, UK, Canada, Italy

G-10   G-7 plus Sweden, Switzerland, Belgium and the Netherlands
       (11 countries)

G-20   G-7 plus Russia, Turkey, India, Indonesia, China, Korea, Australia,
       Brazil, Argentina, Mexico, Saudi Arabia and South Africa, and the chair
       of the European Union

IMFC   G-7 plus Belgium, the Netherlands, Finland, Switzerland, Russia,
       Indonesia, China, Australia, India, Brazil, Argentina, Venezuela, Saudi
       Arabia, Egypt, Iran, Gabon and South Africa (24 countries)

NAB   G-10, Luxembourg, Spain, Austria, Finland, Denmark, Norway, Malaysia,
       Singapore, Thailand, Hong Kong, Korea, Australia, Saudi Arabia and
       Kuwait (25 economies)

Emerging market economies are especially vulnerable to currency and banking crises, as shown by the currency crises of Mexico, Asia, Russia and Argentina. However, such crises are not limited to emerging market economies. Banking crises have been common even in advanced countries – for example, the savings and loans crisis in the United States in the early 1980s, banking crises in Sweden in the early 1990s, and banking crises in Japan in the late 1990s.

Since the mid-1980s, the Basel Committee on Banking Supervision (BCBS), a group of banking supervisors, has helped to promote information exchange and develop banking standards. The BIS provides facilities for its meetings. One standard developed by the BCBS is that for bankers' capital adequacy, which was developed in 1988 and which has had a large impact on the soundness of internationally active banks. The 8 per cent rule has been accepted globally as a minimum standard for international banks. A revised standard, recommending more complex risk management, is under review. It is likely to recommend that internationally active banks introduce sophisticated, model-based risk management models. The BCBS has equivalents in the securities industry and the insurance industry – the International Organization of Securities Commissions (IOSCO) and the International Association of Insurance Supervisors (IAIS).

The trio of supervisors – BCBS, IOSCO and IAIS – have become an important group for developing codes and standards for financial institutions. Of course, there are some concerns about a unified global standard. Even the advanced countries have different regulations. For example, Germany has universal banking, while the United States and Japan have traditionally separated banking and securities. Developing countries and emerging market economies often lack basic financial and legal infrastructures. However, if they want to be integrated into the global financial and capital markets, their supervisory regime must usually conform to 'best practices' of the global standard. As investors from advanced countries have increasingly taken positions in emerging market economies, advanced countries have become more demanding about the state of the supervisory regime. If financial institutions from emerging market economies wish to do substantial business in advanced countries, the credibility of their main supervisors will be under scrutiny. Effective supervision requires reliable accounting statements of banks, securities businesses and corporations that borrow from them. The International Accounting Standards Committee (IASC) has developed important international accounting standards to help in this task.

Organisations like BCBS, IOSCO, IAIS and IASC do not practise surveillance activities, but their discussions and standards are extremely relevant for surveillance activities among international financial institutions. Let us cite an example. In future, we need better surveillance for financial soundness. Vulnerability in the banking sector often causes attacks on currencies; conversely, a sharp depreciation in the currency often causes bank failures. The twin crises – in banking and currency – have been observed repeatedly among emerging market economies. After the Mexican crisis, the BCBS developed 'Core Principles for Effective Banking Supervision', which set out broad guidelines on how to set up a supervision regime. The IMF and the World Bank agreed that the principles will be implemented in the IMF surveillance process. Accordingly, progress in financial supervision will be monitored in a financial sector assessment program (FSAP) for each country. This should provide an effective surveillance system.

REGIONAL SURVEILLANCE COOPERATION ORGANISATIONS

The European Payments Union

The EPU was established on 1 July 1950 as a system of multilateral clearing among West European countries. It replaced the bilateral agreements on which intra-European trade had begun again after World War II amid the lack of convertibility of European currencies and the scarcity of internationally usable reserves (gold and dollar holdings). It functioned successfully for nearly eight years until its dissolution on 27 December 1958, when current account convertibility was restored by a majority of EPU member states.

On 19 September 1950, the EPU Agreement was signed by all 18 Organization for European Economic Cooperation (OEEC) countries (Austria, Belgium, Denmark, France, Germany, Greece, Iceland, Ireland, Italy, Luxembourg, the Netherlands, Norway, Portugal, Sweden, Switzerland, Trieste, Turkey and the United Kingdom). It came into force retroactively on 1 July 1950. The agreement created two bodies: a clearing union for payments made in any member currency and a managing board to supervise operations and recommend improvements in the system. The EPU was constituted within the framework of the OEEC (which evolved into today's OECD). It was administered by a managing board of seven independent experts, with final decisions resting with the OEEC Council.

Operation

There were four components of the EPU system. First, during any given month, member central banks granted unlimited credit to each other. Second, at the end of the month, the net balance of each EPU country with every other country was reported to the BIS (the EPU's financial agent), which converted bilateral balances into units of account and cancelled offsetting claims. Each unit of account was defined by the same gold content as the US dollar (0.88867088 grams of fine gold). Third, a net position was established for each country with the union as a whole (not individual countries). Fourth, liabilities and credits were settled between the member and the EPU, partly in gold or dollars and partly in credit, according to the size of the net cumulative position relative to the quota.

Each country received a quota equal to 15 per cent of its total inter-European trade in 1949. So long as its liability to the EPU remained less than 20 per cent of its quota, it was financed entirely by credit: the net position was carried on the books of the EPU without requiring any payment. After the liability had reached 20 per cent of quota, settlement had to be 20 per cent in gold or dollars. Debts of more than 40, 60 or 80 per cent of quota required settlement in 40, 60 or 80 per cent of gold or dollars, respectively. Cumulative surpluses were settled in similar fashion, although the proportions of gold or dollar payments escalated at a different rate. Once the quota was exceeded, the country had to settle with the EPU, using gold or dollars only; under exceptional circumstances additional credits were extended by the EPU's managing board. The system allowed trade to be 'multilateralised' and its volume to be stimulated by the availability of EPU credit lines (Eichengreen 1993). Table 6.1 shows the initial EPU settlement schedule.

Under this system, what was the incentive for creditors to be in persistent surplus with the EPU? Eichengreen and de Macedo (2001) say:

> Accumulated claims could be converted into commodities or hard currency only partially and with delay. Until its quota was exceeded, a surplus country would receive gold amounting to only 40 per cent of its cumulative net exports to other EPU countries. For debtor countries securing loans and relieved of the need to settle bilaterally, the attraction of this system was obvious. But what was the attraction to a creditor like Belgium in persistent surplus with the Union?

The answer comes in three parts. First, a lower proportion of gold payments was initially required of debtors than was extended to creditors. This increased the likelihood that surplus countries, which would otherwise be trading their exports for inconvertible claims, would wish to participate. Giving creditor countries more gold than was contributed by debtors required working capital:

Table 6.1   Initial schedule of settlements in the EPU (% of current deficit or surplus)[a]

Cumulative surplus or deficit (% of EPU quota)	Country with cumulative deficit		Country with cumulative surplus	
	Gold	Credit	Gold	Credit
0–20	0	100	0	100
20–40	20	80	50	50
40–60	40	60	50	50
60–80	60	40	50	50
80–100	80	20	50	50
Overall	40	60	40	60

Note
a   At the start, the ratio of gold or dollars to credit was set on average (overall) at 40 to 60. In 1954, the increase of international reserve holdings of the OEEC countries since 1953 allowed a move to a flat ratio of 50:50 and in 1955 to a ratio of 75:25.

Source: Kenen (1991).

this the United States contributed in the form of a grant of $350 million of Marshall Plan money to the EPU.

Second, financial assistance came with conditionality minimising the scope for exploitation of creditors by debtors. When a member exhausted its quota, the EPU managing board, comprising independent financial experts reporting to the OEEC council, met to advise it and compel the adoption of corrective policies. Thus, the creditors had reason to anticipate that the debtors would be forced to adjust.

Third, EPU membership required the liberalisation of trade. When countries joined, they pledged to eliminate discrimination against other participants based on balance of payments considerations. Participants were required to reduce trade barriers by a given percentage of their existing level – initially by half, escalating to 60 and 75 per cent. The most internationally competitive European countries, such as Belgium, stood to gain disproportionately from such liberalisation.

Managing board and multilateral surveillance

The managing board of the EPU comprised independent financial experts reporting to the OEEC council; it had seven voting members, each nominated by a government and elected by the OEEC council. The terms were for one year, but members could be re-elected. Members served as individuals, not as representatives of their governments. The meetings of the board were attended by the chairman of the OEEC Payments Committee, representatives of the Secretary General of the OEEC and the BIS, and an observer appointed by the US government.

Over the life of the EPU, the managing board extended supplementary credits to deficit countries that exhausted their quotas. Such credits were subject to economic policy conditions. One of the main activities of the board was to discuss such conditions (which formally were set by the OEEC council) and monitor the progress of domestic policy adjustments in the debtor countries. Government experts from countries receiving exceptional credits cooperated by appearing before the board to review the economic situation of their country in unprecedented detail. These procedures were the first comprehensive arrangement of 'multilateral surveillance' of economic developments for a group of countries.

The first credit of $120 million under this facility went to Germany during the balance of payments crisis of 1950–51 in connection with the Korean War. Germany's quota of $320 million was too small, and in the first four months of the EPU's operation (July–October 1950) Germany exhausted most of its quota. Moreover, the outbreak of the Korean War in June 1950 worsened the terms of trade of countries like Germany that imported raw materials. The board sent two prominent experts to Germany to assess the situation, and to make recommendations on possible German adjustment policies. On 6 November 1950, the board agreed that the EPU would give Germany a special credit if it would accept certain conditions, in substance those recommended by the experts. Those conditions included commitments to maintain the present exchange rate of the German mark, to abstain from any form of deficit financing, and to increase taxes. On 13 December, given the German package of adjustment policies, the OEEC council approved the board recommendations and the extension of $120 million to Germany. In March 1951, Germany's monthly balance of payments turned from deficit to surplus. By the end of May, Germany paid off its special credit, and by the end of 1951 it shifted to perennial creditor status in the EPU.

Trading

The main objective of the EPU clearing mechanism was to restore the current account convertibility of European countries and thus to permit and induce them to remove restrictions on trade in goods and services in Western Europe. The EPU was closely linked to new trading arrangements. The OEEC agreement had established regulations for the gradual removal of trade restrictions on a multilateral basis. On 15 January 1949, the target for the reduction of import quotas was set at 50 per cent of total private imports. When the EPU began on 1 July 1950, the target was raised to 60 per cent; on 1 February 1951 it was raised to 75 per cent; and on 14 January 1955 it was raised to 90 per cent. Trade liberalisation within Europe rose from 56 per cent just before the EPU was instituted to 89 per cent at the end of 1958 (Kaplan and Schleiminger 1989). Intra-European trade expanded vigorously under the EPU, from $10 billion in 1950 to $23 billion in 1959. This suggests that the EPU's liberalising effect was considerable (Eichengreen 1993).

Implications

The EPU was dissolved at the end of 1958 when it became feasible to restore the convertibility of currencies on current account. But full convertibility (on capital as well as current account) was not achieved until the 1980s or even the early 1990s. Currencies on current account are convertible in East Asia, so the example of the EPU does not appear to provide direct lessons for financial cooperation there. But some lessons can be learned.

Future financial arrangements in East Asia should allow countries whose currencies are not yet convertible on capital account to open capital accounts more easily and safely. This should allow both creditor countries and debtor countries to enjoy more open capital movements, because creditor countries will be attracted by trade liberalisation.

The success of the EPU was due to the cooperation between the managing board and the participating countries through multilateral surveillance. The success of financial arrangements in East Asia will also depend on how we arrange mutual multilateral surveillance – in other words, policy dialogue.

The EPU example also shows the advantages of a close linkage between financial cooperation and trade liberalisation. The various moves for free trade agreements within East Asia should be continued vigorously in tandem with the building of financial cooperation.

European Monetary Cooperation Fund

Role

The EMCF was set up on 3 April 1973 and continued through the time of the 'snake'[3] (1972–78) and the European Monetary System (EMS) (1978 on). The European Monetary Institute took over its functions in 1994. The EMCF had a legal basis. It was directed by a board of governors consisting of the members of the Committee of Central Bank Governors, and was required to run within the overall guidelines of economic policy adopted by the ECOFIN Council, composed of the finance ministers of the member states.

The EMCF was to contribute to the progressive establishment of economic and monetary union by promoting reduced fluctuation margins between European Community (EC) country exchange rates, intervening in EC currencies in exchange markets, and promoting settlements between central banks, leading to a concerted policy on reserves. Initially, the organisation was to be responsible for the concerted action necessary for the functioning of the 'snake' agreement, the multilateralisation of creditor and debtor positions and of settlements in the 'snake', and administration of the very short-term financing (VSTF) facility and the short-term monetary support (STMS) facility. The BIS acted as agent for the fund, carrying out its transactions through an arrangement similar to those with the EPU.

Although the tasks of the EMCF as enumerated in the council regulation sounded quite ambitious, the organisation did not acquire a policy role and was limited to an accounting function. Its most important task turned out to be the multilateralisation of 'snake' transactions. Prior to the EMCF, 'snake' interventions resulted in bilateral creditor and debtor positions. After it was established, liabilities and claims resulting from interventions were cleared through the EMCF after conversion into European monetary units of account.[4] The EMCF board met formally for a few minutes each month in Basel after the meeting of the Committee of Central Bank Governors. All issues of importance were discussed in the committee, not by the board. Nobody was employed by the EMCF. Gros and Thygesen (1992) have said:

> ... the main reason why the fund developed only a shadowy existence was its formal subordination to the ECOFIN Council ... Since this was unacceptable to several [central bank] governors, substantive work remained firmly with 'their' committee.

The EMS and EMCF

The EMS was designed in the late 1970s to overcome three weaknesses of the Bretton Woods system: the asymmetric operation of the system, which freed the United States from subjecting domestic monetary policies to smooth the functioning of the world monetary system, while shifting to other countries the burden of adjustment; the difficulties of coping with a world of increasing capital mobility; and the dramatisation of exchange rate parity realignments, which often motivated their postponement, leading to speculative attacks and to the build-up of large current account imbalances. To operate successfully, an adjustable peg needs three conditions: a set of rules governing monetary policy and exchange market interventions that determines whether the system works symmetrically or asymmetrically; provisions for fending off speculative attacks and defending a parity grid; and a set of rules for changing central parities (Giavazzi and Giovannini 1989).

Intervention rules

First of all, a new monetary unit, the European currency unit (ECU), was created. The ECU is a composite unit of account, made up of a basket of fixed amounts of nine EC currencies. The units of each currency that make up one ECU were reviewed every five years, or on request when the weight of any currency changed by 25 per cent or more.

EMS intervention rules worked as follows. Each community currency had an ECU central rate, expressed as the price of one ECU in terms of that currency. ECU central rates were fixed and revised only when there was realignment. The ratio of any two ECU central rates was the bilateral central rate of any pair of currencies that together form the parity grid of the system. Through the exchange rate mechanism (ERM) of the EMS, a central bank agreed to keep its market exchange rate vis-à-vis any other currency participating in the mechanism within prearranged margins from the bilateral central parity. These bilateral margins were set at 2.25 per cent on each side of the central parity, so the fluctuation band for any bilateral rate was 4.5 per cent. Currencies that had been floating could opt for temporarily wider margins of up to ± 6 per cent. Italy made use of this provision until January 1990.

Intervention was compulsory only when two currencies reached their bilateral margin – that is, when the bilateral exchange rate diverged by 2.25 per cent from the central parity. This was called marginal intervention. Marginal intervention had to be carried out by both central banks involved in buying and selling each other's currency at the bilateral limit. The amount of financing for marginal intervention was unlimited. Interventions within the margins (intra-marginal intervention) were not expressly provided for under the terms of the ERM but were not excluded. If intervention was carried out in participating currencies, it was subject to the approval of the central bank whose currency was being sold or bought. If it was carried out in non-EC currencies – usually in dollars – it was always permitted and was not subject to mutual authorisation.

Financing facilities in the EMS[5]

There were three financing facilities in the EMS: the VSTF facility, the STMS facility and the medium-term financial assistance facility (MTFA facility). The latter two facilities are provided to member states with balance-of-payments difficulties.

The VSTF facility was established in 1972 to implement the European exchange rate system, the 'snake'. Following the creation of the EMS, its function was to provide credibility to bilateral EMS parities by securing unlimited financing for marginal intervention. It consisted of mutual credit lines among the central banks for unlimited amounts for the financing of obligatory intervention at the intervention limits.[6]

The terms and conditions of this facility of the 1979 EMS agreement between central banks, with important amendments introduced in the 1987 Basle–Nyborg agreement, were as follows.

The claims and liabilities resulting from intervention were converted into ECUs and entered the books of the EMCF. The credit lines matured 75 days after the end of the month in which the intervention had taken place (before the 1987 Basel–Nyborg agreement, it was 45 days), and would be renewed for a further three months at the request of the debtor central bank. This request was granted automatically provided the total amount of indebtedness of the central bank in the VSTF facility did not exceed a ceiling equal to twice the country's quota in the STMS facility (before the 1987 agreement, it was 100 per cent). Moreover, any debt already renewed automatically for three months could be renewed for another three months subject to the agreement of the creditor central bank. Any debt exceeding the 200 per cent ceiling could be renewed once for three months, subject to the agreement of the creditor central bank.

When a reimbursement of a financing operation fell due, settlement by the debtor central bank was to be effected as far as possible in the creditor's currency. Any debt not settled in the creditor's currency could be wholly or partly settled by transfers of ECU assets and/or by transferring other reserve components in accordance with the composition of the debtor central bank's reserves. In general, the creditor central bank was not obliged to accept settlement in ECUs of an amount exceeding 50 per cent of the claim. But the 1987 amendment allowed this limit to reach 100 per cent provided this did not bring about an ECU disequilibrium in the creditor's composition of reserve assets.

The unit of account of the VSTF facility managed by the EMCF was the ECU (under the EMS), so debtor and creditor balances were denominated in ECUs. However, loans and reimbursements were usually effected in assets denominated in national currencies, so the conversion from the national units of account to the ECU was made on settlement day on the basis of the daily rate for the ECU established by the commission. Under those rules of accounting, a central bank that lent its currency would find itself reimbursed, months later, after its currency has appreciated against the ECU, in fewer units of its own currency.

The interest on outstanding claims was set as the average of the official discount rates of all EC central banks weighted by their shares in the ECU basket.

Pursuant to the 1987 agreement, central banks could also use the credit lines of the VSTF facility for intra-marginal intervention. In this case access to the VSTF facility was not automatic, but was subject to the authorisation of the central bank whose currency was being drawn.

The central banks participating in the ERM were obliged to deposit 20 per cent of their gold reserves and 20 per cent of their dollar reserves with the EMCF against the issue of ECUs. These transactions took the form of revolving three-month swaps between the national central banks and the EMCF. Thus, funds did not really belong to the EMCF, and each central bank continued to manage the gold and dollar reserves it deposited with the EMCF. These ECUs were used primarily as a means of settling debts arising from intervention.

The STMS facility was established in 1970 on the basis of an agreement between the central banks of the EC countries. It was administered by the EMCF following that organisation's establishment in 1973. The participating central banks agreed to provide each other with credits not exceeding their debtor quotas for three months in the case of temporary balance of payments deficits. Credits were granted without economic policy conditions, but they triggered subsequent consultations. Originally they could be renewed for another three months; amendments introduced in the context of the EMS allowed them to be renewed for an additional three months, raising the maximum duration from six to nine months.

The 1974 amendment enlarged quotas; each central bank received a 'debtor quota' (borrowing ceiling) to determine the amount of support it could receive and a 'creditor quota' (commitment ceiling) to determine the amount it agreed to finance. The latter was twice as high as the former to safeguard the viability of the system. In addition, extensions beyond the debtor and creditor quotas (so called *rallonges*) could be applied to any member state. Under the STMS facility, the central bank of a member state could borrow from its partners a total amount equal to its debtor quota plus one-half of the total available (creditor) *rallonge*. At the same time, it was committed to lend to its partners a maximum amount equal to its creditor quota plus the total (creditor) *rallonge*. Accordingly, a central bank would have had to have lent twice the amount that it could have borrowed.

The STMS facility was activated only by Italy, in 1974, but was not used during the life of the EMS.[7]

The MTFA facility was established in 1972. Credits are granted by the central banks, but the Council of Ministers decides whether the facility will be used. Credits are extended to member states with balance of payment difficulties (current or capital account). They have a maturity of two to five years and are subject to economic policy conditions laid down by the council. In formulating conditions and in monitoring the performance of a debtor country, important advisory roles are assigned to the EC and the Monetary Committee. The MTFA facility has creditor ceilings, but no debtor ceilings, for individual countries; however, no country can normally draw more than 50 per cent of the total credit ceilings.

Like the STMS facility, the MTFA facility has been activated only once, by Italy in December 1974. It has not been used since the establishment of the EMS.

The community loan mechanism (CLM) was established in 1975 to assist member states experiencing current account problems arising from the oil price shock. Unlike the MTFA facility, it does not use external funds guaranteed by other member states subject to specified ceilings. In June 1988, the MTFA and the CLM were merged into a single new credit facility called the medium-term financial support (MTFS) facility, allowing both financing methods to be used. In other words, countries can use outside sources or, if necessary, appeal directly to member states. Under the MTFS facility, borrowing is subject to conditions aimed at re-establishing a sustainable balance of payments position.

The MFTS facility has been activated twice. Greece obtained a credit in 1991, and Italy was granted a loan of ECU 8 billion in January 1993.

Realignment rules

Realignments are necessary to correct nominal central rates when these reflect a fundamental disequilibrium in relative price levels. One of the weaknesses of the Bretton Woods system had been the lack of a set of rules for changing central parities. Parity realignments were sometimes dramatic events and often delayed, leading to the build-up of large imbalances. In the 'snake, parity realignments were essentially unilateral and had often resulted in the abandonment of the system by one or more of its members. In the EMS, realignments were made subject to mutual consent, though there were not any clear-cut criteria or rules governing by how much or when a currency should be realigned. The parity change seemed to be the result, more or less, of effective bargaining, and it became apparent that the actual outcome of the negotiations rarely met the initial request of the realigned countries. Although the proceedings of realignment meetings were not made public, it has become clear over the years that realignments were rarely used just to accommodate diverging inflation rates. There was an interplay between corrective realignments and internal adjustment policies. The success of the EMS can be attributed to the fact that it did not operate as a crawling peg regime, but that nominal exchange rate rigidity was used in different ways to support domestic adjustment policies. This is the essence of the so-called 'disciplining effect' of the EMS (Collignon et al. 1996). It is one of the important distinctions between the EMS and the snake as a simple common exchange rate system.

The ERM crises of September 1992 to August 1993

The ERM crisis began in September 1992 and continued in 1993. In 1992–93, there were five realignments of bilateral central rates; two currencies (the British pound and the Italian lira) withdrew from the ERM; and the exchange rate bands were widened from ±2.25 per cent to ±15 per cent. Only the German mark, the French franc, Benelux currencies and the Danish krone were not realigned against each other. The French franc, the Danish krone and the Belgian and Luxembourg francs probably could not have maintained their bilateral central rates against the two 'hard currencies' (the German mark and the Dutch guilder) if the margins of fluctuation had not been widened to ±15 per cent in August 1993.

The causes of the crisis were the weakness of the US dollar in the final phase of the Bush administration, which led to a disproportionate strengthening of the German mark within the ERM; a substantial increase in cross-border investment between member states in the several years preceding the crisis; the effects of German reunification, with its domestic inflationary tendencies; and the uncertainties surrounding the ratification of the Maastricht Treaty.

In the crisis of September 1992, the Bundesbank, through the VSTF facility of the EMCF and its own interventions, provided DM92 billion to the foreign exchange market. Of this, DM33 billion and DM11 billion were lent to the

Bank of England and the Banca d'Italia, respectively, when the pound sterling and the lira touched their weak edge of the intervention band against the German mark on 16–17 September. Despite the United Kingdom's efforts to support the parity of the pound sterling and a sharp increase in the key interest rate by the Bank of England, the UK authorities eventually withdrew the pound from the EMS, as the Italians had done earlier with the lira. France succeeded in maintaining the franc in the margins of fluctuation against the mark. On 23 September 1992, the Banque de France and the Bundesbank issued a joint statement offering unequivocal support for the existing bilateral central rate of the franc and the mark. The statement was backed by heavy intra-marginal intervention on the foreign exchange market by the two central banks.

In July 1993, the French franc came under severe attack again. A new French government had been elected in March and had not yet demonstrated its commitment to monetary and fiscal stability. In these circumstances, the Bundesbank was unwilling to provide unlimited credit to Banque de France, although it did intervene massively. As mentioned above, the problem was dealt with by widening the bilateral margins of fluctuation from ±2.25 per cent to ±15 per cent. As long as the French franc did not depreciate by 15 per cent, this obviated the need for intervention.

The way in which the Bundesbank intervened in the crisis shows that, even if the amount of funding available under the VSTF facility is said to be unlimited, this is not literally true. Because of the fear that domestic price stability might have to be sacrificed for external exchange rate stability, the Bundesbank made it clear that it was not prepared to finance interventions of unlimited amounts in favour of countries whose fundamental exchange rate misalignment required adjustment. The German government acknowledged this opt-out clause by saying that 'the Bundesbank has the responsibility to intervene and the option not to intervene if it is of the opinion that it is unable to do so' (Apel 1998).

Implications

During the 1992–93 crisis, European countries were forced to widen fluctuation margins from ±2.25 per cent to ±15 per cent. If we introduce a common exchange rate system in East Asia, it would be better to begin with a relatively wide band and to narrow the band as economic convergence proceeds among member states, taking into account the fact that economic fundamentals are quite different among East Asian countries.

If a common exchange rate system is adopted in East Asia, it will be important to decide the extent to which credit facilities for intervention should be available and in what circumstances there should be realignment to obviate such intervention. This is necessary in case a given country's currency falls to the bottom of the band. As with the Bundesbank in the EMS, there may be an opt-out clause to avoid interventions of unlimited amounts in favour of countries whose fundamental exchange rate misalignment requires adjustment. At the same time, realignments should be made subject to mutual consent, even though there may not be any clear-cut criteria or rules for when a currency should be realigned and by how much. If policy dialogue includes discussions on such realignment processes, as it should, then it should be sufficiently stringent to have a 'disciplining effect' on member governments to ensure that alignments are not unilateral.

People have different opinions as to whether the EMS was symmetric or asymmetric. But unlike the Bretton Woods system, it was designed as a symmetric multi-currency system, in which the same rules and obligations applied to all participants. All member states tried to stabilise exchange rates. In East Asia we could introduce a common exchange rate system pegged to a basket of three major currencies (the US dollar, the euro and the Japanese yen). We think that such a system would be more asymmetric than the EMS and more like the Bretton Woods system. It would also require Japanese monetary and fiscal policy to be closely attuned to the system. This would allow East Asian countries to monitor Japanese policy, and to apply peer pressure when necessary, so that the Japanese yen did not fluctuate significantly against the US dollar or the euro.

Arab Monetary Fund

The Arab Monetary Fund is a regional financial institution whose headquarters are in Abu Dhabi, United Arab Emirates. It was established in April 1976 and started operations in 1977. It comprises all members of the League of Arab States (Algeria, Bahrain, Djibouti, Egypt, Iraq, Jordan, Kuwait, Lebanon, Libya, Mauritania, Morocco, Oman, Palestine, Qatar, Saudi Arabia, Somalia, Sudan, Syria, Tunisia, the United Arab Emirates, and Yemen).[8] The authorised capital was initially set at 250 million Arab accounting dinars (AADs) – the equivalent of SDR750 million – and currently stands at AAD 600 million (the equivalent of SDR1.8 billion). At the end of 2000, the Arab Monetary Fund's paid-up capital was AAD 324 million (SDR972 million). One AAD is defined as three SDRs.[9]

Objectives

The Arab Monetary Fund has seven objectives: to correct disequilibria in the balance of payments of member countries; to remove restrictions on current account payments between member states; to establish policies and modes of Arab monetary cooperation; to render advice, when called upon to do so, with regard to policies related to the investment of the financial resources of member states; to promote the development of Arab financial markets; to pave the way towards the creation of a unified Arab currency; and to promote trade among member states.

In order to accomplish these objectives, the AMF sets out seven functions: to provide short-term and medium-term credit facilities to help member states to finance overall balance of payments deficits; to liberalise and promote trade and the resulting current payments and encourage capital movements between member states; to allocate from its resources, paid in the currencies of the member states, sufficient funds to provide the necessary credits to settle their current payments, in accordance with the rules and regulations to be laid down by the board of governors and within the framework of a special account to be opened by the fund for that purpose; to manage any funds placed under the charge of the fund by a member state or member states; to hold periodic consultations with member states on their economic conditions and the policies they pursue in support of the realisation of the goals of the fund and the states concerned; to conduct the research required to achieve the goals of the fund; and to provide technical assistance to banking and monetary institutions in member states.

Member states are required to cooperate among themselves and with the fund for the realisation of the goals of the fund. In particular, they must reduce restrictions on current payments among member states and restrictions on the transfer of capital and the transfer of profits therefrom, with a view to the total elimination of such restrictions; and endeavour to achieve the necessary degree of coordination between Arab economic policies, particularly financial and monetary, in a manner that will contribute to Arab economic integration and assist in creating the necessary conditions for the establishment of a unified Arab currency.

Organisational structure

The Arab Monetary Fund consists of a board of governors, a board of executive directors, a director general and staff. The board of governors consists of one governor and one deputy governor appointed by each member country of the fund, and holds all management power. It convenes once a year. The board of executive directors is composed of the director-general of the fund and eight non-resident members elected by the board of governors for a renewable term of three years. The board is entrusted with the supervision of the fund's activities. The board of governors appoints the director-general of the fund for a renewable term of five years. He serves *ex officio* as chairman of the board of executive directors, is the head of the staff and is responsible for all the work of the fund.

Credit facilities

Balance of payments deficits have been a big problem for all Arab deficit countries since the Arab Monetary Fund was created. The main work of the fund has therefore been to help deficit member countries cope with their deficits by providing credit facilities to them. The fund finances member countries' global deficits, not regional deficits. This is because there is only limited inter-Arab trade. The Arab Monetary Fund's credit facilities come mainly from its paid-up capital in convertible currencies and reserves, but it may borrow up to twice the value of its capital from international financial markets.

At present, there are four types of loans for balance of payments support (automatic loan, ordinary loan, extended loan and compensatory loan) and one other facility (the structural adjustment facility) to assist in the reform of the financial and banking sector and public finance.

Automatic loan

An automatic loan of up to 75 per cent of the country's paid-up subscription in convertible currencies may be extended without conditions; it must be repaid within three years. A member is considered eligible for this loan if its balance of payments is in deficit and the volume of its gross international reserves is below the critical limit during the current year or was below it in the preceding year.

Ordinary loan

An ordinary loan is given to a member when its balance of payments needs exceed the limit of the automatic loan. It is extended in support of a financial program which aims at reducing the deficit in the member's balance of payments. This loan is subject to a ceiling of 100 per cent of the member's paid-up subscription and can be extended to 175 per cent in given conditions. Each disbursement of the loan must be repaid within five years.

Extended loan

An extended loan may be granted to a member suffering from a chronic overall deficit in the balance of payments resulting from structural imbalances in the economy, in support of a comprehensive adjustment program agreed upon between the fund and the member, extending over at least two years. This loan is given up to 175 per cent of the member's paid-up subscription and can be extended up to 250 per cent in given conditions. Each disbursement of the loan must be repaid within seven years.

Compensatory loan

A compensatory loan may be given to support countries experiencing an unexpected overall deficit in the balance of payments from a fall in exports or a large increase in agricultural imports due to poor harvests. This loan can be extended to an amount not exceeding 50 per cent of the member's paid-up subscription, and must be repaid within three years.

Structural adjustment facility

The structural adjustment facility was established in 1998 to help members reform and modernise their financial and banking sector and public finance. It has become the core of the Arab Monetary Fund's lending activity. This facility can be extended up to 75 per cent of the member's paid-up subscription, and must be repaid within four years. An important criterion of eligibility is that the member concerned has begun to implement structural reforms and has achieved a satisfactory degree of overall stability in the economy.

Arab Trade Financing Program

The Arab Monetary Fund also provides trade credit to Arab exporters and importers through the Arab Trade Financing Program, designed to promote inter-Arab trade.

Performance and difficulties

Monetary integration

The Arab Monetary Fund has two main objectives for monetary integration: to stabilise the cross-rates of Arab currencies and to bring about their inter-convertibility; and to investigate possible means of expanding the use of the AAD, thereby laying the groundwork for a common Arab currency.

In 1980, nine Arab countries pegged their currencies to the US dollar, five to the SDR and four to a special basket of currencies. The pegging of Arab currencies to different currency blocs makes it difficult to stabilise cross-rates. It has been suggested that all Arab currencies could be pegged to the AAD, but member countries still have a great variety of foreign exchange regimes. Six countries have a floating exchange rate; five peg their currency to the US dollar (one of which is a currency board); six peg their currencies to the SDR (five of which are de facto pegged to the US dollar); two peg their currencies to a currency basket; and some have different arrangements. Table 6.2 shows exchange rate arrangements in the Arab Monetary Fund.

As for inter-Arab currency convertibility and the removal of exchange controls, many currencies are not traded in the markets. At the end of 1999, six countries lacked even mutual convertibility of their currencies, let alone a common currency. Mutual convertibility was a characteristic of the EPU at the beginning of financial cooperation.

Trade integration

Trade integration and the development of trade flows among Arab countries is not a direct objective of the fund, but is closely related to its objectives. The fund was supposed to contribute to it through the removal of restrictions on current account payments, which would have the effect of impeding trade and inhibiting moves towards economic integration. However, it seems that the Arab Monetary Fund has not contributed much in this respect.

Monetary integration is said to be closely related to the degree of trade integration, but this does not seem to be the case for the countries of the Arab Monetary Fund. For example, intra-Arab exports as a share of total Arab exports increased marginally from 4.9 to 8.2 per cent between 1975 and

Table 6.2   The exchange arrangements of Arab Monetary Fund member countries[a]

Country	Currency arrangement	31 December 2000	30 June 1980
Algeria	Dinar	Managed float	Peg to a currency basket
Bahrain	Dinar	Peg to the SDR (±7.25%)[b]	Peg to the SDR (±7.25%)
Djibouti	Franc	Currency board (peg to the US dollar)	Peg to the US dollar
Egypt	Pound	Peg to the US dollar	Peg to the US dollar
Iraq	Dinar	Peg to the US dollar	Peg to the US dollar
Jordan	Dinar	Peg to the SDR[b]	Peg to the SDR
Kuwait	Dinar	Peg to a currency basket	Peg to a currency basket
Lebanon	Pound	Peg	Float
Libya	Dinar	Peg to the SDR (±7.25%)[b]	Peg to the US dollar
Mauritania	Ouguiya	Managed float	
Morocco	Dirham	Peg to a currency basket	Peg to a currency basket
Oman	Rial	Peg to the US dollar	Peg to the US dollar
Qatar	Riyal	Peg to the SDR (±7.25%)[b]	Peg to the SDR (±7.25%)
SaudiArabia	Riyal	Peg to the SDR (±7.25%)[b]	Peg to the SDR (±7.25%)
Somalia	Shiling	Independent float	Peg to the US dollar
Sudan	Dinar	Managed float	Peg to the US dollar
Syria	Pound	Peg to the US dollar	Peg to the US dollar
Tunisia	Dinar	Managed float	Peg to a currency basket
UAE	Dirham	Peg to the SDR (±7.25%)[b]	Peg to the SDR (±7.25%)
Yemen	Rial	Independent float	Peg to the US dollar

Notes
a   No information is available for Palestine.
b   Effectively, a peg to the US dollar.
Sources: IMF (2001); Abdul-Rasool and Faik Ali (1982).

1998, and they still account for only a small portion of total trade compared with trade with other regions (Al-Atrash and Yousef 2000).

Various reasons have been offered as to why intra-Arab trade is relatively low. There are fundamental barriers to trade, such as the lack of product complementarity; high trade costs, including transport and communication, stemming from the distance and difficult geographic terrain between some Arab countries; and disparity in per capita income, especially between oil-producing countries and non-producing ones.[10] Furthermore, trade policies are said to be restrictive. Al-Atrash and Yousef (2000) have summed up the situation as follows:

While some countries in the area, specifically the GCC (the Gulf Cooperation Council) countries, maintain a relatively open trade regime, others have imposed significant barriers to trade. The average tariff for the region as a whole is higher than that of any other region, except Africa. Moreover, non-tariff barriers are extensive in many countries in the region. ... Many countries employ a variety of measures, including restrictive licensing, bans, state trading/monopolies, restrictive foreign exchange allocation, and multiple exchange rates, to discourage imports.

Further, overall economic strategy and policy are different across the region. While some countries are market oriented (for example, Jordan, Morocco and Tunisia), other countries maintain a high degree of government involvement (for example, Libya and Syria).

Policy dialogue

The Arab Monetary Fund requires the same level of information and conditionality as the IMF, despite the fact that its loans are much smaller. Many states are reluctant to accept this kind of interference in their internal affairs. Consequently, it is difficult for the Arab Monetary Fund to obtain necessary data and reach agreement on corrective policies with the borrower states (Al-Sagban 1982).

By the end of 2000, the Arab Monetary Fund had approved 115 loans, valued at AAD 827.6 million (US$3.24 billion) since its inception in 1978. On 31 December 2000, total financial obligations in arrears from three defaulting member countries (Sudan, Somalia and Iraq) amounted to AAD 215.3 million, of which AAD 94.9 million was principal and AAD 120.4 million was interest.

To date, the Arab Monetary Fund has not achieved its objectives of correcting disequilibria in the balance of payments, promoting trade among member countries, or creating a unified Arab currency.

Implications

The experience of the Arab Monetary Fund suggests that, even if an institution for financial cooperation is created in a given region, the desired result cannot be achieved unless trade liberalisation among member countries occurs at the same time as financial cooperation and unless there is appropriate policy dialogue between the institution and member countries.[11]

Latin American Reserve Fund

FLAR has its headquarters in Bogota, Colombia. It was established in March 1991 as the successor of the Andean Reserve Fund, which had been created in 1978 in the framework of the Cartagena agreement for subregional integration of Andean countries. The current members are Bolivia, Colombia, Costa Rica, Ecuador, Peru and Venezuela.[12]

Previously, Article 40 of the FLAR constitution provided that only signatories of the Cartagena agreement could be members of the Andean Reserve Fund.

In the mid-1980s, the foreign debt crisis in the Third World led to suggestions that the Andean Reserve Fund could be expanded to form a Latin American reserve fund. At its seventh extraordinary meeting in Caracas, Venezuela, on 15 January 1988, the Andean Reserve Fund Assembly of Representatives decided that the fund should become the Latin American Reserve Fund, and that membership should be enlarged to members of the Latin American Integration Association (ALADI). The agreement was signed in Lima, Peru, on 10 June 1988, and entered into force on 12 March 1991. At the general meeting held on 30 March 1999, Article 40 was again amended, and any Latin American country can now be a member of FLAR.

Objectives

FLAR is a regional financial institution with an independent juridical basis. It has three main objectives: to support the balance of payments of member countries by granting loans or guaranteeing loans from other lenders; to contribute to the harmonisation of exchange, monetary and financial policies of member countries; and to improve the conditions of reserve investment of member countries.

To achieve these objectives, FLAR, as a financial and monetary institution, undertakes asset and liability operations which seek to attend the financing requirements of member countries. It offers central banks opportunities to invest their international reserves. And it manages its own investments, one of the main sources of which are the international reserves maintained by member countries as capital contributions to FLAR. Further, FLAR plays a role as a fundamental element in the development of the economic and institutional base required to achieve monetary and exchange stability in the region and thus increase opportunities for trading goods and services between these economies.

The subscribed capital today is US$2 billion (it was US$240 million in 1978), to which Colombia, Peru and Venezuela each contribute US$468.75 million, Bolivia and Ecuador each contribute US$234.375 million, and Costa Rica contributes US$125 million. As at the end of June 2001, the paid-up capital was US$1.1 billion.

Organisational structure

FLAR consists of a board of directors, executive president and staff. The general meeting is the highest authority and is composed of the ministers of public finance or their equivalent as indicated by the government of each member country. Each representative is entitled to one vote. The board of directors comprises the executive president and the governors of the central banks of member countries. The board guides operations in general and exercises powers delegated to it by the general meeting. It meets at least twice a year and as often as required. The board of directors elects the executive president for three years. The president serves as the non-voting chairman of the board, and is responsible for the conduct of operations and the appointment of staff.

Lending facility

FLAR offers member countries finance to help them make macroeconomic adjustments when there are structural problems in the balance of payments or transient situations of liquidity that are mainly caused by external distortions. Member countries have access to five kinds of loans, described below. The total amount of credit of all kinds granted to Colombia, Costa Rica, Peru and Venezuela or potential new members may not exceed 2.5 times paid capital. Bolivia and Ecuador may be granted 3.5 times paid capital, this preferential treatment being derived from the Cartagena agreement, which provides for special treatment for 'relatively lower economic development'.

Balance of payments loans and guarantees

This is the most important service for supporting member countries that have a structural imbalance in their balance of payments. The service is granted by making loans to their central banks or issuing guarantees to other lenders at the request of central banks for up to four years with one year's grace. This credit is extended when a country decides to adopt an economic adjustment program to solve its imbalances and when it submits detailed plans of its proposed economic and financial measures that are acceptable to FLAR. The board is responsible for approvals. The maximum amount of loans and guarantees available to any given country for balance of payments supports is 3.5 or 2.5 times its paid capital depending on the relative economic development of the country making the request (see above).

Liquidity loans

Central banks have access to liquidity loans to meet special needs for foreign currency in the event of temporary problems, for up to one year. The executive president is responsible for granting these loans. The maximum amount available for a given country is 1 or 1.25 times its paid capital, depending on the relative economic development of the country making the request (see above).

Emergency loans

The emergency loan service was introduced in 1998 to help member countries to increase international reserves in the face of speculative pressure and adverse expectations in the exchange market. In circumstances of great uncertainty and speculation due to internal or external causes, the FLAR credit line can help to counter negative expectations, and this itself may make the loan unnecessary or only partly necessary. For this reason emergency loans are also called standby or contingent loans. The maximum term is six months. Loans are granted by the executive president and must be secured by collateral securities that are rated to the satisfaction of FLAR and whose face value is higher than the principal amount of the loan. The maximum amount available to a given country is 1.5 or 2 times its paid capital, depending on the relative economic development of the country making the request (see above).

External public debt restructuring loans

This mechanism was created in February 1995 to support member countries in negotiations for restructuring their external public debt. Credit is granted under co-financing schemes with other multilateral organisations. The central bank making the request delivers a document to the executive president containing the principal terms of the restructuring agreement reached with that country's creditors. The board is responsible for approving the loans. The maximum term is four years, including one year of grace. The maximum amount available to a given country is 1.5 or 2.2 times its paid capital, depending on the relative economic development of the country making the request (see above).

Export finance

In addition to the above-mentioned loans, FLAR offers an export finance service, acting through commercial and official banks of the region approved by the fund. Facilities are short- and medium-term operations for goods, services and capital goods, based on LIBOR. A high proportion of FLAR's loans since the 1990s have been of this type.

Performance

Between 1978 and April 2000, FLAR made loans of about US$9.8 billion (about nine times paid-up capital) (Table 6.3). About half (US$4.8 billion) were export finance, 23 per cent liquidity loans and 22 per cent balance of payments loans. The role of FLAR has recently shifted towards providing export finance and offering member central banks opportunities to invest their international reserves. Between 1991 and 2000, three-quarters of the loans were for export finance. As of June 2001, FLAR's balance sheet showed that securities were just over 75 per cent of total assets and balance of payments loans a mere 12 per cent (Table 6.4).

FLAR has been able to serve the needs of all its members without affecting its financial soundness.[13] It has never experienced any difficulty in recovering its loans and there are no arrears. This is despite the fact that FLAR's conditions for each type of credit have been less strict than those of the IMF and other multilateral organisations. However, FLAR's loans are supplemented by the use of the IMF facilities (del Valle 1982).

One of FLAR's long-term objectives is perfect monetary and exchange stability. Substantial progress still needs to be made in this area. FLAR economies need to be liberalised; the evolution of macroeconomic variables needs to be synchronised; and there must be open mobility of production factors, in particular capital and labour. Modest progress has been made so far in the region.[14]

Table 6.3 Value of loans made by the Latin American Reserve Fund to its members since 1978 (as of April, 2000, US$ million)

		Balance of payments loans	*Debt restruct- uring loans*	*Liquidity loans*	*Emerg- ency loans*	*Export finance*	*Total*
Bolivia	1978–90	296.9	–	530.4	–	0	827.3
	1991–2000	0	0	68.1	0	377.4	445.5
	Total	296.9	0	598.5	0	377.4	1,272.8
Colombia	1978–90	229.0	–	435.0	–	0	664.0
	1991–2000	0	0	0	375.0	490.2	865.2
	Total	229.0	0	435.0	375.0	490.2	1,529.2
Ecuador	1978–90	296.7	–	549.9	–	0	846.6
	1991–2000	411.3	200.0	149.7	0	1,080.7	1,841.7
	Total	708.0	200.0	699.6	0	1,080.7	2,688.3
Peru	1978–90	232.5	–	518.5	–	0	751.0
	1991–2000	403.0	0	0	0	2,605.9	3,008.9
	Total	635.5	0	518.5	0	2,605.9	3,759.9
Venezuela	1978–90	271.0	–	22.6	–	0	293.6
	1991–2000	0	0	0	0	214.1	214.1
	Total	271.0	0	22.6	0	214.1	507.7
Total	1978–90	1,326.1	–	2,056.4	–	0	3,382.5
	1991–2000	814.3	200.0	217.8	375.0	4,768.3	6,375.4
		(12.8%)	(3.1%)	(3.4%)	(5.9%)	(74.8%)	(100%)
	Total	2,140.4	200.0	2,274.2	375.0	4,768.3	9,757.9
		(21.9%)	(2.0%)	(23.3%)	(3.8%)	(48.9%)	(100%)

Notes: The values are on the basis of disbursement except the contingency finance for Colombia (US$ 375 million). Debt restructuring loans and contingency loans were created in 1995 and 1998 respectively.

Source: FLAR website at <http://www.flar.net>.

Table 6.4 Latin American Reserve Fund: balance sheet at 30 June 2001 (US$ million)

Assets		*Liabilities*	
Deposits	8.0	Liabilities	561.2
Securities	1,436.0	Sight deposits	248.7
Managed Funds	125.8	Term deposits	309.9
Balance of payments loans	222.3	Others	2.6
Export financing	60.4	Equity	1,308.6
Others	17.3	Paid capital	1,094.3
Total	1,869.8	Reserves	99.5
		Others	114.8
		Total	1,869.8

Source: FLAR website at <http://www.flar.net>.

Implications

Economic integration has not progressed far to date, but FLAR seems to have been successful in supporting balance of payments and liquidity difficulties of member countries. One reason is the connection with IMF operations; another is the relatively small membership of the fund and the fact that Andean countries (unlike those of the Arab Monetary Fund) are geographically adjacent.

In future financial arrangements in East Asia, we should cooperate closely with the IMF in setting lending conditions, as is institutionalised in the current scheme of the Chiang Mai Initiative. It would be better to begin financial cooperation with members who are positive about it – but to keep membership open to all East Asian countries – than to initially include countries with negative views.

The Asian situation

Financial or trade cooperation in the Asian region requires a well-functioning surveillance mechanism. Deep integration will also require a mechanism to make sure the system enhances the economic welfare of member countries and maintains fair competition in the region, without harming countries outside the region. The difficulty of achieving deep integration and effective surveillance should not be underestimated.

Manila Framework Group

The Manila Framework Group (MFG) was created in November 1997 in the aftermath of the failed attempt to establish the Asian Monetary Fund (AMF). The mandate was to provide a mechanism for regional surveillance to complement global surveillance by the IMF; enhance economic and technical cooperation, particularly by strengthening domestic financial systems and regulatory capacities; take measures to strengthen the IMF's capacity to respond to financial crisis; and introduce a cooperative financing arrangement that would supplement IMF resources.

The MFG was created specifically to enhance surveillance in the region. The MFG member list includes larger Asian countries, the United States, Canada, Australia, New Zealand and representatives of the IMF, the World Bank, BIS and the ADB. Both ministry of finance officials and central bankers attend the meetings, which are now held once a year to discuss macroeconomic and financial issues in the East Asian region.[15] Participants review economic conditions, financial and capital markets development and exchange rate issues. No other official meeting of leaders, foreign ministers or trade ministers includes representatives of the same countries.

The effectiveness of the MFG can be questioned. The meetings rarely have an agenda unique to the region. Instead, agenda items often reflect global issues (those of the FSF, G-20 and IMF) or those of other regional meetings (ASEAN and APEC). The MFG membership is wider than ASEAN+3, but the group is a subset of APEC members. The agenda and membership also fall between those of ASEAN+3 and APEC. There is no common interest among its members.

The MFG was created in the midst of the Asian currency crisis, but it did not play a critical role in managing the ongoing Indonesian and Korean currency crises of the time. However, the first MFG meeting was instrumental in creating the Supplemental Reserve Facility (SRF), a mechanism to increase lending for a crisis-hit country or get around the access limit of the standby agreement. There was no incremental financing (described as the fourth mandate) at the height of the Asian crisis. The frequency of the meetings is not sufficient to review economic developments or properly monitor rapidly changing financial market conditions. The MFG has no permanent secretariat.

Asia Pacific Economic Cooperation

APEC was established in 1989 and now has 21 member countries, extending from Russia to Peru and Chile, in addition to the Asian economies. It holds leaders meetings, ministerial meetings in foreign affairs and trade, and finance ministers meetings. The finance ministers meetings focus on macroeconomic issues, exchange rate issues, freer and stable flows of capital, private sector participation in infrastructure development, and the development of financial and capital markets. Reports on macroeconomic conditions of major member countries are often subject to approval by the country concerned; if the country opposes the assessment, the report is rarely published.

Association of Southeast Asian Nations

ASEAN was originally established in 1967 as a group of five large countries (Indonesia, Malaysia, the Philippines, Singapore and Thailand). Brunei joined soon after; Vietnam, Laos, Myanmar and Cambodia joined much later. ASEAN now has 10 member countries. It holds meetings at several levels, including leaders meetings, foreign ministers meetings and finance ministers meetings. There are frequent formal and informal dialogues, made easier by the geographical proximity of the countries involved. Objectives range from free trade to environmental protection, social, cultural and scientific development and the development of economic and financial markets.

In 1998, ASEAN introduced the idea of a surveillance process with technical assistance provided by the Asian Development Bank (ADB) to the ASEAN secretariat in Jakarta. Despite the secretariat, the surveillance process has not been established. The secretariat is too small to conduct its own surveillance over member countries. The institutional bodies consist of the ASEAN finance ministers meeting (AFMM), the ASEAN select committee, and the ASEAN central bank forum. The objectives of the surveillance process are to exchange information and discuss economic and financial development; provide an early warning system and peer review process to enhance macroeconomic stability and improve the financial system; highlight possible policy options and encourage early unilateral or collective actions to prevent a crisis; and monitor and discuss global economic and financial developments.

ASEAN+3

The ASEAN+3 group includes the 10 ASEAN countries plus Japan, China and South Korea. It was established in 2000 following the 'Joint Statement on East Asia Cooperation' issued by the ASEAN+3 leaders at their informal meeting in 1999. ASEAN+3 now meets at leader, foreign minister and finance minister levels. The finance ministers meeting focuses on enhancing policy dialogues and regional cooperation activities, particularly in the areas of regional self-help and support mechanisms, international financial reform and the monitoring of short-term capital flows. Unfortunately, ASEAN+3 does not have a secretariat and is based on voluntary actions rather than formal consensual mechanisms. The monitoring of capital flows is one area of cooperation. However, the group must think carefully about how often its members should communicate (once a month or every day), who should exchange information (central banks or finance ministries) and what kind of information should be exchanged (balance of payment statistics or more market-oriented information).

One concrete outcome of the ASEAN+3 process has been the Chiang Mai Initiative. The joint ministerial statement of the ASEAN+3 finance ministers meeting in Chiang Mai in May 2000 states:

> … we agreed to strengthen our policy cooperation activities in, among others, the area of capital flows monitoring, self-help and support mechanism and international financial reforms …

This led to the creation of a network of bilateral swap agreements.

Central bank network

In addition to the regional groupings described above, central banks have an intra-regional grouping, the Executives Meeting of East Asia and Pacific Central Banks (EMEAP). EMEAP was established in 1991, with strong leadership from the Bank of Japan. It includes the 11 economies of Australia, China, Hong Kong, Indonesia, Japan, South Korea, Malaysia, New Zealand, the Philippines, Singapore and Thailand. Another central bank grouping is SEANZA (South East Asia, New Zealand and Australia), established in 1956. Box 6.2 shows the different groupings.

Regional mechanisms

The Asian region has not had a regional group for financial cooperation. The Asian financial crisis has been a catalyst in thinking about regional financial cooperation. Let us review the Mexican and Asian crises to see why regional mechanisms became an important topic of discussion.

The Thai baht was floated on 2 July 1997. It quickly depreciated by 15 per cent.[16] However, it did not depreciate more than 20 per cent before the IMF,

Box 6.2	Membership of Southeast Asian organisations
ASEAN-10	Indonesia, Malaysia, the Philippines, Singapore, Thailand, Brunei Darussalam, Vietnam, Laos, Myanmar, Cambodia
ASEAN+3	ASEAN plus Japan, China, and Korea
Manila Framework Group	Australia, Brunei, Canada, China, Hong Kong, Indonesia, Japan, Korea, Malaysia, New Zealand, the Philippines, Singapore, Thailand and the United States (14 economies)
APEC	Australia, Brunei, Canada, Chile, China, Hong Kong, Indonesia, Japan, Korea, Malaysia, Mexico, New Zealand, Papua New Guinea, Peru, the Philippines, Russia, Singapore, Taiwan, Thailand, United States and Vietnam (21 economies)

with Japan and Asian countries, put together a package of $17.2 billion in late August. The IMF contributed $4 billion, Japan $4 billion, other Asian countries – China, Australia, Hong Kong, Malaysia and Singapore – $1 billion each, and South Korea, Indonesia and Brunei $500 million each. The remaining funds came from the World Bank and the ADB. The United States was conspicuously absent. On the day the IMF announced the package, the Bank of Thailand was forced to reveal forward contracts amounting to $23.4 billion that would result in foreign reserve losses in the near future. As a result, the market viewed the package for Thailand as too small.

The kind of package put together for Thailand was necessary because of the IMF's access limit: under the standby agreement, the IMF cannot lend more than three times the quota of the country. A similar arrangement was necessary for Mexico after its devaluation in December 1994. In the Mexican case, a large amount of money was necessary for the country not to default on outstanding *tesobonos*,[17] so the United States agreed to co-finance IMF support. As a result, Mexico was treated as an exceptional case and its access limit was raised to five times quota. In the package of $50 billion, the IMF contributed only $17.8 billion – even with the higher than usual access limit – with the United States providing $21 billion.

In the cases of both Mexico and Thailand, the motivation for the regional arrangement (by the United States in the former case, and by Japan and the Asian countries for Thailand) was the access limit and the lack of resources in the IMF.

After the Thai crisis, but before those of Indonesia and South Korea, Japan and some ASEAN countries put forward a proposal for an AMF. The idea was that the participating countries would contribute some of their foreign reserves to a central fund, which would be used to help liquidity shortages in a currency crisis of a member country. This was a response to a frustrating realisation that the IMF did not have the resources to cope with a currency crisis of the type experienced in recent times and that putting together a package with bilateral help would take time and effort, as was the case for Thailand. The AMF proposal was opposed by the United States and the IMF, as well as China, on two grounds. The first was soft conditionality. Providing financial help without stringent conditions could lead to easy money. The crisis would not be resolved, and money would be at risk. The second was duplication. Large numbers of high-quality staff are needed to carry out strict surveillance and there was concern that the AMF would duplicate existing organisations, especially the IMF. The idea of the AMF died at the annual meeting of the IMF and the World Bank in Hong Kong in September 1997. Instead, the MFG was created in November 1997 to enhance regional surveillance.

Unfortunately, the MFG was not effective in the Indonesian or South Korean crises. The initial Indonesian package (November 1997) and Korean package (December 1998) were large in dollar terms ($40 billion for Indonesia and $57 billion for Korea), but bilateral supports, including those from Japan and the United States, were labelled as the 'second line of defence'. Without clear guidelines on how to trigger the second line of defence, the market discounted the effectiveness of the package.[18] The actual disbursement from the IMF and bilateral partners for Indonesia and Korea was not large enough to calm the market. The exchange rate did not rebound for either country on the day the IMF announced the program. For the lender of last resort operations, IMF packages for the Asian countries were too small and thus failed to stabilise the market quickly.

The Asian currency crises made it clear that contagion is dangerous. The crisis spread from Thailand to Indonesia to Korea in several months. Likely contagion is another reason why regional help is desirable.

There have been several attempts to form regional economic cooperative arrangements in East Asia. Some were successful, like the ASEAN free trade arrangement (AFTA); some were unsuccessful, like the AMF. Some arrangements have only regional members (e.g. AFTA); some have other Pacific Rim countries (e.g. APEC). Some groupings are new and some are old.

The new arrangements in Asia have three characteristics. First, there is a tendency to form intra-regional groupings such as ASEAN+3 rather than pan-Pacific groupings such as APEC. Second, free trade arrangements seem to be in vogue. Third, Japan and China seem to be more enthusiastic about an intra-regional grouping than before. The creation of ASEAN+3 is the result of changes in attitude by both Japan and China.

Traditionally, trade arrangements are the most important regional arrangements in the world. Many existing regional groupings started with some sort of preferential trade arrangements. European economic cooperation started with a customs union, and developed into a single-currency, full-fledged economic entity. MERCOSUR and the North American Free Trade

Agreement are two free trade arrangements in the Americas. Asia has lagged behind other regions in the world. Progress through AFTA has been slow, because any member has veto power. For example, the most recent ASEAN drive to accelerate progress towards free trade was halted by Malaysian reluctance to open its automobile market. The APEC Bogor Declaration envisages free trade in the Asia Pacific region by 2010 for advanced countries and 2020 for other countries.

Until 2001, Japan and South Korea had been the only OECD countries without preferential trading arrangements. However, this is changing. Japan and Singapore have signed a free trade agreement in 2001. Korea and Japan have discussed a free trade agreement, but no arrangements have yet been made. China has proposed a free trade agreement with ASEAN, but it is unlikely to occur any time soon. The ASEAN countries have proposed an ASEAN+3 free trade agreement, which would create a large market in Asia. The greater focus on trade integration in East Asia dovetails with the greater focus on financial cooperation in East Asia, embodied most clearly in the formation of ASEAN+3 and the creation of the Chiang Mai Initiative (CMI).

CONCLUSIONS

Under the CMI, the ASEAN+3 countries are creating bilateral networks of swap agreements. Such arrangements will require mutual multilateral surveillance through policy dialogue at MFG and ASEAN+3 meetings. As bilateral networks of swap agreements are formed, mutual surveillance among members that conclude agreements will be more and more important. If the swap agreements are to work effectively, there must be mutual confidence that macroeconomic policies of member countries are relatively sound. If a country which requests a swap under speculative attacks does not seem to have been running a sound macroeconomy, swap-providing countries will hesitate to participate and they will not be able to act promptly. Such a situation will harm the credibility of the system. We should try to have much more frequent policy dialogues than we do now – both formal and informal dialogues – and, as a matter of course, should cooperate closely with the IMF, including the conditionality on lending, as institutionalised in the current scheme of the CMI.

The bilateral networks of swap agreements will help to resolve the problems of the access limit and lack of resources in the IMF. They could also help countries whose currencies are not yet convertible on capital account to open the capital account more easily and safely. In this way, both debtor and creditor countries may be able to enjoy more open and stable capital movements.

Effective cooperation will require constant dialogue and mutual surveillance. Arrangements to discipline member countries' economic policies may also be appropriate. Looking forward, regional exchange rate coordination could be one such mechanism. For example currencies could be pegged to a currency basket of the US dollar, euro and yen, taking into account the weight of trade of East Asian countries so that the volatility of those three currencies does not significantly affect their economies. The discipline imposed by a regional exchange rate mechanism may be more acceptable to member countries than one imposed under an IMF program.

The Bretton Woods and EMS experiences suggest that, if such a common exchange rate system is to be symmetric, Japanese economic policy should be to some extent related to the system. To ensure that Japanese economic policy is also disciplined, East Asian countries need to be able to monitor and apply peer pressure to Japanese policy so that the Japanese yen does not fluctuate significantly against the US dollar and euro.

Fluctuation margins should be set relatively wide to begin with and narrowed as there is increasing economic convergence among member states, taking into account the different economic fundamentals among East Asian countries. Realignments should require mutual consent, even though there will not be any clear-cut criteria or rules of by how much and when a currency should be realigned. Policy dialogue on such realignment should impose a discipline on such actions. Common exchange rate coordination should initially be restricted to countries that are receptive to the idea, but with membership open to every East Asian country.

There is a close linkage between financial cooperation and trade liberalisation. Recently there have been intra-regional moves for a free trade agreement in East Asia. Japan and Singapore have just signed a free trade agreement. The Prime Minister of Japan, Junichiro Koizumi, proposed an 'Initiative for Japan–ASEAN Comprehensive Economic Partnership' and expressed his expectation of creating a 'community that acts together and advances together', in which the countries of ASEAN, Japan, China, South Korea, Australia and New Zealand will be core members. Trade liberalisation is very difficult, as we can see from the experience of APEC in the last decade. We should, however, make efforts to pave the way for future financial arrangements in East Asia to develop in tandem with trade liberalisation.

NOTES

The views expressed here are personal and not necessarily those of the Ministry of Finance of Japan.

1   See de Brouwer (2001) for a discussion and analysis.
2   See Eichengreen (1999) and Kenen (2001) for reviews on new international financial architecture.
3   In December 1971, the G-7 agreed to restrict their currency realignments to a floating band of 2.25 per cent, with the US dollar as the reference. In March 1972, the EC members agreed to limit exchange rate fluctuations to 1.5 per cent with respect to the US dollar and 2.5 per cent with respect to each other. This tighter fluctuation band was called the 'snake'.
4   One European monetary unit of account (EMUA) had a value of 0.88867088 grams of fine gold, equivalent to the gold content of the pre-Smithsonian dollar.

It was replaced by the European unit of account (EUA), which was introduced on 21 April 1975, defined by a basket of fixed amounts of EC currencies. In December 1978, in connection with the creation of the EMS, the EUA was replaced by the ECU, which initially had the same composition as the EUA.

5   For details, see Apel (1998).

6   Although it has been said to have been unlimited, it was, in fact, not literally unlimited, as shown later.

7   The STMS and MTFA facilities were not used more than once, because, as a consequence of the internationalisation of credit markets, debtor countries found it comparatively easy to satisfy their needs on the international markets without going through the politically and procedurally cumbersome process of consultation and approval within the EC. In this respect, the existence of the EC credit facilities may have acted as a 'security umbrella', making it easier for the countries concerned to obtain loans on the markets (Ungerer 1997).

8   Although the board of governors of the Arab Monetary Fund approved the membership of Comoros, the agreement has not yet come into effect because some requirements have not been fulfilled.

9   The group's web site gives further details at <http://www.amf.org.ae>.

10 The classification of countries in the region by the World Bank according to the per capita income in 1998 are as follows: Yemen is classified as low income; Kuwait, Qatar and the UAE are classified as high income; the rest are either 'low middle income' or 'higher middle income'.

11 It is encouraging that, in 1998, 14 Arab countries established the Pan-Arab Free Trade Agreement (PAFTA), under which tariffs will be reduced for participating members by 10 per cent annually (establishing free trade from 2007).

12 Costa Rica became a member on 1 September 2000.

13 FLAR homepage at <http://www.flar.net>.

14 FLAR homepage at <http://www.flar.net>.

15 Before 2002, the MFG met twice a year.

16 In Thailand, initially the impact of floating the exchange rate of 2 July 1997 was not substantial. The exchange rate depreciated by 15 per cent, but not by about 50 per cent, as was the case in Mexico. Some thought that a successful exit from the *de facto* dollar peg had been achieved. However, confidence was not restored when the IMF program was announced, accompanied by the disclosure of the amount that the central bank owed to the market by forward contracts. This delayed recovery; in the meantime, the economy went into recession, partly due to an austerity plan introduced as IMF conditionality. Many people believe the IMF's prescription for the Asian crisis was wrong, especially its imposition of fiscal austerity on a weakening economy. Even the IMF admitted later that fiscal austerity was a mistake. Unlike the Latin American situation, the fiscal deficits were not the core problem. Therefore, the planning of fiscal surpluses did not enhance investor confidence.

17 Short-term Mexican bonds in US dollars.

18 See Parkinson, Garton and Dickson, this volume, for a similar criticism of SLOD.

REFERENCES

Abdul-Rasool and A. Faik (1982) 'The role of the Arab Monetary Fund in achieving Arab monetary integration', in Khair El-Din haseeb and Samir Makdisi (eds), *Arab Monetary Integration; Issues and Prerequisites*, London and Canberra: Croom Helm: 390–417.

Al-Atrash, H. and T. Yousef (2000) 'Intra-Arab Trade: Is It Too Little?', Working Paper WP/00/10, International Monetary Fund (January).

Ali, Abdul Munim Al-Sayyed (1982) 'The external economic and monetary positions of the Arab countries and the role of financial surpluses in promoting Arab monetary integration', in Khair El-Din haseeb and Samir Makdisi (eds), *Arab Monetary Integration; Issues and Prerequisites*, London and Canberra: Croom Helm: 299–336.

Al-Sagban, Abdul Aal (1982) 'The Arab Monetary Fund: Objectives and Performance', in Khair El-Din haseeb and Samir Makdisi (eds), *Arab Monetary Integration; Issues and Prerequisites*, London and Canberra: Croom Helm: 152–186.

Apel, E. (1998) *European Monetary Integration: 1958–2002*, London: Routledge.

Arab Monetary Fund (n.d.) *Annual Report 2000*, AMF, Abu Dhabi, United Arab Emirates.

Collignon, S, P. Bofinger, C. Johnson and B. de Maigret (1996) *Europe's Monetary Future*, London: Pinter.

de Brouwer, G. (2001) *Hedge Funds in Emerging Markets*, Cambridge: Cambridge University Press.

del Valle, J. G. (1982) 'Monetary integration in Latin America', in Khair El-Din haseeb and Samir Makdisi (eds), *Arab Monetary Integration; Issues and Prerequisites*, London and Canberra: Croom Helm: 205–227.

Eichengreen, B. (1993) *Reconstructing Europe's Trade and Payments: The European Payments Union*, Manchester: Manchester University Press.

—— (1994) 'International Monetary Arrangements for the 21st Century', Washington DC: Brookings Institution.

—— (1999) 'Toward a New International Financial Architecture', Washington DC: Institute for International Economics.

Eichengreen, B. and J.B. de Macedo (2001) 'The European Payments Union: History and Implications for the Evolution of the International Financial Architecture', mimeo, University of California, Berkeley.

FLAR (Fondo Latinoamericano de Reservas) (n.d.) *Annual Report 1998–99*, FLAR, Bogota, Colombia.

—— 'Attractions of Membership of Fondo Latinoamericano de reservas', mimeo. FLAR, Bogota, Colombia.

Giavazzi, F. and A. Giovannini (1989) *Limiting Exchange Rate Flexibility: The European Monetary System*, Cambridge MA: MIT Press.

Gros, D. and N. Thygesen (1992) *European Monetary Integration: From the European Monetary System to European Monetary Union*, New York: St Martins Press.

IMF (International Monetary Fund) (2001) Annual Report on Exchange Arrangements and Exchange Restrictions.

Kaplan, J.J. and G. Schleiminger (1989) *The European Payments Union: Financial Diplomacy in the 1950s*, Oxford: Clarendon Press.

Kenen, P.B. (1991) 'Transitional arrangements for Trade and Payments among CMEA Countries', IMF Staff Papers, 38: 235–67.

—— (2001) 'The International Financial Architecture: What's New? What's Missing?', Washington DC: Institute for International Economics.

Morsi, F. (1982) 'Basic economic and political prerequisites for achieving Arab monetary integration', in Khair El-Din haseeb and Samir Makdisi (eds), *Arab Monetary Integration; Issues and Prerequisites*, London and Canberra: Croom Helm: 422–447.

Nashashibi, K. (1982) 'Trade and exchange regimes and the exercise of monetary policy in the Arab countries', in Khair El-Din haseeb and Samir Makdisi (eds), *Arab Monetary Integration; Issues and Prerequisites*, London and Canberra: Croom Helm: 103–124.

Ravenhill J. (2001) *APEC and the Construction of Pacific Rim Regionalism*, Cambridge: Cambridge University Press.

Takagi, S. (2001) 'Regional Financial Arrangements in East Asia: A Reflection on the Modalities of Regional Monetary Cooperation: Lessons from the European Payments Union, the CFA Franc Zone, and the Arab Monetary Fund', mimeo, International Monetary Fund.

Ungerer, H. (1997) *A Concise History of European Monetary Integration: From EPU to EMU*, Westport: Quorum Books.

Williamson, J. (1977) *The Failure of World Monetary Reform*, New York: New York University Press.

7 Strengthening regional financial cooperation in East Asia

Haruhiko Kuroda and Masahiro Kawai

INTRODUCTION

The financial crisis of 1997–98 highlighted the importance of regional financial cooperation in East Asia. Before the crisis, increasing economic interdependence through trade, direct investment and finance in the region was not matched by the development of mechanisms and institutions for regional financial cooperation. There is a strong perception in the region that more effective regional institutions and frameworks might have prevented the crisis or at least allowed it to be better managed. The crisis prompted the region's economies to realise that stronger regional cooperative institutions could help to prevent and manage crises in a way that complements the role of the International Monetary Fund (IMF) in the global framework.

This paper argues that a new regional financial architecture needs to be firmly established in East Asia, outlines recent developments in financial cooperation in the region, and provides possible directions for the future. We recommend that the regional surveillance process be made more effective, and consider the option of creating a common pool of foreign exchange reserves to allow more flexible financial support at times of crises and contagion while minimising the problem of moral hazard. The arrangement must be consistent with the global framework; in particular, it must ensure private sector involvement for crisis management and resolution at the global level. In this paper we suggest that exchange rate regime choice should be coordinated at the regional level, with a long-term vision of regional monetary integration.

The organisation of the paper is as follows. First, we summarise some lessons to be learned from the East Asian crisis. Then we discuss the logic of financial cooperation at the regional level in East Asia, emphasising the increasing economic interdependence among the regional economies. Next, we outline several initiatives for financial cooperation, including the ASEAN+3 Economic Review and Policy Dialogue Process and the formation of a network of bilateral swap arrangements under the Chiang Mai Initiative (CMI). This section also identifies future challenges for regional financial cooperation. Finally, we provide some concluding remarks.

LESSONS FROM THE EAST ASIAN CRISIS

The 1997–98 crisis

The East Asian financial crisis of 1997–98 was triggered by massive reversals of capital flows and contagion. Though deeper, structural causes of crises vary, there was a common factor across countries: imprudently managed domestic financial institutions over-extended loans to corporations that in turn invested the borrowed funds in unproductive projects. Furthermore, an initially benign-looking currency crisis evolved into a full-blown economic crisis due to the mutually reinforcing impacts of currency depreciation, financial sector deterioration, and corporate sector distress. Essentially the crisis was the result of interactions between the forces of financial globalisation and domestic structural weaknesses (World Bank 1998, 2000).

Forces of financial globalisation

The affected countries had liberalised international capital flows and had been integrated with the international capital markets before the crisis. Many East Asian economies clearly benefited from the liberalisation and globalisation of financial markets. From the mid-1980s to the mid-1990s, large inflows of capital, particularly long-term capital such as foreign direct investment (FDI), helped finance the region's rapid economic development and growth. In the several years leading up to the crisis, however, countries had received large inflows of capital in the financial and corporate sectors, particularly in the form of unhedged short-term capital. As a result, the ratios of short-term external debt to foreign exchange reserves had risen to levels greater than one. When market perceptions changed rapidly in 1997, these economies saw sudden outflows of capital and consequent large downward pressures on the currency. The currency crisis was triggered by the sudden reversal of capital flows, which is why the crisis is often called the 'capital account crisis' (Yoshitomi and Shirai 2000; Kawai et al. 2001).

Regional contagion of the crisis was spectacular. The Thai baht crisis spread to Malaysia, Indonesia, the Philippines and eventually South Korea within a few months. At a later stage, Hong Kong was also affected, but the authorities managed successfully to contain its impact using unconventional policy measures.

Domestic structural weaknesses

The crisis-hit countries also had domestic structural weaknesses. Some foreign capital was intermediated by domestic financial institutions that extended loans to domestic sectors, including non-tradable real estate and construction; some found its way directly into domestic corporations. Investment in real estate and other assets contributed to the generation of asset bubbles, which left financial institutions with serious problems of non-performing loans when the bubble ultimately burst. In this way, financial institutions that intermediated foreign capital to domestic sectors were exposed to currency and maturity mismatches. Domestic corporations that were highly leveraged were also exposed to interest and exchange rate shocks. Inadequate regulatory and supervisory frameworks had left banks and corporations with imprudent financial management and, more generally, weak corporate governance. Steep exchange rate depreciation, high interest rates and tight budgets, induced by the eruption of a currency crisis in 1997, aggravated financial and corporate sector distress and led to a sharp contraction of economic activity in 1998.

Reform of the international financial architecture

Lessons

There are at least two important lessons from this experience. First, greater attention needs to be paid to managing the forces of financial globalisation, particularly in a world of rapid short-term capital flows. Until the crisis, implications of the scope and magnitude of short-term capital flows were not fully understood by international investors, policymakers of the borrowing countries, or international financial institutions. More fundamentally, there was a lack of concern over the volatile nature of capital flows, the need for monitoring capital flows, and the need to respond to rapid capital flows. Management of financial globalisation requires frameworks that reduce capital flow volatility and enhance domestic capacity to manage undesirable impacts of globalisation.

Second, emerging market economies need to strengthen domestic economic systems, in particular their financial and corporate sectors. This task requires the establishment of effective regulatory and supervisory frameworks for the better management and governance of financial institutions and corporations. Specifically, economies in the region need to improve banks' asset-liability management capacity so as to avoid over-extension of loans and excessive currency and maturity mismatches; improve corporations' financial management capacity so as to maintain their sound financial discipline; and develop sound capital markets so as to provide alternative financing sources for corporations. If the domestic economic system becomes robust and resilient, a crisis could be prevented, or its impact on the economy would be mitigated even if a crisis occurred.

Reflecting on these lessons, there has been an increasing recognition that putting effective mechanisms in place to manage the forces of globalisation and to strengthen domestic economic systems is key to crisis prevention, management and resolution. Various efforts to reform the functioning of international financial markets and to strengthen domestic economic underpinnings have been made under the title of the 'international financial architecture'.[1]

Strengthening the international financial system

At the global level, various reforms for crisis prevention, management and resolution have been proposed and some have been put in place.

First, the workings and functions of the IMF have been strengthened. In particular, the IMF has increased its liquidity position. Its usable resources – the amount it can lend to member countries in financial need – doubled from SDR54 billion in 1998 to SDR110 billion in 2001. Its stock of net uncommitted usable resources – usable resources less resources committed under current arrangements and considered likely to be drawn, and less working balances of usable currencies – rose to SDR75 billion in 2001. In case its own resources are inadequate, the IMF can borrow up to SDR34 billion under the New Arrangements to Borrow and the General Arrangements to Borrow.

The IMF has also introduced new lending facilities to meet the greater financial needs of member countries at times of crises or as preventive measures. The Supplemental Reserve Facility was established in December 1997 and has been used in South Korea, Brazil, Argentina and Turkey. It provides large financial assistance, without access limit, to members facing exceptional balance of payments difficulties resulting from a sudden and disruptive loss of market confidence. The Contingent Credit Line was created in 1999 as a precautionary line of defence to help protect member countries in the event of an exceptional balance of payments need arising from the spread of financial crises, provided that the countries have pursued strong policies. Furthermore, the IMF has improved the transparency of its operations and policy deliberations. It has also decided to streamline its conditionality, particularly structural conditionality, in order to enhance the ownership and effectiveness of its program.

Second, private sector involvement has been an important focus of reform. Given that the volume of private resources far exceeds that of official resources, private sector involvement is vital for crisis prevention and resolution. If official intervention were to bail out private investors without making them pay for their bad investment decisions, this would create a serious moral hazard problem. While private financial institutions decided to share the burden in helping crisis-hit countries in several cases, such as South Korea and Brazil, a definitive framework has yet to be developed. This is particularly the case for the restructuring of emerging economy bonds because of the large number and dispersion of bond-holders involved.

The international community has begun to explore possible mechanisms for the debt restructuring of international sovereign bonds in the recognition that, at the time of a liquidity crisis, holders of sovereign bonds, along with other creditors, would need to contribute to the resolution of such crises. Two methods have been recommended: a contractual approach and a statutory approach. A contractual approach considers collective action clauses in sovereign bond contracts as a useful device for orderly resolution of crises; their explicit inclusion in bond documentation would provide a degree of predictability for the restructuring process. A statutory approach (Krueger 2002) attempts to create the legal basis – through universal treaty rather than through a set of national laws in a limited number of jurisdictions – for establishing adequate incentives for debtors and creditors to agree upon a prompt, orderly and predictable restructuring of unsustainable debt.[2]

Third, the G-20 and the Financial Stability Forum were created to broaden input into international financial policymaking, including systemically important developed and emerging market economies. A wide range of issues has been taken up, including highly leveraged institutions, offshore financial centres, and measuring vulnerabilities. But the reforms have not been fully satisfactory, owing to inadequate progress on private sector involvement, information disclosure by highly leveraged institutions, and use of contingent credit lines.

National efforts to strengthen domestic policies and institutions

At the national level, there are efforts to strengthen domestic policy and institutional frameworks with an emphasis on macroeconomic management capacity and financial sector reform. Attention has focused particularly on the need to improve regulatory and supervisory frameworks in the financial system, to strengthen corporate governance, and to establish effective domestic insolvency procedures to deal with non-viable banks and corporations.

One of the principal tools for strengthening domestic policies and institutions is international best practice information in macroeconomic policymaking, financial sector regulation and supervision, and capital market infrastructure. Reports on the Observance of Standards and Codes (ROSCs), supported by various international organisations and agencies and adopted by the IMF in September 1999, cover 12 issues in three main areas. In the macroeconomic policy area, these include monetary and financial policy transparency, fiscal transparency, and special data dissemination standards in addition to the general data dissemination system. In the area of financial sector regulation and supervision, they include banking supervision, securities regulation, insurance supervision, payments systems, and anti-money-laundering. In the area of capital market infrastructure, they include corporate governance, accounting standards, auditing standards, and insolvency and creditor rights.

An important instrument is the Financial Sector Assessment Program (FSAP) supported jointly by the IMF and the World Bank.[3] These processes are undoubtedly useful, but take time to be effectively implemented. And even if ROSCs are fully in place, crises may still occur.

Creating a new regional financial architecture

While the international community and emerging market economies have focused on global and domestic policy reforms, a well-designed regional framework can also contribute to the stability of the international financial system for three reasons.[4] First, the global efforts are still inadequate and national efforts take more time to become effective. Second, there is increasing regional integration in trade, FDI and financial flows, so an effective regional framework for policy coordination and concerted action is desirable. Third, as economic contagion tends to begin with a geographic focus, a regional framework for financial cooperation to address crisis prevention, management and resolution is a logical way to proceed.[5] Thus it is important to improve regional financial architecture.

A framework for regional financial cooperation may include three areas: regional surveillance and monitoring for crisis/contagion prevention; schemes to augment international liquidity for crisis management; and programs to assist crisis-affected countries to resolve the systemic impact of the crisis and accelerate the recovery process. Any regional framework must be consistent with the global framework in order to secure efficient responses to, and management and resolution of, future crises.

Crisis prevention

Regional information sharing, policy dialogue, consultation, surveillance and monitoring are instrumental to crisis prevention at the regional level. The process should include sharing of information on both macroeconomic and structural issues, such as monetary and exchange rate policies (including domestic and foreign assets and liabilities of the central banks), fiscal positions and debt management, capital flows and external debts, financial system conditions, and corporate sector developments. Monitoring capital flows at the regional level is particularly important. Prudential capital controls in the face of large inflows of short-term capital can be effective, as evidenced in the case of the Chilean experience in the 1990s. Developing a reliable early warning system is useful in detecting macroeconomic, external and financial sector vulnerabilities and preventing currency and financial crises in the future. With effective surveillance mechanisms in place, each economy in the region is expected to be under peer pressure to pursue disciplined macroeconomic and structural policies that are conducive to stable external accounts and currencies.

The consultation process may include efforts toward intra-regional exchange rate stability for economies that are highly integrated with, or complementary to, one another through trade and FDI. Avoiding competitive currency depreciation and mutually incoherent exchange rate policies is essential for preserving financial stability for mutually interdependent economies. These economies may wish to support an informal arrangement for stable exchange rates, introduce a formal mechanism for intra-regional exchange rate stability, or form a regional currency union.

Crisis management

Once an economy is hit by a currency crisis, appropriate policy responses and timely provision of international liquidity are needed to prevent the economy from slipping into a serious economic contraction of systemic proportions. The pace of liquidity disbursement at the global level may be slow in times of crisis or contagion, because of cumbersome bureaucratic processes and disagreements over policy conditionality. To avoid long delays and to augment globally available resources, a regional financing facility can help close the gap. This need is particularly apparent today because the IMF appears to be moving away from large-package operations to smaller packages with private sector involvement (PSI) (Kenen 2001). A financing facility that can rapidly mobilise a large amount of liquidity to head off a speculative attack is an obvious benefit if the attack is the result of irrational herd behaviour. For such a financing facility to be effective, its provision must be accompanied by appropriate policy measures to address the problem and restore investor confidence in the market.

When an effective PSI cannot be expected, an alternative might be a unilateral imposition of a standstill and/or a capital outflow control. Outflow controls have more frequently been a failure than a success in emerging market economies, but the Malaysian experience suggests that the deployment of this instrument can be useful in the right environment. In Malaysia, controls had a salutary effect mainly because they were temporary, supported by a strong macroeconomic framework, accompanied by bank and corporate restructuring, and implemented with credible supervision (see Kawai and Takagi 2003).

Some experts and academics have heavily criticised the recent IMF conditionality on certain East Asian countries, notably Indonesia, for not focusing sufficiently on containing the immediate currency crisis.[6] A regional initiative, including liquidity support, may allow an economy hit by a currency attack or contagion to respond with more focused policy measures that are designed to address the immediate need for fire-fighting without compromising on moral hazard problems. This initiative, however, must be consistent with, and complementary to, the global framework, in order to exploit the synergy between the two, ensure policy coherence, and involve private creditors from outside the region.

Crisis resolution

To resolve a crisis, international efforts are needed to ensure that a crisis-affected economy returns to a sustainable growth path. In the face of a systemic crisis in the banking, corporate and social sectors, fiscal resource mobilisation is essential for the quick resolution of the crisis. Fiscal resources that are needed to recapitalise weak banks, facilitate corporate debt restructuring and strengthen social safety nets may be limited by the lack of fiscal headroom or constraints to external financing on market terms. Because the resources from the multilateral development banks are also limited, regionally concerted action to mobilise such resources, particularly from the core countries in the region, should contribute greatly to crisis resolution.

In this sense, the so-called New Miyazawa Initiative contributed to crisis resolution. In October 1998, under the leadership of Finance Minister Kiichi Miyazawa, Japan pledged US$30 billion to support the economic recovery of the crisis-affected countries. Half of the pledged amount was to be dedicated to short-term capital needs during economic restructuring and reform; the rest was earmarked for medium-term and long-term reforms. A commitment to provide a large amount of resources helped stabilise the regional markets and economies, thereby facilitating the recovery process.

LOGIC OF REGIONAL FINANCIAL COOPERATION IN EAST ASIA

Economic interdependence in the region

Strong regional economic interdependence is the most important rationale for regional financial cooperation. More broadly, regional spillover effects and externalities due to economic interdependence call for regional economic cooperation in various areas, including the establishment of regional common policies toward trade and FDI, harmonisation of standards and regulations, financial sector supervision, intra-regional exchange rate stability, and macroeconomic policy coordination. Though financial cooperation focuses on issues pertinent to financial spheres, it cannot be sustained as a productive tool without broader economic integration at the regional level.[7]

Trade and FDI integration

The East Asia region has long enjoyed market-driven integration through trade and FDI, while embracing a multilateral liberalisation framework under the World Trade Organization (WTO) and open regionalism under Asia Pacific Economic Cooperation (APEC) and avoiding discriminatory trade arrangements. The APEC process was successful in encouraging China to pursue trade and FDI liberalisation outside the WTO framework, and inducing other economies in the region to pursue the same objectives. Regional economic integration has been strengthened through FDI. FDI flows to the East Asian economies expanded rapidly in the second half of the 1980s, driven largely by Japanese multinational corporations after the Plaza Accord. FDI flows have generated greater intra-industry trade within the region and contributed to deeper economic integration.

The degree of regional integration through trade in East Asia is already high and comparable to levels seen in the North American Free Trade Agreement (NAFTA) or the European Union (EU). Table 7.1 summarises intra-regional trade intensity indices for various groupings in the world over the period 1980–2000. The table demonstrates that within groups of East Asia, whether including Japan or not, the indices are larger than those for NAFTA or EU-15.[8]

The ASEAN free trade arrangement (AFTA) used to be the only formal regional trade arrangement in East Asia.[9] Despite the slow pace of trade liberalisation, AFTA has been in effect among the original five ASEAN members – Indonesia, Malaysia, Singapore, Thailand and the Philippines – since January 2002. Although the exclusion list is long and individual country circumstances

Table 7.1   Intra-regional trade intensity index[a]

Region	1980	1985	1990	1995	1996	1997	1998	1999	2000
East Asia-15, including									
Japan[b]	2.6	2.3	2.3	2.1	2.2	2.2	2.3	2.4	2.2
Emerging East Asia-14[c]	3.0	2.9	2.8	2.3	2.4	2.4	2.6	2.5	2.4
ASEAN-10	5.1	6.1	4.6	3.8	3.8	3.8	4.3	4.1	3.7
NAFTA	2.1	2.0	2.1	2.4	2.4	2.3	2.3	2.3	2.1
European Union-15	1.5	1.6	1.5	1.7	1.7	1.7	1.6	1.7	1.7
MERCOSUR	6.6	4.9	9.7	13.3	14.4	14.0	14.2	14.7	15.0

Notes

a   The trade intensity index is defined as $(X_{ij}/X_{i.})/(X_{.j}/X_{..})$ where X_{ij} represents exports from region i to region j, $X_{i.}$ represents total exports from region i, $X_{.j}$ represents total exports from the world to region j (or total imports of region j), and $X_{..}$ represents total world trade. In the table, the index is defined only for countries within the same region, so that $i=j$.

b   East Asia-15 includes Emerging East Asia-14 and Japan.

c   Emerging East Asia-14 includes ASEAN-10, China, Hong Kong, South Korea and Taiwan.

Source: Kawai and Urata (2002).

vary, most goods traded between these countries are already subject to tariffs of only zero to 5 per cent. Vietnam is to comply with the same tariff standards by 2003, Laos and Myanmar by 2005, and Cambodia by 2007.

Recently, several economies in East Asia have indicated a willingness to embark on regional trade arrangements on a larger scale. Japan concluded a bilateral economic partnership arrangement (EPA) with Singapore, made effective in November 2002.[10] China and ASEAN are negotiating a free trade agreement (FTA) to be completed within 10 years. Japan has also proposed an EPA with ASEAN, and is discussing the possibility of similar arrangements with Mexico (under negotiation), Malaysia, the Philippines, South Korea and Thailand (under study). Many other countries in the region have concluded or are negotiating bilateral FTAs with countries inside and outside the region.[11]

Japan's conclusion of a bilateral FTA–EPA with Singapore symbolises a change in its longstanding trade policy of pursuing only multilateral liberalisation. Japan is shifting its trade policy to a three-track approach based on multilateral, regional and bilateral liberalisation. For Japan, regional and bilateral liberalisation is an attempt to achieve deeper integration with trading partners on a formal basis, going beyond reductions in border restrictions, and pursuing investment liberalisation, greater competition in the domestic market, and harmonisation of standards (Box 7.1). This approach not only is consistent with, but also promotes, the multilateral approach, which remains an important element of Japanese trade policy.

Financial integration

Financial integration has also proceeded as a result of the increased liberalisation of the financial system and the capital account. Commercial

---

Box 7.1   Regional trade arrangements in East Asia

There has recently been a heightened interest in regional trade and investment arrangements in East Asia, with regional trade agreements (RTAs) as well as several bilateral free trade agreements under active discussion. RTAs, if properly designed for trade creation, can be a positive force, especially for smaller economies, for stimulating trade in a global context. There are two main ways in which an RTA can have a positive economic impact in the region. The first is through an enlargement of the market as a whole, with the resulting economies of scale, improved efficiency and greater competitiveness of regional producers. Forming an ASEAN+3 free trade area may be particularly useful for achieving a large-scale regional market. Realising these gains requires inefficient sectors and firms to contract as market pressure develops. The second is through trade and location effects, through the induced improvements in technologies and institutions. Any negative impact from trade diversion to less efficient producers is likely to be offset by the positive impact of technology transfers and modernisation of standards and procedures – as has been the case with the expansion of the ASEAN Free Trade Area to countries such as Vietnam and Cambodia. Growing regional activities can also stimulate demand for intermediate inputs from non-regional sources.

Hence, an RTA could generate significant welfare gains for both the East Asian and global economies if properly designed to expand trade. Gains would also depend on the depth of integration (reductions in tariffs and non-tariff barriers), including investment liberalisation, deregulation of domestic markets to enhance competition, and harmonisation of regulations and standards.

---

banks operating throughout the region have contributed to a closely connected banking sector within East Asia. Opening of securities markets, particularly equity markets, has attracted foreign portfolio capital flows. As a result, there have been positive correlations of stock price movements within the region. Greater commercial bank lending and portfolio flows have linked the economies in the region financially.

Macroeconomic interdependence

Macroeconomic interdependence within the region has recently become stronger, as evidenced by a simultaneous contraction of economic activity throughout East Asia in 1998 and a simultaneous expansion in 1999–2000. Though the regional economies may have been affected by some common factors such as US economic and information technology stock price cycles, much of the recent, synchronised economic activities in the region can be attributed to strong macroeconomic interdependence.

Indeed, earlier studies by Eichengreen and Bayoumi (1999) found that, in terms of supply shocks, some East Asian nations were just as closely connected with one another as European countries were. In terms of demand shocks, ASEAN countries were also well connected.[12] The Kobe Research Project Study on Regional Financial Cooperation and Surveillance, conducted by the Japanese team (IIMA 2002), also found increasing macroeconomic interdependence in East Asia in the 1990s, in terms of movements of real output and shocks to real investment.[13]

Information sharing and regime setting for regional financial cooperation

The presence of deepening economic interdependence in East Asia suggests that there is a case for economic policy cooperation at the regional level. The pace and extent of crisis contagion observed in the region in the second half of 1997 also suggest that regionally coordinated action to contain contagion is logical. An efficient cooperative framework for regional financial management can be useful in coping with serious currency crises and contagion. In a region where economic fluctuations, policies and shocks are transmitted across countries, positive outcomes can be expected from cooperative financial policies and frameworks. In this context, three types of financial cooperation could be pursued in the region: policy optimisation, regime setting or information sharing.[14]

Policy optimisation is a joint maximisation of a weighted sum of economic welfare of the countries concerned. It often takes the form of policy exchanges where one country pursues monetary policy expansion while another pursues monetary policy contraction. This type of policy coordination was a hot topic in academic and policy circles from the mid-1980s to the early 1990s for the G-7 countries. In particular, the United States, Japan and Germany took coordinated action to induce US dollar depreciation in 1985 and, when the dollar declined too far, to prevent its fall in 1987.[15] The European economies have been coordinating their monetary policies at least since 1979 under the European Monetary System (EMS). While one may question whether the approach taken by these industrialised countries can be a useful guide to emerging market economies, coordinated action in macroeconomic policy could be productive under the right circumstances.

Not all East Asian economies have the capacity to carry out credible national economic policies or regionally coordinated policies. For example, Indonesia continues to suffer from the fallout of the crisis, and setting the right macroeconomic framework is proving to be a challenge. The primary objective of economic policies of less developed countries such as Cambodia, Laos, Myanmar and Vietnam is to accelerate economic development and poverty reduction by promoting industrialisation, structural changes, and human resource development. It may be difficult for these economies to follow internationally agreed economic policies. Nonetheless, regional financial cooperation would eventually require coordinated policy action on the part of many economies in the region.

Regime setting is a joint exercise to agree on a set of rules within which individual countries can conduct independent policymaking to pursue their own economic interests. This type of policy cooperation includes agreements on such issues as regional trade and FDI arrangements, regional exchange rate regimes, regional financing arrangements, other regional frameworks for action at the time of a crisis, and initiatives for regional bond market development. An example is a joint setting of exchange rate policies for intra-regional exchange rate stabilisation, which can prevent competitive depreciation at the regional level. Another example is the creation of a regional financing facility, which can contain regional currency attacks and contagion quickly, supplement IMF roles and resources, and economise on resources through reserve pooling at the regional level. Yet another example is an initiative for regional bond market development, which encourages the economies in the region to make concerted efforts to develop national bond markets as well as regional infrastructure, including clearance, settlements, and rating agencies.

A third profitable approach for interdependent economies in the region would be to establish a cooperative framework that encourages frequent information sharing. Regional policy dialogue and surveillance mechanisms facilitate greater information sharing, closer monitoring of regional economic conditions and short-term capital flows, and peer pressure to develop better policies. These improve each country's understanding of its peers' economic performance, macroeconomic and structural issues, policy objectives, and policy choices. A cooperative framework enhances the economic welfare of the countries concerned because it enables each country to use more accurate information about other countries in its own policymaking.

Though policy optimisation is an unrealistic option at this stage, there is scope for the East Asian economies to pursue at least two types of policy cooperation: regime setting and information sharing. These would probably be the most productive mechanisms for cooperation at present. Given the already strong economic interdependence among the region's economies, they will benefit by establishing a framework for exchange rate stabilisation and then gradually moving toward collective efforts in monetary–fiscal policy coordination based on policy exchanges.

Challenges for closer financial cooperation in East Asia

Both advocates and sceptics of East Asian financial cooperation have argued that the regional economies face several challenges for closer cooperation.[16]

The most serious challenge reflects the fact that the regional economies are diverse and heterogeneous in terms of per capita incomes, stage of economic development, institutional capacity, and economic systems and structures. Such diversity and heterogeneity create obvious difficulties for any attempt to agree on coordinated policies. In order for the economies to take joint action at the regional level, there must be substantial economic convergence.

The second challenge is how to create conditions for political leadership to emerge. Currently there is no strong political leadership in the region, due to differences in political systems and the lack of full mutual trust. In East Asia no single economic power plays a dominant role like that of the United

States in the Western hemisphere, nor is there any bipolar relationship like the Franco-German alliance in Western Europe. Japan is currently suffering economic stagnation, and China, while rapidly emerging as an economic power, has yet to achieve transition from a planned to a market economy and from one-party rule to democracy. It will take time for any bipolar alliance to emerge in East Asia.

The third challenge is how to go beyond the so-called 'consensus' culture. Cooperation in East Asia has been characterised by consensus decision-making and a presumption of non-intervention in domestic affairs. The emphasis on consensus, non-interference and good manners has nurtured a shallow form of regional financial cooperation so far. For much deeper policy cooperation, the economies in the region must be ready to accept constructive comments and criticisms on their policymaking and, hence, a certain degree of friendly intrusion from their peers.

The fourth challenge is how to create sufficient incentives for regional financial cooperation given that the region is economically open to the rest of the world. While intra-regional trade and investment interdependence are rising, East Asia is not self-contained in terms of trade and financial flows. The region needs North America and Europe as destinations for its export products. The region also allocates a substantial amount of financial wealth in US dollar denominated assets. Essentially, the challenge is how to make East Asian regionalism attractive when it is embedded in the larger global system.

The difficulties underlying these challenges may have prevented the economies in East Asia from pursuing serious financial (as well as broader economic) cooperation so far. However, the East Asian crisis has revealed the importance of regional financial cooperation, possibly by raising the perceived payoffs to cooperation. Despite heterogeneity and differences in political systems among the economies in the region, countries have increasingly come to realise the strength of the economic logic for further cooperation. As the region makes progress on economic and financial cooperation, the resulting institution building would provide further impetus for more ambitious cooperation.

EAST ASIAN INITIATIVES FOR REGIONAL FINANCIAL COOPERATION

Initiatives to strengthen regional financial cooperation in East Asia have so far fallen into three broad areas: information sharing, policy dialogue and economic surveillance; regional financing arrangements; and coordination of exchange rate policies.

Regional policy dialogue and surveillance mechanisms

There are several mechanisms for regional information sharing, policy dialogue, and economic surveillance. Three major initiatives are the ASEAN Surveillance Process, the ASEAN+3 Framework, and the Manila Framework

Group (MFG). Other initiatives include SEANZA (South East Asia, New Zealand and Australia), SEACEN (South East Asian Central Banks), and EMEAP (Executives Meeting of East Asia and Pacific Central Banks) for central banks, APEC and ASEM (Asia-Europe Meeting) for trans-regional policy dialogue, and smaller groups (see Table 7.2).

Table 7.2 Regional forums for finance ministries and central banks

	Finance ministries and/or central banks					Central banks		
Year established	ASEAN 1967	ASEAN+3 1999	MFGᵃ 1997	APEC 1994	ASEMᵇ 1997	SEANZA 1956	SEACEN 1966	EMEAP 1991
Japan		√	√	√	√	√		√
China		√	√	√	√	√		√
South Korea		√	√	√	√	√	√	√
Hong Kong		√	√			√		√
Taiwan			√				√	
Singapore	√	√	√	√	√	√	√	√
Brunei	√	√	√	√	√			
Cambodia	√	√						
Indonesia	√	√	√	√	√	√	√	√
Laos	√	√						
Malaysia	√	√	√	√	√√	√	√	√
Myanmar	√	√					√	
Philippines	√	√	√	√	√	√	√	√
Thailand	√	√	√	√	√	√	√	√
Vietnam	√	√		√	√			
Mongolia						√	√	
Macao						√		
Papua New Guinea				√		√		
Australia, New Zealand				√	√	√		√
Nepal, Sri Lanka						√	√	
Bangladesh, India, Iran, Pakistan								√
USA, Canada			√	√				
Chile, Mexico, Peru				√				
Russia				√				
EU-15					√			

Notes
a Includes the International Monetary Fund, the World Bank, the Asian Development Bank and the Bank for International Settlements.
b Includes the European Commission.
  APEC = Asia Pacific Economic Cooperation; ASEAN = Association of Southeast Asian Nations; EMEAP = Executives Meeting of East Asia and Pacific Central Banks; MFG = Manila Framework Group; SEACEN = South East Asian Central Banks; SEANZA = South East Asia, New Zealand and Australia

ASEAN Surveillance Process

While the economic goal of ASEAN has been the promotion of trade and investment flows in the region, the recent success of European countries to complete economic and monetary integration has encouraged ASEAN to think that it might productively pursue similar goals.

The ASEAN Surveillance Process was established in October 1998 when the ASEAN finance ministers signed a 'terms of understanding' for regional cooperation. The objective of the process was to strengthen policy dialogue and policymaking capacity in monetary, fiscal and financial areas through information exchanges, peer reviews and recommendations for action at the regional and national levels. For this purpose, the ASEAN Surveillance Process is designed to monitor macroeconomic developments, capital flows, exchange rates, and structural and social policies, and to include provisions for capacity building, institutional strengthening, and information sharing. The ASEAN finance ministers meet twice a year for policy coordination under this process.

The ASEAN Surveillance Coordinating Unit (ASCU), established at the ASEAN Secretariat in Jakarta, prepares an ASEAN Surveillance Report. Using the same data supplied to the IMF in conjunction with its Article IV consultations and program negotiations, the ASCU performs an analysis of the latest economic and financial conditions in ASEAN while taking into account global developments that affect the regional economies. The exercise has recently been strengthened by the establishment of national surveillance units in several ASEAN countries (Cambodia, Indonesia, Laos, the Philippines, Thailand, and Vietnam), which produce drafts of country chapters. The Asian Development Bank (ADB) supports this process by preparing an ASEAN Economic Outlook and special issue studies, as well as providing technical assistance.[17] The ASEAN Surveillance Report is considered and finalised by the ASEAN finance and central bank deputies before it is submitted for discussion by the ASEAN finance ministers during their peer review session.

The ASEAN Surveillance Process is the first concrete attempt by a group of developing countries to establish mechanisms for information sharing, policy dialogue, and individual and collective responses to events that could adversely affect subregional economies. It has two components. The first is a monitoring mechanism that allows early detection of any irregular movement in key economic and financial variables; the second is a peer review mechanism that induces appropriate policy responses to issues emerging from the monitoring exercise.

ASEAN+3 Economic Review and Policy Dialogue Process

The Asian financial crisis in 1997 highlighted the need to strengthen regional cooperation and urged the heads of state or government of the ASEAN+3 group, consisting of ASEAN-10 and China, Japan and South Korea, to meet for the first time in December 1997 to discuss regional peace, stability and prosperity. To promote regional financial cooperation in particular, the first

ASEAN+3 Finance Ministers Meeting was held in April 1999 on the sidelines of the ADB annual meeting in Manila. The ASEAN+3 leaders recognised the need for 'enhancing self-help and support mechanisms in East Asia through the ASEAN+3 Framework' in November 1999.[18] Following this recognition, the ASEAN+3 Economic Review and Policy Dialogue (ERPD) was introduced in May 2000. Under this process, the ASEAN+3 finance ministers have met annually, in principle to exchange information and discuss policy issues.

The purpose of the ASEAN+3 ERPD process is to strengthen policy dialogue, coordination and collaboration on the financial, monetary and fiscal issues of common interest. Its major focus is on issues related to macroeconomic risk management, better corporate governance, monitoring of regional capital flows, strengthening of the banking and financial systems, reform of the international financial architecture, and enhancement of self-help and support mechanisms in East Asia. Steps have been taken for cooperation in monitoring short-term capital flows and developing a regional early warning system to assess regional financial vulnerabilities, with a view to preventing financial crises in the future.

The first peer review meeting under the ASEAN+3 ERPD process was held in May 2000 on the sidelines of the ADB annual meeting. Like the ASEAN Surveillance Process, the ASEAN+3 ERPD process has not yet been as effective as it should be. There is no secretariat to support the logistics of the process, and there is no organisational structure to provide substantive inputs into the process, except that the ADB provides some data on developing member economies. Recognising the importance of enhanced monitoring of economic conditions in the region, the ASEAN+3 finance ministers agreed at their fourth meeting, in Honolulu in May 2001, to establish a study group to discuss feasible mechanisms for economic reviews and policy dialogue.[19]

Manila Framework Group

Inspired by the success of the Tokyo meeting to create a much-needed financial support package for Thailand in August 1997, Japan, with support from South Korea and the ASEAN countries that participated in the Thai package, proposed to establish an Asian Monetary Fund (AMF) to supplement IMF resources for crisis prevention and resolution. The United States and the IMF opposed this proposition on grounds of moral hazard and duplication. They argued that an East Asian country hit by a currency crisis would bypass the tough conditionality of the IMF and receive easy money from the AMF, thereby creating potential for moral hazard; and that an AMF would be redundant in the presence of an effective global crisis manager, the IMF.

The idea was dropped, but in November 1997 the East Asian economies, together with the United States, Canada, Australia and New Zealand, agreed to establish the MFG.[20] Its objective is to develop a concerted framework for regional financial cooperation in order to restore and enhance the prospects for financial stability in the region.[21] Its initiatives include the establishment of a new mechanism for regional surveillance to complement global surveillance by the IMF; enhancement of economic and technical cooperation, particularly in strengthening domestic financial systems and regulatory capacities; strengthening the IMF's capacity to respond to financial crises; and development of a cooperative financing arrangement for the region to complement IMF resources.

One notable feature of the MFG is its establishment of a new mechanism for regional surveillance. This mechanism would provide a basis for an intensive and high-level process of surveillance and dialogue among participating finance ministries and central banks with support from the IMF, World Bank, ADB and Bank for International Settlements (BIS). The MFG is a process for finance and central bank deputies. By March 2003, the group had met 10 times.

As indicated by the IMF's characterisation of the MFG as the 'preeminent forum for Asian regional surveillance and peer pressure',[22] the MFG's strength lies in its capacity to carry out more effective policy dialogue than any other regional forum. It has no permanent secretariat or funding of its own.

Central bank forums

Asian central banks also have their own policy dialogue processes, including SEANZA, SEACEN and EMEAP.

The SEANZA group grew out of a 1956 meeting of central bank governors from the Asia–Oceanic region and is one of the oldest and largest regional forums in terms of membership. It is a forum for exchanges of information on issues and problems of common interest among central banks and for providing training courses for central bank staff.

SEACEN was established in February 1966, initially as a training and research organisation. It has evolved into a more substantive forum for discussion of central banking issues. Membership includes the major Southeast Asian economies as well as South Korea and Taiwan. It runs a training centre in Kuala Lumpur.

EMEAP was organised in February 1991 with the leadership of the Bank of Japan and the Reserve Bank of Australia. Its major objectives include enhanced regional surveillance, exchanges of information and views, and the promotion of financial market development. Its activities include annual meetings of EMEAP central bank governors, semi-annual meetings of the deputy governors, and three working groups concerned with bank supervision, financial markets, and payments and settlement systems.[23] Like the MFG, EMEAP has no secretariat; instead, the responsibility for organisational matters, along with the meetings themselves, is rotated among the participating central banks.

Since late 1997, central banks of ASEAN members have started to meet for policy dialogue as the ASEAN Central Bank Forum.

APEC and ASEM

The region has also developed trans-regional arrangements with the Americas (APEC) and the European Union (ASEM).

The objective of APEC has long been trade and investment liberalisation and facilitation among the Asia Pacific countries, including the United States and Canada. The APEC Finance Ministers Meeting was established in March 1994 as a main forum for the exchange of views and information on macroeconomic conditions, capital flows, and financial market development. The IMF, the World Bank and the ADB help to prepare papers on relevant issues. A distinctive feature of APEC is that ministers invite representatives from the private sector – Asian Bankers Association Council, APEC Financiers Group, and Pacific Economic Cooperation Council – to briefly report on their work and discuss issues.

At the first Asia-Europe Meeting in March 1996, the heads of states of Asian and EU countries initiated a process for strengthening partnership between Asia and the EU. The ASEM Finance Ministers Meeting was established in September 1997. By March 2003, three meetings had been held. From 2002, the meetings began to be held annually. The European Commission is a regular member and the IMF, European Central Bank and ADB contribute to discussions. One hallmark activity was the Kobe Research Project, which was designed to promote regional monetary cooperation in East Asia, by taking into account the lessons learned from the European integration experience.

Smaller-scale regional groups

There are several smaller-scale meetings for information exchange in the region, including the Four Markets Meeting (Australia, Hong Kong, Japan and Singapore, established in May 1992), the Six Markets Meeting (China, the United States and the Four Markets Meeting members, starting in March 1997), and the Trilateral Finance Ministers Meeting (China, South Korea and Japan, starting in September 2000). These groups discuss such regional issues as macroeconomic conditions, capital flows, foreign exchange markets, and financial market developments. By March 2003, the Four Markets Meetings had been held 16 times and the Six Markets Meetings twice. They are attended by finance and central bank deputies. A second Trilateral Finance Ministers Meeting was held in May 2002.

Regional financing facilities

The IMF has a limited role as an international lender of last resort, so a regional financing facility can play a useful role in crisis prevention and management. With good policies and disciplines, it can do this through timely and adequate provision of international liquidity at times of currency attack, contagion and crisis. Under the CMI, the longstanding ASEAN Swap Arrangement (ASA) has been strengthened and bilateral swap arrangements for the ASEAN+3 members, including China, Japan and South Korea, have been introduced.

ASEAN Swap Arrangement

In August 1977 the original five ASEAN central banks and monetary authorities
– Indonesia, Malaysia, the Philippines, Singapore, and Thailand – signed the
first memorandum of understanding on the ASA. The total facility was US$100
million, with each member contributing US$20 million. In 1978, the total was
increased to US$200 million, with each member contributing US$40 million.
The objective was to provide immediate, short-term swap facilities to any
member facing a temporary liquidity shortage or a balance of payments
problem.[24]

However, the Asian financial crisis highlighted the importance for the
facility to be able to respond more effectively to the needs of its members in
a world of increased financial globalisation. At the ASEAN Finance Ministers
Meeting in March 2000, it was decided to extend membership to include
Brunei, Cambodia, Laos, Myanmar and Vietnam. In November 2000, 10 ASEAN
members signed a new memorandum of understanding to expand the ASA
membership to all 10 ASEAN central banks and monetary authorities and to
enlarge the size of the swap facility from US$200 million to US$1 billion. This
reflected the CMI objectives. The founding ASEAN members and Brunei now
contribute US$150 million each, while the other members contribute smaller
amounts (Vietnam US$60 million, Myanmar US$20 million, Cambodia US$15
million, and Laos US$5 million). The ASA allows member central banks to
swap their domestic currencies with major international currencies, such as
the US dollar, Japanese yen and euro, for an amount of up to twice their
commitment amount under the facility, and for a period of up to six months.[25]

Bilateral swap arrangements under the Chiang Mai Initiative

The finance ministers of ASEAN+3 who met in Chiang Mai in May 2000 also
agreed to establish a regional network of bilateral swap arrangements (BSAs)
under the CMI. In addition to expanding the existing ASA, the CMI is designed
to create a new network of bilateral swap and repurchase arrangements
among Japan, China and South Korea as well as between each of these and
any one of the ASEAN countries (see Figure 7.1).[26] By the end of March
2003, 12 BSAs had been concluded in line with the main principles, reaching
a total of US$39 billion (see Table 7.3).[27] Negotiations for two BSAs are
under way.[28]

At Chiang Mai, the ASEAN+3 countries agreed on the basic framework
and main principles of bilateral swap arrangements, including linkages to
the IMF, maturity and interest. For example, countries can borrow liquidity
collateralised by domestic currencies with government guarantees, rather
than offering US treasury bonds as collateral. The swap will be for 90 days,
renewable up to seven times, at an interest rate equivalent to the LIBOR plus
150 basis points for the first drawing and first renewal. Thereafter, the premium
rises by 50 basis points every two renewals, subject to a maximum of 300
basis points. Negotiations on the swap arrangements are to be concluded
bilaterally, based on the agreed main principles.

Figure 7.1 Network of Bilateral Swap Arrangements (BSAs) under the Chiang Mai Initiative

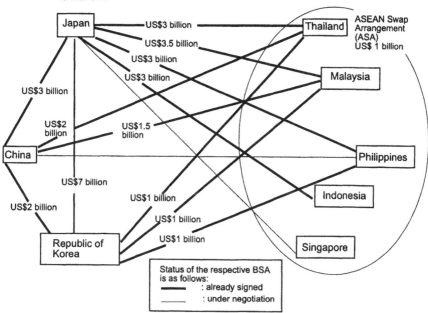

Note
1 The BSAs for Japan–Korea and Japan–Malaysia include the BSAs under the New Miyazawa Initiative (US$5 billion and US$2.5 billion, respectively).
2 The BSAs for Japan–China, China–Korea, Korea–Malaysia, and Korea–Philippines are local currency swap arrangements.

Members requesting liquidity support under the CMI can immediately obtain short-term financial assistance for the first 10 per cent of the BSA facility. The remaining 90 per cent is provided to the requesting member under an IMF program or an activated contingent credit line. This linkage of disbursements to IMF conditionality is designed to address the concern that balance of payments difficulties may be due to fundamental problems and that the potential moral hazard problem could be non-negligible in the absence of an effective adjustment program.[29]

MFG cooperative financing arrangements

One of the MFG's objectives is the development of a cooperative financing arrangement (CFA) for the region that would supplement resources from the IMF and other international financial institutions. Under this arrangement CFA participants could provide supplemental financial resources for IMF-supported programs, in consultation with the IMF and on a case-by-case basis. In exceptional circumstances, such support could augment a country's

Table 7.3   Progress on the Chiang Mai Initiative (as of end-December 2002)

BSA	Currencies	Conclusion date	Size (US$ billion)
Japan–Korea	USD–won	4 July 2001	7.0[a]
Japan–Thailand	USD–baht	30 July 2001	3.0
Japan–Philippines	USD–peso	27 August 2001	3.0
Japan–Malaysia	USD–ringgit	5 October 2001	3.5[b]
China–Thailand	USD–baht	6 December 2001	2.0
Japan–China	Yen–renminbi	28 March 2002	3.0[c]
China–Korea	Renminbi–won	24 June 2002	2.0[c]
Korea–Thailand	USD–won or USD–baht	25 June 2002	1.0
Korea–Malaysia	Won–ringgit	26 July 2002	1.0[c]
Korea–Philippines	Won–peso	9 August 2002	1.0[c]
China–Malaysia	USD–ringgit	9 October 2002	1.5
Japan–Singapore	Under negotiation		
Japan–Indonesia	Under negotiation		
China–Philippines	Under negotiation		

Notes
a Includes US$5 billion committed under the New Miyazawa Initiative.
b Includes US$2.5 billion committed under the New Miyazawa Initiative.
c US$ equivalents.
BSA=bilateral swap arrangement

foreign exchange reserves after it had used resources made available by the IMF.[30]

Regional exchange rate arrangement

Not much progress has been made in the area of exchange rate coordination or stabilisation in the region, despite the desirability of stable exchange rates in East Asia. One of the reasons for the lack of progress could be the fact that there is no international rule or best practice with regard to exchange rate regimes. The popular 'two-corner solution' view focuses exclusively on crisis prevention. However, countries can rightly pursue growth, trade, investment promotion and other objectives through exchange rate policy. As Frankel (1999) has argued, the optimal exchange rate regime depends on the circumstances of a particular country and time, and there is no single regime to fit all emerging market economies.

For the emerging East Asian economies that depend heavily on trade and investment, exchange rate stability is desirable for the promotion of trade and investment and economic development. In addition, intra-regional exchange rate stability is a public good for the East Asian economies that have increasingly integrated with one another. In the pre-crisis period, *de facto* US dollar pegged exchange rate regimes ensured extra-regional as well as intra-regional exchange rate stability on an informal basis. However, a US dollar based regime was susceptible to fluctuations in effective exchange rates when the dollar–yen rate became volatile in 1995 and 1998.

When the currency crisis led to a collapse of the then prevailing *de facto* US dollar based exchange rate regimes in crisis-hit economies, East Asian countries moved to more flexible exchange rate regimes. In the post-crisis period, they began to show a diversity of exchange rate arrangements. Some economies reverted to US dollar based regimes – notably Malaysia, which restored a formal US dollar peg. Indonesia and the Philippines increased exchange rate flexibility; South Korea and Thailand appear to have shifted to a currency basket type arrangement (see Kawai 2002).

For emerging market economies in East Asia, a pure float is not desirable because of a potential for excessive volatility and misalignment. Nor is a hard peg desirable except in small open economies like Hong Kong and Brunei. However, the region is beginning to take action to coordinate exchange rate policies – for example, through the ASEAN Task Force on ASEAN Currency and Exchange Rate Mechanism, established in March 2001.

Moving forward

More effective regional surveillance

There are already several forums for information sharing, policy dialogue, and economic surveillance in the region,[31] but none is effective at this point. To be effective, the surveillance process needs to put more emphasis on technical discussions and create an environment for serious policy discussions by taking an appropriate balance between consensus, non-interference and good manners on one hand and strong peer pressure on the other. The surveillance process must encourage frank discussions on the technical substance without being abrasive and confrontational.

This process is particularly important as the CMI may develop into an important source of financial facilities and the ASEAN+3 ERPD process will have to be strengthened beyond the peer review process. While this may imply a challenge in the tradition of a presumption of non-interference in domestic affairs, ASEAN+3 policymakers need to appreciate the necessity of constructive engagement. One feasible option in this direction would be to set up a technically competent third party unit. Its role would be to assist the ERPD process by providing high-quality and in-depth economic reviews and assessments, timely identification of emerging issues and vulnerabilities affecting the region, and effective policy advice.

It is important to provide sufficient incentives for countries in the region to participate in the economic surveillance process. Each economy in the region must be convinced that going through the surveillance process focusing on its own economy would be to its benefit because it sends positive signs to the international community and investors and helps establish its own credibility and reputation. In addition, potential recipients of regional liquidity can benefit from participation in the surveillance process through implementation of liquidity support at times of a crisis or contagion.

Regional bond market development

The region needs to develop bond markets as an alternative source of financing in view of the heavy dependence on bank-based financing. In particular, the development of market infrastructure for local currency-denominated bonds is desirable to reduce the double mismatch problem – that is, the mismatch of maturity and currency, which was at the heart of the East Asian currency crisis. The basic idea is to mobilise the region's vast pool of savings to be intermediated directly to regional long-term investment, without going through financial intermediaries outside the region. Regional financial intermediation through bond markets would diversify the modes of financing in the region and reduce the double mismatch.

Once such markets become sufficiently deep and liquid, foreign investors would also be induced to purchase Asian currency-denominated bonds, thereby enabling the region to overcome the so-called 'original sin' problem.[32] This effort should begin first at the country level with sovereign bonds and then private bonds, and second at the regional level to encourage the development of regional bond markets. At the country level, a useful step would be to allow non-residents – such as multinational corporations – to issue local currency-denominated bonds to satisfy their local financing needs. At the regional level, the countries must make concerted efforts and coordinate on clearance and settlement, information disclosure, accounting and auditing standards, and rating agencies. In addition, the region may embark on the issuance of common currency-denominated bonds, such as Asian Currency Unit (ACU) bonds (see below).

Regional reserve pooling

The CMI BSAs are to be reviewed in 2004. At that time, East Asian countries may decide to amend the arrangement, to make it permanent, or even to begin the process to transform it into a more formal institution like a regional monetary fund. One option is for each monetary authority of the ASEAN+3 group to set aside a modest share of its foreign exchange reserves and place the funds in a common pool with the other 12 central banks. The funds could be drawn to support countries that are affected by currency speculation, contagion or crisis. Such regional reserve pooling makes sense because Japan, China and others collectively have abundant foreign exchange reserves and could economise on their use through the establishment of a common pool.

Several mechanisms have been proposed for such reserve pooling schemes. They include a Framework for Regional Monetary Stability (IIMA 2000), an East Asian Fund (Ito et al. 1999) and two versions of a regional financing arrangement (Yoshitomi and Shirai 2000; Chaipravat 2001). To go beyond the CMI and operate such a formal institution for foreign exchange reserve pooling, the region must address the earlier concern that an AMF that could lend too generously with too little conditionality might create moral hazard for the government at the receiving end as well as for investors with stakes in the countries in question. To minimise moral hazard, it is essential to strengthen the surveillance process, improve the capacity to formulate appropriate adjustment policy in the event of liquidity provision and, to the extent necessary, enforce effective private sector involvement.

Regional common unit of account

It is time to introduce a regional common unit of account in East Asia. One way to do this is to construct a basket of regional currencies that include 13 currencies for ASEAN+3 – the Japanese yen, the Chinese renminbi, the South Korean won, the Singapore dollar, the Malaysian ringgit, the Thai baht and so forth. Just like the European currency unit under the EMS (1979–98), the weights of the regional currencies would reflect the relative importance of the countries in the region. Such a currency basket could be called the Asian currency unit (ACU). The ACU could be used to denominate economic transactions (trade and capital flows) and asset stocks (foreign exchange reserves and cross-border bonds) and to measure the degree of each currency's exchange rate deviation from the regional average.

When the regional emerging market economies adopt a G-3 currency basket arrangement based on the Japanese yen, the US dollar and the euro, the ACU will also become a *de facto* basket of the G-3 currencies. This will create a zone of currency stability within East Asia. Even without a G-3 currency basket arrangement, creation of an ACU would be a significant step toward closer financial cooperation in the region.

Exchange rate coordination

There have been several proposals for developing a cooperative framework for regional exchange rate stability.

First, McKinnon (2001) and Mundell (2001) have suggested using the US dollar standard to achieve regional exchange rate stability. The advantage is that the emerging East Asian economies can use simply the most dominant international currency; the US dollar standard is simple and involves no additional cost in ensuring exchange rate stability extra- and intra-regionally. However, it would result in undesirable fluctuations in effective exchange rates in the face of volatile movements in yen–dollar exchange rates.

Second, Williamson (1999a,b), Kawai and Takagi (2000), French and Japanese Staff (2001), Ito (2001), Kawai (2001, 2002) and Ogawa and Ito (2002) have suggested a G-3 currency basket system in which a currency's central rate is linked to a basket of major currencies – the US dollar, the Japanese yen, and the euro – rather than to the US dollar alone. Initially, the tightness of the link and the currency weights could be left to each authority's choice. As the authorities realised the importance of intra-regional exchange rate stability, there could be closer coordination on the choice. The virtue of this system is that it would prevent excessive fluctuations in effective exchange rates in the face of volatile yen–dollar or euro–dollar rate movements, while allowing the currencies of East Asian countries some flexibility to move within a certain range. It is also consistent with inflation targeting if the latter is defined appropriately (Box 7.2).

Finally, there is a view that a basket system based on the G-3 currencies is unfair because it gives the Japanese yen special advantages by treating it asymmetrically vis-à-vis other East Asian currencies. Wang (2002) suggests that, in the spirit of regional cooperation, a more symmetric approach, such as the joint formation of a common currency union like the EMS or the euro area, is more appropriate.

Such an approach makes sense but only in the long run. In the long run, the region may develop a common currency arrangement, like the euro regime. However, it cannot be expected to develop in the very near future because there is no convergence of macroeconomic conditions and economic

---

Box 7.2   Recommending a G-3 currency basket system for emerging East Asia

The yen–US dollar exchange rate has been fluctuating, reflecting market demand and supply. China, South Korea and a few other economies in East Asia often express their concerns over the weakness of the yen when the yen happens to depreciate, but do not complain when the yen appreciates. Given that yen–dollar volatility is expected to continue, emerging market economies in East Asia are encouraged to adopt exchange rate regimes that can cope with such volatility. A reasonable move may be a shift to a free float with inflation targeting. But many economies in the region, including those that have already shifted to floating rate regimes such as South Korea and Thailand, do not want to see wild fluctuations of their exchange rates. They prefer a certain degree of exchange rate stability due to their 'fear of floating'. This fear is understandable. For outward-oriented development and growth, relatively stable exchange rates are desirable. The emerging market economies in the region are better off by moving to a *de facto* managed float, with the central rate linked to a basket of the world's major currencies: the US dollar, the yen, and the euro. This will allow the effective exchange rate to remain relatively stable in the face of volatile yen–dollar or euro–dollar exchange rates. A G-3 currency basket system preserves both flexibility and stability, promoting trade, foreign direct investment and economic development. Inflation targeting with a band can be consistent with the basket system if the target inflation rate is a weighted average of the G-3 inflation rates, with the inflation weights set equal to the currency basket weights.

(Kawai and Takagi 2000)

structures and systems. A monetary union would require relatively closely coordinated economic policies and similar market infrastructures to be in place long before it was implemented. A more realistic approach would be for emerging East Asian countries to shift to a currency basket system now, thereby minimising the impact of yen–dollar exchange rate volatility on their economies. They could then start to build institutions, strive for deeper economic interdependence, and achieve economic convergence for future monetary integration.

CONCLUDING REMARKS

Regional financial cooperation in East Asia is still in its infancy. Institutions and initiatives are not sufficiently developed for significant regional economic integration. Nonetheless, some important steps have been taken. The CMI is dealing with the issues of regional liquidity support, and several forums have been created for information sharing, policy dialogue and economic surveillance among the financial authorities. As yet, there have been no visible steps towards exchange rate stabilisation or for macroeconomic policy coordination. East Asian countries maintain open regionalism in the global system governed by the WTO, the IMF and the World Bank, while keeping close dialogues with the Americas and the EU.

Further regional cooperation will require freer movements of goods, services and labour; convergence of per capita incomes, economic structures and systems, and institutions; and creation of a sound financial system and development of deeper capital markets. A stronger surveillance process is essential not only for better information sharing and policy dialogue, but also for in-depth understanding of the region's economies, more effective policymaking to avoid crises, and better responses to a crisis once it breaks out. The CMI could lead to the creation of a more formal, reserve pooling institution; then minimising the moral hazard problem would be an important challenge for the region. A framework for exchange rate and monetary policy coordination will have to be developed.

Regional financial cooperation in East Asia is unlikely to be of a North American type, where a US-centred, asymmetric approach has driven regional joint initiatives – mainly in trade and investment liberalisation. For East Asia, a European-style, symmetric approach would be more realistic. Japan and China are big powers in Asia, but neither is dominant. Regional financial cooperation can be beneficial to all economies given the potential for dynamic economic growth and the availability of abundant financial resources. Japan, China and South Korea and ASEAN must work jointly towards further financial cooperation in the region. Strong political will and a vision for regional integration will be required for such endeavours.

NOTES

This is a revised version of the paper presented to the Seminar on 'Regional Economic, Financial and Monetary Co-operation: The European and Asian Experiences,' organised by the European Central Bank in Frankfurt am Main, 15–16 April 2002. The views expressed in this paper are those of the authors and do not necessarily represent the views of the Japanese government.

1   See Eichengreen (1999) and Kenen (2001) for a discussion of reforms of the international financial architecture.
2   Similar approaches might be needed for private debt instruments as well, because of the surge in private-to-private capital flows – as was the case in East Asia.
3   The FSAP is intended to strengthen the monitoring and assessment of financial systems in view of the fact that financial sector weaknesses have played an important role in damaging a country's overall economic health.
4   See also Bird and Rajan (2002).
5   Some countries generate more contagion effects than do other countries. Allocating resources to only one country in the midst of a regional crisis might not be very effective, because other neighbouring countries may suffer contagion. Moreover, preventing and containing crises in the countries that generate more spillover is relatively more effective for controlling regional and global shocks. See Kawai et al. (2001).
6   For example, see Feldstein (1998).
7   Sakakibara and Yamakawa (2001) provide a comprehensive treatment of these issues.
8   The trade intensity index measures closeness between regions (in the case of Table 7.1, closeness among economies within a region) relative to the region's weight in the global economy. It is interesting to note that MERCOSUR has a trade intensity index that is higher than any other regional grouping.
9   AFTA is complemented by the ASEAN Industrial Complementation Scheme for investment liberalisation. This scheme has moved more slowly than AFTA; its main focus is on the rationalisation of the automotive industry.
10   More precisely, the Japan–Singapore agreement is called the 'Agreement between Japan and the Republic of Singapore for a New-Age Economic Partnership' and goes beyond a conventional FTA.
11   These include China with Hong Kong; Hong Kong with New Zealand (and China); South Korea with Chile; Singapore with Australia, the United States, Canada, Mexico and Chile; Thailand with Australia; Australia with the United States (and Singapore and Thailand); and New Zealand with Chile (and Hong Kong).
12   More specifically, Eichengreen and Bayoumi (1999) have found that two groups of economies in the region – one for Japan, South Korea and Taiwan, and another for Hong Kong, Indonesia, Malaysia, Singapore and possibly Thailand – are natural groups of countries that are closely integrated. See also Bayoumi and Eichengreen (1994) and Bayoumi et al. (2000).
13   See specifically a paper by Goto (2002) in IIMA (2002) as well as Goto and Kawai (2001).
14   See Kenen (1994), and Hamada and Kawai (1997).
15   In 1985, when the US dollar was overvalued and the US current account deficits were deemed unsustainable, the foreign exchange market intervention and macroeconomic policies of the United States, Japan and Germany were coordinated in order to guide the US dollar downward, thereby containing the protectionist pressure in the United States. Once the US dollar began to decline rapidly, the G-3 countries attempted to prevent the free fall of the dollar so as to avoid a hard landing of the US economy.

16 See for example Eichengreen (2001).

17 The ADB is also invited for discussions with the finance ministers and/or finance and central bank deputies.

18 See ASEAN+3 Heads of State/Government, 'Joint Statement on East Asia Cooperation,' Manila, 29 November 1999, available at < http://www.aseansec.org/5469.htm>.

19 A task force called the 'ASEAN+3 Study Group to Examine Ways of Enhancing Effectiveness of Economic Reviews and Policy Dialogues' has recommended a two-phase approach. In phase one, the existing arrangement for economic reviews and policy dialogue is strengthened by making the current ERPD process more credible and subject to serious discussion by finance ministers and their deputies. In phase two, an enhanced ERPD process will be introduced with support from an independent, professional third party that prepares reviews, assessments and issue papers on emerging problems affecting the region. It has also been proposed that the process should consider soliciting inputs from international financial institutions.

20 Many, but not all, of these economies participated in the Thai financial package – Japan, Australia, China, Hong Kong, Malaysia, Singapore, Brunei, Indonesia and South Korea.

21 See Asian Finance and Central Bank Deputies, 'A New Framework for Enhanced Asian Regional Cooperation to Promote Financial Stability', Manila, 18–19 November 1997, available at <http://www.mof.go.jp/english/if/if000a.htm>.

22 The IMF's Regional Office for Asia and the Pacific provides a technical secretariat function for the MFG.

23 While this forum is considered the most influential for regional central banks, it has its own weaknesses such as irregularity of meeting schedules and lack of continuity. According to Eichengreen (2001), each meeting has a different theme, and themes have ranged over everything from social safety nets to capital flows.

24 A member's swap request for temporary liquidity or balance of payments assistance is confirmed through the agent bank, which informs and consults with the rest of the members to assess and process the request as expeditiously as possible. The agent bank is appointed on a rotation basis in alphabetical order for a term of two years; its primary task is to coordinate ASA implementation. The ASA was activated by Indonesia in 1979, Malaysia in 1980, Thailand in 1980, and the Philippines in 1981 (Henning 2002).

25 More precisely, the term of swap arrangements is for a period of one, two, or three months and renewable, at most once, for up to three months.

26 In principle, there could be 30 bilateral agreements between any one of China, Japan and South Korea, on the one hand, and the 10 ASEAN members on the other, plus three additional agreements among the three non-ASEAN participants. In practice, the main agreements have so far been reached (or are close to agreement) among China, Japan and South Korea, as well as between any one of the non-ASEAN countries and the former crisis-affected members of ASEAN.

27 This is the sum of all BSAs, including the amount that Japan committed under the New Miyazawa Initiative – a total of US$7.5 billion, or US$5 billion with South Korea and US$2.5 billion with Malaysia – except that two-way BSAs are doubled for calculation purposes. Excluding the amount committed under the New Miyazawa Initiative, the total sum is US$31.5 billion.

28 While Indonesia has proposed BSAs with China and South Korea, actual negotiations have yet to begin.

29 Although up to 10 per cent of the BSA drawings under the CMI can be provided for a limited period without an IMF program, subsequent disbursements have to be linked to an IMF program and, therefore, to the government's willingness to

meet IMF conditionalities. The participating countries agreed to review the issue of the IMF linkage and other main principles in May 2004.

30 While recognising the benefits of such an arrangement, the group has not agreed on whether the financing should function as the first line of defence, the second line of defence, or both, whether the financing arrangement is for a short term or a medium term, and who should play the coordinating role at the time of a crisis.

31 Some duplications are unavoidable.

32 'Original sin,' as hypothesised by Eichengreen and Hausmann (1999), is a situation where emerging economy residents cannot borrow abroad in domestic currency or borrow long term, even domestically. Hence domestic banks and corporations tend to face a currency or maturity mismatch or both, thus facing balance sheet vulnerabilities to sharp changes in exchange rates and/or interest rates.

REFERENCES

Bayoumi, T. and B. Eichengreen (1994) 'One Money or Many? Analyzing the Prospects for Monetary Unification in Various Parts of the World', *Princeton Studies in International Finance*, No. 76, International Finance Section, Princeton University.

Bayoumi, T., B. Eichengreen and P. Mauro (2000) 'On Regional Monetary Arrangements for ASEAN', *Journal of the Japanese and International Economies*, 14: 121–148.

Bird, G. and R.S. Rajan (2002) 'The Evolving Asian Financial Architecture', *Essays in International Economics*, 226 (February), International Economics Section, Princeton University, Princeton.

Chaipravat, O. (2001) 'Towards a Regional Financing Arrangement in East Asia', paper presented to the ADBI/FIMA Symposium, 'From the Asian Financial Crisis of 1997 to a Regional Financing Arrangement' (10 May), Honolulu.

Eichengreen, B. (1999) *Toward a New International Financial Architecture: A Practical Post-Asia Agenda* (February), Institute for International Economics, Washington, DC.

—— (2001) 'Hanging Together? On Monetary and Financial Cooperation in Asia', mimeo (October), University of California, Berkeley.

Eichengreen, B. and T. Bayoumi (1999) 'Is Asia an Optimum Currency Area? Can It Become One?', in: S. Collignon, J. Pisani-Ferry and Y.C. Park (eds.), *Exchange Rate Policies in Emerging Asian Countries*, London: Routledge, 347–66.

Eichengreen, B. and R. Hausmann (1999) 'Exchange Rates and Financial Fragility', *NBER Working Paper*, No. 7418 (November), National Bureau of Economic Research, Cambridge.

Feldstein, M. (1998) 'Refocusing the IMF', *Foreign Affairs*, 77: 20–33.

Frankel, J.A (1999) 'No Single Currency Regime Is Right for All Countries or at All Times', *Essays In International Finance*, No. 215 (August), International Finance Section, Princeton University.

French and Japanese Staff, Ministries of Finance (2001) 'Exchange Rate Regimes for Emerging Market Economies', Discussion Paper (14 January), Paris and Tokyo.

Goto, J. (2002) 'Economic Preconditions for Monetary Cooperation and Surveillance in East Asia', in Institute for International Monetary Affairs (ed.), *Report on the Study Group on Strengthening Financial Cooperation and Surveillance* (February), 1–26, Tokyo.

Goto, J. and M. Kawai (2001) 'Macroeconomic Interdependence in East Asia', paper presented to the international conference on 'Economic Interdependence: Shaping Asia-Pacific in the 21st Century' (22–23 March), International Monetary Fund and World Bank, Tokyo.

Hamada, K. and M. Kawai (1997) 'International Economic Policy Coordination: Theory and Policy Implications', in Michele U. Fratianni, Dominick Salvatore, and Jurgen von Hagen (eds), *Handbook of Comparative Economic Policies, Volume 5, Macroeconomic Policy in Open Economies*, Westport and London: Greenwood Press, 87–147.

Henning, R.C (2002) 'East Asian Financial Cooperation', *Policy Analyses in International Economics*, No. 68 (September), Institute for International Economics, Washington, DC.

Institute for International Monetary Affairs (IIMA) (2000) *Workshop on the Framework for Regional Monetary Stabilisation in East Asia* (July), Tokyo.

—— (IIMA) (2002) Report on the Study Group on Strengthening Financial Cooperation and Surveillance: Kobe Research Project (February), commissioned by the Ministry of Finance Japan, Tokyo.

Ito, T. (2001) 'The Role of the Yen in East Asia', paper presented to the international conference on 'Monetary Outlook on East Asia in an Integrating World Economy' (5–6 September), Chulalongkorn University, Bangkok.

Ito, T., E. Ogawa and Y. Sasaki (1999) 'Establishment of the East Asian Fund', Institute for International Monetary Affairs (ed.) *Stabilisation of Currencies and Financial Systems in East Asia and International Financial Cooperation*, Tokyo.

Kawai, M. (2001) 'Recommending a Currency Basket System for Emerging East Asia', paper presented to the conference on 'Regional Financial Arrangements in East Asia' (12–13 November), Australian National University, Canberra.

—— (2002) 'Exchange Rate Arrangements in East Asia: Lessons from the 1997–98 Currency Crisis', *Monetary and Economic Studies*, Special Edition, 20 (December), Institute for Monetary and Economic Studies, Bank of Japan, 167-204.

Kawai, M., R. Newfarmer and S. Schmukler (2001) 'Crisis and Contagion in East Asia: Nine Lessons', Policy Research Working Paper, No. 2610 (June), World Bank, Washington, DC.

Kawai, M. and S. Takagi (2000) 'Proposed Strategy for a Regional Exchange Rate Arrangement in Post-Crisis East Asia', Policy Research Working Paper, No. 2502 (December), World Bank, Washington, DC.

—— (2003) 'Rethinking Capital Controls: The Malaysian Experience', PRI Discussion Paper Series, No. 03A-05 (May), Policy Research Institute, Japanese Ministry of Finance, Tokyo. [A revised version of the paper presented to the international conference on 'Monetary Outlook on East Asia in an Integrating World Economy' (September 5-6, 2001), Chulalongkorn University, Bangkok.]

Kawai, M. and S. Urata (2002) 'Trade and Foreign Direct Investment in East Asia', paper presented to a conference on 'Linkages in East Asia: Implications for Currency Regimes and Policy Dialogue' (September 23-24), Seoul.

Kenen, P.B. (1994) *The International Economy*, 3rd edition, Cambridge: Cambridge University Press.

—— (2001) *The International Financial Architecture: What's New? What's Missing?*, Washington DC: Institute for International Economics.

Krueger, A. (2002) 'New Approaches to Sovereign Debt Restructuring: An Update on Our Thinking', paper presented to a conference on 'Sovereign Debt Workouts: Hopes and Hazards' (April 1), Institute for International Economics, Washington, DC.

McKinnon, R.I. (2001) 'After the Crisis, the East Asian Dollar Standard Resurrected', paper presented to the international conference on 'Monetary Outlook on East Asia in an Integrating World Economy' (September 5-6), Chulalongkorn University, Bangkok.

Mundell, R. (2001) 'Currency Area Formation and the Asian Region', paper presented to the international conference on 'Monetary Outlook on East Asia in an Integrating World Economy' (September 5-6), Chulalongkorn University, Bangkok.

Ogawa, E. and T. Ito (2002) 'On the Desirability of a Regional Basket Currency Arrangement', *Journal of the Japanese and International Economies*, 16: 317–334.

Sakakibara, E. and S. Smith Yamakawa (2001) 'Regional Integration in East Asia: Challenges and Opportunities', mimeo, Global Security Research Center, Keio University, Tokyo.

Wang, T. (2002) 'Policy Recommendations on How to Strengthen Financial Cooperation in Asia', Institute for International Monetary Affairs (ed.), *Report on the Study Group on Strengthening Financial Cooperation and Surveillance* (February), 198-211, Tokyo.

Williamson, J. (1999a) 'The Case for a Common Basket Peg for East Asian Currencies', Stefan Collignon, Jean Pisani-Ferry and Yung Chul Park (eds.), *Exchange Rate Policies in Emerging Asian Countries*, London and New York: Routledge, 327–343.

—— (1999b) 'Future Exchange Rate Regimes for Developing East Asia: Exploring the Policy Options', mimeo (May), South Asia Region, World Bank, Washington, DC.

World Bank (1998) *East Asia: The Road to Recovery*. Washington, DC.

—— (2000) *East Asia: Recovery and Beyond*. Washington, DC.

Yoshitomi, M. and S. Shirai (2000) 'Policy Recommendations for Preventing Another Capital Account Crisis', Technical Background Paper (July 7), Asian Development Bank Institute, Tokyo.

8 The management of financial crises: theory and policy

Prasanna Gai

INTRODUCTION

The recent spate of financial crises in emerging market economies has focused attention on the importance of improving the international framework for crisis management. In a recent speech, Krueger (2001) makes the case for a 'new' global approach to sovereign debt restructuring involving the International Monetary Fund (IMF), and calls for a framework analogous to corporate insolvency regimes like the US bankruptcy court. In Europe and Canada, the merits of sovereign debt standstills and other policy measures that target short-term debt are currently topics of hot debate. And in East Asia, concerted efforts are being made to create stronger regional financial arrangements to deal with temporary liquidity shortfalls.

Despite the emphasis accorded to the topic in the policy sphere, theoretical work on financial crisis management has developed slowly. There has been little substantive progress on the topic since Sachs (1995), Cornelli and Felli (1995) and Eichengreen and Portes (1995) drew informal attention to the analogy between domestic insolvency and international debt workouts. In part, this reflects the exposure of the world financial system to new kinds of risks. The theoretical literature is only just beginning to address issues of contagion, financial fragility, and the potentially catastrophic impact of small exogenous shocks.[1] But it also reflects a tendency for analyses to focus on mistakes in government policy, and to seek explanations of crisis mainly through macroeconomic channels or by appeal to multiple equilibria.[2] This has limited study of the welfare costs of crisis. Welfare-oriented analyses about the best policies for managing financial crises and the design of appropriate institutional structures are more naturally posed using a microeconomic approach. Recent theoretical advances in the literature on coordination games, incentives, sovereign debt and the pricing of risky assets have much to contribute to a better understanding of crisis management policy.

This paper explores some of the micro-foundations of financial crises and highlights the implications for crisis management policy. The central theme of the paper is that creditor coordination problems result in disorderly workouts and/or the premature liquidation of assets during a financial crisis. This generates deadweight losses that are potentially costly, *ex post*. But public policy measures that seek to ameliorate these inefficiencies must, as noted by Eichengreen and Portes (1995), strike a balance between *ex ante* and *ex post* efficiency. They should encourage adherence to the *ex ante* provisions of loan contracts while seeking to maximise the *ex post* value of the debtor in the event that the terms cannot be met. Attention to this tradeoff and pinpointing the economic costs of crisis are, arguably, central to any serious assessment of proposals put forward by financial architects. I assess the recent proposal to introduce orderly debt workouts, and explore the consequences of such changes in the architecture for creditor behaviour. The finer detail of microeconomic modelling also allows the role played by the IMF in shaping debtor and creditor incentives to be cast in sharper relief.

The paper proceeds as follows. First, I sketch a model that nests the key features of earlier crisis models, but which is better suited to allow an assessment of welfare losses and the impact of different public policy measures. Then I examine the balance between *ex ante* and *ex post* efficiency, and illustrate the circumstances under which official sector intervention can be beneficial. Next I consider the merits of some frequently encountered criticisms of formal crisis management mechanisms, and argue that they do not constitute a decisive argument against a coherent debt restructuring framework. Finally, I draw some policy lessons for East Asia.

THE CAUSES OF CRISIS

Before tackling the normative question of optimal policy towards crisis, it is important to address the positive question of the causes of crisis. The theoretical literature on financial crises is typically divided into two strands. Both focus on currency crises, though the methods of analysis are applicable to capital market crises more generally. This section reconciles the key features of these theoretical models, highlighting some welfare and policy implications.

A cross-generational representation

'First-generation' models were motivated by the Latin American crises of the late 1970s and 1980s. These crises were typically preceded by over-expansive macroeconomic policies that were inconsistent with the prevailing fixed exchange rate regime. Mistakes in government policy provide the analytical bedrock for these models.[3] The actual and expected deterioration of fundamentals – for example, uncontrolled domestic credit expansion – *pushes* the economy into crisis. With rational expectations about these fundamentals among atomistic investors, efficient asset-price arbitrage ensures that the currency collapse is anticipated and brought forward to today.

The Exchange Rate Mechanism crises of the early 1990s cast doubt on the notion that weak economic fundamentals and irresponsible credit expansion are the main factors behind currency crises. This prompted a second strand of literature – 'second-generation' models – to suggest that sound fundamentals, on any definition, may be neither a sufficient nor indeed a necessary condition for averting crisis.[4] The crisis mechanism in these models is a coordination failure among international investors that leads to multiple equilibria. If no one believes that a crisis is about to occur, there will be no speculative attack. But if everyone believes that a crisis is about to occur, it becomes optimal for each investor to attack if others do. An economy can thus be *pulled* into crisis by the actions of fleeing investors, in much the same way as a Diamond–Dybvig (Diamond and Dybvig 1983) bank 'run'. And because countries can be driven into crisis independently of fundamentals (that is, by extraneous variables or 'sunspots') there may be a range of seemingly robust fundamentals over which an economy is susceptible to a financial crisis.

Chui et al. (2002) capture the key features of both classes of model in a simple liquidity crisis framework. There are two types of agent: a single debtor and a large number of atomistic creditors. The debtor is a sovereign borrower which would like to invest in a project that takes two periods to complete. The project is financed from the debtor's own resource endowment (illiquid assets, E) and from foreign borrowing (L). Both of these inputs are fixed prior to the start of the project. The returns to the investment project depend on the factor inputs, and on the outcome of a random productivity shock, θ. The parameter θ is assumed to be a summary measure of fundamentals that is normally distributed. So gross income from the project is given by

$$y = \theta (E+L) \tag{1}$$

Creditors lend to the debtor at an interest rate, r_L. The debt contract between the debtor and creditors is assumed to take a particular form. Specifically, it gives creditors the option to withdraw their funds before the project is completed. Thus, the project is effectively financed by short-term loans that need to be rolled over. If creditors choose to exercise their option and refuse to roll over their loan ('flee'), they face an exit cost, c. If they choose to stay for the full two periods ('stay'), then they receive repayment with interest if the debtor is solvent ('repay'), but nothing if the debtor is insolvent and fails ('default'). The payoff matrix for each representative creditor under the four possible scenarios is shown in Table 8.1.

The debtor's ability to pay depends on the returns to the project. This, in turn, depends crucially on two factors: the outcome of the productivity shock, θ; and the proportion of creditors that flee, λ. In the event of creditors fleeing, the debtor meets these payments by drawing down liquid reserves, A. But fleeing also causes disruption to the investment project. This can be thought of as the cost of prematurely liquidating the investment project – a half-built bridge or an abandoned factory. Denote the marginal cost of this disruption

Table 8.1　Payoff matrix for creditors

			Debtor action	
		Time of payoff	Repay	Default
Creditor action	Flee	Stage 1	$L(1-c)$	$L(1-c)$
	Stay	Stage 2	$L(1+r_L)$	0

by α. The solvency constraint facing the debtor at the end of the game, which determines the ability to repay, is:

$$\theta(E+L)-\alpha\lambda L+(1+r_A)(A-\lambda L)\geq(1-\lambda)(1+r_L)L \tag{2}$$

where r_A is the rate of interest on A. The left-hand side of Equation 2 defines the debtor's return on the project at the end of period 2, while the right-hand side defines the debtor's debt repayments. Default will occur only when the inequality in Equation 2 is violated, that is, when gross repayments exceed gross income.

If creditors have perfect knowledge of θ before deciding on their rollover decision, we can partition the space of fundamentals into three regions of interest using the solvency constraint. If fundamentals are particularly weak, there will be values of θ for which the country always defaults. Denote by θ_1 that value of θ such that the country will be unable to meet debt repayments even if all creditors choose to remain in the country ($\lambda=0$)

$$\theta_1=[(1+r_L)L/(E+L)]-[(1+r_A)A/(E+L)] \tag{3}$$

If $\theta<\theta_1$, it is always optimal for the individual creditor to liquidate his position, even if all other creditors roll over their loans. Similarly, denote by θ_2 that value of θ such that the country is able to repay its loans even if all creditors flee. If $\lambda=1$,

$$\theta_2=[\alpha L/(E+L)]+[(1+r_A)L/(E+L)]-[(1+r_A)A/(E+L)]. \tag{4}$$

If $\theta>\theta_2$, it is always optimal for creditors to remain in the country. This defines the range of fundamentals over which the economy is solvent irrespective of the investors' expectations.

When θ lies in the range $[\theta_1, \theta_2]$, a coordination problem among creditors arises. This stems from the presence of strategic complementarities in creditor payoffs (that is, the decision to flee by creditor i raises the marginal profitability of fleeing for investor j). If all other creditors opt to stay, then the payoff to staying, $L(1+r_L)$, exceeds the payoff from early liquidation, $L(1-c)$. But if all creditors opt to flee, the payoff from staying is 0, which is less than the payoff from early liquidation. In the presence of complete information, λ and θ cannot be simultaneously determined. And with many creditors, there is a potentially infinite number of equilibria when fundamentals lie in the range $[\theta_1, \theta_2]$.

The two generations of crisis model can be represented schematically (Figure 8.1). Below θ_1, the economy is fundamentally insolvent. The zone to the left of θ_1 defines the range of fundamentals over which the economy might be subject to a first-generation crisis, with the insolvency trigger being determined by the debtor's net liquidity position. It is the zone of fundamentals-based crises. The zone to the right of θ_2 can be regarded as a region of strong solvency where the debtor can withstand a run. With fundamentals in the range $[\theta_1, \theta_2]$ the economy is susceptible to a beliefs-based crisis resulting from creditor coordination failure – the economy behaves as in a second-generation model.

Welfare costs of crisis

The sharp distinction between fundamental and belief-based theories of crisis does not sit comfortably with the evidence from recent crises in Asia and elsewhere. Fischer (1999) suggested that both fundamentals and expectations played a role and interacted in a subtle fashion. Some models – such as

Figure 8.1 Classification of fundamentals

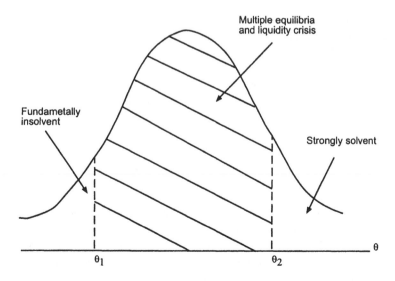

Krugman (1999) and Chang and Velasco (1998) – allow for an explicit interaction between fundamentals and beliefs, so that crises can be based partly on beliefs and partly on fundamentals, rather than on one or the other in isolation. They also broaden the notion of fundamentals to allow for micro-prudential policies and frictions induced by government guarantees. But such models again generate multiple equilibria. This poses two problems for policymakers. First, if the trigger for crisis is a random, unpredictable event (a 'sunspot'), it hinders analysis because it is difficult to determine what policy measures might best be put in place to avert crisis. Second, with multiple equilibria, it is difficult to conduct meaningful welfare analysis of crisis management measures, because equilibrium is not precisely defined.

Recent work (Morris and Shin 1998, 2000) tackles this shortcoming. These papers argue that second-generation models make the unrealistic assumption that economic actors have common knowledge of the underlying fundamentals. Once small amounts of imperfect information across creditors are introduced, a unique equilibrium can be obtained in the coordination problem region $[\theta_1, \theta_2]$. At the interim stage, the creditor observes a private signal and updates his beliefs concerning his expected payoff and the possible signals obtained by other creditors. Based on this information he decides to stay or flee. If the signal is below a certain trigger value (determined in equilibrium), then it is optimal for him to run. If a sufficient number of creditors also have signals below this trigger, the run is sufficient to trigger default. Observing this, all remaining creditors run as well. Fundamentals and beliefs interact explicitly – the weaker the fundamentals, the more fragile the situation becomes in the sense that fewer participants are required to trigger the crisis. The weaker the underlying macroeconomic outlook, the more susceptible is an economy to a creditor run. There is a systematic mapping between fundamentals and the probability of crisis, even though the mapping is a complicated, non-linear one.

Chui et al. (2002) formally demonstrate the uniqueness result in the model outlined above. But the welfare implications of the approach can be given a simple graphical treatment. The unique value for fundamentals, θ^*, at which crisis is triggered is shown in Figure 8.2. This lies above θ_1, the value at which a fundamentals-based solvency problem occurs. The welfare cost of creditor coordination is directly related to the shaded area between θ_1 and θ^* in Figure 8.2. It reflects the cost of liquidation, as the disruption caused by fleeing creditors results in lost production in stage 2. When creditors have to realise the value of their assets in a hurry, they are typically unable to realise the full value that they would receive if they could wait until maturity. This is captured in a reduced-form fashion by the parameter α.

Since closed form solutions are typically unavailable, the size of the welfare burden must be obtained from numerical simulations. Because α is difficult to gauge in practice, Chui et al. (2002) consider a range of illustrative values. When $\alpha=0.06$ – that is, every dollar withdrawn by creditors reduces the return on investment by 6 cents – the welfare costs of creditor coordination

Figure 8.2 Unique equilibrium

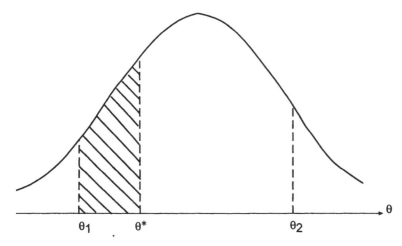

θ_1 θ^* θ_2 θ

are nearly 10 per cent of the debtor's *ex ante* expected output, given plausible choices for the other parameters. By contrast, if $\alpha=0.4$, these costs rise to some two-thirds of expected output. Although the deadweight losses posed by a creditor run are difficult to pin down precisely, such results appear plausible. Direct empirical attempts to measure the output costs of recent crises have suggested that the costs of financial crises may lie between 10 per cent and 20 per cent of annual pre-crisis GDP.[5]

A natural criticism of models that are based on a Diamond–Dybvig liquidity framework is that they assume that the moneys leaving the project when creditors flee cannot be replaced. Does a secondary market in debt contracts resolve the problem of deadweight losses associated with liquidation? After all, if assets are sold during a run, the seller 'loss' is the buyer 'gain' *ex post* – there is a transfer of value, not an economic cost. Allen and Gale (1998) argue that efficiency losses may arise nevertheless. This is because sub-optimal risk sharing leads to transfers being made only in the worst states of the world. Market provision of liquidity to a distressed debtor will be provided only if the terms are sufficiently profitable. So the country gets a bad price in states of the world where its demand for liquidity is high, but a good price in those states where demand for liquidity is low. Financial crises are costly not because of runs per se, but because of the deadweight losses from disorderly workouts and premature liquidation of projects.

The central policy implication of the recent theoretical literature is that measures aimed at tackling creditor coordination may bring significant welfare benefits. Of the many proposals that have been put forward, I mention four.

The first is country clubs. These are standing committees of creditors that might serve as a coordinating device for creditors' actions. They can also be used to share information between the debtor and creditors, and amongst creditors themselves. G-20 policymakers recently supported the introduction of country clubs by emerging market borrowers.[6] If these help creditor coordination problems, they could help ameliorate the costs of disorderly workouts.

The second is swap arrangements. East Asian economies have actively attempted to develop bilateral and multilateral swap arrangements as part of the Chiang Mai initiative.[7] One benefit of these swap arrangements is as a confidence building measure. If the accumulation of these 'extra' reserves is publicly observed, theory suggests that speculators will anticipate that other speculators will be less aggressive in attacking the currency. So in regions of fundamentals where a self-fulfilling attack is in fact feasible, it will not occur.

The third is liquidity management. Several policy working groups have proposed a risk management framework for national balance sheet monitoring.[8] Greenspan (1999) has gone further, proposing that, as a rule of thumb, countries should hold enough foreign exchange reserves to cover a year's maturing external obligations. In terms of the framework above, lowering the short-term debt reserve ratio has a dual effect. It improves fundamentals because the trigger for solvency crisis depends importantly on net liquidity. And it also reduces the probability of belief-based crisis by positively shaping expectations of future repayment. Improvements in liquidity management thus serve to reduce the welfare costs of crisis.

The fourth is payments standstills. Recent policy discussion has considered the merits of international payments suspensions. Some have argued that standstills play a useful role in mitigating the effects of creditor runs.[9] A coherent standstill procedure may help break the circuit of self-fulfilling creditor expectations in much the same way as a credible 'bank holiday' eliminates the possibility of a bank run in the Diamond–Dybvig model. It may also help promote orderly workouts by providing time for debtors to put in place remedial policy measures, and by convincing (forcing) creditors to act in a coordinated fashion.

NEW APPROACHES TO SOVEREIGN DEBT RESTRUCTURING

The analysis outlined above assumed that the debtor could not default strategically and that the quantum of foreign lending was fixed up front. These assumptions were useful in focusing attention on the *ex post* costs of financial crisis. But this contrasts with the literature on sovereign debt theory (for example, Eaton and Gersovitz 1981) which emphasises the importance of the *ex ante* moral hazard problem of enforcing contracts. The lack of collateral means that a threat is necessary to provide the incentives for the repayment of sovereign debt. The implication is stark – the coordination problem among private creditors, and the associated economic cost for the debtor, is the feature of the international financial system that makes international lending possible. This section illustrates the incentive effects and tradeoffs in the design of sovereign debt contracts, and explores the role played by the official sector in influencing them.

Crises as market discipline – *ex ante* vs *ex post* efficiency

Gai et al. (2001) consider the interaction between a single debtor country and a continuum of small creditors. Production in the country depends on its ability to attract foreign capital. There are three dates (0, 1, and 2 respectively), during which events proceed as follows. At the initial date (date 0), the debtor is granted a loan of size L and promises to repay rL at the interim date (date 1). It is assumed that when the resources loaned are invested at date 0, the production process generates an interim output at date 1 which is used to repay creditors. The final output in date 2 depends on the amount repaid by the debtor at the interim date. If the debtor repays the full promised amount, then production is allowed to mature to date 2 without intervention from creditors. But if there is a shortfall in the amount repaid, creditors can force costly liquidation commensurate with the amount of the shortfall. If x denotes the amount repaid by the debtor at the interim date, then the proportional shortfall, s, is the amount repudiated as a proportion of the amount owed:

$$s=(rL-x)/(rL) \tag{5}$$

Output in the final date (period 2) is increasing in the scale of initial investment, L, and decreasing in the extent of costly liquidation arising from s at date 1:

$$y=(1-\alpha s)L^v \tag{6}$$

where $0<\alpha, v<1$. The parameter α again captures the extent of the damage done by the premature liquidation of creditors at date 1. If there is a repudiation of s, output in date 2 is reduced by the amount αs. The inherent coordination problem is not formally modelled, but can be thought of as a run akin to the type described above.

The output available to the debtor at the interim stage, x^{**}, is assumed to be random. The debtor may choose to repay the full amount owed if interim output is sufficient. But the debtor may instead choose not to honour its promise and repudiate some or all of its obligations, even if it can afford to pay in full. In other words, there can be 'strategic default' by the debtor. If interim output falls short of debt obligations, then the debtor is forced into defaulting on some of its debt. This means that payments shortfalls could arise from 'bad luck' defaults. Importantly, whether non-payment is strategic or due to bad luck is not verifiable for the purpose of the loan contract between debtors and creditors. More formally, suppose that x^{**} is uniformly distributed on the interval $[0, rL]$ with probability $1-\varphi$, and takes the value rL

with probability φ. The proportional natural shortfall in resources at the interim date, z, can be defined as:

$$z=(rL-x^{**})/rL \tag{7}$$

where z is a random variable that takes the value 0 with probability φ, is uniformly distributed over the interval [0,1], and can be thought of as reflecting the state of economic fundamentals in the debtor economy.

These building blocks are sufficient to characterise the optimal contract in a world without public intervention. The optimal contract solves for the amount of lending, L, that maximises expected output, net of debt repayments, taking into account the possible disruptions caused by premature liquidation; the requirement that the debtor be better off with the debt contract than without (the participation constraint); and the requirement that the optimal contract generates truthful behaviour by the debtor (the incentive compatibility constraint).

Given the realisation of z (the realised shortage in debtor country resources), the debtor decides on the amount of the actual shortfall, s, in the repayment to creditors, subject to s being no smaller than z. So the debtor's problem is to maximise

$$(1-\alpha s)L^{v}- (1-s)rL \tag{8}$$

subject to $s \geq z$. Since this expression is linear in s, the debtor would choose to repay all available resources at the interim date if $\alpha L^{v}>rL$, but would choose to repudiate all of its debt if $\alpha L^{v}<rL$. So the set of incentive constraints reduces to a single condition on the size of the loan L. The initial loan must be small enough so that $\alpha L^{v} \geq rL$,

$$L \leq (\alpha/r)^{1/(1-v)} \tag{9}$$

It remains to determine when this constraint will be binding in the optimal contract. The unconstrained maximisation problem entails solving for L that maximises

$$\varphi[L^{v}-rL]+(1-\varphi)[(1-\alpha E(z\,|\,z>0))L^{v}-(1-E(z\,|\,z>0))rL] \tag{10}$$

where $E(z\,|\,z>0)$ is the expectation of z conditional on its being strictly positive. If z is uniformly distributed on the unit interval, then $E(z\,|\,z>0)=1/2$. The first-order condition of the unconstrained problem is given by

$$vL^{v-1}[\varphi+(1-\varphi)(1-(\alpha/2))]-r[\varphi+((1-\varphi)/2)]=0 \tag{11}$$

which yields

$$L=((v/r)(2-\alpha(1-\varphi))/(1+\varphi))^{1/(1-v)} \qquad (12)$$

Thus the incentive compatibility constraint fails to bind if, and only if:

$$\alpha \geq (2v)/(1+\varphi+v(1-\varphi)) \qquad (13)$$

If α is large enough, there are no impediments to borrowing the *ex ante* optimal amount. Conversely, if it is too small, incentive problems limit the amount of borrowing. So to summarise, the solution to the optimal contract is given by

$$L^*=min\{ (\alpha/r)^{1/(1-v)}, ((v/r)(2-\alpha(1-\varphi))/(1+\varphi))^{(1/(1-v))} \} \qquad (14)$$

The intuition is straightforward. If the costs of premature liquidation, α, are large enough, there is no impediment to borrowing the *ex ante* optimal amount. The threat that arises from the coordination problem of creditors is enough to discipline the borrower to repay as much as it can. Knowing this, creditors lend the first best amount. But if α is too small – that is, if the productivity of real investment is not very sensitive to premature liquidation – then incentive problems result in the rationing of credit. This captures the point made by Corrigan (2000), Dooley (2000) and creditor groups such as the Institute of International Finance (1996), who argue that policies designed to promote orderly *ex post* crisis resolution could have the adverse effect of lowering the aggregate capital inflow to emerging economies or shortening the maturity of debt contracts.[10]

'Orderly workout' mechanisms

Although the disciplining role of the threat of a disorderly creditor run allows the borrower greater access to credit, it comes at a cost. If the borrower is genuinely unlucky and is forced into default by adverse conditions, and if the potential damage that the coordination problem inflicts on the economy, α, is large, the implications may be severe. Merely to focus on the incentive mechanism determining the access to credit markets understates the potential role that public policy can play in crisis management. Policy can potentially have a twofold effect. First, it is possible that increased scrutiny from the official sector may substitute for private sector discipline by distinguishing publicly between 'bad luck' and 'strategic' defaults. Such 'whistleblowing' can help ensure *ex ante* good behaviour by the debtor. Second, if the framework for public intervention is effective, policymakers can mitigate *ex post* coordination costs (that is, act as 'fire-fighters'). This might be achieved by providing limited official finance, mediating in workouts or endorsing temporary controls on capital outflows.

There is a legitimate question about whether policymakers, any more than private creditors, are capable of distinguishing between strategic and bad luck default. But Gai et al. (2001) demonstrate that, even taking into account such concerns, public sector actions that mitigate the costs of disorderly liquidation may be capable of generating similar levels of lending as a regime in which the threat of liquidation is the sole source of discipline on the debtor's willingness to pay. This, together with the elimination of *ex post* inefficiencies, can generate an improvement in welfare.

To illustrate this, suppose there is a third party ('the IMF' for short) which plays a role in the interim stage of the story. At date 1 it observes an imperfect signal concerning the state of the debtor's finances at that time. Specifically, through its surveillance activity, the IMF has access to a signal as to whether the borrower has sufficient resources to repay the loan in full – that is, whether z is positive or zero. Based on this information, the IMF makes a pronouncement of its views on the current state of fundamentals and reaches a judgment about the need for official intervention. The information available to the IMF is presumed to be coarse – it can receive two messages about the state of fundamentals [good, bad]. Such signals are also noisy. It is possible for the international community to make an error of judgment and incorrectly opt for intervention when, in fact, it is unnecessary. Denoting this probability by ε, we can describe the joint distribution over messages and the underlying fundamentals by the matrix in Table 8.2 below.

Crucially, in the model, the announcement by the IMF that fundamentals are bad results in the implementation of policies to limit the effects of creditor liquidation. The effects of these actions are captured in reduced form fashion by σ, which reflects the extent to which the public sector is able to reduce the output losses generated by premature liquidation. In essence, σ measures the efficacy of the official community's framework for crisis management. The framework might include the sorts of mechanisms envisaged by Krueger (2001), namely bankruptcy arrangements and officially sanctioned standstills that lock in creditors while orderly workout procedures are put in place. In addition, it could involve policies that entail limited official assistance to offset the output costs of creditor coordination, such as IMF lending into arrears.

Table 8.2 Messages and fundamentals

| | | *Message that fundamentals are* | |
		Good	*Bad*
Fundamentals	Good ($z=0$)	$\varphi(1-\varepsilon)$	$\varphi\,\varepsilon$
	Bad ($z>0$)	$(1-\varphi)\,\varepsilon$	$(1-\varphi)(1-\varepsilon)$

There are four main effects of official intervention.

First, there is an attenuation of the effect of the costs of disorderly liquidation (α). In particular, the IMF action reduces this parameter by a factor s, where $0 \geq s \geq 1$ and $s \to 0$ reflects increasing efficacy of public intervention. So output in the final period given shortfall s when the IMF has intervened is given by

$$(1 - \sigma \alpha s)L^v \tag{15}$$

Second, when a standstill is correctly called (the event represented by the bottom right-hand cell of the matrix in Table 8.2), the debtor's true resources become verifiable to the IMF, so the debtor repays within its reduced means without precipitating a costly crisis. This means that the realised shortfall, s, is equal to the true shortage of resources, given the realisation of fundamentals, z.

Third, if a standstill is called incorrectly (the event given by the top right-hand side of the matrix in Table 8.2) the IMF mistakenly attributes deliberate default as having arisen from bad luck. In this case, creditors are inappropriately locked into the workout process, the IMF acts to limit the impact of liquidation, and the debtor cheats successfully. This possibility has a cost. The greater its likelihood, the lower is the level of initial lending.

Fourth, if the IMF mistakenly fails to intervene (the bottom left-hand corner of the matrix in Table 8.2), it makes the opposite error. Even if the shortfall in payments is due to genuine bad luck, the failure to intervene exposes the country to the full impact of a creditor grab race.

The consequences of imperfect public intervention are now twofold. On the one hand, by reducing liquidation costs, the IMF can mitigate output losses when fundamentals are poor. On the other hand, there are costs from the reduced disciplining effect of a country run, leading to a lower level of initial lending. The net benefit from IMF intervention arises only when the first effect outweighs the second.

The optimal contract in the presence of the IMF is described in detail by Gai et al. (2001). The level of lending under policy intervention depends on the ability of the official sector to identify the correct state of fundamentals and its efficacy in limiting the disorderly effects of liquidation. The two factors work in different ways. As the ability of the official sector to spot a bad luck default improves ($\varepsilon \to 0$), the discipline of official surveillance increasingly substitutes for market discipline, and the level of *ex ante* lending approaches the first best. If the official sector's ability to limit the disorderly run is limited ($\sigma \to 1$), the official sector has relatively little influence over the payoffs of creditors and debtors. So the threat of punishment once again permits full access to credit. Outside these extremes, the borrower is unable to obtain full access to credit compared with a world without policy intervention.

The focus on lending is, however, only half the story. There is a beneficial aspect to public intervention, namely the ability to mitigate the *ex post* inefficiencies that result from a bad luck default. Once this is taken into account, the effects of intervention depend on the quality of the IMF's (*ex ante*) judgment and the efficacy of its *ex post* action.

Figure 8.3 illustrates the importance of the official sector's dual role as 'whistleblower' and 'fire-fighter'. It compares expected output in an IMF regime with expected output in a no-IMF regime. We vary the efficacy of intervention σ for given levels of judgment error ε and output cost α. The deadweight costs of coordination are taken to be high (α=0.6). As can be seen, in the case where the IMF's judgment is perfect (ε=0) but its ability to mitigate the costs of crisis is poor ($\sigma\rightarrow 1$), expected output in the two regimes is the same. But as the ability of the IMF to contain crises improves ($\sigma\rightarrow 0$), output in the regime with the IMF rises above that in the regime without. If the IMF is less than perfect in exercising judgment (ε=0.2 or ε=0.3 in Figure 8.3), expected output in the IMF regime can still be higher than in the regime with no intervention. This is because the value of a reduced cost of crisis outweighs the effects of lower lending. But if $\sigma\rightarrow 0$, expected output in the IMF regime falls below that in a no-IMF world. The moral hazard effects, created by the combination of weak public monitoring and extremely effective crisis management, overwhelm the gains from the elimination of the creditor coordination problem.

Figure 8.3 Expected output and the efficacy of measures to mitigate disruption costs

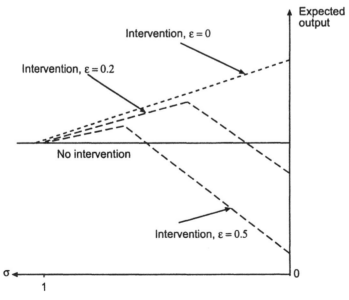

Although the model is an extremely simple characterisation of the mechanisms currently being considered in policy circles, it offers some useful insights. It shows, for example, how the efficacy of new workout proposals is likely to depend critically on the quality of public sector monitoring of debtor country conditions. This disciplining effect plays an important part in determining the *ex ante* terms of the debt contract (that is, the level of lending and the conditions of the loan). The greater the transparency and accountability of the debtor, the more effective public monitoring is likely to be. The results underline the important role played by IMF surveillance and data disclosure by debtor countries.

The analysis also suggests that a coherent framework of crisis management and resolution can bring welfare benefits. Although the introduction of standstills or similar measures can reduce the level of capital inflows *ex ante*, they confer benefits *ex post*. And there is no reason why lower *ex ante* lending should be a general result. If orderly crisis resolution means that a country recovers more swiftly and is monitored effectively, investors are likely to be faced with a greater number of profitable investment opportunities over time. The benefits of a coherent crisis resolution framework are most likely to accrue if the official sector is capable of identifying the source of financial problems and utilising emergency finance accordingly.

COUNTER-ARGUMENTS

Implementation of a formal sovereign debt restructuring mechanism poses some important questions. First, would the official sector be better able to mitigate moral hazard by pursuing a policy of 'constructive ambiguity' in crisis resolution, in the same way as with domestic lender of last resort facilities? Second, what is the credit supply-side reaction to changes in the financial architecture? For example, does the use of crisis management measures heighten financial fragility by encouraging creditors to pre-empt each other by lending at ever shorter maturities?

Rules vs discretion in the international financial architecture

The analysis in the above section on 'New approaches to sovereign debt restructuring' presumed an orderly approach by the official sector in pronouncing and then implementing intervention. An alternative is to intervene on a case-by-case basis according to the perceived merits of the case. In the framework above, if it is assumed that the underlying ability of the public sector to identify fundamentals remains unchanged, such a policy amounts to intervening only in a subset of cases for which the policymaker has received a signal of a bad outcome. This (mixed) strategy can be described below:

signal of good outcome	$\rightarrow$	no action
signal of bad outcome	$\rightarrow$	intervene with probability p
		no action with probability $1-p$

How does one interpret such policymaker behaviour? One interpretation of such a strategy is that it reflects the fact that international investors are unsure of the type of policymaker with whom they are dealing. Thus, creditors and debtors assign some probability of intervention taking place. We can modify the joint probabilities over states and signals described in Table 8.2 to construct a table of joint probabilities over states and intervention policies generated by the discretionary strategy (see Table 8.3).

There is a sense in which discretion is an intermediate policy that lies between the regime without intervention and the regime with intervention based on rules and guidelines. The possibility that the policymaker might not intervene cuts across both good and bad states, so that the *ex post* effects of failing to stem the run lowers expected output in the bad state relative to the IMF regime. But since intervention does take place some of the time, some of the detrimental effects are contained, relative to a regime with no public sector intervention.

A more satisfactory framework to examine this issue would be one in which the signal received by the IMF had many values, so that it would make sense to talk about varying degrees of certainty that the fundamentals of the debtor country were good or bad. Case-by-case intervention would amount to a policy in which intervention took place only when the signal was sufficiently strong that the underlying fundamental was one of bad luck default. In such a framework, the decision of the IMF is to choose the optimal cut-off point for the value of the signal at which intervention takes place. A policy of case-by-case intervention that allows the IMF to choose this cut-off optimally given the joint distribution over signals and outcomes will bring benefits over a regime in which the cut-off is set at an artificially low level.

Another way to frame the debate on a case-by-case approach is to suppose that there are cross-sectional differences in the noise parameter ε across debtor countries. Some countries may have high ε due to the opaqueness of their disclosure policies, for instance. A case-by-case approach would then imply a partitioning of debtor countries in terms of the size of their ε. Only countries that satisfy certain preconditions (for example, of providing sound information about fundamentals) would be eligible for IMF support in a

Table 8.3 Probabilities over states and intervention

		Policy action	
		No action	*Intervention*
Fundamentals	Good	$\varphi(1-\varepsilon)+(1-p)\varphi\varepsilon$	$p\varphi\varepsilon$
	Bad	$(1-\varphi)(\varepsilon+(1-p)(1-\varepsilon))$	$p(1-\varphi)(1-\varepsilon)$

crisis. In terms of the model, the implication is that intervention should take place only when ε is less than some (low) critical threshold value. Again, this points in favour of a coherent crisis management framework.

'Rushes for exits'

The use of voluntary rollovers to facilitate crisis resolution in Brazil in 1998 – in the aftermath of a concerted rollover in South Korea – led creditors to shorten maturities pre-emptively and cut interbank lines sooner than would otherwise have been the case. The experience has lead to scepticism about the efficacy of rollovers and other measures that target short-term debt, such as stays on creditor litigation. It is argued that, by encouraging creditors to 'rush for the exits' (that is, lend at shorter and shorter maturities to ensure that they get their money out before others), such measures merely bring forward financial crises (for example, Geithner 2000; Mathieson et al. 2000).

The issue of debt maturity structure cannot be considered in isolation from the issue of the pricing of risky debt. In general, it is difficult to study the two simultaneously as the failure rate of a project and the pricing relationship are both endogenous and depend on each other. Thus, the recent finance literature has focused on asset pricing issues, taking the maturity profile as given. In reduced-form credit models (for example, Jarrow and Turnbull 1995; Duffie and Singleton 1999), default is an event that is entirely governed by an exogenous failure rate of default. To examine the effects of crisis management measures on the maturity profile, it is necessary to focus on the complementary issue, the failure rate of a project that is implied by a given pricing structure.

Gai and Shin (2002) model the equilibrium maturity profile of debt that is implied by this approach. Their results suggest that debt workouts which improve the recovery process for bond-holders do not necessarily skew the maturity profile towards the shorter term. Higher recovery rates influence creditor behaviour in two ways. First, there is a direct effect: any increase in the recovery rate increases the amount that the bond-holder can recover in the event of a default. Second, there is a strategic effect – an increase in the recovery rate lowers the payoff from pre-empting, relative to the payoff from maintaining a longer-maturity instrument.

Figure 8.4 illustrates this result. It plots the equilibrium expected payoff to the representative claim-holder as a function of the recovery rate, ρ. As can be seen, the expected payoff is increasing in ρ and lies above the 45 degree line. In other words, marginal improvements in the recovery rate lead to a more than one-for-one increase in the expected payoff. This 'overall' effect can be decomposed into its direct and strategic components. Figure 8.4 also shows how the direct effect influences the expected payoff on its own. As ρ exceeds the reference point ρ', the wedge between the overall and direct effects becomes larger. Improvements to the recovery process amplify the role played by the strategic effect and dampen creditors' desire to pre-empt. So an increase in expected payoffs from higher recovery rates need not just

Figure 8.4 Expected payoffs and the recovery rate

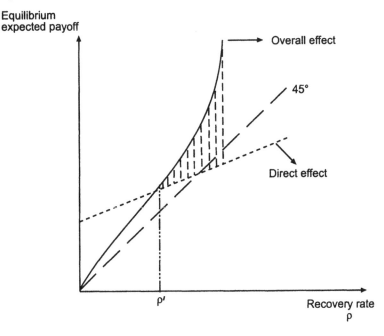

reflect improved debt collection – creditor behaviour is altered in the workout regime. Intuitively, if the amount that can be recovered in the event of default is sufficiently high, the desire to pre-empt one's opponent diminishes.

Gai and Shin also demonstrate how the equilibrium maturity profile depends critically on whether policy measures are temporary or long-lived. Different assumptions about the duration of rollovers generate different maturity profiles for debt. Measures that permanently improve the recovery rate do not necessarily skew the maturity profile towards the shorter term. Similar results obtain if the reorganisation process is a short-lived one that culminates in permanently higher recovery rates in the future. But in more intermediate cases, the results are ambiguous. If an orderly workout is moderately lengthy, creditors are faced with weighing up the relative benefits of staying or pre-empting. In such circumstances, the maturity profile can even be 'double peaked' as creditors opt for very long or very short maturities. The ultimate implications for the debt maturity profile are likely to depend on the duration of the policy measure and on the effectiveness of the recovery process.

IMPLICATIONS FOR EAST ASIA

What sort of actions can be taken at the East Asian level to develop a market-oriented crisis management infrastructure? A full discussion of actual arrangements is beyond the scope of this paper. Nevertheless, the issues raised above (destabilising speculation, private sector involvement and IMF reform) have all been the focus of policy attention in the region. The analysis points to two modest alterations to existing proposals that could help further crisis management in East Asia.

A first possibility could be to develop forums that focus on creditor coordination and regional surveillance in unison. The Manila Framework Group could be a useful starting point for this. It could be expanded to include more explicit involvement by private creditors. By acting as a 'country club' it could subject members to thorough peer reviews and provide an opportunity for countries to share information with the IMF and private sector participants. By offering scope for a frank dialogue and the means for creditors to exchange information between each other, it could act as an informal way of coordinating creditor actions. As noted by Morris and Shin (1998), increasing transparency is unlikely to provide a panacea against crisis, but the sharper discipline and scrutiny that such a forum might entail could bring significant welfare benefits.

A second possibility might be to build on the Korean proposals (see Kim et al. 2000) for an 'Asian Arrangement to Borrow' (AAB). The AAB is envisaged as a regional pool of funds that can be made available to countries facing crisis. As de Brouwer (2003) noted, regional arrangements need to be designed to complement global solutions. The AAB may be a useful means of accomplishing this. Once a standstill is imposed by the official sector (the IMF), an AAB could contribute to the 'fire-fighting' tasks of crisis management. A significant AAB fund would place Asian policymakers in a better position to influence the direction of conditionality and take a leadership role in the workout solution. As argued in the paper, more focused conditionality and official sector leadership are important elements in catalysing private sector finance. And, to the extent that such a process allows for IMF conditions to be better aligned with debtor incentives, an AAB might also encourage greater ownership of reform programs.

Improving the international financial system to better cope with crises is an important task for regional and global policymakers. The process for developing a framework for crisis management is in its early stages. Economic theory can contribute to this debate and help discipline policy thinking, but there is more research to be done and there is much that is still to be agreed upon.

ACKNOWLEDGMENTS

I am grateful to Gordon de Brouwer for encouraging me to bring my thoughts on this topic together, and to Professor Koichi Hamada for his thoughtful comments. I am particularly indebted to Michael Chui, Andy Haldane, Simon Hayes, Hyun Shin, and Nick Vause for the substantial intellectual input that forms the basis of this paper. I also thank Adrian Penalver and Paul Tucker for their perceptive advice and encouragement. The opinions expressed, and the errors that remain, are mine alone.

NOTES

1　A comprehensive survey of the recent literature in this field in offered by de Bandt and Hartmann (2000).
2　See, for example, the many models surveyed in Flood and Marion (1998), and the conference volume on managing currency crises by Edwards and Frankel (2002).
3　The key references are Krugman (1979) and Flood and Garber (1984).
4　The seminal reference is Obstfeld (1996). Flood and Marion (1998) provide a comprehensive survey of first- and second-generation models.
5　See, for example, Allen and Gale (1998) and IMF (1998).
6　See the communique by G-20 Finance Ministers and Central Bank Governors, October 2000.
7　De Brouwer (2003) offers a concise review of East Asian responses to the recent financial crises.
8　See the findings of the G-22 working group on strengthening financial systems (1998), and the Financial Stability Forum working group on capital flows (2000).
9　This view has most recently been advanced by the IMF (Krueger 2001), the Canadian government (Martin 1998; Dodge 2001), and the Bank of England (King 1999; Clementi 2000; Haldane and Kruger 2001). The academic case has been put forward by Sachs (1995), Radelet and Sachs (1998), Radelet (1999) and Miller and Zhang (2000).
10　A similar argument is put forward by Calomiris and Kahn (1991) in the literature on banking. They argue that the threat of withdrawal of demand deposits provides bank managers with incentives to undertake monitoring.

REFERENCES

Allen, F. and D. Gale (1998) 'Optimal financial crises', *Journal of Finance* 53: 1254–84.
Calomiris, C. and C. Kahn (1991) 'The role of demandable debt in structuring optimal banking arrangements', *American Economic Review* 80: 93–106.
Chang, R. and A. Velasco (1998) 'Financial crises in emerging markets: a canonical model', *Federal Reserve Bank of Atlanta Working Paper* No. 98–10.
Chui, M., P. Gai and A. Haldane (2002) 'Sovereign liquidity crises: analytics and implications for public policy', *Journal of Banking and Finance* 26: 519–46.
Clementi, D. (2000) 'Crisis prevention and resolution: two aspects of financial stability', *Financial Stability Review*, December, Bank of England.
Cornelli, F. and L. Felli (1995) 'The theory of bankruptcy and mechanism design', in B. Eichengreen and R. Portes (eds), *Crisis? What Crisis? Orderly Workouts for Sovereign Debtors*, London: CEPR.
Corrigan, G. (2000) 'Resolving financial crises: a shared responsibility', *Goldman Sachs Economic Weekly*, May.
de Bandt, O. and P. Hartmann (2000) 'Systemic risk: a survey', *European Central Bank Working Paper* No. 35, Frankfurt.
de Brouwer, G. (2003) 'The IMF and East Asia: a changing regional financial architecture', in Chris Gilbert and David Vines (eds), *The IMF and International Financial Architecture*, Cambridge: Cambridge University Press.
Diamond, D. and P. Dybvig (1983) 'Bank runs, deposit insurance, and liquidity', *Journal of Political Economy* 91: 401–19.
Dodge, D. (2001) 'The Bank of Canada and Financial Stability', speech to the Montreal Society of Financial Analysts, 20 March, Montreal.

Dooley, M. (2000) 'Can output losses following international financial crises be avoided?', *NBER Working Paper* No. 7531.

Duffie, D. and K. Singleton (1999) 'Modelling term structures of defaultable bonds', *Review of Financial Studies* 12: 687–720.

Eaton, J. and M. Gersovitz (1981) 'Debt with potential repudiation: theory and estimation', *Review of Economic Studies* 48: 289–309.

Eichengreen, B. and R. Portes (1995) *'Crisis? What Crisis? Orderly Workouts for Sovereign Debtors'*, London: CEPR.

Edwards, S. and J. Frankel (eds) (2002) 'Preventing Currency Crises in Emerging Markets', NBER Conference Proceedings, University of Chicago Press.

Fischer, S. (1999) 'Reforming the international financial system', *Economic Journal* 109: F557–76.

Flood, R. and P. Garber (1984) 'Collapsing exchange rate regimes: some linear examples', *Journal of International Economics* 17: 1–13.

Flood, R. and N. Marion (1998) 'Perspectives on the recent currency crisis literature', *IMF Working Paper* No 98/130.

Gai, P., S. Hayes and H.S. Shin (2001) 'Crisis costs and debtor discipline: the efficacy of public policy in sovereign debt crises', *Bank of England Working Paper*, No. 136 (May).

Gai, P. and H.S. Shin (2002) 'Debt maturity structure with pre-emptive creditors', mimeo, Canberra: Australian National University.

Geithner, T. (2000) 'Sovereign Risk Management in an Integrated World', Washington DC: US Treasury.

Greenspan, A. (1999) 'Testimony before the Committee on Banking and Financial Services', US House of Representatives, Washington DC (May).

Haldane, A. and M. Kruger (2001) 'The resolution of international financial crises – private finance and public funds', *Financial Stability Review*, December, Bank of England.

Institute of International Finance (1996) *'Resolving Sovereign Financial Crises'*, Washington DC.

IMF (International Monetary Fund) (1998) *World Economic Outlook*, Washington DC.

Jarrow, R. and S. Turnbull (1995) 'Pricing derivatives on financial securities subject to credit risk', *Journal of Finance* 50: 53–86.

Kim, T.J., J.W. Ryou and Y. Wang (2000) *'Regional Arrangements to Borrow – A Scheme for Preventing Future Asian Liquidity Crises'*, Seoul: Korean Institute for International Economic Policy.

King, M. (1999) 'Reforming the international financial system: the middle way', *Financial Stability Review*, November, Bank of England.

Krueger, A. (2001) 'International financial architecture for 2002: a new approach to sovereign debt restructuring', speech to the American Enterprise Institute, Washington DC.

Krugman, P. (1979) 'A model of balance of payments crises' *Journal of Money, Credit and Banking* 11: 311–25.

—— (1999) 'Balance sheets, the transfer problem and financial crises', mimeo, MIT.

Mathieson, D. and others (2000) 'International capital markets: developments, prospects and key policy issues', Washington DC: IMF.

Martin, P. (1998) 'Statement to the Interim Committee of the IMF', Ottawa, 4 October.

Miller, M. and L. Zhang (2000) 'Sovereign liquidity crises: the strategic case for a payments standstill', *Economic Journal* 110: 309–34.

Morris, S. and H.S. Shin (1998) 'Unique equilibrium in a model of self-fulfilling currency attacks', *American Economic Review* 88: 587–97.

—— (2000) 'Rethinking multiple equilibria in macroeconomic modelling', *NBER Macroeconomics Annual*, MIT Press.

Obstfeld, M. (1996) 'Models of currency crisis with self-fulfilling features', *European Economic Review* 40: 1037–47.

Radelet, S. (1999) 'Orderly workouts for cross-border private debt', *Harvard Development Discussion Paper* No. 721, HIID, Harvard.

Radelet, S. and J. Sachs (1998) 'The East Asian financial crisis: diagnosis, remedies, prospects', *Brookings Papers on Economic Activity* 1: 1–78.

Sachs, J. (1995) 'Do we need an international lender of last resort?', Frank Graham Lecture, April, Princeton University.

9 Instruments and techniques for financial cooperation

Yunjong Wang

INTRODUCTION

Since the East Asian financial crisis, various proposals have been put forward for financial cooperation in East Asia in an effort to better prevent and manage future financial crises and to enhance economic efficiency through the development of sound financial markets. Terms like 'financial cooperation' and 'financial arrangements' can cover a range of activities and it is probably helpful to be more specific about what they mean. Financial cooperation, for example, may comprise nothing more than a common international reserve pooling or mutual credit arrangement such as bilateral swaps, without any commitment to pegging the exchange rates of the participating countries to each other. At present, East Asian countries appear to be pursuing this line of financial cooperation. Even in the absence of monetary cooperation, this more limited form of financial cooperation can serve a number of important purposes.[1]

In this paper, I critically review existing multilateral and regional financial arrangements in East Asia, focusing on the Chiang Mai Initiative (CMI), and I propose an augmented CMI, consisting of a unified framework equipped with the instruments and techniques necessary for financial cooperation.

RATIONALE AND BACKGROUND FOR REGIONAL FINANCIAL COOPERATION

The Asian financial crisis provided a strong impetus for East Asia to reform and strengthen its domestic financial systems, markets and institutions. In particular, there is a strong need for a framework that can support regional financial cooperation that will help to prevent and manage such crises in the future. However, the term 'regional financial cooperation' needs to be more clearly specified. No one denies the need for genuine regional financial cooperation, but there is considerable disagreement about the details of concrete proposals. One clear example of such disagreement concerns the proposed Asian Monetary Fund (AMF), which was rejected in 1997.

Progress update

Today there is a growing sense of an East Asian identity. After the rejection of the AMF proposal, ASEAN invited China, South Korea and Japan to join it in an effort to seek economic cooperation in the region. In 1999, the idea of an ASEAN+3 arrangement began to take hold.

The ASEAN+3 summit in November 1999 in Manila released a 'Joint Statement on East Asian Cooperation' that covers a wide range of possible areas for regional cooperation. Recognising the need to establish regional financial arrangements to supplement the existing international facilities, the finance ministers of ASEAN+3 at their meeting in Chiang Mai, Thailand, in May 2000 agreed to strengthen the existing cooperative frameworks in the region. The CMI involves an expanded ASEAN Swap Arrangement (ASA) that includes all ASEAN members and a network of bilateral swap and repurchase agreement facilities among ASEAN countries and China, Japan and South Korea.

Implementation of the CMI has strengthened self-help and support mechanisms in East Asia. For example, by 17 November 2000, the ASA had increased to US$1 billion and encompassed all ASEAN member countries. There has also been progress on the network of bilateral swap arrangements (NBSA) and repurchase agreements. The chapter by Kuroda and Kawai in this volume contains details. Government officials of the ASEAN+3 countries will continue to establish a network of bilateral swap and repurchase agreement facilities among ASEAN+3 countries.

Under the CMI, the NBSA has been linked with the IMF, thereby contributing to both regional and global financial stability. In fact, the bilateral arrangements require 90 per cent of the committed currency swaps to be activated along with International Monetary Fund (IMF) financial support. In other words, financial support under the NBSA is activated under IMF conditionality. By nesting regional facilities into the existing global facilities, the IMF and outsiders can no longer maintain an outright objection to East Asian financial arrangements.

Rationale for regional financial arrangements

The adoption and implementation of the CMI can be regarded as a major step toward strengthening financial cooperation among the 13 East Asian countries. However, ASEAN+3 countries will face much tougher challenges and tasks in exploring developments beyond the CMI. East Asian countries need to clarify their motivations, how they will develop an action plan, and how they believe such a plan fits in with the existing global financial system.

The United States, European countries and the IMF strongly opposed the creation of a regional monetary fund in East Asia. Eichengreen (2000) and others dismissed the contention that an East Asian regional fund might have a comparative advantage in diagnosing regional economic problems and prescribing appropriate solutions, and would increase the competition for ideas. The CMI is acceptable to many detractors of the regional monetary fund proposal: it does not require a new institution and it is tightly linked to IMF facilities and conditionalities.

However, one strong argument against the regional monetary fund concerned the issue of moral hazard. Eichengreen (2000) argued that at this stage of development East Asians may not be prepared to negotiate an international treaty that includes provisions for sanctions and fines for countries that do not adjust their domestic policies as required under an agreement. This unwillingness would make it difficult for a regional monetary fund to impose politically unpopular policies on member countries and hence may pose a serious problem in policy discipline. But it is not clear why an East Asian monetary fund would suffer more from moral hazard than the IMF. An East Asian monetary fund could provide the IMF with additional resources, while joining forces to work on the prevention and management of financial crises. At the same time, it could support the IMF by monitoring economic development in the region and taking part in the IMF's global surveillance activities.

Eichengreen (2001) finds it useful to distinguish between technical assistance and financial assistance. It is true that there is no reason to discourage competition in the market for technical assistance: governments should be free to choose the source of technical assistance with the best track record. However, Eichengreen seems to believe that AMF conditionalities would be much softer than IMF conditionalities. He was concerned that, if multiple monetary funds were available, East Asian governments would have an incentive to shop around for the most generous assistance and the least onerous terms. Institutional duplication and the problem of moral hazard are serious issues and should be fully considered in the design of regional financial arrangements as they develop further. Several developments have encouraged the formation of a regional financial arrangement in East Asia. One has been the slow progress of the reform of the international financial system. Architectural reform in the G-7 countries has slowed considerably, and there is a perception in East Asia and elsewhere that the existing international architecture is defective. As long as there are structural problems in the supply side of international capital – such as volatile capital movements and gyrations in the G-3 exchange rate – East Asian countries will be as vulnerable to future crises as they were before. Instead of waiting for the G-7 to create a new architecture, whose effectiveness may be questionable, East Asians could work together to create their own self-help arrangements. The CMI, established by ASEAN+3, is one such option (Park and Wang 2001).

Many of the victims of the East Asian financial crisis are increasing their foreign exchange reserves above the level regarded as adequate for their import requirements. Korea has built a level of reserves equivalent to 20 per cent of its GDP (over US$120 billion at the end of 2002), largely because of the increased volume of its capital account transactions. By any measure, this level is excessive, is costly, and represents a clear case of resource misallocation. To reduce the amount of reserve holdings and to use them more efficiently for financing development projects, these funds could be drawn on by regional countries as precautionary lines of credit. This notion is already partially reflected in the CMI. ASEAN+3 countries have about US$1 trillion of foreign reserves. If these reserves are pooled and managed well, a mere 10 per cent of the total amount would be sufficient to provide a first line or second line of defence against any speculative attack.

When the Asian crisis broke in 1997, advocates of the AMF stressed the need for a regional monetary fund, referring to the fact that the IMF did not allocate enough funds for East Asia to meet the needs of sizeable emerging market economies. At that time, the international community recognised that the IMF did not have the financial resources to provide emergency assistance to mid-size emerging market economies such as Russia and Brazil. In its September 1997 annual meeting in Hong Kong, after the Asian financial crisis, the IMF decided to increase the quota of 182 member countries by 45 per cent.[2] It also established the 'New Arrangements to Borrow' (NAB), effective from November 1998.

The IMF is now in a better financial position than it was before the Asian financial crisis, but the IMF alone cannot provide all necessary liquidity to crisis countries. As in the case of the 1994–95 Mexican peso crisis, a group of countries including the United States provided liquidity support in tandem with the IMF to fill the financing gap. Instead of just being an *ad hoc* arrangement determined on a geopolitical basis, a more formalised arrangement could act as a mechanism for parallel lending.

More seriously, most East Asian countries are underrepresented in the IMF quota formula. East Asian countries are willing to contribute more to the IMF. If they contribute more, they should be accorded greater representation both on the board of directors and in management. They could also be entitled to greater liquidity based on their increased quota. However, quota reform is not simple politics. Increased voting rights for currently underrepresented members would be allowed only if currently overrepresented members agreed to reduce their proportionally greater voting rights. Since any reallocation of quotas and voting rights is seen as a zero-sum game, even a perfectly designed quota formula would not satisfy the political interests of members involved.

The Supplemental Reserve Facility (SRF) created on 17 December 1997 is one way of providing enlarged liquidity assistance exceeding the normal standby quota disbursement. In principle, any country may use the SRF. However, it is intended for situations where difficulties in one country have the potential to destabilise the international financial system. The disbursement takes place when there is a chance of improvement in the balance of payments during a short period, based on bold restructuring and monetary policies. Korea, Russia and Brazil have received funds from the SRF. However, it is not clear whether those countries were recipients simply because of systemic consequences of their financial collapse.

As Ito et al. (1999) have argued, contagion is geographically concentrated, so a regional grouping for support is logical. Whether or not the primary source of the Asian financial crisis was the sudden shift in market expectations and confidence, foreign lenders were so alarmed by the Thai crisis that they abruptly pulled their investments out of the other countries in the region, causing the crisis to be contagious. Geographical proximity and economic similarity (or similar structural problems) of these Asian countries prompted the withdrawal of lending and portfolio investment, while differences in economic fundamentals were often overlooked. If channels of contagion cannot be blocked by multilateral cooperation in the early stages of a crisis, countries lacking sufficient foreign reserves will be adversely affected. Hence, neighbours have a stake in helping to stop the financial crisis before it spreads to them (Ito et al. 1999). As long as a crisis remains country-specific or regional, there is no urgent political need for unaffected countries outside the region to pay the significant costs associated with providing support.

Policy dialogue, including monitoring and surveillance, is the bedrock of coherent policy formation under the regional financial arrangements. ASEAN+3 is exploring ways to advance this. A monitoring and surveillance unit or process would provide prompt and relevant information for assessing countries in trouble and for assessing the potential for contagion to neighbouring countries. A joint exercise based on a region-wide early warning system would make it easier to examine financial vulnerabilities in the region. Furthermore, the regional policy dialogue process would provide discipline and so help to ensure high-quality accounting and auditing standards, strong disclosure requirements, credible rating agencies and appropriate corporate governance.

APPRAISAL OF EXISTING MULTILATERAL FINANCIAL ARRANGEMENTS

IMF facilities

The IMF provides a number of financing facilities, and here I focus mainly on two.[3]

The General Arrangements to Borrow

IMF funds come mainly from quota subscriptions of member countries. In 1962, the largest industrial countries became concerned about what would happen if any one of them were to draw on the resources of the IMF, because the amount they could potentially borrow would significantly reduce the amount of usable resources readily available to other countries. Accordingly, they agreed to stand ready to lend the IMF supplemental funds if such funds were needed to forestall, or cope with, an impairment of the international monetary system. This agreement was named the 'General Arrangements to Borrow' (GAB). Since then, the GAB has remained the IMF's longest lasting borrowing arrangement.

The GAB are a conditional credit line that were incorporated within the IMF's ordinary lending procedures and could be drawn on only with the consent of the participants. The credit arrangements assigned to the participants are based on their present and prospective balance of payments and reserve positions. The IMF can call on GAB participants to finance either a standby arrangement or an 'exchange transaction' which does not require a standby arrangement. Each GAB participant reserves the right to decide whether or not to lend to the IMF.

Loans by GAB participants are essentially for up to five years. However, the IMF can repay earlier if the GAB beneficiary is committed to repaying the IMF within five years. The interest paid by the IMF on GAB loans is relatively low, partly because the arrangements are seen as a cooperative effort to protect the international monetary system, and partly because the GAB claims are secured. In 1975, a new interest formula was adopted, requiring the IMF to pay GAB creditors interest each quarter at the same rate levied on drawings financed by the GAB, but not less than 4 per cent per annum.

Between 1964 and 1970, the GAB were activated six times to help the IMF finance four large drawings by the United Kingdom and two by France. The total GAB borrowings during this period amounted to US$2.155 billion, all of which had been repaid by August 1971. In the 1970s, the GAB were used to help finance large drawings by the United Kingdom (January 1977), Italy (May 1977) and the United States (November 1978).

The GAB have always been controversial, and some members, including industrial and developing countries, were overtly critical of their non-global characteristics at the time. There have been three main criticisms. First, the GAB were exclusive. The number of participants was limited, and participants had agreed to lend to the IMF only to finance their own transactions with it. Several countries, and not solely developing countries, resented this exclusiveness. Second, the GAB were seen as reducing the IMF's authority. They gave a small club of rich members an effective veto over important decisions by the IMF to enter into transactions. Third, the GAB were the *raisons d'être* of the G-10, which played a much greater role in discussing IMF issues, such as the creation of the special drawing right (SDR). This later prompted the developing countries to form their own group, the G-24, in November 1971, to protect their interests in the international monetary field.

The GAB stayed virtually the same from 1962 to 1982. On several occasions, participants examined the problems raised against them, but very little was done. Reform of the GAB came as a direct response by the major industrial countries to the debt crises. In the summer of 1982, Mexico and then Brazil were unable to obtain new loans or to roll over existing ones. The results were higher spreads for virtually all borrowers, irrespective of their particular circumstances, and an abrupt reduction in the availability of credit for specific countries. Eventually, the major borrowing countries defaulted on their loans.

The immediate crisis was averted by a series of *ad hoc* rescue packages involving the Bank for International Settlements (BIS), central banks, governments, commercial banks and, crucially, the IMF. However, the debt crisis, and the consequent requests for IMF support on a large scale, highlighted the inadequacy of IMF resources. In September 1982, US Treasury Secretary Donald T. Regan proposed two new initiatives: to increase the fund quota so that it would cover the members' need for temporary financing in normal circumstances at the annual joint meetings of the IMF and the World Bank; and to adopt an additional permanent borrowing arrangement that would be available to the IMF on a contingency basis for use in extraordinary circumstances. The GAB were reformed and enlarged as a result of this proposal.

The revision of the GAB was agreed by the G-10 and the executive board in January and February 1983, respectively, and the new arrangements came into effect in December 1983. There were seven main changes.

First, the total of individual credit lines under the GAB was increased to SDR17 billion.

Second, the shares of individual participants in the increased total were rearranged to reflect changes in their economic and financial positions since 1962 and their ability to provide resources to the IMF. The shares of the original and revised GAB are shown in Table 9.1.

As in 1962, the size of individual credit lines was decided rather informally. There was no single or precise formula.

Third, the Swiss central bank became a new participant in the GAB. The fact that Switzerland is not a member of the IMF means that the IMF cannot call on the revised GAB to finance transactions with Switzerland.

Fourth, the revised GAB allows the IMF to enter into borrowing arrangements with members that are not GAB participants. In this case, a non-participant now has virtually the same rights and responsibilities as a GAB participant.

Fifth, the IMF concluded an associated borrowing arrangement with Saudi Arabia. Under the arrangement, Saudi Arabia agreed to stand ready to lend the IMF up to SDR1.5 billion on a revolving basis over five years. The procedure for making calls, the interest rates and most other terms and conditions are essentially the same as those in the revised GAB.

Sixth, the IMF can call on participants to finance drawings by non-participants according to the revised GAB only in certain well-defined circumstances. Such drawings were only to be made in support of adjustment programs. Furthermore, special criteria have to be met in order for the managing director to propose calls on the GAB to finance transactions with non-participants. The criteria are stricter than those for participants. In particular, the criterion referring to problems which could 'threaten' the stability of the international monetary system was much more severe than that which allowed the GAB to be activated for the benefit of participants to forestall or cope with an 'impairment' of the system.

Finally, GAB creditors are expected to earn interest at a rate equal to the combined market interest rate. The market interest rate is determined on the

Table 9.1   Original and revised GAB: individual credit arrangements

Participant	1962		1983	
	Amount (US$ million)	%	Amount (SDR million)	%
United States	2,000	33.33	4,250	25.00
Deutsche Bundesbank	1,000	16.66	2,380	14.00
Japan	250	4.16	2,125	12.50
France	550	9.16	1,700	10.00
United Kingdom	1,000	16.66	1,700	10.00
Italy	550	9.16	1,105	6.50
Canada	200	3.36	892.5	5.25
Netherlands	200	3.36	850	5.00
Belgium	150	2.50	595	3.50
Sveriges Riksbank	100	1.66	382.5	2.25
Swiss National Bank	–		1,020	6.00
Total	6,000		17,000	

Source: Ainley (1984).

basis of a weighted average of yields on short-term market instruments denominated in the five currencies that make up the SDR basket. It was also agreed to denominate the individual credit lines in SDR. This would avoid unintended changes in the value caused by exchange rate fluctuations.

The New Arrangements to Borrow

Following the Mexican financial crisis in December 1994, participants in the June 1995 G-7 Halifax Summit called on the G-10 and other financially strong countries to develop new financing arrangements. Following the meeting, the IMF's executive board adopted a decision establishing the NAB on 27 January 1997. The NAB were not immediately implemented, mainly due to delay in US congressional approval. Only after the Thai crisis spread to neighbouring countries, and many East Asian countries came to support Japan's proposal for the AMF in late 1997, did the United States and the other developed countries become aware of the severity of the Asia-wide crisis. The compromise plan, envisioned during the gathering in Manila in November 1997, was to strengthen the ability of the IMF to provide funds through early approval of the NAB and cooperative lending.

The NAB finally became effective on 17 November 1998 and remain in effect for five years. They are a set of credit arrangements between the IMF and 25 members and institutions to provide supplementary resources to the IMF, enabling it to forestall or cope with an impairment of the international monetary system. They also aim to deal with an exceptional situation threatening the stability of the system, as under the GAB. The NAB do not replace the existing GAB, which remain in force. However, the NAB are to be the first and principal recourse in the event that supplementary resources are needed by the IMF. The total amount of resources available to the IMF under the NAB and GAB combined is SDR34 billion (about US$46 billion), double the amount available under the GAB alone. The main criterion for commitment from individual participants is relative economic strength as measured by the country's actual IMF quota.

A proposal for calls on the NAB by the IMF's managing director becomes effective only if it is accepted by the NAB participants, and then approved by the executive board. The NAB may also be activated to finance drawing on the Fund by non-participants, as in the GAB. The NAB have been activated once, to finance an extended arrangement for Brazil in December 1998, when the IMF called on funding of SDR9.1 billion, of which SDR2.9 billion was used. The Fund repaid the outstanding amount in March 1999, when its liquidity position improved substantially due to the bulk of the quota increases following the Eleventh General Review of Quotas.

Credit facilities of the European Community[4]

The credit mechanisms of the European Union (EU) originated in the late 1960s, when the inflation rates and external balances of member states of the European Community (EC) began to diverge. A speculative attack against the French franc in favour of the German mark in May 1968 put a great deal of pressure on the bilateral parities of EC currencies and resulted in heated discussions on the need for coordinating economic and monetary policies among the member states and establishing monetary facilities for mutual balance of payments assistance.

The credit mechanisms of the EC are composed of three distinctive but mutually complementary instruments: the very short-term financing facility (VSTF), the short-term monetary support (STMS) facility and the medium-term financial assistance (MTFA) facility. These facilities have the common goal of providing international liquidity to member states experiencing balance of payments deficits. However, they differ in their maturity and conditions attached to borrowing.

With the introduction of the euro and the creation of the Economic and Monetary Union (EMU), the VSTF and STMS facilities are no longer necessary for maintaining bilateral exchange rates through intervention. Such financing is available directly from the European Central Bank under ERM II – the exchange rate mechanism to stabilise European currencies against the euro, of which the Danish krone is the only present member. Notwithstanding the European monetary union, the MTFA remains in place but is unused at the moment (Henning 2002).

The Short-Term Monetary Support Facility

The STMS facility aimed at providing a certain amount of credit to its members in return for their commitment to lend on request from other members. It became operational in February 1970 on the basis of an agreement between the central banks of the six member states. Under the agreement, the central bank of each member state agreed that on request it would provide funds (not exceeding a given ceiling, equal to its debtor quota) to the other central banks of the member states experiencing short-term balance of payments difficulties.

Initially, this facility had a total quota of one billion units (one unit of account = US$1) available to the central banks of the member states. The total quota was broken down in the following way: 300 million units for France and Germany respectively, 200 million units for Italy, and 100 million units for the Netherlands and Belgium (together with Luxembourg). The central bank of a participating country was able to borrow from the other four central banks up to its quota and was obliged to lend up to the same quota to the other banks. In addition, the total extension (or *rallonge*) of the quotas can attain a maximum of one billion units of account.

The STMS facility was governed by an agreement between the central banks of the member states and was administered by the European Monetary Cooperation Fund (EMCF), with the BIS as its agent.[5] The granting of short-term monetary support was linked to the need for short-term financing caused by a temporary balance of payments deficit. Credits were granted without economic policy conditions, but they trigger subsequent consultations. They were extended for three months originally, with the possibility of renewal for another three months. With the amendments introduced in the context of the European Monetary System (EMS), credits under the STMS facility could be renewed for an additional three months, raising the maximum duration from six to nine months.

The STMS facility was fully revised and strengthened in February 1974. The central banks of nine member states agreed to increase the total amount of the quotas; more importantly, a debtor quota (borrowing ceiling) and a creditor quota (commitment ceiling) were separately arranged, the latter being twice as high as the former. In addition, extensions beyond the debtor and the creditor quotas (so-called *rallonges*) could be applied to any member state. Under the STMS facility the central bank of a member state could borrow from its partners a total amount equal to its debtor quota plus one-half of the total available (creditor) *rallonge*. The central bank of a member state is committed to lend to its partners a maximum amount equal to its creditor quota plus the total (creditor) *rallonge*.

The STMS facility was used by Italy in 1974, but has not been used since the launch of the EMS. Table 9.2 shows the participants and the amount of debtor and creditor quotas. As of January 1995, all 15 EU member states took part in the STMS facility; the total amount of credit available from the facility was ECU15.45 billion.

The Very Short-Term Financing Facility

In the midst of increased uncertainty about the prospects for the Bretton Woods system, the central banks of the six member states of the EC and the three prospective member states signed an agreement to narrow the margins of fluctuation between EC currencies. Under the Smithsonian agreement, any EC currency could fluctuate within a margin of plus or minus 2.25 per cent of its parity against the US dollar. Meanwhile, under the Basel Agreement, which is sometimes referred to as the 'snake in the tunnel', any two EC currencies could fluctuate within the much narrower margin of just 2.25 per cent.

The VSTF facility was established in April 1972 to finance the marginal intervention required to stabilise bilateral exchange rates between community currencies. It required the central banks of strong currencies to provide a sufficient amount of their currencies to allow official intervention to defend the existing exchange rate margin. For example, if the exchange rate of the French franc per unit of the German mark increased sharply, the French central bank needed to intervene in the foreign exchange market by selling marks. Through the VSTF facility, France can borrow marks from Germany. This obligation came about because the official reserve holdings that one country could use in order to intervene in the foreign exchange market were

Table 9.2 Short-term monetary support facility

Participant	Amount of quota, March 1979 (ECU million)			Amount of quota, January 1995 (ECU million)		
	Debtor quota	Creditor quota	Percentage	Debtor quota	Creditor quota	Percentage
Belgium	580	1,160	7.34	580	1,160	5.81
Denmark	260	520	3.29	260	520	2.60
Germany	1,740	3,480	22.03	1,740	3,480	17.43
France	1,740	3,480	22.03	1,740	3,480	17.43
Ireland	100	200	1.27	100	200	1.00
Italy	1,160	2,320	14.67	1,160	2,320	11.62
Netherlands	580	1,160	7.34	580	1,160	5.81
UK	1,740	3,480	22.03			
Greece				150	300	1.50
Spain				725	1,450	7.26
Austria				350	700	3.50
Total	7,900	15,800	100.0	9,985	19,970	100.0
Rallonge	4,400	8,800		4,400	8,800	

Note: ECU = European currency unit.

Source: Apel (1998): 71.

not sufficient to cope with the unprecedented magnitude of private capital movements. In addition, the ERM crisis in 1992–93 shows that the EMS institutional framework alone was not sufficient to fend off speculative attacks.

In the case of European monetary cooperation, the German Bundesbank assumed the role of the regional lender of last resort. For example, during the EMS crisis in September 1992, the credit supplied by the Bundesbank reached about DM93 billion. Because the liabilities that weak currency countries incur can be repaid in European currency units (ECUs), the value of German credits decreased after the devaluation of some European currencies. The expected loss of the Bundesbank from the use of the VSTF facility is estimated to be in excess of DM1 billion (Collignon et al. 1996).

The terms and conditions of the VSTF facility were revised several times after the introduction of the EMS in 1979. According to the 1987 agreement between the central banks, which is known as the Basel–Nyborg Agreement, there are five major features of the VSTF.

First, the debtor central bank is given 75 days from the end of the month in which the debt is incurred to reimburse the principal and interest. At the request of the debtor central bank, this initial settlement date may be extended for three months. This request is automatically granted, provided the total amount of indebtedness of the central bank in the VSTF facility does not exceed a ceiling equal to 200 per cent of the debtor quota of the central bank concerned under the STMF facility. Moreover, any debt already renewed automatically for three months may be renewed for a further three months, subject to the agreement of the creditor central banks.

Second, any debt exceeding the 200 per cent ceiling may be renewed once for three months, subject to the agreement of the creditor central bank or central banks if the debtor central bank has loans outstanding with more than one creditor central bank.

Third, when the reimbursement of a financing operation falls due, settlement by the debtor central bank is to be effected preferably in the creditor's currency. Any debt not settled in the creditor's currency may be settled by transfers of ECU assets or other reserve components in accordance with the composition of the debtor central bank's reserves. Fourth, since the unit of account of the VSTF facility managed by the EMCF is the ECU, debtor and creditor balances are also denominated in ECU. However, the loans and reimbursements are usually effected in assets denominated in national currencies, so national units of account are converted to ECUs on settlement day on the basis of the daily rate for the ECU established by the commission.

Finally, interest payments apply to loans granted under the VSTF operations. Following the 1985 amendment, the interest rate is calculated as a weighted average of the most representative rates on the domestic money market of the countries whose currencies make up the ECU basket.

To summarise, the VSTF facility was closely linked to the STMS facility in its purpose of stabilising bilateral exchange rates between Community currencies. Determination of the creditor and debtor ceilings was also linked to those under the STMS facility. In addition, appropriate market interest rates were applied to loans under the VSTF facility.

The Medium-Term Financial Assistance Facility

The MTFA facility was established in 1972 to extend loans to any member state in difficulty, or seriously threatened with difficulties, in its balance of payments. Whether difficulties with the balance of payments resulted from the current account or the capital account did not matter. Under the MTFA facility, credits are extended for two to five years. The debtor country is subject to economic policy conditions decided by the Council of Ministers. In formulating conditions and monitoring the performance of the debtor country, the Commission and the Monetary Committee assume the key advisory roles. The MTFA facility has creditor ceilings, but no specified debtor ceilings, for individual countries except that the borrowing of a member state normally cannot exceed half of the total creditor ceilings. The creditor ceilings for participants are as follows: 600 million units of account each for Germany and France, 400 units for Italy and 200 units each for Belgium, Luxembourg and the Netherlands.

Meanwhile, the community loan mechanism (CLM) was established in 1975 to assist member states experiencing current account problems arising from the oil price shock. Unlike the MTFA facility, the CLM used outside funds, with the community allowed to borrow up to US$3 billion. In 1988, the MTFA and CLM were merged to form a new credit facility called the medium-term financial support (MTFS) facility. This decision was made to provide a flexible financial safety net in order to encourage full liberalisation of the member states' capital flows. Borrowing under the MTFS facility is subject to conditions aimed at re-establishing a sustainable balance of payments status. The ceiling for total borrowing under the MTFS facility was ECU16 billion.

EXISTING REGIONAL FINANCIAL ARRANGEMENTS IN ASEAN+3

ASEAN swap arrangement

In August 1977, the five original ASEAN countries, in pursuit of their common objective to promote financial cooperation, established an ASEAN swap arrangement (ASA) for one year. The ASA has been renewed several times in accordance with Article X laid down in the memorandum of understanding of the ASA. The latest renewal, for an additional five years, was made in Kuala Lumpur on 27 January 1999. The ASA has been a very primitive financial arrangement, mainly due to loose financial cooperation in ASEAN. Furthermore, given that there is no meaningful regional lender of last resort, the total outstanding amount of US dollars provided by each participant was US$40 million. This amount was far from enough to fend off the volatile capital reversal that occurred during the Asian financial turmoil. The ASA was not utilised during the Asian financial crisis of 1997–98. Instead, seriously battered economies – with the exception of Malaysia – sought financial assistance from the IMF.

On 17 November 2000, the ASA was enlarged to US$1 billion and included all ASEAN member countries. However, the total outstanding amount currently available is relatively small and falls short of the amounts needed to deal with a major withdrawal of capital. A major drawback of the existing ASA stems from the 'equal partnership' condition, which stipulates that the amount of swap to be granted to a swap-requesting member country shall be provided by the other member countries in equal shares, which fails to take into account the relative size and strength of the economies of different countries. In addition, a participant may refrain from providing committed lending by merely informing other member countries of its decision, and may, at its discretion, provide reasons for its decision.

As long as the ASEAN members cannot find a country to contribute a meaningful amount of credit, the ASA must link this regional arrangement to global liquidity facilities provided by the IMF or other regional liquidity facilities. The ASA could be further expanded to include China, Japan and South Korea. However, key characteristics of the scheme – namely, that contributions are voluntary and identical between countries – limits the potential size and reach of the scheme. Serious revision should be required to secure firm commitment and enlarged contributions.

Network of bilateral swap arrangements

In May 2000, China, Japan and South Korea jointly drafted a statement of principal points of the standard agreement for bilateral swap arrangements (BSA) under the CMI. Each pair of countries is expected to choose feasible arrangements and negotiate the swap amount and other specific conditions of arrangements bilaterally.

Given the CMI principles and objectives, the network of BSA (NBSA) is not meant to be simply a collection of BSAs, although it is not there yet. The NBSA need to be designed to develop a mechanism for joint activation and quick disbursement of swaps. It should establish a coordinated decision making process for activation and disbursement and create a monitoring and surveillance unit to support the swap operations. The current NBSA is not sufficiently structured. Park and Wang (2000b) consider a structured NBSA beyond the CMI. They suggest that the current CMI discussions would be much improved if the ASEAN+3 countries agreed to incorporate such structured elements into the current version of the CMI.

REGIONAL LIQUIDITY FACILITIES BEYOND THE CMI

As schemes for mobilising financial resources, the IMF's GAB and NAB can be useful benchmarks for regional borrowing arrangements. Just as those multilateral borrowing arrangements have been operated under the IMF's supervision and accountability, a regional body is required to be accountable for the operation of regional borrowing arrangements. An AMF could assume such a role. I will discuss the future prospects for the Asian Arrangements to Borrow (AAB) and Asian Monetary Fund (AMF) later in this section.

The motivation for the CMI has always been different from that for similar European facilities. The European facilities were created to limit exchange rate fluctuations under the coordinated exchange rate mechanism. The CMI started with high capital mobility and flexible exchange rates, although some members of ASEAN+3 have maintained various types of fixed exchange rate regimes. The CMI has not presumed any manifest exchange rate coordination. Even before the region starts thinking about common exchange rate arrangements, it should address particular structural shortcomings in the present strictures of the CMI. Unlike the proposal for the AMF, these would require minimal institutional development.

I now turn to consider various possible regional facilities. A structured NBSA, AAB and AMF all seek closer regional financial cooperation. However, they have different institutional arrangements. For example, the NBSA is the product of bilateral negotiations, whereas the AAB and AMF depend on region-based multilateral negotiations and the NBSA and AAB are contractual arrangements (less institutional) whereas the AMF is a full-fledged institution like the IMF. The choice of arrangement will depend on the economic benefits and costs of each regional financial arrangement as well as the political preferences of ASEAN+3 countries.

At this stage, the ASEAN+3 countries do not have a strong political incentive to pursue further drastic institutional development, so a structured NBSA (as discussed below) would be a feasible regional financial facility. However, it would require several amendments. The structure of the NBSA would need to take into account the actual financing capacity and needs of each participating country. The BSA is by definition reciprocal: contracting parties have both swap-providing and swap-requesting status. In practice, however, the swap positions are not symmetrical. If the positions are clearly defined in the BSA, the overall and individual size of the credit available under the NBSA could be determined in a transparent way.

Further negotiations on bilateral swaps among ASEAN+3 countries are expected in coming years, but the uncertainty of the overall size of the swap borrowing available under the NBSA remains a critical problem. Even as a supplement to IMF resources, the CMI swap borrowings may not be large enough to meet potential needs.

Extended network of bilateral swap arrangements

The structure of the network

There are three different groups of participants or contracting parties in the current system of BSAs in the CMI: one between the three Northeast Asian countries, China, Japan, and South Korea; one between the ASEAN members; and one between each of the three Northeast Asian countries on the one hand and the ASEAN members on the other.

The network consists of one-way and two-way swap arrangements. In one-way swaps, one contracting party is a swap-providing country and the other is a swap-requesting country. Japan, for example, is only a swap-providing country. In two-way swaps, contracting parties have both swap-providing and swap-requesting status. Each swap arrangement is divided into two tranches. The first is a standing tranche, from which swap-requesting countries can draw automatically and without an agreement with the IMF as the first line of defence. The second is a conditional tranche, which requires approval by the decision-making body of the NBSA and serves as the second line of defence. It can be disbursed in multiple stages. This structure of the NBSA has several conceptual and operational merits.

First, a total of 78 BSAs can be formed among the ASEAN+3 member countries if each member country seeks BSAs with the 12 other members. As Henning (2002) describes, there would be no bilateral swaps among ASEAN members. If so, the CMI would provide for 33 BSAs to be negotiated: 30 agreements between three Northeast Asian countries and the 10 ASEAN members and three agreements between the three Northeast Asian countries. Contracting parties would voluntarily determine the placement of the amount in each swap arrangement. The aggregate value of the credit available under the NBSA can be estimated. Based on this total, the credit provided by the various participants can be determined by considering economic conditions such as the size of their GDP and foreign reserves. The amounts provided by each country – either an ASEAN country or a Northeast Asian country – could vary.

Second, this structure takes into account the actual financing capacity of each participating country. The BSA is, by definition, reciprocal in that contracting parties have both swap-providing and swap-requesting status. In practice, however, the swap positions would not be symmetric. This conceptual demarcation would be useful in estimating the actual positions of lending and borrowing, not nominal ones. If these positions are clearly defined, the overall and individual size of the credit available under the NBSA could be determined in a transparent way.

Third, further to the classification of one-way vis-à-vis two-way swap arrangements, the classification of standing vis-à-vis conditional tranches in each swap arrangement can be introduced to maintain a balance between automaticity and conditionality. Quick disbursement from a standing tranche is comparable to automatic drawing from the reserve tranche, as is the case with the IMF, which does not require approval by the IMF executive board.

How useful are these conceptual categorisations of different types of BSAs? It could be argued that each BSA should be formed on a voluntary and bilateral basis, or that a simpler structure of the BSA would be more efficient and effective. But the history of financial cooperation elsewhere suggests that the NBSA under the CMI will be but a first step toward more integrated and structured financial cooperation in East Asia. Further deliberation on other cooperative initiatives will emerge sooner or later. At the same time, the European experience of monetary cooperation would be a point of reference for mindful policymakers and economic leaders in East Asia. A more concerted and structured framework would pave the way for member countries to be interlocked in various multilateral arrangements.

Given these structures of the NBSA, an integral part of the network will be a decision-making body and a monitoring and surveillance unit. These need not be costly and bureaucratic, unlike the AMF proposal.

The NBSA can supplement the ASA and can be jointly activated if an ASEAN member so requests. At the same time, the NBSA could be supplementary to the IMF facilities if the requesting member sought IMF assistance. The NBSA initiative would be a complement and supplement to the IMF by strengthening the financial capacity of the international and regional community.

The existing repurchase agreements could operate on a commercial basis without links to the NBSA or the ASA.

Phase-in drawings: two-tranche swaps

Under the current CMI framework, an initial drawing (standing tranche) of up to 10 per cent can be disbursed without an agreement with the IMF. However, the remaining 90 per cent of subsequent drawings (conditional tranche), including the renewal of the initial drawing, are subject to an IMF program. At this stage, it is unclear whether the linkage to the IMF will be untied at some later time. Even if the regional CMI facility is independent from IMF conditionality, there should be a clear structure of phase-in drawings.

In the extended NBSA, the standing arrangements on which the initial drawing would be activated could have the following structure.

For one-way swaps, swap-providing countries would deposit 10 per cent of their total NBSA commitments in US dollars at an NBSA operating agency. The swap-using countries would deposit 10 per cent of the committed amount in their own currencies as collateral at the operating agency. The operating agency would pay interest (less operation fees) on deposits made by the swap-providing countries, while local currencies deposited as collateral would not receive any interest.[6]

For two-way swaps, each participating country would deposit 5 per cent of its total NBSA commitment at the operating agency in US dollars, because the country would have both swap-providing and swap-requesting status. On the other hand, each participating country would deposit 10 per cent of the committed amount in its own currency at the operating agency. The agency would pay interest (less operation fees) to countries depositing US dollars; there would be no interest for local currencies deposited as collateral.

The inclusion of both US dollars and local currency deposits in the operational fund would have two main consequences. First, at an early stage of its development, prearranged swaps fixed as a proportion of the total

NBSA commitment would lay a strong foundation for enhancing the credibility and effectiveness of the NBSA. This structure would also help to ensure that the initial tranche is jointly activated and quickly disbursed. Park and Wang (2000b) propose 10 per cent of the total NBSA commitment as a predetermined ceiling for standing arrangements, but this is an open issue and participating countries could determine a different proportion of standing vis-à-vis conditional arrangements in the total NBSA commitment.

Certainly, the creation of an operating agency would impose additional costs. One way to minimise these costs would be to use an existing institution as the operating agency – such as the ADB. To minimise the operational costs of managing the fund, a swap-providing country could entrust the ADB with highly liquid and convertible financial assets in return for US dollars. Any interest earnings from those financial assets in the custody of depository institutions would accrue to the swap-providing country. However, the agreement would have to include a provision that the ADB had an authorisation to dispose of those financial assets when activation was needed.

Subsequent drawings which exceed the predetermined ceiling (including the renewal of the initial drawing) would need to be approved by the decision-making body, composed of swap-providing countries. Conditional swaps subject to approval would not require any prior currency deposit at the operating agency. Appropriate policy conditionality should be attached to the second tranche in cooperation with the IMF. The conditional tranche could be jointly activated with IMF facilities if the requesting member sought IMF assistance. Through constant monitoring and surveillance of participating members, the NBSA would be managed more effectively and efficiently.

For one-way swap arrangements, the swap-providing country would be entitled to exercise its veto power if the swap-requesting country refused policy conditionality attached to its drawing from the second tranche. The swap-requesting country could also provide US Treasury bills as collateral instead of accepting the policy conditionality.

Drawing amount and allocation of swaps

Before the specific size of the ASA and actual placement of each BSA are determined, the overall size of the swap borrowing available under the NBSA would need to be sufficient to meet potential needs. In particular, two-way swap arrangements by themselves would limit the overall amount of financing available. An effective NBSA would require a large number of one-way swap arrangements. In the last episodes of the Asian financial crisis, for example, Japan, with other industrial countries, committed to providing a further defence to crisis-affected countries: US$4 billion to Thailand, US$5 billion to Indonesia, and US$10 billion to South Korea.

Countries not covered by IMF Article VIII – specifically, Cambodia, Lao PDR, Myanmar and Vietnam – could use overseas development assistance rather than the BSA. These countries need long-term development assistance rather than short-term measures to manage a liquidity crisis. When they become more deeply integrated into international capital markets, the source of financing will be more diversified and the role of private capital will be more important. They could then seek such preventive measures as the ASA and the BSA to ward off volatile capital movement.

For a given total available credit, the actual placement of the NBSA would depend on the economic characteristics of the borrowing countries. A formula would be needed to calculate swap commitments of participating countries. It could include various country data profiles such as external financing requirements (external debt profile), GDP and foreign exchange reserves. Given that such data profiles change, such a scheme would largely serve as a benchmark.

Terms and conditions for the NBSA

Currencies

As the recent Asian financial crisis has shown, the international financial institutions provided liquidity assistance in US dollars. Unlike liquidity facilities under the EMS, regional currencies, including the Japanese yen, are not widely used in East Asia. Internationalisation of the Japanese yen or other regional currencies is an important issue that needs to be further explored when promoting monetary cooperation in East Asia. The Japan–China BSA under discussion is a symbolic step towards this, because it is a yen for renminbi swap.

Given these constraints, it would be more realistic for the BSA to be a US dollar–local currency swap. A swap-providing country must provide US dollars in exchange for local currency. However, in principle, a swap-providing country can provide any equivalent amount denominated in the currencies the swap-requesting country requests. The swap-requesting country in need of foreign exchange liquidity purchases US dollars from the counter-party country with a contract of future selling, in exchange for selling its local currency with a contract of future repurchase at a specified price.

Maturity

Each new or renewed drawing by the swap-requesting country under the NBSA would mature 90 days after the day when such drawing or renewal of drawing took place. If the swap-drawing country wants to renew its initial drawing from the standing tranche, the 90 days can be extended if approved by the decision-making body. However, renewal of the initial drawing will be treated as a drawing from the conditional tranche. If the swap-drawing country did not seek IMF assistance, but requested renewal of the initial drawing, the interest rate would be LIBOR plus 150 basis points for the first renewal. The rate on subsequent renewals would rise by 50 basis points at every other renewal, to a limit of 300 basis points over LIBOR.[7]

For the conditional tranche, maturity times should be in line with those of similar IMF facilities when the swap-drawing country also seeks IMF assistance. If the swap-drawing country did not seek IMF assistance, each drawing of the swap-requesting country would mature in 90 days. The interest rate would be LIBOR plus 150 basis points for the first drawing from the conditional tranche. The rate on subsequent renewals would rise by 50 basis points at every other renewal, to a limit of 300 basis points over LIBOR.

Interest rates

When a repurchase in any swap transaction is made, the swap-requesting country repays the counter-party the original amount and interest. For the standing tranche, the interest rate would be lower than the IMF SRF rate. If a swap-requesting country is eligible for IMF contingent credit lines (CCLs), a new IMF CCL rate could be applicable.[8] If the swap-requesting country is not eligible for the IMF CCL, LIBOR plus 100 basis points could be charged on the swap borrower. Therefore, countries eligible for the CCL would be treated more favourably.

For the conditional tranche, the interest rate should be in line with the IMF lending rates. If an economic program for financial assistance agreed between the IMF and the swap-requesting country is already in existence, or the swap-requesting country intended to request IMF assistance, any applicable IMF lending rate could be charged. If an arrangement for the CCL between the IMF and the swap-requesting country is already in existence, and the swap-requesting country has made a purchase thereunder or the swap-requesting country is eligible for the CCL and prepared to request it, the CCL rate could be charged. On the other hand, if a swap-requesting country does not seek IMF assistance, the interest rate could be LIBOR plus 150–300 basis points.[9]

It is worth considering the case where a country seeks assistance from the NBSA but not from the IMF even though the NBSA interest rate is higher than the IMF lending rate. This could occur if the country wanted to avoid IMF conditionality. However, the NBSA would impose its own conditionality on countries that drew from the conditional tranche. To prevent a country that in reality should go to the IMF from relying on the NBSA, the decision-making body should not ease the conditionality required. However, this would not mean that a country seeking lending from the NBSA would necessarily also seek IMF assistance. If a country experiences a pure liquidity crisis, then, in preference to using its standby arrangement with the IMF, it could draw short-term liquidity support from the NBSA, which should be sufficient to prevent a liquidity crisis from developing into a full-fledged crisis. As seen below, the maturity of NBSA is mostly shorter than for IMF loans.

Collateral

Swap-providing countries would provide collateral in their own currencies. Maintaining the value of good collateral is critical in the context of the regional lender of last resort.[10] For the standing and conditional tranches, the operating agency would adjust the deposit value of local currencies periodically – say, annually or quarterly.

Opt-out clause

Since a crisis can be contagious to neighbouring countries, some member countries might decide to opt out from the NBSA. The decision to opt out would be allowable under the jurisdiction of the decision-making body. The NBSA would need to maintain a balance between flexibility and commitment. If the decision to opt out was completely discretionary, a serious coordination problem may arise, weakening the credibility and effectiveness of the NBSA. If the opt-out clause was to be included, conditions for non-participation should be specified. A regular monitoring and surveillance process should be installed to promptly provide relevant information for assessing the economic conditions of the country exercising the opt-out clause.

The economic conditions of the country exercising the opt-out clause could be based on quantitative measures such as the degree of nominal exchange rate depreciation, the depletion of foreign reserves, and so on. However, a qualitative assessment would reflect the true state of the member countries' vulnerability to the crisis.

Establishment of the decision-making body

A ministerial-level decision-making body is required to ensure and coordinate joint activation. Simultaneous activation will be a key ingredient for the effective containment of a crisis. Under the current CMI framework, a group of swap-providing countries agree that one of them serve as the coordinating country for joint activation of the swaps. But if some countries were hesitant to provide swaps or postponed the immediate activation of swaps, the NBSA would not be a credible instrument. Some enforcement mechanism to commit participating countries to this bilateral contractual arrangement is required, because there is no central organising body to disburse the tranche.[11] However, the BSA is in essence a product of bilateral agreement, so a decision-making body would not have legal status to enforce the contractual arrangement. The decision-making body would coordinate joint activation and specify the conditions for exercising the opt-out clause.

The decision-making body would have the following functions: facilitate and coordinate joint activation and disbursement; assess and supervise regular monitoring and surveillance activities; conduct performance evaluation of swap-requesting countries; impose and enforce conditionality and covenants specified under the framework of the NBSA; identify the sources of systemic risks and causes of individual crisis; determine conditions under which swap-providing countries can exercise their opt-out clauses; provide liaison services for ASEAN+3 countries; and coordinate the activities of the NBSA with those of the IMF and other IFIs.

If this decision-making body and process is put in place, the proposed NBSA could be independent from the IMF or provide parallel lending with the IMF. If the NBSA is somehow jointly activated with IMF facilities, there must be some potential conflicts between the competing conditionalities of the NBSA and the IMF. The IMF conditionality could be used but it should be coordinated by the NBSA secretariat.[12]

Establishing a monitoring and surveillance unit

A regular monitoring and surveillance process is essential for the prevention of crises. The collected information helps to detect and identify the characteristics of a looming crisis at an early stage so that proper remedial action can be taken in a timely manner.

Economic and financial sector monitoring would keep a close watch over macroeconomic trends and policy changes; financial market developments, including cross-border capital flows; and institutional and legal changes. This rather broad coverage of economic monitoring would support effective management of the NBSA, promote orderly economic integration in the region, and facilitate policy consultation and deepening financial cooperation among NBSA members.

The independent monitoring and surveillance unit would also develop a surveillance mechanism to enforce the implementation of common standards agreed upon by members; policy changes and reforms required of the swap-drawing countries from the NBSA (including policy conditionality attached to the swap borrowing); and economic policy coordination or consultation agreed upon by the members.

Relationship with the IMF

Liquidity assistance other than assistance under the standing arrangements could be arranged in cooperation with the IMF. In particular, conditional arrangements could be supplementary to IMF facilities if the swap-requesting country sought IMF assistance. The IMF program could play a role as a credible guarantee to enhance the swap-requesting country's commitment to policy reform. The NBSA initiative would be a complement and supplement to the IMF by strengthening the financing capacity of the international and regional community.

As explained above, the IMF would be invited onto the board of directors responsible for managing an independent unit of monitoring and surveillance owned by the members of the NBSA. The decision-making body of the NBSA could also consult the IMF and Asian Development Bank.

Establishment of the Asian Arrangements to Borrow

As mentioned above, the NBSA and the ASA could be merged into the AAB. The AAB would not require the raising of quota subscriptions, which would be based on the credit arrangements among members, as in the case of the ASA. While the swap size of the NBSA is determined through bilateral negotiations, the AAB credit allocations among members would be determined by considering various economic criteria. It would be useful to have a fixed formula for calculating the credit commitments of participating countries. By using various country data profile such as external financing requirements (external debt profiles), GDP and foreign exchange reserves, an elaborate scheme could be developed. However, data profiles are also changing, so such a scheme would act mainly as a benchmark.

If the amount of AAB credit commitment was too large, some countries would not be willing to participate. Because the total borrowing of an individual participant should be proportional to its own credit commitment, too excessive a credit assignment to each participant could lead to a failure to repay, which would threaten the stability of the system. On the other hand, the AAB would be of no value if its total credit quota were not sufficient to ease the liquidity problem of crisis-hit countries. Using the asymmetry of the one-way swap arrangements as the basis for a proposed AAB is one solution. As in the IMF and other credit unions, the AAB would operate in partnership with all its members, based on their shared interests. But, unlike a typical credit union, there would be a clear demarcation between net lenders and net borrowers. Of its members, Japan, China, South Korea and Singapore are likely to do most of the lending, with the other ASEAN countries likely to do most of the borrowing. If this bifurcation between lenders and borrowers is applied to the AAB, the gearing ratio of the AAB would be even greater than otherwise and more funds would be available to potential borrowing countries.

To address the moral hazard problem, there should be a penalty rate for lending under the AAB facility. If the interest rate is too low and there is no, or insufficient, conditionality attached, borrowers might not have sufficient incentive to set policy well. In addition, borrowers that are not currently in trouble might take excessive risk, knowing that there was a cheap source of credit available if things turned out badly. Monitoring and surveillance activities could mitigate the moral hazard problem to some extent. However, to prevent frequent borrowing from the AAB, the decision-making body should be able to impose stringent conditionality after thoroughly reviewing the track records of recent economic and financial sector performances.

Establishment of an Asian Monetary Fund

It is probably too costly to have a regional monetary fund which has a large bureaucratic organisation. However, the management of the AMF could be less costly if the AAB served as an instrument for mobilising funds provided under the AMF, together with quota contributions from the participants. If the AAB is to operate under the AMF in a similar way to the IMF's GAB or NAB, strict conditionality has to be imposed on the borrowing country. The AAB would technically be an agreement between the AMF and its corresponding creditors, because the AMF would utilise the AAB to mobilise the funds needed to assist countries in an emergency situation. If the AMF did not attach IMF-like conditionalities, the international financial community might raise the issue of moral hazard. In this regard, relevant but binding policy recommendations should be imposed on the borrowing countries. Without due lending discipline in place, the AMF would probably be exhausted due to lax supervision of financial assistance.

CONCLUSION

East Asians may begin to examine the possibilities and desirability of cooperation and coordination in exchange rate policies – creation of a regional exchange rate mechanism and eventually an East Asian common currency. Although a full-fledged form of monetary integration is not viable at this stage, regional financial arrangements could be structured and managed in order to support the coordinated ERM. However, we must note that – as seen in the ERM crisis of 1992–93 – even this institutional framework for exchange rate coordination would not be sufficient to ward off speculative attacks. More complicated issues beyond the development of regional financial facilities would emerge if exchange rate coordination mechanisms were introduced. In this regard, the CMI could be regarded as a significant step, providing a basis for further regional financial and monetary cooperation (Henning 2002).

Looking into the future, financial arrangements in East Asia will be evolutionary. The East Asian Vision Group (EAVG) submitted its report to the leaders of ASEAN+3 in Brunei on 5 November 2001. In this report, the 26 EAVG members proposed that East Asian governments adopt a staged, two-track approach towards greater financial integration: one track for establishing a self-help financing arrangement, the other for coordinating a suitable ERM among countries in the region. Regarding regional financial arrangements, the EAVG proposed that a full-fledged regional financing facility such as the East Asian arrangements to borrow or an East Asian Monetary Fund be established. At this stage, it is unclear whether the leaders and finance ministers of ASEAN+3 would reach a consensus to explore new instruments and techniques beyond the CMI. However, it is worth noting that European monetary integration was also evolutionary. Wyplosz (2001) explains that, although exchange rate stability has been considered as the linchpin of efforts to achieve trade integration, there was never any detailed master plan or any set deadlines.

At its inception, the EC almost completely dismissed monetary cooperation as a regional project, although the European Payments Union, which was set up in 1950, could be credited with having contributed to the resumption of intra-European trade. There was no serious consideration of a regional ERM, because the Bretton Woods system provided stability for European currencies. The Werner Plan was completed in 1970 and endorsed by the Council of Ministers in 1971 just before the Bretton Woods system collapsed in 1971–73. The Werner Report recommended the rapid adoption of a single currency. However, not surprisingly, the plan was deemed wholly unrealistic, and was immediately rejected. As late as 1988, when the idea of monetary union resurfaced, it was widely met with the same scepticism. It took an exceptional event, the collapse of the Berlin Wall, to trigger a serious reassessment. Even the celebrated countdown to monetary union, with a terminal date set in concrete, was accepted in Maastricht only at the last minute (Wyplosz 2001: 15). Wyplosz concluded that Europe's number one lesson is that what matters is the political will to seek closer economic and financial integration; precisely defined plans and schedules are not necessary.

For over a half century, European countries have worked very hard to develop a wider web of political and diplomatic agreements which encouraged their cooperation on monetary and financial matters. There is no such web in East Asia. In the sense that the political preconditions for monetary unification are not in place, Eichengreen (1997, 2000) has a point. If the European experience is any guide, East Asia may take many years to develop effective cooperative arrangements and institutions. However, some observers also note that East Asia may be on the brink of a historical evolution, as Europe was half a century ago (see Bergsten 2000; Bird and Rajan 2001; Dieter 2001). Having suffered such a painful and costly financial crisis, the East Asian countries seem to be prepared to work together to develop a region-wide self-help system against future crises.

East Asian governments have different views about the pace, extent and direction of regional financial cooperation. This is mainly due to the fact that East Asian economic systems, patterns of trade and levels of economic development are far more diverse than those manifest in the EC. Political willingness could be the most important trigger, as shown in the experience of post-war Europe, but the region still needs to reduce economic disparities if an integrated East Asian economic community is to emerge. East Asia has a long way to go before it implements the CMI and launches other regional financial arrangements. At this critical juncture, however, East Asia should not miss the opportunity if regional financial arrangements are thought to be desirable in the long run.

NOTES

This chapter draws heavily on previous joint work with Yung Chul Park. The opinions presented here are my own, however.

1 See also Henning (2002).
2 The quota increase was not immediately put into force, mainly due to the delay in approval by the US Congress. During the 11th General Review of Quotas (22 January 1999), the quota was finally increased from SDR145.6 billion to SDR212 billion.
3 See Ainley (1984) and IMF (2000) for details.
4 For details, see Apel (1998).
5 The European Monetary Cooperation Fund was established in April 1973 with a view to promoting economic and monetary union. It was given three tasks: the cooperation necessary to facilitate the gradual narrowing of the margins of

fluctuation of EC currencies against each other; the administration of the short-term monetary support facility; and the multilateralisation of positions in the very short-term financial support financing facility resulting from intervention carried out by the central banks in EC currencies. This was a more limited system than originally planned. See Apel (1998: 40).

6   By the definition of swap arrangements, currencies involved would be mutually exchanged. However, local currencies exchanged in return for US dollars are inconvertible in most cases and would play only a limited role as good collateral in the event of default, although the operating agency could adjust the deposit value of local currencies periodically.

7   Currently, under the CMI framework, the interest rate on the initial drawing and first renewal is paid at LIBOR plus 150 basis points. The rate on subsequent renewals rises by 50 basis points every other renewal, to a limit of 300 basis points over LIBOR, as in my proposed scheme.

8   The IMF board agreed to reduce the rate of charge and the commitment fee on CCL resources. The initial surcharge (which is currently the same as that on the SRF) will be reduced from 300 basis points to 150 basis points, and the surcharge will then rise with time at the same rate as the surcharge under the SRF, to a ceiling of 350 basis points. Given that the basic charge, which is set as a proportion of the weekly SDR interest rate, is currently around 4.7 per cent, the initial CCL rate will be around 6.2 per cent.

9   LIBOR plus 150–200 basis points would probably be higher than IMF lending rates. In this sense, the interest rate would not be concessional. Nevertheless, some participating countries might enjoy lower spread than those of their sovereign bonds in the international market during the normal period. To prevent moral hazard on the part of borrowers and habitual use of the NBSA, higher spread will be charged on renewal of drawing.

10 The principles governing the lending activities of a lender of last resort should be reconciled with the classic Bagehot rules of lending freely to solvent borrowers against good collateral and at a penalty rate.

11 This point is also rightly recognised by Ito et al. (1999). If the NBSA is just a collection of non-committed pledges, it may take time to activate and disburse funds in the case of a crisis. Firm commitment must mean that, once the decision-making body of the NBSA decides to disburse funds for a swap-requesting country, it should not require any further approval from national authorities of the member countries.

12 Henning (2002) asserts that a division of labour whereby Asian governments provide financing while the IMF provides conditionality is attractive from the standpoint of staff resources and energy. He also points out that because such a division of labour enables Asian officials to avoid specifying political adjustments required of their regional partners, it is attractive for political reasons as well.

REFERENCES

Ainley, M. (1984) 'The General Arrangements to Borrow', Washington DC: International Monetary Fund.

Apel, E. (1998) *European Monetary Integration: 1958–2002*, London: Routledge.

Bergsten, C.F. (2000) 'Toward a tripartite world,' *The Economist*, 15 July.

Bird, G. and R.S. Rajan (2001), 'Regional Arrangements for Providing Liquidity in a Financial Crisis: Developments in Asia', Discussion Paper No. 0127, Adelaide University: Centre for International Economic Studies.

Collignon, S., P. Bofinger, C. Johnson and B. de Maigret (1996) *Europe's Monetary Future*, London: Pinter.

Dieter, H. (2001) 'Monetary Regionalism: Regional Integration without Financial Crises', CGSR Working Paper No. 52/00, May.

Eichengreen, B. (1997) 'International Monetary Arrangements: Is There a Monetary Union in Asia's Future?', *Brookings Review* 15: 33–35.

—— (2000) 'Strengthening the international financial architecture: where do we stand?' *ASEAN Economic Bulletin* 17 (2): 175–192.

—— (2001) 'Comments on "What Kind of International Financial Architecture for an Integrated World Economy",' written by Yung Chul Park and Yunjong Wang, *Asian Economic Papers* (MIT Press).

Henning, R.C. (2002) 'East Asian Financial Cooperation', Policy Analyses in International Economics, No. 68, September, Washington DC: Institute for International Economics.

IMF (International Monetary Fund) (2000) 'Review of Fund Facilities: Preliminary Considerations', paper prepared by the Policy Development and Review Department, Washington DC: IMF.

Ito, T., E. Ogawa and Y. Sasaki (1999) 'Establishment of the East Asian Fund,' Chapter 3 in *Stabilization of Currencies and Financial Systems in East Asia and International Financial Cooperation*, Tokyo: Institute for International Monetary Affairs.

Kim, Y.H. and Y. Wang (2001) *Regional Financial Arrangements in East Asia*, Seoul: Korea Institute for International Economic Policy.

Kim, T.-J., J.-W. Ryou and Y. Wang (2000) 'Regional Arrangements to Borrow: A Scheme for Preventing Future Asian Liquidity Crises', Seoul: Korea Institute for International Economic Policy.

Park, Y.C. and Y. Wang (2000a) 'Reforming the International Financial System: Prospects for Regional Financial Cooperation in East Asia', in Jan Joost Teunissen (ed.), *Reforming the International Financial System: Crisis Prevention and Response*, The Hague, FONDAD.

—— (2000b) 'Beyond the Chiang Mai Initiative: Rationale and Need for Decision-Making Body and Extended Regional Surveillance under the ASEAN+3 Framework', paper presented at the deputies meeting of ASEAN+3, Prague, 24 September.

—— (2001) 'What kind of international financial architecture for an integrated world economy', forthcoming in *Asian Economic Papers* (MIT Press).

Wang, Y. (2000) 'The Asian financial crisis and its aftermath: do we need a regional financial arrangement?', *ASEAN Economic Bulletin* 17 (2): 205–217.

Wyplosz, C. (2001) 'Regional Arrangements: Some Lessons from Postwar Europe,' paper presented at the conference on 'The Role of Regional Financial Arrangements in Crisis Prevention and Management: The Experience of Europe, Asia, Africa, and Latin America', organised by the Forum on Debt and Development (FONDAD), Prague, 21–22 June 2001.

10 The compatibility of capital controls with the development of financial markets

Menzie D. Chinn

INTRODUCTION

A number of recent studies have identified financial development as a key empirical determinant of growth. It is easy to forget how much of a sea change this finding represents. As recently as 1992, Levine and Renelt concluded that investment was the only determinant of growth that was not fragile and that trade openness was the only variable robustly related to investment. Now, after waves of interest in human capital, political factors and other variables, it appears that finance has reasserted its central role. However, this role appears to be significant only in the Organisation for Economic Co-operation and Development (OECD) countries, and not more generally, although the debate over this issue is far from over.[1]

Capital controls have also taken on heightened significance in recent years, in the wake of the East Asian crises. Some people have asserted that 'soft' capital controls, of the Chilean type, have transformed the composition of capital inflows, thereby discouraging unstable hot capital. In contrast, little attention has been paid to an equally interesting question – whether capital controls are compatible with financial development. In this paper I assess this issue. My discussion is based on an econometric analysis, using aggregate data on a large sample of countries over the 1970–97 period.

The analysis in this paper differs in three main ways from that found in much of the existing literature. First, it skirts the links between financial development or capital liberalisation and growth, and focuses on the link between capital liberalisation and financial development. Second, it covers a relatively large set of financial development measures, including those pertaining to equity markets. Third, it uses a relatively large set of measures on restrictions on international financial transactions, specifically using all the IMF's indicators of exchange restrictions and the Quinn (1997) measure of international financial regulation. After discussing the econometric analysis, I make some observations on banking development and equity market development that cannot be easily addressed in the context of large cross-country regression analyses. I also outline some directions for future research.

The paper concludes with speculation on why capital controls, and financial regulation more generally, are likely to become more important in the future. As noted in a recent study (APEC Economic Committee 2001b), assimilation and development of high technology activities around the Pacific Rim may very well require differing modes of financing. Capital controls may directly or indirectly hinder development and use of those alternative modes. Even if capital controls are not direct hindrances, they may signal a policy stance inconsistent with allowing market forces to work, thereby raising the risk associated with ventures that already have uncertain payoffs.

AGGREGATE MEASURES OF FINANCIAL DEVELOPMENT AND CAPITAL CONTROLS

Literature review

There is a long line of papers investigating the link between finance and growth. However, there is a much smaller literature examining the link between capital controls and/or financial openness and financial development. One paper of interest is by De Gregorio (1998). He examines the related question of whether economies exhibiting greater financial integration experience greater financial development. He does not equate integration with financial restrictions of a regulatory nature. Rather, he investigates the effect of a lack of integration characterised by deviations from two no-arbitrage profits conditions: the international arbitrage pricing model (IAPM) of Levine and Zervos (1995), and the international capital asset pricing model (ICAPM) of Levine and Zervos (1998). These measures may reflect the effects of capital controls, but they could also be driven by non-regulatory imperfections in the capital markets. De Gregorio also examines two other measures of capital market openness – the ratio of gross capital flows to GDP and a subjective, polychotomous variable based upon the ratio of gross capital flows to GDP, the Feldstein–Horioka savings–investment correlation coefficient, Euler equation estimates, and uncovered interest parity (UIP) deviations, obtained from Montiel (1995).

De Gregorio uses four measures of financial deepening: total lending to the private sector divided by GDP (by far the most commonly used measured); the ratio of the value of listed shares to GDP; the ratio of the total value of shares traded per year to GDP; and the volatility of the stock market, as measured by a rolling one-year standard deviation.

After controlling for inflation rates and trade openness, De Gregorio finds that, in a cross-section of developing and industrialised countries, the no-arbitrage profits conditions have a positive and statistically significant effect on the lending, stock market capitalisation and volatility measures of financial deepening. The measure of total value of shares traded per year appears to depend only on the ICAPM measure.

In these analyses, one important distinction is that between behaviour in developed and developing countries. In the sample for which De Gregorio has data on gross capital flows and the composite measures, the observations are restricted to developing countries. In these samples, he finds only mixed evidence for either of these two measures having an effect. Gross capital flows appear to be correlated with the lending measure of financial deepening, an intuitive finding, but this is the least convincing measure of the variable of interest.[2]

In one of the more relevant papers in the literature, Klein and Olivei (2001) examine a cross-section of 87 industrialised and less developed countries over the 1976–95 period. They examine both the link between financial development and economic growth and the nexus between liberalisation and finance that we are interested in. Here I merely recount the results pertinent to the question at hand. Their regressions take the form:

$$FD_t^i - FD_{t-k}^i = \beta_0 + \beta_1 FD_{t-k}^i + \beta_2 KALIB_{t-k,t}^i + \beta_3 X^i + \varepsilon_t^i \qquad (1)$$

where *FD* is the financial development variable, *KALIB* is the capital account liberalisation variable, and X is a set of control variables, including regional and time dummies. Klein and Olivei's measures of financial development include the ratio of liquid liabilities to GDP, the ratio of financial intermediates' claims on the private sector to GDP, and the ratio of private bank to private plus central bank assets. Each of these measures has strengths and weaknesses. The liquid liabilities measure is the most common measure of financial development; it consists of the sum of currency outside the banking system, plus demand and interest-bearing liabilities of the banking system.[3] However, the liquid liabilities measure does not distinguish between allocation to private and public sector entities, so it could indicate that a country with directed lending to state-owned enterprises had an advanced financial system when in fact the banking system was failing in its role as project monitor. The private claims measure addresses this deficiency, and is similar to the series used by De Gregorio. Both data series are readily available. The commercial bank assets ratio focuses on the development of services that are most related to financial management.

For *KALIB*, Klein and Olivei use the most common measure of capital account liberalisation – the indicator variable on capital account restrictions of the International Monetary Fund (IMF) from the *Annual Report on Exchange Restrictions and Exchange Arrangements* or, for a subset of industrialised countries, the OECD measure of capital account liberalisation. Comfortingly, Klein and Olivei find a relationship between capital account liberalisation and financial development. However, a notable characteristic of their sample is that the identified correlation is driven entirely by the developed countries. In other words, there is no detectable relationship between liberalisation and development for the less developed countries. Klein and Olivei conjecture that this result obtains because the less developed countries were latecomers to the liberalisation game and that time will tell whether it is just that the effects of liberalisation have not yet been felt.

Empirical analysis

The analysis that I conduct takes a broad view of financial development: it includes the lending measures typically used, but also incorporates various measures of the equity markets. In some respects, the development of equity markets may be a better measure of the ability of an economy to mobilise capital in an efficient manner; conventional measures of lending activity are susceptible to mis-characterising government-directed lending as market-driven lending. Hence, a variety of financial deepening measures are used, although I report results from only a subset of the measures analysed.

Specification

In principle, one would like to estimate the long run equilibrium relationship in

$$FD_t^i = \gamma_0 + \gamma_1 KC_t^i + X_t^i \Gamma + u_t^i \qquad (2)$$

where KC is a measure of capital controls, and X is a vector of economic variables. The capital controls variables are described in greater detail under 'Data' below. Here I focus on the economic rationale underpinning the other right-hand-side variables, in the X vector, which could in principle include a very large number of variables. In this analysis, the set is kept fairly small to allow the correlations to be interpreted. The economic variables include log per capita income in purchasing power parity (PPP) terms, the inflation rate, and trade openness, measured as the ratio of the sum of exports and imports to GDP.

Log per capita income is included because many authors ascribe financial deepening not only to regulation but also to the increasing complexity of economic structures associated with rising income. The inflation rate is included because it (or its volatility)[4] may cause distortions in decision-making on nominal magnitudes. In particular, moderate to high inflation may discourage financial intermediation and encourage saving in real assets. Finally, trade openness is included as an *ad hoc* control variable; many empirical works find a correlation of trade openness with any number of economic variables.

It is difficult to control for apparently secular trends in financial deepening in the context of the panel regression in levels (Equation 2). This is probably due to large cyclical variations in the financial deepening variables, along with trending behaviour of the variables of interest. Hence, an alternative specification, akin to a panel error-correction model, is estimated:

$$FD_t^i - FD_{t-s}^i = \gamma_0 + \rho FD_{t-s}^i + \gamma_1 KC_{t-s}^i + X_{t-s}^i \Gamma + u_t^i \qquad (3)$$

This regression carries with it the following interpretation: the rate of financial development depends inversely on the level of financial development, negatively upon the extent of capital controls (or positively on the degree of financial openness) and on a series of economic control variables.

The use of the long horizon of five years (the average annual growth rate over a five-year period) has two advantages. First, it serves to minimise the effect of correlations due to business cycle fluctuations. Second, relating the growth rate between period t-5 and period t to the level of variables dated at time t-5 serves to mitigate endogeneity problems. Specifically, in regressions of either the level or the growth rate of financial development on variables such as per capita income or, more importantly, capital controls, one could easily imagine two-way causality at the annual frequency. For instance, increases in the ratio of M2[5] to GDP might cause more rapid GDP growth, or increasing stock market capitalisation might induce policymakers to have a less sanguine view of the effects of capital controls. Analysing the data at five-year horizons mitigates (but of course does not completely solve) this problem.

The drawback, of course, is that one is throwing away some data by using average growth rates and sampling the 'initial conditions' at every five years. The ideal solution would be to purge the data of cyclical fluctuations and instrument the right-hand-side variables; in a large panel study of this nature, it is difficult to implement such econometric techniques in a manner that is appropriate, so I resort to simpler and more readily interpretable methods. In any event, this approach is common in the literature (and in my opinion is preferred to pure cross-section regressions that examine growth over a very long horizon such as 20 years).

DATA

The data are drawn from a number of sources, primarily the World Bank's *World Development Indicators*, the IMF's *International Financial Statistics* and the database associated with Beck et al. (2000). The analysis is based upon 1970–97 data, recorded each year, and covers 105 countries. Details are reported in the Data Appendix.

Financial development indicators

A large number of indicators are examined. Below, I discuss only a subset that is actually used in the analysis or mentioned in the text; the others are described in the Data Appendix.

The first set is the most familiar: LLY is the ratio of liquid liabilities to GDP; M2Y is the ratio of M2 to GDP; PCGDP is the ratio of private credit from deposit money banks to the private sector.

The second set is slightly less familiar and applies to the equity markets. SMKC is the ratio of the stock market capitalisation to GDP, SMTV is the ratio of total value of stocks traded to GDP, and SMTO is the stock market turnover ratio. EQTY is the ratio of equity issues to GDP.

Finally, there are a series of measures that pertain to the bond markets. Unfortunately, the number of observations is quite small, and the cross-country coverage quite narrow.[6] For instance, there are only about 140 annual observations on long-term private debt issues, while there are over 1,600 on liquid liabilities measures. When the specification involves five-year growth rates, the number of observations is so small that we are unable to obtain any interesting results for this particular aspect of financial development, even though long-term financing through bonds is likely to be an important factor in economic development (see, for example, Herring and Chatusripitak 2000).

Figure 10.1 shows annual observations on three key measures of financial deepening: liquid liabilities, private credit and stock market capitalisation. There is a clear correlation between the two banking sector related measures; the relationship with capitalisation is less obvious. The top five rows of Table 10.1 report summary statistics for these variables; Table 10.2 reports the correlation coefficients. The correlation between liquid liabilities and M2 ratios is quite high, and the results do not differ substantially when using one or the other variable, so M2 will not be discussed further.

Capital controls

Almost all analyses of effects of either capital controls or their determinants rely on the IMF's categorical enumeration reported in the *Annual Report on Exchange Restrictions and Exchange Arrangements*. Here, for example, k_1 is

Figure 10.1 Selected measures of financial deepening

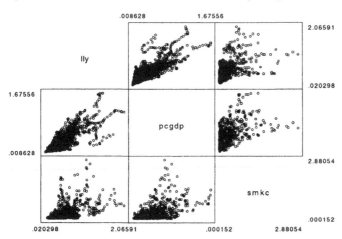

Source: See Data Appendix for explanation of terms.

Table 10.1 Descriptive statistics (full sample)[a]

	Mean[b]	Average growth rate (%)[c]	SD of average growth rate (%)[c]	n
Measure of financial deepening				
Liquid liabilities to GDP ratio	0.6949401	0.011967	0.0107174	558
Private credit to GDP ratio	0.5642643	0.0237751	0.0201916	558
M2 to GDP ratio	0.6377639	0.0106012	0.032067	541
Stock market capitalisation to GDP ratio	0.3449102	0.069905	0.1055967	393
Stock market total value traded to GDP ratio	0.1626606	0.1920002	0.6132919	415
Capital control measures				
k_1: multiple exchange rates	0.0890756	–0.090000	0.3013323	595
k_2: current account	0.1129848	–0.0790598	0.3310367	593
k_3: capital account	0.5234783	-0.0786266	0.1392699	575
k_4: surrender of export proceeds	0.4016807	–0.0953565	0.2522137	595
Other measures				
Estimated financial openness (Quinn)	10.9526	0.0127034	0.0194603	599
Per capita income (in PPP) ('000)	15.10267	0.0590587	0.0376519	464
Trade openness	0.5993367	–0.0116554	0.1188412	591
Inflation	0.0700355	–0.0000891	0.2680427	597

Notes: SD= standard deviation; see text for explanation of other abbreviations
a   Sample periods differ.
b   Mean pertains to the untransformed variable.
c   Growth rates calculated using log differences.

Source: Author's estimates.

an indicator variable for the existence of multiple exchange rates, while k_4 is a variable indicating the surrender of export proceeds. Perhaps the most relevant capital controls are k_2 and k_3. They indicate restrictions on current account and capital account transactions, respectively.

These restrictions on current account transactions limit the private sector's ability to obtain foreign exchange for payments related to imports and to retain foreign exchange earned through exporting. They also limit the ability of foreign direct investors to repatriate interest and profits. The argument for including them as a form of capital controls is that transactions on the current account have often been used to evade capital account controls. Considerable ingenuity is used to do this, through methods such as manipulating the timing of payments and over- or under-invoicing exports and imports. The more obscure provisions pertaining to surrender requirements, bilateral payments

Table 10.2 Correlation coefficients[a] for selected financial deepening measures: full sample

	LLY	PCGDP	M2Y	SMKC	SMTV
Liquid liabilities to GDP ratio	1				
Private credit to GDP ratio	0.814	1			
M2 to GDP ratio	0.8482	0.7752	1		
Stock market capitalisation to GDP ratio	0.4425	0.5063	0.3508	1	
Stock market total value traded to GDP ratio	0.4759	0.538	0.3799	0.687	1

Notes: See Data Appendix for explanation of terms.
a   Correlation coefficients for common samples.

Source: Author's estimates.

restrictions and multiple exchange rates are typically included as a proxy for the intensity of controls explicitly aimed at capital transactions.

Rows 6–9 of Table 10.1 report summary statistics for these capital control measures. Restrictions on the capital account and the surrender of export proceeds appear to be the most pervasive compared to current account restrictions and multiple exchange rates. However, the use of these capital controls appears to be decreasing – although one cannot conclude that their restrictiveness is also decreasing.

Financial regulation

The deficiencies of these dichotomous measures of capital controls are well known. The most critical and obvious is that they do not measure the intensity of the controls, or their efficacy, which might be better assessed using the outcome-based measures of De Gregorio. This criticism can be illustrated by noting that capital controls might be as stringent – and as strongly oriented to command and control measures – as those imposed by Latin American governments in the wake of the 1980s debt crises, or of a less *dirigiste* form, such as Chilean controls.[7]

Quinn (1997) recently compiled a composite measure of financial regulation which ranges from 0 to 14, with 14 representing the least regulated and most open regime. The bulk of the index is based upon Quinn's coding of the qualitative information contained in the various issues of the *Annual Report on Exchange Restrictions and Exchange Arrangements* pertaining to k_2 and k_3, augmented by information on whether the country in question has entered into international agreements with international organisations such as the OECD and European Union (EU).

There is a complete tabulation for the OECD members, but the coverage for the less developed countries is much less extensive, with values reported only for certain years (1958, 1973, 1982 and 1988).[8] Figure 10.2 shows changes in the index for Argentina and the United States. The lack of observations on the developing countries is frustrating as researchers are particularly interested in the role of financial liberalisation in emerging economies.

As an expedient, I estimate a Quinn measure of financial regulation for developing countries. This 'pseudo-Quinn' measure is estimated in the following manner. The entire sample is used to estimate the following relationship between the Quinn measure and the variables k_1 through k_4:

$$Quinn_t^i = \theta_0 + \sum_{j=1}^{4} \theta_j k_j^i + v_t^i \qquad (4)$$

When this regression is implemented over the entire sample of industrialised and less developed countries, all the coefficients enter with the expected negative, and statistically significant, sign. The k_i variables take a value of unity when a control is in effect, and the Quinn measure takes on a higher value the weaker the restriction. This is a very blunt instrument to use to estimate the Quinn variable, but, remarkably, these four variables explain most of the variation in the index; the adjusted R^2 is 0.71.

One might think that the relationship between the Quinn measure and capital control dummy variables differs over groups. One obvious distinction is that between the industrialised and less developed countries. Equation 4 is estimated allowing for an intercept shift and differential slope coefficients.

Figure 10.2 Financial openness measure (Quinn) for United States and Argentina

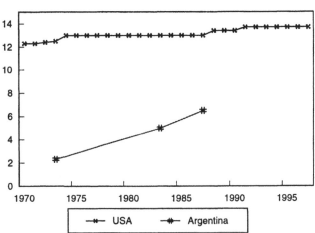

The intercept shift is statistically significant, but this may represent the fact that there are no observations on emerging market Quinn indexes for the 1990s. The only differential slope coefficient that is significant is for k_3 (the capital account), at the 7 per cent marginal significance level. Since the evidence for differential effects is limited, the estimated measure is based upon the regression coefficients in Equation 4, and closer investigation of this issue is reserved for further research.

At this point I will digress a little. There is a variety of alternative estimates of financial openness, some of which have been described above. One set of alternatives relies upon cumulated net foreign assets or liabilities, an index analogous to trade openness. The IMF research staff (IMF 2001) use this measure in their discussion of capital restrictions. However, it is obvious that these stock measures suffer from the same limitations as flow measures of openness – they can be greatly influenced at the high to medium frequency by economic and policy influences other than capital controls.

Another approach attempts to measure intensity, akin to Quinn's approach. Montiel and Reinhart (1999) allow the capital control proxy to vary between 0 (no controls) and 2 (severe controls); unfortunately, they tabulate figures only for 1990–96 for 15 countries.

There are other variations. Kraay (1998) identifies major episodes of capital account liberalisation as those episodes in which a control that has existed for at least five consecutive years is eliminated and stays eliminated for five consecutive years. This approach certainly has an intuitive appeal. Indexes based upon the more finely detailed divisions of the IMF categories have also been constructed by Miniane (2000); however, this index shares the limitation of the standard IMF-based $k_1 - k_4$ variables, in that they can only take values of 0 to 1.[9]

RESULTS

In a preliminary set of regressions, capital controls are proxied by $k_1 - k_4$. It turns out that none of these capital control variables robustly exhibits any statistical significance, even though they had the expected effect of depressing financial deepening regardless of the indicator. Hence, I will focus the discussion below on the results using Quinn's measure of financial openness.

Figure 10.3 illustrates the correlation between private credit (PCGDP) and stock market capitalisation (SMKC) on one hand, and the estimated Quinn measure of financial openness on the other. Both financial development series appear to co-vary in the expected manner with the capital control proxy (positively in the case of the Quinn variable). Indeed, when Equation 3 is estimated omitting X (per capita income, inflation, trade openness), all financial development variables appear to depend significantly upon the degree of financial openness. However, financial development and the absence of capital controls are both positively correlated with per capita income. Hence, the positive association visible in Figure 10.3 may not survive multiple regression analysis.

Figure 10.3 Selected measures of financial deepening and Quinn's measure of financial openness

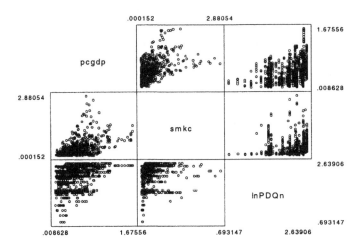

Source: See Data Appendix for explanation of terms.

Table 10.3 reports the results of estimating Equation 3, including *X*, over the entire sample. Neither the change in liquid liabilities (column 1) nor the change in private credit (column 2) appears to be closely linked to financial openness. Per capita income enters with the expected positive sign, as does trade openness. The results using the equity market measures are stronger. The growth rate of new equity issued (columns 3 and 6) responds to the financial openness measure at borderline significance level. More interestingly, stock market total value traded and stock market turnover (columns 4 and 5) – which are better indicators of equity market activity than stock market capitalisation – are both significantly affected by financial openness. The proportion of variation explained is also higher than in the cases using the bank credit measures.

It is possible that these observed patterns are being driven by the decision to pool both industrialised and less developed economies into one sample. This applies to both the apparent sensitivity of equity market indicators to financial openness and the absence of any relationship of bank credit measures to financial openness. As mentioned earlier, some studies have identified sample-specific results pertaining to financial development. Table 10.4 presents the results for a developing country sample.

Bank credit indicators (columns 1 and 2) do not appear to be depressed by capital controls. Nor does stock market capitalisation (column 3). However,

Table 10.3 Financial development and financial openness: full sample, five-year panels, 1972–97

	Pred sign	Liquid liabilities [1]	Private credit [2]	Stock mkt capital'n [3]	Stock mkt total value [4]	Stock mkt turnover [5]	Equity issued [6]
Financial openness[a] [t-5]	(+)	0.0009 (0.0045)	0.0055 (0.0044)	0.0043 (0.0124)	0.0245*** (0.0077)	0.0299* (0.0181)	0.0026 (0.0017)
Financial deepening [t-5]	(–)	–0.0067 (0.0088)	–0.0022 (0.0090)	–0.0014 (0.0326)	–0.0804 (0.0573)	–0.1154*** (0.0304)	–0.0383* (0.0222)
Per capita income [t-5]	(+)	0.0026 (0.0018)	0.0033** (0.0015)	0.0062 (0.0060)	0.0046 (0.0038)	0.0109 (0.0082)	–0.0009 (0.0007)
Inflation [t-5]	(–)	–0.0034 (0.0110)	0.0152 (0.0130)	–0.0690** (0.0260)	–0.0347** (0.0164)	0.0176 (0.0669)	–0.0001 (0.0027)
Trade openness [t-5]	(+)	0.0058* (0.0036)	0.0054* (0.0028)	–0.0208 (0.0171)	0.0022 (0.0073)	–0.0149 (0.0098)	–0.0006 (0.0006)
R^2		0.04	0.09	0.20	0.26	0.35	0.16
N[b]		299	297	148	154	150	54
RMSE[c]		0.022	0.021	0.04	0.036	0.066	0.003

Notes: Point estimates from ordinary least squares (OLS) estimation, heteroskedasticity robust standard errors in parentheses. Dependent variable is the average annual growth rate over a five-year period.
Observations of inflation rates in excess of 100% are dropped from the sample.
a   Financial openness variable is Quinn's measure of financial openness, predicted using the IMF's individual capital control measures.
b N is the number of observations.
c   RMSE is the root mean squared error of the regression. Regressions include fixed time effects (estimates not reported).
*** = significant at the 1% marginal significance level; ** = significant at the 5% marginal significance level; * = significant at the 10% marginal significance level

the preferred measures of equity market development (value traded, turnover and new equity issued)[10] all appear to significantly depend on financial openness. Fixed effects regressions are also implemented, although I do not report the results here. In these estimates, the statistical significance of the financial openness variable is largely eliminated. This outcome is partly to be expected. The country fixed effects are highly correlated with the financial openness of an individual country.

The econometric analysis thus confirms what other studies have found: the relationship between capital controls and bank credit measures of financial development does not hold for developing countries. On the other hand, equity market development does appear to be linked to financial openness in a significant manner, thus yielding a perspective on the relationship between capital controls and financial development that is drastically different from that in the extant literature.

Table 10.4 Financial development and financial openness; less developed countries, five-year panels, 1972–97

	Pred sign	Liquid liabilities [1]	Private credit [2]	Stock mkt capital'n [3]	Stock mkt total value [4]	Stock mkt turnover [5]	Equity issued [6]
Financial openness[a] [t-5]	(+)	−0.0014 (0.0057)	−0.0009 (0.0044)	0.0014 (0.0018)	0.0178* (0.0094)	0.0282 (0.0217)	0.0047** (0.0022)
Financial deepening [t-5]	(−)	−0.0226* (0.0130)	−0.0039 (0.0157)	−0.0091 (0.0442)	−0.0362 (0.1172)	−0.0929** (0.0401)	−0.0256 (0.0235)
Per capita income [t-5]	(+)	0.0046** (0.0019)	0.0019 (0.0014)	0.0111 (0.0094)	0.0019 (0.0049)	0.0142 (0.0118)	0.0002 (0.0009)
Inflation [t-5]	(−)	−0.0035 (0.0113)	0.0192** (0.0131)	−0.0643* (0.0374)	−0.0089 (0.0143)	0.035 (0.0714)	−0.0069 (0.0045)
Trade openness [t-5]	(+)	0.0101** (0.0048)	0.0084** (0.0040)	−0.0253 (0.0241)	0.0102 (0.0078)	−0.0098 (0.0142)	−0.0026* (0.0013)
R-squared		0.09	0.15	0.16	0.12	0.26	0.40
N^b		227	225	85	91	87	31
RMSE[c]		0.021	0.018	0.047	0.032	0.074	0.003

Notes: Point estimates from ordinary least squares estimation, heteroskedasticity robust standard errors in parentheses. Dependent variable is the average annual growth rate over a five year period.

Observations of inflation rates in excess of 100% are dropped from the sample.

a   Financial openness variable is Quinn's measure of financial openness, predicted using the IMF's individual capital control measures.

b N is the number of observations.

c   RMSE is the root mean squared error of the regression. Regressions include fixed time effects (estimates not reported).

*** = significant at the 1% marginal significance level; ** = significant at the 5% marginal significance level; * = significant at the 10% marginal significance level

CAVEATS

Empirical work is always fraught with hazards. When estimating non-structural relationships, the challenges to interpretation of the statistical results are compounded. Here I flag two key issues: two-way causality and mis-attribution of influences.

In the simple two-variable case, endogeneity will tend to bias the regression coefficients toward finding a non-zero relationship. In a multiple regression, the impact is not easily determined, but in principle will be an issue. In using the five-year growth rates and the lagged initial conditions, I have attempted to mitigate the problem of endogeneity. However, to the extent that the right-hand-side variables, such as per capita GDP and the capital control measures, exhibit high serial correlation, simultaneity bias may still be a concern.

Financial development and capital controls might be influenced by a third factor, such as political stability or the strength of the legal system (both the laws and the enforcement thereof). In that case, it would be inappropriate to attribute financial development to the absence of capital controls *per se*.

BANK-CENTRED FINANCIAL DEVELOPMENT: A DISAGGREGATE LOOK

There is a limited amount that one can learn from these analyses at the aggregate level. In particular, a rising stock is not necessarily a good indicator of increasing financial development in a deep sense. In order to examine such issues, one has to consider the efficiency with which resources are used to conduct financial intermediation. To take a stark example, in the years leading up to the Korean financial crisis, one would have witnessed increasing liquidity (LLY) measures. But at the same time, the ratios of incremental capital to output were declining (Chinn and Kletzer 2001).

Detailed microeconomic data are needed to examine the efficiency of the banking sector; even then, one might not be able to measure the true economic efficiency with which resources are being used. Cross-country studies assessing banking efficiency are few and far between; indeed, the appropriate measures are in doubt. Beck et al. (2000) suggest overhead cost and net interest margin. The former is the accounting value of a bank's overhead cost expressed as a proportion of its overall assets; thus a lower figure suggests greater efficiency, assuming the accounting data accurately reflect the economic values. The latter measure is the net interest revenue to total assets, and suffers from similar limitations in relying upon accounting data. In a recent study, the APEC Economic Committee (2001a) compiled these series for 1990–97; they found that both indexes were highly correlated and, further, that they are generally lowest for the developed economies. However, the fact that the indexes for Korea and the People's Republic of China are lower than the corresponding figures for the United States gives one pause for thought.

Figure 10.4 depicts the correlation between overhead costs and the Quinn measure for 1988, along with a non-parametric best-fit line.[11] There appears to be some sort of negative relationship in that a more open capital account in 1988 is associated with a more 'efficient' banking system over most of the 1990s. However, one would not want to make too much of the apparent relationship, given the above caveats. Nevertheless, this finding suggests that it might be profitable to obtain better (economic) measures of bank efficiency, and to relate those measures to the prevalence of capital controls.

EQUITY MARKETS AND AN ALTERNATIVE MEASURE OF CAPITAL CONTROLS

The econometric results for equity markets outlined above are striking in that they suggest that the existence of controls is likely to exert a negative effect on the development of equity markets as well as on credit formation, although

Figure 10.4 Bank overhead cost and Quinn measure for APEC economies, 1988

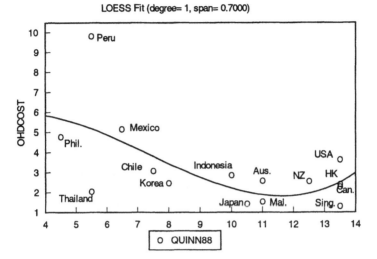

Source: APEC (2001a) and personal communication with Dennis Quinn.

the effect is most pronounced for developed economies. This observation is important because there are some indications that equity markets are better equipped to finance the emerging technologies and business ventures of recent years than are bank-oriented systems (Leahy et al. 2001; US President 2001).[12] Levine (2000) argues that the financing mode is less important than the enforcement of laws pertaining to property and finance when determining whether an economic environment is conducive to growth.

Suppose that the capital control measures discussed earlier are not well suited to indicating whether markets are open. What are the alternative means of measuring capital controls, and hence determining their influence? Bekaert and Harvey (2000) and Bekaert et al. (2001) document how to date the integration of equity markets with global markets, using structural breaks in the correlations of returns. They then associate these breaks with observable changes in regulatory regimes. Using the breaks, they have been able to determine the impact of integration on capital flows and the subsequent change in the behaviour of asset prices. Similarly, Henry (2000) found that the size of equity markets increases after discrete breaks. This work is definitely interesting; however, like all work that infers breaks from behavioural changes, credulity is sometimes stretched when there are a plethora of regulatory breaks and only a rare instance of observable changes (see, for example, Chinn and Maloney 1998, for money market returns in Korea and Taiwan). Moreover, the difficulties are compounded by uncertainty over the correct model for equity returns, so that differing models yield differing conclusions regarding integration versus non-integration.

Recently, Ahearne et al. (2000) proposed an alternative means of indicating the presence and extent of capital controls that impede cross-border equity market transactions. Specifically, they constructed measures of capital controls based upon the proportion of the equity market open to international investors. To do this, they took advantage of the International Finance Corporation (IFC) investable index, which is aimed at measuring that component of the equity market that foreigners can access. Dividing the capitalisation of the IFC investable index by a measure of the overall market capitalisation (the IFC global index),[13] and subtracting that ratio from unity, yields an index that is continuous and that can in principle indicate the degree of openness.

Edison and Warnock (2001) find that their liberalisation breaks accord well with the ones identified by Bekaert and Harvey (2000). However, the 'biggest' openings are not always contemporaneous with the Bekaert–Harvey break. For instance, Bekaert and Harvey time the Taiwan break in 1991, while Edison and Warnock identify the largest decline in restrictiveness in late 1998. On the other hand, it is reassuring that the Edison–Warnock measures correlate quite well with the Quinn measure of openness for the 29 countries these authors examine. Relating this alternative measure of capital controls to equity market characteristics would seem to be an obvious direction for future research.

CONCLUSION

Thus far, I have laid out the empirical evidence from my study and from an admittedly selective survey of the literature. I have reserved until the end the main point of the paper – assessing the compatibility of capital controls with financial development. The basic results from the regression analysis conducted here indicate two main conclusions.

First, if one's measure of financial development is the amount of 'credit' being extended to the private sector, there appears to be a relatively weak relationship between the extent of capital controls and financial development.

Second, financial development, as proxied by the capitalisation of the equity market, does not appear to be closely linked to the extent of capital controls; and, to the extent that a relationship does exist, it is for the developed economies. A caveat is necessary, though. If the measure of financial market development is either total value traded or the turnover ratio, which are indicators of equity market activity rather than size, then financial development appears to depend in a statistically significant manner on the presence of capital controls. This relationship holds in both the aggregate sample and a sample of less developed economies.

This second point is important. It suggests that the potential costs of repressing development of the equity markets may be high; in that case a minimum–maximum criterion may suggest erring on the side of avoiding capital controls.

To extend this assertion, I will focus my argument on the Asia Pacific countries, since the stakes may be highest there. Many of the countries of East Asia have long relied on bank-directed financing, and this type of financing may have been the most appropriate for early- to middle-term industrialisation. However, as I have alluded to in my earlier discussion of equity markets, the changing economic environment, and emerging technologies, may be less amenable to bank-directed financing. As the 2001 *Economic Report of the President* observed:

> The efficiency of capital markets in the United States has also contributed to the superior economic performance we have seen. The more widespread availability in this country of equity finance, including venture capital, facilitates business creation and propels the development of new technologies. In contrast, in Japan and some European countries, banks and other large financial institutions provide most business financing, hold some firm equity, and usually exert a measure of corporate control. These differences between the two systems give rise to different incentive structures. Returns to bank loans are limited by the interest rate; returns to equity investments are determined by profits and capital gains. This makes bank lending better suited to financing low-risk activities, whereas an equity-based system has the potential to generate greater capital investment in activities where expected returns are high but uncertain.
>
> When most job creation and investment are undertaken by large and established firms, these differences in the mode of financing are not likely to be important, since such companies finance most investment out of their own retained earnings. However, it is likely that the performance of the two systems will diverge in sectors such as information and communications technologies, for at least two reasons. In the telecommunications sector, the large outlays required to finance the emerging new technologies could well exceed the financing available from retained earnings and from banks. In other areas of information technology, banks have not been especially successful in supporting the new firms that play an important role in generating innovation. These considerations put the bank-centered systems of Europe and Japan at a relative disadvantage. (US President 2001: 167)

It is tempting, in the wake of the bursting of the dot.com bubble and the deceleration of economic growth in the United States, to dismiss the importance of new technologies. However, even the more sceptical observers believe that some acceleration in trend growth has occurred in the United States (McKinsey 2001), and the economies of developing Pacific Asia will probably need to move up the quality ladders of production and export if they are to sustain their trend growth rates.

The fact that the East Asian economies are rapidly becoming more like the developed economies in terms of economic structure suggests that the relationships previously associated with only the OECD countries may soon apply with some force to the newly industrialising countries. Hence, I believe financial development in the form of equity market development will become increasingly incompatible with capital controls. Although this is conjecture, it is apparently a conjecture shared by others:

> Research suggests that best practice in finance rebounds to benefit all users of financial transactions (that is, the whole economy benefits when the financial system works well). Thin non-bank financial markets (bond, stock, and venture) stymie the New Economy, particularly holding-back new firms. Transparent public listing requirements, along with strong accounting standards will help deepen financial markets. *Economies should give priority attention to, in an orderly way, liberalizing barriers to cross-border financial transactions and institutions* to bring in best practice. (APEC Economic Committee 2001b: 7) (Emphasis added by author.)

DATA APPENDIX

Definition of variables

Indicator	Description	Source
BGD	Budget surplus (+) or deficit (-)	IMF-IFS
BTS	Deposit Money Bank Assets to Total Financial Assets,	BLL, 1970–97
CN	Country code (1-105)	
CPI	Consumer price index (64)	IMF-IFS
DMCB	Deposit money vs central bank assets,	BLL, 1970–97
DMGDP	Deposit money bank bank assets to GDP	BLL, 1970–97
EQTY	equity issues to GDP, Beck, Loazya and Levine data set	BLL data set
EXPORTS	National currency (from national account, 90c)	IMF-IFS
GDP	Nominal in national currency (ny, 99b)	IMF-IFS
QM	Quasi-money; M2, units (35)	IMF-IFS
IDC	idc = 1 if industrialised country; idc = 0 otherwise	
IMPORTS	National currency (from national account, 98c)	IMF-IFS
k1	Multiple exchange rates,	IMF
k2	Restrictions on CA trans,	IMF
k3	Restrictions on KA trans,	IMF
k4	Surr. exp. proceeds,	IMF
LLY	Liquid Liability to GDP (LLY), currency demand and interest-bearing liabilities of banks and other financial intermediaries divided by GDP.	Levine Database[a]
LTPD	long-term private debt issues to GDP,	BLL data set
M1	M1, Stock End of Period, units (34)	IMF-IFS
M2Y	RATIO OF M2 TO NOMINAL GDP	IMF-IFS, (1970–99)
MQM	Money plus Quasi-money, units (M1 + M2)	IMF-IFS
NY	GDP, nominal, local currency, units (99b)	IMF-IFS
SPRDL	Spread between average deposit and lending rates, % (60p – 60l)	IMF-IFS
CAB	Current account balance (78al)	IMF-IFS
OPN	Openness to trade (nominal exports plus imports)/ nominal GDP	IMF-IFS
OPENN	Quinn financial liberalisation indicator,	Quinn (1997)
PBBM	Public bond market capitalisation to GDP ratio	BLL data set
PCGDP	Private credit by deposit money banks to GDP	BLL, 1970–97
POP	Population, 99z	IMF-IFS
PVBM	private bond market capitalisation to GDP	
RY	GDP, real, local currency, units (line 99b)	IMF-IFS
SMKC	Stock market capitalisation ratio to GDP	BLL data set
SMTV	Stock market total value traded to GDP	BLL data set
SMTO	Stock market turn over ratio	BLL data set

Note: BLL = Beck et al. (2000).
a The data are available up to 1997.

Country list (105 countries)

1	ARG	Argentine	53	KEN	Kenya
2	AUS	Australia	54	KOR	'Korea, Rep.'
3	AUT	Austria	55	KWT	Kuwait
4	BDI	Burundi	56	LKA	Sri Lanka
5	BEL	Belgium	57	LSO	Lesotho
6	BEN	Benin	58	MAR	Morocco
7	BFA	Burkina Faso	59	MDG	Madagascar
8	BGD	Bangladesh	60	MEX	Mexico
9	BHR	Bahrain	61	MLI	Mali
10	BHS	'Bahamas, The'	62	MLT	Malta
11	BLZ	Belize	63	MRT	Mauritania
12	BOL	Bolivia	64	MUS	Mauritius
13	BRA	Brazil	65	MWI	Malawi
14	BRB	Barbados	66	MYS	Malaysia
15	BWA	Botswana	67	NER	Niger
16	CAF	Central African Republic	68	NGA	Nigeria
17	CAN	Canada	69	NIC	Nicaragua
18	CHE	Switzerland	70	NLD	Netherlands
19	CHL	Chile	71	NOR	Norway
20	CIV	Cote d'Ivoire	72	NPL	Nepal
21	CMR	Cameroon	73	NZL	New Zealand
22	COG	'Congo, Rep.'	74	OMN	Oman
23	COL	Colombia	75	PAK	Pakistan
24	CRI	Costa Rica	76	PAN	Panama
25	CYP	Cyprus	77	PER	Peru
26	DNK	Denmark	78	PHL	Philippines
27	DOM	Dominican Republic	79	PNG	Papua New Guinea
28	DZA	Algeria	80	PRT	Portugal
29	ECU	Ecuador	81	PRY	Paraguay
30	EGY	'Egypt, Arab Rep.'	82	RWA	Rwanda
31	ESP	Spain	83	SAU	Saudi Arabia
32	FIN	Finland	84	SEN	Senegal
33	FJI	Fiji	85	SGP	Singapore
34	FRA	France	86	SLE	Sierra Leone
35	GAB	Gabon	87	SLV	El Salvador
36	GBR	United Kingdom	88	SWE	Sweden
37	GHA	Ghana	89	SWZ	Swaziland
38	GMB	'Gambia, The'	90	SYC	Seychelles
39	GRC	Greece	91	SYR	Syrian Arab Republic
40	GTM	Guatemala	92	TCD	Chad
41	HND	Honduras	93	TGO	Togo
42	HTI	Haiti	94	THA	Thailand
43	IDN	Indonesia	95	TTO	Trinidad and Tobago
44	IND	India	96	TUN	Tunisia
45	IRL	Ireland	97	TUR	Turkey
46	IRN	'Iran, Islamic Rep.'	98	TZA	Tanzania
47	ISL	Iceland	99	UGA	Uganda
48	ISR	Israel	100	URY	Uruguay
49	ITA	Italy	101	USA	United States
50	JAM	Jamaica	102	VEN	Venezuela
51	JOR	Jordan	103	ZAF	South Africa
52	JPN	Japan	104	ZMB	Zambia
			105	ZWE	Zimbabwe

NOTES

I thank Ashok Mody and Dennis Quinn for providing data, and Hiro Ito for excellent research assistance. Helpful comments were received from the participants at the Conference on East Asian Financial Markets and Centres, Sydney, 11–12 November 2001, organised by the Asia Pacific School of Economics and Management at the Australian National University. Faculty research funds of UC Santa Cruz are gratefully acknowledged.

1   See for instance Leahy et al. (2001) for OECD-specific results. Klein and Olivei (2001) document the linkage for developed countries, and its absence for less developed countries. Spiegel (2001) examines an APEC sample, while Arteta et al. (2001) document the fragility of many of these group-specific results. IMF (2001, Chapter 4) surveys the literature on growth and finance and on finance and liberalisation.

2   Unfortunately, De Gregorio (1998) does not report results for the no-arbitrage profits measures broken down by developing and developed countries. This is probably due to the small number of observations (there are about 24 observations per integration measure).

3   Hence, it is essentially the underlying series used in calculating 'credit booms' in financial crisis models. See for example, Chinn et al. (1999).

4   In most cases, the volatility of inflation rises with the inflation rate, so the inflation rate could proxy for either or both of these effects.

5   Money plus 'quasi-money', comprising the sum of currency outside banks, demand deposits other than those of the central government, and the time, savings, and foreign currency deposits of resident sectors other than the central government.

6   Data are available for the following series: PVBM, the ratio of private bond market capitalisation to GDP; PBBM, the ratio of public bond market capitalisation to GDP; and LTPD, the ratio of long-term private debt issues to GDP.

7   Specifically the unremunerated reserve requirements, which sought to discourage short-term capital inflows and hence outflows.

8   Personal communication from Dennis Quinn.

9   See the discussion in Edison and Warnock (2001) and a comparison of various measures.

10 The equity issue results have to be treated with caution, as the sample is fairly small.

11 A nearest-neighbour fit with window size equal to 70 per cent of total sample.

12 There is a separate issue about whether equity markets are equally, or even more, susceptible to fads and bubbles, relative to banking systems, in the wake of the collapse of equity prices in 2000–01. Even if there was some 'irrational exuberance' in equity markets, the key issue remains whether equity financing was better able to foster high technology investment.

13 The IFC measure of capitalisation does not measure the entire market capitalisation (usually coverage is about 60–70 per cent), but is designed to be representative of the entire market.

REFERENCES

Ahearne, A., W. Griever and F. Warnock (2000) 'Information Costs and Home Bias: An Analysis of U.S. Holdings of Foreign Equities', *International Finance Discussion Paper* #691. Washington: Board of Governors of the Federal Reserve System.

Arteta, C., B. Eichengreen and C. Wyplosz (2001) 'When Does Capital Account Liberalization Help More Than It Hurts?' *NBER Working Paper* #8414.

APEC (Asia-Pacific Economic Cooperation) Economic Committee (2001a) 'Financial Development and Efficiency: Relations with Economic Growth in APEC Economies', *Economic Outlook 2001*, Singapore: APEC (October): Chapter 2. Available at http://www.apecsec.org.sg/download/pubs/Ec2001.exe

—— (2001b) *The New Economy and APEC*, Singapore: APEC, and Washington DC: Institute for International Economics (October). Available at http://www.iie.com/apec/apec-report.htm

Beck, T., A. Demirgüc-Kunt and R. Levine (2000) 'A New Database on Financial Development and Structure,' *Policy Research Paper* No. 2147, Washington DC: World Bank.

Beck, T., R. Levine and N. Loayza (2000) 'Finance and the source of growth', *Journal of Financial Economics* 58: 261–300.

Bekaert, G. and C.R. Harvey (2000) 'Capital flows and the behavior of emerging market equity returns,' in S. Edwards (ed.) *Capital Inflows to Emerging Markets*, Chicago: University of Chicago Press and NBER.

Bekaert, G., C.R. Harvey and R. Lumsdaine (2001) 'The Dynamics of Emerging Market Equity Flows', mimeo, Columbia University, available at <http://www-1.gsb.Columbia.edu/faculty/gbekaert/>.

Chinn, M.D. and W.F. Maloney (1998) 'Financial and capital account liberalization in the Pacific Basin: Korea and Taiwan', *International Economic Journal* 12(1): 53–74.

Chinn, M.D., M.P. Dooley and S. Shrestha (1999) 'Latin America and East Asia in the context of an insurance model of currency crises', *Journal of International Money and Finance* 18 (4): 659–681.

Chinn, M.D. and K. Kletzer (2001) 'Imperfect information, domestic regulation and financial crises', in Reuven Glick, Ramon Moreno and Mark Spiegel (eds), *Financial Crises in Emerging Markets*, Cambridge: Cambridge University Press.

De Gregorio, J. (1998) 'Financial integration, financial development and economic growth', mimeo, Department of Industrial Engineering, Universidad de Chile (July).

Edison, H.J. and F.E. Warnock (2001) 'A Simple Measure of the Intensity of Capital Controls', International Finance Discussion Paper #708, Washington: Board of Governors of the Federal Reserve System (September).

Henry, P.B. (2000) 'Stock market liberalization, economic reform, and emerging market equity prices', *Journal of Finance* 55 (2): 529–564.

Herring, R.J. and N. Chatusripitak (2000) 'The Case of the Missing Market: The Bond Market and Why it Matters for Financial Development', paper prepared for the ADB–Wharton seminar on 'Financial Structure for Sustainable Development in Post-Crisis Asia,' Tokyo, 26 May 2000.

IMF (International Monetary Fund) (2001) *World Economic Outlook*, IMF (September).

Klein, M. and G. Olivei (2001) 'Capital Account Liberalization, Financial Depth and Economic Growth', mimeo, Tufts University and FRB Boston (April).

Kraay, A. (1998) 'In Search of the Macroeconomic Effects of Capital Account Liberalization', mimeo, Washington DC: World Bank.

Leahy, M., S. Schich, G. Wehinger, F. Pelgrin and T. Thorgeirsson (2001) 'Contributions of Financial Systems to Growth in OECD countries', OECD Economic Department Working Paper No. 280.

Levine, R. (2000) 'Bank-Based or Market-Based Financial Systems: Which is Better?', mimeo, Minneapolis: Carlson School of Management, University of Minnesota, (12 June).

Levine, R. and D. Renelt (1992) 'A sensitivity analysis of cross-country growth regressions', *American Economic Review* 82 (4): 942–963.

Levine, R. and S. Zervos (1995) 'Capital Control Liberalization and Stock Market Development,' mimeo, Washington DC: World Bank.

—— (1998) 'Stock markets, banks, and economic growth', *American Economic Review* 88 (3) (June): 537–558.

McKinsey and Company (2001) *Productivity in the United States* (October). Available at http://www.mckinsey.com/knowledge/mgi/reports/Productivity.asp

Miniane, J. (2000) 'A New Set of Measures of Capital Account Restrictions', mimeo, Baltimore: Johns Hopkins University.

Montiel, P. (1995) 'Capital mobility in developing countries: some measurement issues and empirical estimates', *World Bank Economic Review* 8: 311–350.

Montiel, P. and C.M. Reinhart (1999) 'Do capital controls and macroeconomic policies influence the volume and composition of capital flows? Evidence from the 1990s', *Journal of International Money and Finance* 18: 619–635.

Quinn, D. (1997) 'The correlates of change in international financial regulation', *American Political Science Review* 91 (3): 531–551.

Spiegel, M. (2001) 'Financial Development and Growth: Are the APEC Nations Unique?', paper presented to the 2001 APEC Economic Outlook Symposium, Hong Kong, 28–29 June 2001.

US President (2001) 'Economic Report of the President', Washington DC: US Government Printing Office (February).

11 Unilateral, regional and multilateral options for East Asia

Ramkishen S. Rajan

INTRODUCTION

Referring to the Mexican crisis of 1994–95 and the Thai crisis of 1997–98, Montiel (1999: 41) observed that 'the similarities between Mexico and Thailand mattered much more than the differences, and the policy message from the two experiences is the same'. Two similarities stand out: devaluation seemed to trigger an outright financial and economic collapse; and recessionary impulses were transferred from 'ground zero' countries (Mexico and Thailand) to neighbouring countries. An important point underscored by these new financial crises is that sound macroeconomic policies and robust domestic financial systems are certainly *necessary* but clearly *insufficient* to make a country resistant to the effects of sharp reversals in capital flows of the type experienced by East Asia between 1996 and 1998.

The severity of these crises, in terms of both depth and breadth, are important characteristics of 'capital account' crises.[1] Stanley Fischer (2001a:2) recently made the following observation:

> ... the huge expansion of international capital flows of the last decade has delivered significant economic benefits to borrowers and lenders alike. But as we have seen all too often in recent years, this silver lining has a cloud. Countries have been exposed to periodic crises of confidence when large inflows of capital suddenly go into reverse. As capital flows have increased relative to the size of national economies, so too has the disruption that such reversals can cause.

> The spread of financial crises is far from random: contagion tends to hit weaker economies more quickly and more forcefully than strong ones. But even so, it is hard to believe that the speed and severity with which crises spread can be justified entirely by economic fundamentals ... One reason to take excess contagion seriously is that an investor panic can itself push an economy from a good to a bad equilibrium: when a country's policies and institutions are subjected to pressure from a reversal of capital inflows, they may crack, appearing in retrospect to justify the reversal of flows that caused the crisis to begin with.

Managing a conventional current account crisis involves a judicious combination of adjustment and financing, but tackling a capital account crisis predominantly entails the restoration of 'market confidence'. It is therefore a much more imprecise and difficult task, and the emphasis is best placed on crisis prevention rather than crisis management. In this regard, developing and emerging economies must supplement sound economic policies with appropriate financial safeguards to shield themselves from externally induced shocks and liquidity crises (Bussiere and Mulder 1999; IMF 2001d; World Bank 2000b). Ways to increase resilience to capital account shocks include measures aimed at liquidity enhancement, the selective imposition of restrictions on currency or financial flows, and adoption of 'best practice' financial codes, standards and prudential regulations. This paper focuses narrowly on the first issue of liquidity support as an insurance policy against capital account crises.[2]

It has long been recognised that inadequate liquidity can threaten the stability of international financial regimes. Illiquidity can create crises even when economic fundamentals are sound, or it can make a bad situation worse when the fundamentals are weak. Moreover, once it becomes problematic, illiquidity further undermines the confidence of international capital markets. Capital outflows accelerate, thereby reducing liquidity still further. The intensity of economic adjustment following a crisis is largely dictated by the scarcity of liquidity. Thus, Eichengreen and Rose (2001) stress that the East Asian process of 'V-shaped' adjustment has not been very different from the stylised patterns of previous currency crisis episodes in developing countries. However, the degree of initial contraction and subsequent recovery has been far greater in East Asia, attributable to the severe liquidity crisis that was triggered by investors' panic (Rajan and Siregar 2002).

Recognising that private capital flows tend to be procyclical rather than countercyclical and that they intensify shocks rather than offset them, this paper examines potential ways of enhancing the availability of liquidity in crisis conditions so as to minimise the potential for future crises and their social costs if they do occur. Liquidity enhancement measures are commonly seen in terms of being either unilateral or multilateral, the latter invariably involving an expanded role for the International Monetary Fund (IMF). These measures are discussed below. As noted, the contagious transmission of impulses across borders appears to be an important characteristic of liquidity crises. A high-profile Independent Task Force on the Future of the International Financial Architecture sponsored by the Council on Foreign Relations (1999) recently recognised the existence and importance of contagion and the need for some sort of facility to deal with the problem. According to them, such a facility should work in concert with the IMF but not actually be part of the IMF's lending facility. They also argued that only countries afflicted by 'systemic crises' or episodes of contagion ought to be provided with funding, which should be disbursed quickly and be heavily front-loaded. As will be noted, contagion, which is discussed in detail below, often tends to have a largely regional, as opposed to global, dimension (although there are certainly exceptions). This feature of contagion provides the rationale for exploring regional approaches to tackling illiquidity concerns. Following on from this, I briefly examine and assess below the regional initiatives that are currently under way in East Asia. I then offer a summary and conclude with a few remarks on the nexus between monetary and financial regionalism and multilateralism.

UNILATERAL SAFEGUARDS AGAINST CAPITAL ACCOUNT CRISES

Beyond attempts to implement prudential measures on banks' borrowing in foreign currency and to diversify financial systems, some East Asian economies have unilaterally imposed restraints on capital flows.[3] For instance, Malaysia imposed capital controls in September 1998. While the Malaysian controls have since been modified and somewhat loosened, an exit tax remains in place to try and prevent the build-up of 'hot money'. Other countries, such as Thailand and Indonesia, have taken measures to curb currency speculation by imposing quantitative restrictions on foreign currency flows. The IMF has been fairly supportive of such unilateral actions to restrain international financial flows. For instance, a recent IMF study concluded that measures to limit the offshore trading of currencies 'could be effective if they were comprehensive and effectively enforced, and were accompanied by consistent macroeconomic policies and structural reform' (Ishii et al. 2001: 1).

Reserve build-up

While restraints on currency trading may have merit in some instances, an often ignored danger of such measures is that they could dry up liquidity and widen bid–ask spreads, thereby raising hedging costs. One obvious method of enhancing a country's liquidity positions is through the accumulation of international reserves. This is clearly a policy that has been embraced by East Asia; the regional economies have rapidly built up international reserves despite purporting to have adopted flexible regimes (so-called 'floating with a life-jacket') following the crisis (Table 11.1).[4] The replenishment and accumulation of international reserves, on the one hand, and the lengthening of the average maturity profile of external indebtedness of the regional economies (Table 11.2), on the other, have significantly reduced the region's vulnerability to the destabilising effects of volatile and easily reversible capital flows.[5] Nonetheless, recent weaknesses in regional currencies and the desire by central banks to offset, at least partly, the currency declines relative to the US dollar have led to a slight drain in reserves in some Southeast Asian economies since late 2000 (Figure 11.1).

An important limitation of a reserve-hoarding policy is that it involves high fiscal costs as the country effectively swaps high-yielding domestic assets for lower-yielding foreign ones.[6] Appendix 11.1 provides rough estimates of

Table 11.1 Foreign exchange reserves and current account balances in East Asia

	Foreign ex-change reserve		Current account balance	
	US$ million	% of GDP	US$ million	% of GDP
South Korea				
1996	34,037	6.5	-23,005	-4.4
1997	20,368	4.2	-8,167	-1.7
1998	51,975	16.2	40,365	12.6
1999	73,987	17.8	24,477	5.9
2000	96,131	21.0	11,040	2.4
2001(f)a	105,191	23.5	6,000	1.3
2002(f)	119,323	23.9	2,000	0.4
Taiwan				
1996	88,038	31.5	10,923	3.9
1997	83,502	32.7	7,051	2.8
1998	90,341	32.6	3,437	1.2
1999	106,200	35.9	8,384	2.8
2000	106,742	36.4	9,316	3.2
Malaysia				
1996	27,009	26.7	-4,462	-4.4
1997	20,788	20.8	-5,936	-5.6
1998	25,559	35.0	9,529	13.1
1999	30,588	37.7	12,606	15.9
2000	29,075	32.6	8,850	9.9
2001(f)	30,632	32.6	7,300	7.7
2002(f)	32,640	32.0	5,000	4.9

	Foreign ex-change reserve		Current account balance	
	US$ million	% of GDP	US$ million	% of GDP
China, PR				
1996	107,039	13.1	7,243	0.9
1997	142,762	15.8	36,963	4.1
1998	149,188	15.8	31,472	3.3
1999	157,728	15.9	15,667	1.6
2000(f)a	168,277	15.4	12,000	1.1
2001(f)a	178,387	14.9	7,000	0.6
2002(f)	188,152	14.2	4,000	0.3
Thailand				
1996	37,731	20.7	-14,691	-8.1
1997	26,179	17.3	-3,021	-2.0
1998	28,825	25.7	14,243	12.7
1999	34,063	27.5	12,428	10.0
2000	31,947	26.0	9,200	7.5
2001(f)	33,802	28.2	7,000	5.8
2002(f)	35,050	28.0	4,700	3.8
Philippines				
1996	10,030	12.1	-3,949	-4.8
1997	7,266	8.8	-4,353	-5.3
1998	9,226	14.9	-1,546	2.4
1999	13,242	17.3	7,911	10.3
2000	13,048	27.4	9,349	19.7
2001(f)	14,452	19.1	8,400	11.1
20001(f)	15,971	20.3	8,000	10.2

	Foreign ex-change reserve		Current account balance	
	US$ million	% of GDP	US$ million	% of GDP
Hong Kong SAR				
1996	63,840	41.4	-3,509	-2.3
1997	92,823	54.3	-6,159	-3.6
1998	89,625	55.0	3,891	2.4
1999	96,255	60.5	10,545	6.6
2000	107,560	65.8	8,806	5.4
2001(f)	–	–	4,000	2.3
2002(f)	–	–	1,000	0.6
Indonesia				
1996	24,024	10.6	-8,532	-3.8
1997	20,609	9.6	-5,790	-2.7
1998	22,713	23.0	4,102	4.2
1999	23,540	16.2	578.3	4.1
2000(f)	27,464	18.5	8,400	5.7
2001(f)	31,164	19.2	7,000	4.3
Singapore				
1996	76,976	83.7	13,898	15.1
1997	71,392	85.2	16,912	20.2
1998	75,028	99.9	21,025	23.3
1999	77,176	89.3	21,254	24.0
2000	80,362	82.2	21,715	22.2

Notes

a   Estimates by the International Institute of Finance.

f   = forecast

Source: Park (2001).

Table 11.2 External debt of crisis-hit East Asian economies,[a] 1995–2000 (% of GDP)

	1995	1996	1997	1998	1999	2000
External debt						
Indonesia[b]	56.3	53.4	63.9	149.4	95.5	93.8
Malaysia	37.6	38.4	43.8	58.8	53.4	49.3
Philippines	54.9	55.0	61.6	81.7	75.7	78.9
Thailand	49.1	49.8	62.0	76.9	61.4	51.7
South Korea	26.0	31.6	33.4	46.9	33.4	26.5
Of which short-term debt						
Indonesia[b]	8.7	7.5	27.5	76.4	5.9	5.7
Malaysia	7.2	9.9	11.1	11.7	7.6	6.4
Philippines	8.3	12.0	14.0	15.6	11.3	7.5
Thailand	24.5	20.7	13.3	21.0	11.4	6.8
South Korea	14.6	17.9	23.1	9.7	9.3	7.7

Notes
a   Indonesia, Malaysia, Philippines, South Korea and Thailand.
b   Data for Indonesia exclude trade credits.
Source: IMF (2000).

Figure 11.1 Index of gross international reserves less gold in East Asian economies[a] (June 1997 = 100)

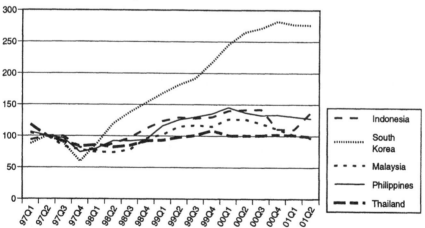

Notes
a   Indonesia, Malaysia, Philippines, South Korea and Thailand.
Source: ARIC website (www.aric.org).

these fiscal costs. They range between 0.3 and 1 per cent of GDP annually. The size of international reserve holdings has also been found to be a theoretically and statistically significant determinant of creditworthiness

(Bussiere and Mulder 1999; Haque et al. 1996; Disyatat 2001), so depleting them as a way of cushioning the effect of capital outflows on the exchange rate may make matters worse by inducing further capital outflows. If capital outflows reflect a perception within private capital markets that a country is illiquid, reducing international reserves and therefore curbing liquidity further is hardly likely to be an effective strategy.

Foreign bank entry and contingent credit lines

In light of the above, it has been suggested that the internationalisation of domestic banking systems in developing countries could be an important additional means of overcoming illiquidity during crisis periods. The argument is that a banking system with an internationally diversified asset base is more likely than another system to be stable and is less prone to bank runs and outright crises because domestic branches of foreign banks can obtain financing from the foreign head office, which effectively acts as a private lender of last resort. In addition, since the portfolios of foreign banks are much less concentrated in any single country, particularly in developing and emerging host countries, they ought to be less susceptible to country-specific crises. Thus, foreign banks in Argentina and Mexico were able to maintain access to offshore financing during the Tequila crisis of 1994 and 1995 while domestic banks were faced with credit squeezes.

There are other potential advantages of allowing foreign bank entry *per se* – for example, lowering overall financial cost structures – which may make it a desirable policy in and of itself.[7] Regardless of the national policy towards foreign bank entry, countries may find it useful to establish contingent lines of credit with foreign banks and private financial institutions as a means of providing additional international liquidity to deal with sudden capital flow reversals. Indonesia, Argentina, Mexico and South Africa are recent examples of countries that have arranged such private lines of credit with international banks.

That said, there are a number of problems and limitations in depending solely on such unilateral credit lines on a private basis rather than regionally or multilaterally through official channels. First, there may be high opportunity costs involved insofar as the individual countries have to commit certain assets or revenue streams as collateral. Second, calling on these lines of credit when needed could lead to a hike in the country's international risk premium. Third, the financial institutions with which the lines of credit have been negotiated could undermine their commitments by reducing their other exposures to that country – so-called dynamic hedging. These institutions could themselves be a source of contagious transmission of crises. For instance, in response to a crisis in one country, they might attempt to liquidate positions in other regional economies to which they have exposures. Fourth, and related to this, if the credit lines are called upon by one country, the international financial institutions may be forced to reduce their exposures in other emerging economies, either to cover losses or in order to reduce portfolio risks and improve the liquidity position ('flight to safety' effects). In view of this, Fischer (2001a) has stressed the need for a multilateral response in the form of IMF lending to complement unilateral measures that countries may take towards liquidity enhancement.

MULTILATERAL SAFEGUARDS: LIQUIDITY, CRISIS AND THE IMF

IMF contingent credit lines

One component of the debate about a new international financial architecture (Box 11.1) has been how to provide adequate liquidity to help forestall a crisis in a distressed economy and prevent its spread to other countries when

---

Box 11.1 Components constituting reform of the international financial architecture

Detecting and monitoring external vulnerability While good macroeconomic policies and adequate foreign reserves remain the key to reducing vulnerability, work has concentrated on improving IMF surveillance of policies, and on tools to help countries better assess the risks they face.

Strengthening financial systems Financial regulators need to upgrade supervision of banks and other financial institutions to keep up with the modern global economy and ensure that risk management and other practices keep institutions from getting into difficulties.

International standards and codes Adherence to international standards and codes of good practice helps ensure that economies function well at the national level, which is a key prerequisite for a well-functioning international system.

Capital account issues Architecture reform aims to help countries benefit from international capital flows, an important element of which is helping them open to such flows in ways that avoid risks and emphasise careful preparation.

Sustainable exchange rate regimes Financial crises have often been marked by inconsistencies between the exchange rate regime and other economic policies. The IMF is advising countries to choose a regime that fits its needs, especially in light of the risks of pegged exchange rates for countries open to international capital flows.

Involving the private sector in forestalling and resolving crises Better involvement of the private sector in crisis prevention and management can limit moral hazard, strengthen market discipline by fostering better risk assessment, and improve the prospects for both debtors and creditors.

Reform of IMF financial facilities and related issues The IMF is implementing important changes to help focus its lending on crisis prevention and to ensure more effective use of IMF funds.

Measures to increase transparency Measures are being taken to make available timely, reliable data, plus information about economic policies and practices, to inform both policymakers and market participants, and to reduce the risk of crisis.

Source: IMF (2001a: 1).

there is reluctance to make concessions in terms of conditionality and to substantially increase the IMF's lending capacity. The IMF's response has been to create a contingent credit line (CCL). Officially, the CCL was conceived as a 'precautionary line of defense to help protect countries pursuing strong policies in the event of a balance of payments need arising from the spread of financial crises' (IMF 2001d: 37). The negotiation of conditionality with potential users of the CCL would therefore take place before the country needed to draw on the fund. The facility underwent some modifications in late 2000, including a reduction in its relatively high costs of borrowing and a review of the conditionality involved as part of obtaining the funding (Fischer 2001a). Box 11.2 gives details of recent CCL changes.

This sort of 'tinkering' fails to recognise a more fundamental drawback of such a scheme. Why should countries sacrifice sovereignty over national policy and subject themselves to strict conditionality when all they receive in return is an option on a drawing? In many cases, countries fail to implement conditionality for one reason or another, so a situation could arise where a country complies with a significant proportion of conditionality and yet is ineligible to draw in the event of experiencing contagion from a crisis. Of most concern, however, has been the possibility that by approaching the IMF to negotiate a CCL a country sends out a negative signal to private capital markets that it is vulnerable to a crisis. Negotiating a CCL may be viewed by financial markets as a sign of a country's weakness rather than a sign of strength. This may make a crisis self-validating.[8] Moreover, there must remain some doubt about whether the facility would be adequately financed and able to provide sufficient net liquidity to a country in times of crisis. This is particularly so as the whole idea of contagion is that a number of countries are simultaneously affected and subsequently in need of financing. In view of this, it should be of no surprise that the facility has remained unutilised (IMF 2001d).

Contagion: regional more than global

The primary reason for the establishment of the CCL was the recognition of the importance of the contagious transmission of currency crises. Yet, with some notable exceptions – such as the Russian debt default in 1998 – contagion has turned out to be more of a regional than a global phenomenon; consequently contagion is also referred to as 'neighbourhood effects'. The East Asian crisis threatened to turn global, but it did not do so. Similarly, the currencies of Thailand, Hong Kong and the Philippines underwent brief periods of speculative attacks during the Tequila crisis, but the crisis predominantly affected Mexico's neighbouring economies. In a recent study using a sample of 20 countries covering the periods of the 1982 Mexican debt crisis, the 1994–95 Tequila crisis and the 1997–98 Asian crisis, De Gregario and Valdes (2001) found contagion to be directly dependent on geographical horizon. Using a panel of annual data for 19 developing economies for the period 1977–93, Krueger et al. (2000) concluded that a currency crisis in a regional

Box 11.2 Recent modifications to the IMF's contingent credit lines

Monitoring arrangements Monitoring arrangements for members that had strong track records on policies and that qualified for the CCL would be less intensive than for members under other IMF arrangements. Accordingly, in its request for a commitment of CCL resources, the member should present a quarterly quantified framework to guide its macroeconomic policies that would be a basis for monitoring, but there would be no need for a detailed definition of program targets. Also, while the initial consideration of the member's eligibility should include an assessment of its structural program and the progress expected under that program, formal structural benchmarks would not be necessary. Finally, in appropriate cases, the midterm review of arrangements with CCL resources could be completed on a lapse-of-time basis (without formal discussion by the IMF's executive board). Between reviews, staff and management would remain in close touch with the member and inform the board if there were concerns that slippages in the member's policies might make it vulnerable to crises. The board agreed that the IMF must continue to have the means to make a member exit formally from the CCL – primarily in the form of the limited (one-year) commitment period under the CCL and the midterm review.

Activation A member approved for a CCL could request financing at any time, which would lead to a special 'activation' review by the board. In September 2000, directors agreed to simplify the conditions for completing the activation review to assure members using the CCL of greater automaticity in the disbursement of resources. The activation review would be divided into an 'activation' review and a 'post-activation' review. The former would be completed quickly and release a predetermined, large amount of resources (normally a third of the total commitments) and the member would be given the strong benefit of the doubt as to any required policy adjustments. In the post-activation review, phasing and conditionality would be specified for access to the remaining resources.

Conditions One formal condition for the completion of the activation review would be eliminated. Under the original policy, the board had to agree that 'up to the time of the crisis, the member has successfully implemented the economic program that it had presented to the Board as a basis for its access to CCL resources.' This condition was intended to guard against the possibility that the member's own policies had contributed to the build-up of its balance of payment difficulties. The board agreed to omit this as a separate condition because this possibility would not be consistent with the member's difficulties being judged to be largely beyond its control (a separate condition for the activation review).

Rate of charge The overall rate of charge and the commitment fee on CCL resources was reduced. The initial surcharge was lowered from 300 basis points to 150 basis points – half the surcharge under the Supplemental Reserve Facility (SRF). The surcharge would then rise with time, to a ceiling of 350 basis points. The commitment fee on the CCL (and other large arrangements) was reduced by replacing the prevailing flat commitment fee of 25 basis points with a new schedule (to be applied to all IMF arrangements) of 25 basis points on amounts up to 100 per cent of quota, and 10 basis points for amounts in excess of 100 per cent of quota. This structure recognises the importance of fixed costs in setting up an arrangement.

Sunset clause To allow for a meaningful period of experimentation with the revised facility, the board extended the sunset clause on the CCL until November 2003. The board will conduct its next review of the CCL in November. The design of IMF-supported programs will be guided by the requirement that the member should be able to meet repurchase obligations. The member's ability to meet the repurchase expectations would signal as a general rule a stronger-than-expected improvement in its external position. Members may request an extension of repurchase expectations at any time. Should a member fail to meet a repurchase expectation not extended by the board, its right to make further drawings, including under ongoing arrangements, would be automatically suspended. The board agreed to review the operation of early repurchase expectations by November 2005.

Source: IMF (2001b: 37 and 38).

economy raises the probability of a speculative attack on the domestic currency by about 8.5 percentage points.[9]

These findings raise the following questions. If the knock-on effects from financial crises are primarily a regional phenomenon, does it not follow that the liquidity provided in an attempt to forestall the contagion effects of crises should be provided regionally in the first instance? Does not the principle of subsidiarity suggest that a regional system of contingent credit lines should be established in a manner similar to the bilateral swaps used to support pegged exchange rates during the Bretton Woods era? There are signs that this is the direction in which the East Asian economies are moving. Before examining recent developments and the unresolved issues to which these developments in East Asia give rise, it is important to define and highlight the various transmission channels through which currency and financial crises may spread contagiously.

CONTAGION: DEFINITIONS AND TRANSMISSION CHANNELS

At a broad level, 'contagion' refers to the simultaneous occurrence of currency crises in two or more economies. It may be more formally defined as a situation where a currency crisis in one economy leads to a jump to a 'bad' equilibrium in a neighbouring economy (Masson 1998).[10] A distinction needs to be made between transmission channels that are related to investor sentiment or psychology (termed 'pure contagion') and linkages between countries that are measurable or observable *ex ante* (referred to as 'spillovers' or 'linkages').[11] Spillovers in turn take the form of trade (real) or financial linkages between countries. Calvo and Reinhart (1996) call this type of crisis propagation 'fundamentals-based contagion'.

Trade spillovers

Glick and Rose (1999) have noted:

> ... trade is an important channel for contagion, above and beyond macroeconomic influences. Countries who trade and compete with the target of speculative attacks are themselves likely to be attacked ...This linkage is intuitive, statistically robust, and important in understanding the regional nature of speculative attacks' (pp. 604–5).[12]

Trade spillovers in turn could be due to either 'complementarity' or 'competition' in export product structures between regional economies.

With regard to the former ('direct channel'), extensive intra-regional trade and investment linkages could lead to contagion due to trade complementarities. For instance, currency devaluation in an emerging or developing economy is often accompanied by a sharp economic downturn (Rajan 2002; Rajan and Shen 2001), thereby compressing imports. This in turn reduces exports of its trading partners, leading to 'demand-driven' trade spillovers. On the other hand, there may be extensive and growing trade, investment and other intra-regional interdependencies leading to contagion due to trade complementarities that are 'supply-driven' ('indirect channel'). For instance, Japanese foreign direct investment (FDI) has developed an intricate division of labour based on both horizontal and vertical differentiation in East Asia (Kawai and Urata 1998). This has stimulated intra-regional trade, which has been about two-fifths of the region's total trade, with parts and components playing a particularly important role in such transactions (World Bank 2000b). Accordingly, any disruption in one economy could interrupt the entire regional production network, leading to a withdrawal of investors from all other trade partners.

In contrast to the complementarity-induced channels, even economies that do not have strong trade and investment linkages with the crisis-hit economies may yet be indirectly affected if their exports to third markets overlap significantly. In other words, currency devaluation in one economy may provoke devaluation in a trade competitor (another economy with similar export structures or comparative advantage) that suddenly finds itself at a competitive disadvantage (Gerlach and Smets 1995; Huh and Kasa 1997). Corsetti et al. (1999) have shown that a game of competitive devaluation could generate currency overshooting if market participants, anticipating that a series of competitive devaluations will take place once there is a successful speculative attack in one country, flee from the trade competitors.[13]

Financial sector spillovers and pure contagion

While trade spillovers appear to be relatively straightforward, in practice it can be difficult to clearly distinguish between trade and financial linkages as 'most countries that are linked via trade channels tend also to be linked via finance channels (Kaminsky and Reinhart 2000a,b). As Dornbusch et al. (2000) note:

> … [a] channel similar to trade links can be financial links. The process of economic integration of an individual country into the world market will typically involve both trade and financial links. In a world or region that is heavily economically integrated – covering trade, investment, and financing links – a financial crisis in one country can then lead to direct financial effects, including reductions in trade credit, FDI and other capital flows to other countries. (p.6)

While acknowledging this fact, it is far more difficult to distinguish between financial spillovers and pure contagion, as both largely pertain to investors' decisions. The one substantive distinction between spillovers and pure contagion is that in the former there must be *ex ante* linkages between the crisis-hit economies, while in the latter the linkages only appear *ex post*. Masson (1998) shows how it is conceptually possible for 'pure contagion' to make an economy relatively more susceptible to a currency crisis. He notes:

... pure contagion is only possible if changes in expectations are self-fulfilling, and this requires that financial markets be subject to multiple equilibria ... Even if each country separately is not subject to multiple equilibria, together they may be, since the fear of crisis in one will increase the devaluation probability in the other, making a crisis more likely in both.

Shifts in market sentiments could lead to jumps between one equilibrium and the other, introducing sharp volatility in financial markets. Theoretically, anything could act as the coordinating device leading to a jump from a 'good' to 'bad' equilibrium.

To illustrate the practical difficulties in distinguishing between the effects of financial sector linkages and pure financial contagion, consider the case of a coincident decline in cross-border bank loans in the ASEAN-5 on the one hand and Hong Kong and Singapore on the other. There could be substantive linkages between the two set of economies, either because the ASEAN-5 economies and Hong Kong share a common creditor – namely, Japanese banks – or because financial institutions in the latter two economies might have large exposures to the ASEAN-5 economies. These are instances of actual pre-crisis linkages and qualify as financial spillovers. However, losses in one economy may lead banks (or other financial entities like open-end mutual funds, for that matter) to rationally unwind positions in other regional economies in which they have exposures. This 'forced portfolio adjustment' behaviour or 'liquidity constrained' effect, which is a perfectly rational behaviour, may occur for a number of reasons. These include an anticipation of higher-frequency redemptions, the need to cover capital losses in other crisis-hit markets ('cash-in' effects), and an attempt to reduce portfolio risks and improve the liquidity position ('flight to safety' effects).[14]

In addition to the direct linkages and liquidity constraints, there is the possibility of 'panic herding' or 'bandwagon' effects, as international creditors and investors choose to reduce exposures to all emerging economies (particularly those in the region) if they are spooked by the crisis in one or more of the regional economies, leading to a Diamond–Dybvig (1983) international bank panic. Krugman (1999: 8–9) stated that there is no way 'to make sense of the ... (East Asian) contagion of 1997–98 without supposing the existence of multiple equilibria, with countries vulnerable to self-validating collapses in confidence'.

One can never be sure what causes these investor panics, sudden shifts in market expectations and indiscriminate withdrawal from many markets. This is what makes explanations based on multiple equilibria difficult to pin down, as a jump between a good (that is, non-attack) and bad (that is, attack) equilibrium is driven by market psychology or changes in the interpretation of existing information. A weakness or attack on one currency could lead to a reassessment of the region's 'fundamentals' and the probability of a similar fate befalling regional economies with broadly similar macroeconomic stances (whether actual or perceived). This is popularly termed the 'wake-up call' effect (Ahluwalia 2000). This phenomenon could also refer to the sudden realisation of how little market participants truly understood about the regional economies, leading to a region-wide downgrading or sell-off (Radelet and Sachs 1998). In related literature, Drazen (1999) has developed a contagion model which is based on economies being in an implicit or explicit currency or monetary union. Devaluation by one economy acts as a wake-up call to investors in the sense that it leads them to question the commitment of other regional economies to maintain 'club membership' by not devaluing. Dooley (2000) suggests that the 'bunching together' of crises may also be due to revisions in the effective size of official lines of credit available to the regional governments to defend the currency (either from international agencies or *ad hoc* bilateral or multilateral agreements).

Such sudden capital withdrawals are not limited to bank flows and do not arise only when financial markets are subject to multiple equilibria or self-validating expectations. For instance, focusing on portfolio flows and assuming that there are some fixed costs of gathering and processing country-specific information, Calvo and Mendoza (1996, 2000) show how just a rumour of such vulnerabilities may generate large-scale reallocation of funds from one destination to another, making small open economies susceptible to large swings in capital flows and costly boom–bust cycles. The Calvo–Mendoza model is best seen as an open economy extension of the information-based herding and cascades genre of models that have been recently developed to explain herding behaviour in domestic financial markets a la Banerjee (1992), Scharfstein and Stein (1990) and others.[15]

The literature has so far not been able to come up with a consistent definition of financial sector spillovers. If trade spillovers include both direct and indirect channels, consistency seems to dictate that financial sector spillovers include both direct financial linkages and indirect or cross-market interconnections through liquidity constraints. This leaves only capital outflows triggered in international financial markets due solely to sudden shifts of sentiment of financial agents (that is, 'animal spirits or herding') following a crisis in another economy as qualifying as 'pure contagion'. This appears closest to the definition by Masson (1998). As Van Rijckeghem and Weder (1999: 5–6) note:

> ... pure contagion refers to those crises triggered by a crisis elsewhere but which cannot be explained by changes in fundamentals or by any sort of the rather 'mechanical' spillovers ... but are possibly caused by shifts in market sentiments (increased risk aversion) or changes in interpretation given to existing information (an increased perception of risk or a 'wake-up call').

REGIONAL RESPONSES: THE CHIANG MAI INITIATIVE

Much work remains to be done to disentangle the various transmission channels documented above. Suffice it to note here that the regional dimension of the 1997–98 crisis, as well as the perceived inadequacies of the IMF's response to it, has motivated a subgroup of East Asian economies to take some small but important steps towards enhancing regional financial stability and protecting themselves against externally induced shocks and liquidity crises. The establishment of the Manila Framework Group (MFG), the ASEAN Surveillance Process (ASP) – which is managed by the newly created ASEAN Surveillance Coordinating Unit (ASCU) – and the recently formed Regional Economic Monitoring Unit (REMU) of the Asian Development Bank (ADB) are all steps in the right direction. These initiatives towards enhanced regional surveillance have been discussed in some detail by Chang and Rajan (2001), Rajan (2000), Manzano (2001) and others, and will not be repeated here. They are important in their own right, but they do not in and of themselves reduce a country's susceptibility to capital account crises, which requires access to international credit lines as discussed previously.

Against this background, and in recognition of the fact that financial stability has the characteristics of a regional public good, it is important to note that selected East Asian economies have recently agreed to create a network of bilateral currency swaps and repurchase agreements as a 'firewall' against future financial crises. This has come to be termed the Chiang Mai Initiative (CMI), following an agreement in Chiang Mai, Thailand, on 6 May 2000. The chapter by Yunjong Wang in this volume gives details of the CMI.

Economic analysis helps to identify some broad principles that need to be incorporated in the initiative. First, the resources need to be capable of being disbursed quickly and of being front-loaded. Speed is of the essence in a crisis. Second, the credit lines need to be large enough to generate confidence in private capital markets and to repel speculative attacks, and need to involve enough countries to avoid potential problems of co-variance and to allow the pooling of risks. Third, the rate of interest needs to be high enough to guard against moral hazard. Countries need to be discouraged from using such credit lines as a matter of course. Fourth, access to such liquidity needs to be separated from the detailed negotiation of conditionality, which would prejudice quick dispersal; links to IMF conditionality are therefore a cause of concern. However, given the part played in the East Asian crisis by weak domestic financial structures, and inadequate prudential standards and supervision, there is a strong argument for making access to the credit lines associated with the CMI conditional upon compliance with some minimum set of financial standards. This would encourage countries to push ahead with reforms to their domestic financial systems. Rajan and Bird (2001) provide a brief progress report on financial restructuring efforts in the region.

A credible system of regional swaps based on these principles has two key attractions. First, it would enable participants to avoid the severe output losses that are associated with extreme shortages of liquidity. Second, by creating confidence that such extreme shortages will not occur, the incidence of crises could be reduced. Of course, confidence would be undermined if the swap arrangements were used to defend disequilibrium real exchange rates. Therefore, the CMI should not be a mechanism for inappropriate currency pegging in the region. The history of bilateral swaps in the context of the Bretton Woods system demonstrates that they are an ineffective means of defending seriously misaligned currencies.[16]

The CMI appears to have been well received, even by the IMF and the US administration. The IMF Managing Director, Horst Kohler, has expressed support for the Asian Monetary Fund (AMF) and other regional initiatives as long as they are complementary to, and not competitive with, the IMF approach (Kohler 2001). China too has expressed open support for the CMI and has become an active participant in it (Goad 2000; Rowley 2000, 2001). Support by these entities is significant, not least because their opposition stifled the initial proposals for fortified monetary regionalism via an Asian monetary facility (Bird and Rajan 2000a; Chang and Rajan 2001). In fact, a successful introduction of a network of regional swap arrangements in East Asia (possibly enlarged to encompass most of Asia as defined by the ADB over time) has been viewed by some observers as an important step towards the eventual creation of a full-fledged regional monetary facility (Rowley 2001).

CONCLUSION

Looking at the issues that have gone to make up the architecture debate, and taking an East Asian perspective rather than a global one, there is reason to believe that there is both more scope for reform and more motivation to pursue it.[17] In the main, it was the East Asian economies that suffered the costs of the 1997–98 crisis. While one could quibble about the exact magnitude of these costs, it is widely agreed that they have been substantial, involving large-scale declines in output and overall living standards.

While the term 'contagion' has gained prominence – notoriety, in fact – following recent currency crises, it should be recalled that the term was used in a positive sense before the crisis to describe the spread of trade and investment liberalisation and economic prosperity in East Asia. According to the logic of this argument, a positive externality of being associated with dynamic open economies involves the transformation of the conventional prisoner's dilemma – which suggests that protectionist policies are the 'dominant strategy' for each country acting in isolation – to one of prisoner's delight, whereby trade liberalisation is the dominant strategy for a country in a region in which some other countries are already reaping the benefits of a liberal trade regime (Garnaut 1994).[18] An important policy conclusion drawn at that time was the need for a formalisation and institutionalisation of these market-driven linkages – that is, the creation of regional economic alliances. In similar vein, the contagious transmission of currency crises, which often tends to be regional, has provided the basis for regional financial and monetary cooperation.

There are at least two further reasons to believe that regional arrangements to augment international liquidity have a comparative advantage over multilateral ones when it comes to the provision of CCLs. First, regional credit lines would have more of the features of a credit union than the IMF possesses. All participants would be able to perceive circumstances in which they might themselves need to use the credit lines, and these vested interests ought to create a stronger motivation to make the system successful than perhaps exists in the case of the IMF's CCL. Second, prudential and supervisory standards might be more appropriately set at the regional level, where special circumstances could be more easily identified and addressed.

For the foregoing reasons, an efficient cooperative arrangement for providing liquidity would be consistent with the central elements of the new international financial architecture. It is still possible to think globally and act regionally.[19] The IMF would continue to stand ready to assist economies where regional arrangements failed to resolve problems, but in this event it might be more reasonable to assume that these problems were not exclusively to do with shortages of liquidity, and this would raise the credibility of IMF conditionality.[20] For poorer developing countries, where balance of payments deficits remain driven by the current account, conventional IMF lending, or even a resuscitated low conditionality compensatory lending facility, could augment the regional credit lines organised by emerging economies. Boughton (1997: 3) has reminded us that:

> ... although the intention was that the availability of the Fund's resources should prevent countries from experiencing financial crisis, in practice, the institution has often found itself helping its members cope with crises after they occur...

Monetary and financial regionalism, as discussed in this chapter, could help the IMF fulfil its stated aim; it is consistent with the principle of 'subsidiarity'. Why choose to deal with a problem at the global level when it can be handled adequately, and perhaps more effectively, at the regional level? Just as multilateral trade liberalisation and multilateral trade institutions have been joined by an increasing array of regional trading arrangements, regional financial crises may be better handled by regional arrangements. To the extent that regional arrangements may help reinvigorate interests in strengthening the international financial architecture, they could act as stepping stones towards multilateral reforms rather than 'stumbling blocs'.

APPENDIX 11.1 ESTIMATING THE FISCAL COSTS OF RESERVE ACCUMULATION IN EAST ASIA[21]

The costs of holding foreign reserves may be quite high. This appendix attempts to offer an illustrative estimate. Following Rodrik (2000), I make two key assumptions. First, all reserves beyond the age-old rule of thumb of three months worth of imports are considered to be 'excess reserves'. I treat these 'excess' levels of reserves as the opportunity cost of maintaining an open capital account. Second, the spread between the yield on foreign reserves (the US Treasury bill rate) and the marginal cost of domestic funds is taken to be six percentage points.[22] Under these assumptions, the annual cost of this 'insurance policy' against financial market unpredictability is in the order of 0.3–1 per cent of GDP for the five crisis-affected economies in East Asia in 1999. These costs are the highest for Thailand and Malaysia and lowest for the Philippines.

Table A11.1 Social cost of excess reserves, 1999

Country	Foreign reserves (US$ million)[a]	Reserves in months of imports	'Excess reserves' (% of GDP)[b]	Annual cost of excess reserves (% of GDP)[c]
Indonesia	26,445.0	7.6	11	0.66
Malaysia	30,588.2	4.8	15	0.90
Philippines	13,299.7	4.3	5	0.30
Thailand	34,062.8	7.3	16	0.96
South Korea	73,987.3	5.9	9	0.54

Notes
a Total reserves minus gold at the end of 1999.
b 'Excess' refers to the level beyond the 3-month benchmark.
c Assuming a 6 per cent spread between the yield on foreign reserves and the marginal cost of borrowing.
Source: Computed from *International Financial Statistics* (IMF).

NOTES

This paper was completed in December 2001 and draws partly on joint work with Graham Bird and Reza Siregar.

1 In recognition of the urgent need to further study and understand the workings and dynamics of international capital markets and flows, the IMF recently established a new International Capital Markets Department. The former Managing Director of the IMF, Michel Camdessus, was among the first to emphasise capital account factors as being the drivers behind recent financial crises in emerging economies in 1995 when he referred to the Mexican crisis of 1994–95 as 'the first financial crisis of the twenty-first century' (see Buira 1999).

2 The issue of restraints of capital flows has been extensively discussed elsewhere – for instance, Bird and Rajan (2000b) and references cited within. Eichengreen (2001) takes up the issue of financial standards. The Financial Stability Forum (2000) has been at the vanguard of recommending such standards. Other important policies to prevent liquidity crises are officially sanctioned standstills to prevent rush to exits and collective action clauses, along with a general 'constructive engagement' among borrowers, lenders and regional and international financial institutions (Eichengreen 2001; IMF 2001b).

3 See Johnston and Otker-Robe (1999) and Abrams and Beato (1998) for in-depth discussions of prudential regulations.

4 The accumulation of international reserves by developing countries is indicative of the 'fear of floating' by developing and emerging economies (Calvo and Reinhart 2000; Hausmann et al. 2000; Rajan 2002).

5 The extent of short-term indebtedness has been found to be a key indicator of (il)liquidity and a robust predictor of financial crises (Bussiere and Mulder 1999; Dadush et al. 2000; World Bank 2000b. According to Dadush et al., on the basis of data for 33 developing economies, the elasticity of short-term debt with GDP growth is 0.9 when there is a positive shock to output and –1.8 when there is a negative shock. This extreme reversibility of short-term debt in the event of negative shock exposes borrowers to liquidity runs and systemic crises. In a somewhat contrarion view, Jeanne (2000) argues that it is not clear that short-term debt contracts ought to be discouraged as they may play a socially advantageous function in reducing agency problems. The World Bank (1999) surveys recent literature on short-term debt and financial crises.

6 There is the additional question of what the appropriate size of reserve holdings is – against what yardstick should reserve adequacy be measured? The generally accepted rule of thumb that a country needs to hold reserves equivalent to short-term debt cover (that is, debt that actually falls due over the year) is true only when a country is running a current account balance and there are no other liabilities that are easily reversible. The optimal level of reserves depends on factors such as the degree of export diversification, size and variability of the current account imbalance, and type of exchange rate regime (Bussiere and Mulder 1999). A related issue pertains to the appropriate currency composition of reserves (Eichengreen and Mathieson 2000). Steps have been taken to improve the IMF's analytical framework for management of international reserves as well as for assessing a country's external financial vulnerability in general (IMF 2001d: Chapter 3).

7 See Bird and Rajan (2001) and Claessens et al. (1999) for discussions about the potential benefits of foreign bank entry. Of course, as with financial liberalisation in general, care must be taken to ensure that foreign bank entry is undertaken in a careful (gradual?) manner so as to avoid any major disruptions to the domestic financial system by enticing domestic banks to opt for increasingly risky investments. Montreevat and Rajan (2001) discuss Thailand's recent experience

with bank restructuring and foreign bank entry.

8 Radelet and Sachs (1998) get the point across in a rather colourful manner when they note that the 'arrival of the IMF gives all the confidence of seeing an ambulance outside one's door'.

9 Other recent empirical studies confirming this regional dimension of currency crises include Calvo and Reinhart (1996), Frankel and Schmukler (1996), Glick and Rose (1999) and Kaminsky and Reinhart (2000a).

10 Other definitions of contagion include an increase in asset price volatility across countries or a significant increase in cross-market linkages after a crisis in one country or group of countries. Dornbusch et al. (2000) provide a comprehensive review of the definitions as well as theoretical and empirical studies on contagion. The World Bank web site on the topic is also useful: <http://www1.worldbank. org/economicpolicy/managing%20volatility/contagion/index.html>.

11 A third category, 'common external shocks' or 'monsoonal effects', refers to all those factors that affect all regional economies (Masson 1998). A number of external shocks have been suggested in the case of the East Asian crisis (Whitt 1999). In a recent study using a comprehensive data set of financial statistics, product information, geographic data and stock returns involving 14,000 companies in 46 economies, Forbes (2000) found all the preceding transmission mechanisms were important in the case of the East Asian crisis, particularly the product competitiveness channel. *A priori*, it is surprising that the common creditor/credit crunch effect (through banks) was not found to be as important. This may be explained by the fact that Forbes focused on international rather than regional propagation and did not explicitly test for the herding channel. Kaminsky and Reinhart (2000b) and Van Rijckeghem and Weder (1999) have concluded that the bank lender channel was particularly important in the East Asian crisis, though the inclusion of a trade competition variable tends to dilute the significance, due possibly to the high correlation between competition for funds and trade.

12 Also see Van Rijckeghem and Weder (1999). In a pioneering study, Eichengreen et al. (1996) emphasised this channel for industrial countries.

13 Rajan et al. (2002) explore the various trade spillover channels noted above as they try to explain the spread of the crisis from Indonesia, Malaysia, Philippines, South Korea and Thailand to the city-states of Hong Kong and Singapore.

14 See Calvo (1999) for a model involving two sets of agents (informed and uninformed), in which margin calls necessitate asset sales in one economy following price declines in another. Folkerts-Landau and Garber (1998) stress risk control systems as a possible reason for region-wide asset sell-offs and resultant contagion; while Van Rijckeghem and Weder (1999) emphasise the value at risk technique in particular. However, Schinasi and Todd Smith (1999) show that such financial contagion could result from normal/textbook portfolio diversification rules, with risk management techniques and rules not having any significantly different consequences on optimal sell-off periods or strategies.

15 Bikhchandani and Sharma (2000) provide a succinct discussion of the various types of recent herding models in financial markets.

16 We should note that the East Asian and Pacific region already has a financial cooperative scheme in the form of the Executives Meeting of East Asia and Pacific Central Banks (EMEAP). EMEAP is a cooperative organisation comprising central banks and monetary authorities of 11 economies: Australia, China, Hong Kong, Indonesia, Japan, South Korea, Malaysia, New Zealand, the Philippines, Singapore and Thailand. Spurred on by the Tequila crisis, substantive steps towards monetary cooperation have been taken by EMEAP. For instance, a number of member economies signed a series of bilateral repurchase (repo) agreements

in 1995 and 1996. Hong Kong and Singapore agreed to intervene in foreign exchange markets on behalf of the Bank of Japan. These creditor regional economies attempted to help defend the Thai baht for some period before the Bank of Thailand succumbed to the speculative pressures (Rajan 2000). There does not appear to have been any discussion in policy circles on the nexus between EMEAP and the CMI.

17 According to some observers, the debate about a 'new international financial architecture' was launched at the Halifax G-7 summit in 1995 and to all extents and purposes concluded at the Cologne summit in 1999 (Kenen 2000). According to Eichengreen and James (2001), one reason why international financial reforms are not occurring at a faster pace is that the recent financial crises do not appear to have threatened the global trading system.

18 Of course, loosely speaking, an infinitely played prisoner's dilemma game predicts that a cooperative strategy could be supported if agents have high enough rates of time preference (the so-called 'Folk theorem').

19 Needless to say, in addition to these regional and multilateral liquidity pools, countries are expected to maintain sound debt and reserve management policies.

20 As Fischer (2001b) has noted, there are two primary objectives of IMF conditionality: 'to ensure that IMF resources are used to promote economic reform and adjustment, rather than to postpone it; and to ensure that the borrower is able to repay the loan on the agreed terms, making the resources available to other members who may need them'.

21 This draws from Rajan and Siregar (2002).

22 Ideally I would like to have obtained data on an individual country's market bond rates and obtain more exact spreads. Rodrik (2000) argues that for a lot of emerging economies this level of spread is likely to be a conservative estimate of the true opportunity cost of holding reserves.

REFERENCES

Abrams, R. and P. Beato (1998) 'The Prudential Regulation and Management of Foreign Exchange Risk', *IMF Working Paper No. 98/37.*

Ahluwalia, P. (2000) 'Discriminating Contagion: An Alternative Explanation of Contagious Currency Crises in Emerging Markets', *IMF Working Paper No.00/14.*

Banerjee, A. (1992) 'A simple model of herd behavior', *Quarterly Journal of Economics* 107: 796–817.

Bikhchandani, S. and S. Sharma (2000) 'Herd Behavior in Financial Markets: A Review', *IMF Working Paper No. 00/48.*

Bird, G. and R. Rajan (2000a) 'Is there a case for an Asian Monetary Fund?', *World Economics* 1: 135–43.

—— (2000b) 'Restraining international capital flows: what does it mean?', *Global Economic Quarterly* 1(2): 57–80.

—— (2001) 'Banks, financial liberalisation and financial crises in emerging markets', *The World Economy* 24(7): 889–910.

Boughton, J. (1997) 'From Suez to Tequila: the Fund as Crisis Manager', *IMF Working Paper No. 97/90.*

Buira, A. (1999) 'An alternative approach to financial crises', *Essays in International Finance*, No.212, International Finance Section, Princeton University.

Bussiere, M. and C. Mulder (1999) 'External Vulnerability in Emerging Market Economies: How High Liquidity Can Offset Weak Fundamentals and the Effects of Contagion', *IMF Working Paper No. 99/88.*

Calvo, G. (1999) 'Contagion in Emerging Markets: When Wall Street is a Carrier', mimeo (May), Department of Economics, University of Maryland.

Calvo, G. and E. Mendoza (1996) 'Mexico's balance-of-payments crisis: a chronicle of a death foretold', *Journal of International Economics* 41: 235–64.

——— (2000) 'Rational contagion and the globalization of securities markets', *Journal of International Economics* 51: 79–113.

Calvo, G. and C. Reinhart (1996) 'Is there evidence of contagion effect', in G. Calvo, M. Goldstein and E. Hochreiter (eds), *Private Capital Flows to Emerging Economies After the Mexican Crisis*, Washington DC: Institute for International Economics.

——— (2000) 'Fear of floating', *NBER Working Paper No. 7993*.

Chang, L.L. and R. Rajan (2001) 'The economics and politics of monetary regionalism in Asia', *ASEAN Economic Bulletin* 18: 103–18.

Claessens, S., A. Demirguc-Kunt and H. Huizinga (1999) 'How Does Foreign Entry Affect the Domestic Banking Market?', *Working Paper No.1918*, World Bank.

Corsetti, G., P. Pesenti and N. Roubini (1999) 'Paper tigers? A model of the Asian crisis', *European Economic Review*, 43: 1211–236.

Council on Foreign Relations (1999) 'Safeguarding Prosperity in a Global Financial System: The Future International Financial Architecture', Washington DC: Institute for International Economics.

Dadush, U., D. Dasgupta and D. Ratha (2000) 'The role of short-term debt in recent crises', *Finance and Development* 37: 54–7.

De Gregario, J. and R. Valdes (2001) 'Crisis transmission: evidence from the Debt, Tequila, and Asian flu crises', in S. Claessens and K. Forbes (eds), *International Financial Contagion*, Boston MA: Kluwer Academic Publishers.

Diamond, P. and P. Dybvig (1983) 'Bank runs, deposit insurance, and liquidity', *Journal of Political Economy* 91: 401–19.

Disyatat, P. (2001) 'Currency Crises and Foreign Reserves: A Simple Model', *IMF Working Paper No. 01/18*.

Dooley, M. (2000) 'A model of crises in emerging markets', *Economic Journal* 110: 256–72.

Dornbusch, R., Y.C. Park and S. Claessens (2000) 'Contagion: understanding how it spreads', *The World Bank Research Observer* 15: 177–97.

Drazen, A. (1999) 'Political contagion in currency crises', in P. Krugman (ed.), *Currency Crises*, Chicago: University of Chicago Press.

Eichengreen, B. (2001) 'Strengthening the International Financial Architecture: Open Issues, Asian Concerns', mimeo (May), University of California, Berkeley, available at <http://emlab.berkeley.edu/users/eichengr/research.htm>.

Eichengreen, B. and H. James (2001) 'Monetary and Financial Reform in Two Eras of Globalization (and in between)', mimeo (April), University of California, Berkeley, available at <http://emlab.berkeley.edu/users/eichengr/research.htm>.

Eichengreen, B. and D. Mathieson (2000) 'The Currency Composition of Foreign Exchange Reserves: Retrospect and Prospect', mimeo (January), University of California, Berkeley, available at <http://emlab.berkeley.edu/users/eichengr/research.htm>.

Eichengreen, B. and A. Rose (2001) 'To Defend or Not to Defend? That is the Question', mimeo (February), University of California, Berkeley, available at <http://emlab.berkeley.edu/users/eichengr/research.htm>.

Eichengreen, B., A. Rose and C. Wyplosz (1996) 'Contagious currency crisis', *Scandinavian Economic Review* 98: 463–84.

Financial Stability Forum (2000) 'Report of the follow-up group on incentives to foster implementation of standards' (13 August).

Fischer, S. (2001a) 'Reducing Vulnerabilities: The Role of the Contingent Credit Line', paper presented at the Inter-American Development Bank, Washington DC, 25 April.

—— (2001b) 'Priorities for the IMF', Remarks to the Bretton Woods Committee, Washington DC, 27 April.

Folkerts-Landau, D. and P. Garber (1998) 'Capital flows from emerging markets in a closing environment', *Global Emerging Markets* 1, Deutsche Bank (London).

Forbes, K. (2000) 'The Asian Flu and Russian Virus: Firm-Level Evidence on How Crises are Transmitted Internationally', *NBER Working Paper No. 7807*.

Frankel, J. and S. Schmukler (1996) 'Crisis, Contagion, and Country Funds: Effects on East Asia and Latin America', *Working Paper No.96-04*, Center for Pacific Basin Monetary and Economics Studies, Federal Reserve of San Francisco.

Garnaut, R. (1994). 'Open regionalism: its analytic basis and relevance to the international system', *Journal of Asian Economics* 5: 273–90.

Gerlach, S. and F. Smets (1995) 'Contagious speculative attacks', *European Journal of Political Economy* 11: 5–63.

Glick, R. and A. Rose (1999) 'Contagion and trade: why are currency crises regional?', *Journal of International Money and Finance* 18: 603–17.

Goad, P. (2000) 'Asian Monetary Fund reborn', *Far Eastern Economic Review*, 18 May: 54.

Hausmann, R., U. Panizza and E. Stein (2000) 'Why Do Countries Float the Way They Float?', *Working Paper No. 418*, Inter-American Development Bank.

Haque, N., M. Kumar, M. Nelson and D. Mathieson (1996) 'The Economic Content of Indicators of Developing Country Creditworthiness', *IMF Working Paper No.96/9*.

Huh, C. and K. Kasa (1997) 'A Dynamic Model of Export Competition, Policy Coordination, and Simultaneous Currency Collapse', *Working Paper PB 97-08*, Center for Pacific Basin Monetary and Economics Studies, Federal Reserve of San Francisco.

IMF (2000). *World Economic Outlook 2000*, Washington DC: IMF (May).

—— (2001a) 'Reforming the International Financial Architecture', *IMF Issues Brief 01/01* (9 March).

—— (2001b). 'Resolving and Preventing Financial Crises: The Role of the Private Sector', *IMF Issues Brief 01/02* (26 March).

—— (2001c) *World Economic Outlook 2001*, Washington DC: IMF (May).

—— (2001d) *Annual Report 2001*, Washington DC: IMF (September).

Ishii, S., I. Otker-Obe and L. Cui (2001) 'Measures to Limit the Offshore Use of Currencies: Pros and Cons', *IMF Working Paper No.01/43*.

Jeanne, O. (2000) 'Foreign currency debt and the global financial architecture', *European Economic Review* 44: 719–27.

Johnston, B. and I. Otker-Robe (1999) 'A Modernized Approach to Managing the Risks in Cross-Border Capital Movements', *IMF Working Paper No.99/6*.

Kaminisky, G. and C. Reinhart (2000a) 'On crises, contagion, and confusion', *Journal of International Economics* 51: 145–68.

—— (2000b). 'Bank lending and contagion: evidence from the Asian crisis', in T. Ito and A. Krueger (eds), *Regional and Global Capital Flows: Macroeconomic Causes and Consequences*, Chicago: University of Chicago Press.

Kawai, M. and S. Urata (1998) 'Are trade and direct investment substitutes or complements? An empirical analysis of Japanese manufacturing industries', in H. Lee and D. Roland-Holst (eds), *Economic Development and Cooperation in the Pacific Basin*, New York: Cambridge University Press.

Kenen, P. (2000) 'Currency Areas, Policy Domains, and the Institutionalization of Fixed Exchange Rates', mimeo (April), Department of Economics, Princeton University.

Kohler, H. (2001). 'New Challenges for Exchange Rate Policy', paper presented at the Asia–Europe Meeting of Finance Ministers, Kobe, Japan, 13 January.

Krueger, M., P. Osakwe and J. Page (2000) 'Fundamentals, contagion and currency crises: an empirical analysis', *Development Policy Review* 18: 257–74.

Krugman, P. (1999) 'Balance sheets, the transfer problem, and financial crisis', in P. Isard, A. Razin and A. Rose (eds), *International Finance and Financial Crises, Essays in Honor of Robert P. Flood*, Dordrecht: Kluwer.

Larsen, F. (2001) 'The IMF's efforts to reduce the risk of financial crises', *Le Monde*, 24 September.

Manzano, G. (2001) 'Is there any value-added in the ASEAN surveillance process?', *ASEAN Economic Bulletin* 18: 94–102.

Masson, P. (1998) 'Contagion: Monsoonal Effects, Spillovers, and Jumps Between Multiple Equilibria', *IMF Working Paper No.98/142*.

Montiel, P. (1999) 'Policy Responses to Volatile Capital Flows', mimeo (March), Williams College.

Montreevat, S. and R. Rajan (2001) 'Banking Crisis, Restructuring and Liberalization in Emerging Economies: A Case Study of Thailand', mimeo (July) University of Adelaide and Institute of Southeast Asian Studies, Singapore.

Ng, F. and A. Yeats (1999) 'Production Sharing in East Asia: Who Does What for Whom, and Why?', *Policy Research Working Paper No. 2197*, World Bank.

Obstfeld, M. (1994) 'The logic of currency crises', *Cahiers Économiques et Monetaries* 43, Banque De France, Paris, 189–213.

—— (1996) 'Models of currency crises with self-fulfilling features', *European Economic Review* 40: 1037–48.

Park, Y.C. (2001). 'Beyond the Chiang Mai Initiative: Rationale and Need for a Regional Monetary Arrangement in East Asia', mimeo (June), paper presented to a seminar on 'Regional Cooperation: The Way Forward', Annual Asian Development Bank meeting, Honolulu, 8 May.

Radelet, S. and J. Sachs (1998) 'The East Asian financial crisis: diagnosis, remedies, prospects', *Brookings Papers on Economic Activity* 1: 1–74.

Rajan, R. (2000) 'Financial and macroeconomic cooperation in ASEAN: issues and policy initiatives', in M. Than (ed.), *ASEAN Beyond the Regional Crisis: Challenges and Initiatives*, Singapore: Institute of Southeast Asian Studies.

—— (2001) '(Ir)relevance of Currency Crises Theory to the Devaluation and Collapse of the Thai Baht', *Princeton Studies in International Economics No.88*, International Economics Section, Princeton University.

—— (2002) 'Exchange rate policy options for post-crisis Southeast Asia: Is there a case for currency baskets?', *The World Economy* 25(1), pp. 137–63.

Rajan, R. and G. Bird (2001) 'Still the weakest link: the domestic financial system and post-crisis recovery in East Asia', *Development Policy Review* 19: 355–66.

Rajan, R., R. Sen and R. Siregar (2002) 'Hong Kong, Singapore and the East Asian crisis: how important were trade spillovers?', *The World Economy* 25(4): 503–37.

Rajan, R. and C.H. Shen (2001). 'Are Devaluations in Emerging Economies Contractionary? Revisiting an Age-Old Debate', mimeo (September), University of Adelaide.

Rajan, R. and R. Siregar (2002) 'Private capital flows in East Asia: boom, bust and beyond', in G. de Brouwer (ed.), *Financial Markets and Policies in East Asia*, 47–81, London: Routledge.

—— (2001) 'Revisiting the economics of international reserve holdings: with reference to Asia', mimeo, University of Adelaide.

Rodrik, D. (2000) 'Exchange rate regimes and institutional arrangements in the shadow of capital flows', mimeo.

Rowley, A. (2000). 'IMF policy shift may revive AMF idea', *Business Times*, Singapore, 2 October.

—— (2001) 'ASEAN + 3 group boosts currency defences', *Business Times*, Singapore, 11 May.

Scharfstein, D. and J. Stein (1990) 'Herd behavior and investment', *American Economic Review* 80: 465–79.

Schinasi, G. and R. Todd Smith (1999) 'Portfolio Diversification, Leverage, and Financial Contagion', *IMF Working Paper No. 99/136.*

Van Rijckeghem, C. and B. Weder (1999) 'Sources of Contagion: Finance or Trade?', *IMF Working Paper No. 99/146.*

Whitt, J. (1999) 'The Role of External Shocks in the Asian Financial Crisis', *Economic Review*, Federal Reserve Bank of Atlanta, Second Quarter, pp.18-31.

World Bank (1999) *Global Development Finance 1999*, New York: Oxford University Press.

—— (2000a). *East Asia: Recovery and Beyond*, New York: Oxford University Press.

—— (2000b). *Global Economic Prospects and the Developing Countries*, New York: Oxford University Press.

12 The role of regional financial arrangements in the international financial architecture

Martin Parkinson, Phil Garton and Ian Dickson

INTRODUCTION

The East Asian economic crisis of 1997–98 has prompted closer examination of measures to strengthen the region against the prospect of recurring crises. Countries in the region have tried to reduce vulnerability by introducing greater flexibility into exchange rate regimes and improving corporate governance and prudential regulation of domestic financial sectors. There has also been constructive dialogue on cooperative regional measures to promote stability and growth. A key outcome of this dialogue is the network of swap agreements contained in the Chiang Mai Initiative (CMI). While the CMI should be welcomed in its own right, some see it as part of evolving regional cooperation that may result in larger, more comprehensive and more elaborate regional arrangements for crisis prevention and resolution.

This paper focuses on some conceptual issues that need to be considered when pondering the potential evolution of regional facilities. Its aim is to identify some key issues and challenges, not to provide definitive answers. In doing so, we also try to provide a sense of the different approaches to these issues.

First, we examine the factors that have led to increased pressures on International Monetary Fund (IMF) resources, particularly in the past decade, and that have given rise to large-scale financing from sources outside the IMF in the midst of crises. We discuss the critical importance of the changing nature of balance of payments crises associated with increasing capital mobility, and the uncertainties about the effectiveness of official financing in resolving crises. We also consider factors that may influence the need for financing in the future.

Next, we discuss regional financing arrangements and alternative conceptual models relating to the role of such arrangements vis-à-vis the IMF. One approach – which might be called 'complementary financing' – would involve both the IMF and any regional facility in an explicitly coordinated approach from the beginning of any crisis. Either the IMF or the regional facility could take the role as lead crisis manager, supplemented by funds from the other in a first or second line of defence. An alternative model – 'concentric lines of defence' – would entail the lead manager initially acting alone, with only implicit back-up from the lender of second resort should the approach of the lead manager fail. Both these models have supporters in East Asia, but the latter has garnered most attention.

We recognise the rationale for a concentric lines of defence approach, but such an approach will need to address some challenges before the feasibility of specific proposals can be assessed. These challenges include appropriate crisis diagnosis; current moves to develop effective mechanisms for private sector involvement (PSI); the credibility of lending conditions; and coordination with the IMF as the lender of second resort.[1]

FACTORS AFFECTING THE NEED FOR ADDITIONAL FINANCING SOURCES

Crisis resolution financing from sources outside the IMF has emerged as a result of several factors. First, there has been increasing pressure on IMF resources as rapid growth in capital flows has resulted in private sector 'adjustments' in the midst of crises that dwarf resources currently available from the public sector, particularly the IMF. Second, the associated change in the nature of financial crises has led to a level of demand for financial assistance that was not anticipated even a few years ago. Finally, there has been – at least in the East Asian region – increasing interest in regional approaches to marshalling additional liquidity support.

Relative size of IMF resources

The size of the Fund relative to world trade and capital flows has fallen considerably since the IMF was first created. In 1946, total IMF resources were equivalent to about 12 per cent of world imports, but this ratio had fallen to just over 3 per cent before the 45 per cent quota increase in 1999 (Figure 12.1). Even after the quota increase, the ratio was just under 5 per cent. The fall in the relative size of the fund largely occurred in the late 1960s and early 1970s, and resources have broadly kept pace with growth in imports since then. Figure 12.1 also shows the relative size of additional resources potentially available to the IMF through the General Arrangement to Borrow (GAB) and New Arrangements to Borrow (NAB), which are discussed in more detail in Box 12.1. These arrangements have not altered the trend of static or declining Fund resources relative to global economic flows that has been apparent since the mid-1960s.

Even more significant in terms of the present-day challenges faced by the IMF may be the dramatic increase in cross-border private capital flows. The growth in such flows has been particularly large for emerging market economies, which are now the primary focus of the IMF's lending activities. Net private capital flows to emerging economies averaged only US$17 billion annually during the 1980s, but rose sharply to average US$120 billion during

---

Box 12.1 General and New Arrangements to Borrow

General Arrangements to Borrow (GAB)

The GAB allows the IMF to borrow specified amounts of currencies from 11 industrial countries or their central banks at market-related rates of interest, where there is mutual agreement that the resources are needed to forestall or cope with an impairment of the international monetary system.

The GAB was established in 1962 in response to the growing pressures on the par value exchange rate system caused by the balance of payments problems of the United States and the United Kingdom (Kim et al. 2000). This reflected concerns that potential borrowing by one of the largest industrial countries could severely impact on the adequacy of useable resources available to other members.

Reflecting its original purpose, funds could only be used to finance borrowing by the GAB participants. The GAB in its original form was activated nine times between 1964 and 1978. The growth of alternative market sources of credit and the move to floating exchange rates by participants meant that its relevance declined over time. Its exclusivity also prompted considerable criticism.

In response to the growing pressures on the IMF's resources caused by the emergence of the debt crisis in Latin America in mid-1982, a review of the GAB was undertaken in February 1983. This review resulted in a substantial enlargement of the potential credit available under the GAB from US$6 billion to SDR17 billion (about US$21 billion), with an additional SDR1.5 billion available under an associated arrangement with Saudi Arabia. In addition, the provisions were amended to allow the IMF to use the GAB to finance transactions with non-participants, where participants agreed that there was a threat to the stability of the international system.

The reformed GAB arrangements were not, however, activated until 1998 when they were used in the financing of an extended arrangement for Russia, due to delays in the NAB coming into effect.

New Arrangements to Borrow (NAB)

Following the Mexican financial crisis in December 1994, concern that substantially more resources might be needed to respond to future financial crises prompted the June 1995 G-7 Halifax Summit to call for the development of financing arrangements that would double the amount available to the IMF under the GAB. The IMF's Executive Board agreed to establish the NAB in January 1997. Owing mainly to difficulties in obtaining legislative approval from the US Congress, however, the NAB did not become effective until November 1998.

The NAB expanded the existing GAB participation to 25 governments and institutions. While the GAB remain in force, the NAB are the first and principal recourse in the event of a need to provide supplementary resources to the IMF. The total amount of resources available to the IMF under the NAB and GAB combined is SDR34 billion (about US$42 billion), equivalent to around 16 per cent of the IMF's existing quota resources. The NAB has been activated once, to finance a standby arrangement for Brazil in December 1998.

Figure 12.1 Ratio of IMF resources to world imports at each quota increase, 1946–99

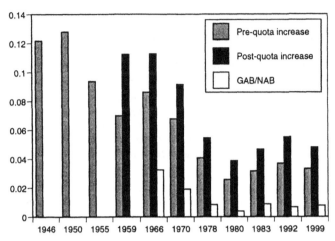

Source: IMF staff, authors' calculations.

the 1990s.[2] These flows have also been exceptionally volatile. From a peak of US$228 billion in 1996, private flows to emerging markets fell sharply to US$53 billion in 1998. In contrast to the eightfold increase in decade average private capital flows, total IMF resources at the time of the Asian crisis were only some 59 per cent larger than total resources in 1983.

Put another way, at the onset of the crisis, the IMF's total net uncommitted usable resources amounted to only around SDR40 billion (around US$57 billion), about the same magnitude as the net capital outflows from the crisis-affected economies that occurred in the final two quarters of 1997. Net private capital flows to the four Asian crisis economies fell by a total of US$106 billion between 1996 and 1998 (around 10 per cent of combined pre-crisis GDP). Net official flows increased by US$22 billion over the same period, offsetting only about one-fifth of the reduction in private flows.

Of course, comparisons of the relative size of IMF resources over time tell us nothing about the appropriate level of IMF resources, either now or in the past. Even if we assume that the level of resources available in 1946 was right, the rationale for IMF lending and the nature of the international monetary system have changed tremendously. In particular, the Fund's original role in the Bretton Woods system of pegged exchange rates meant that most advanced economy members were potential borrowers. That is unlikely to be the case today. Nevertheless, new demands on the Fund – particularly in relation to the financing of capital account crises – have arisen to replace these previous responsibilities.

Changing nature of balance of payments crises

In the past decade, international financial crises have unfolded in a rapid and unanticipated fashion, notably in the Asian crisis in 1997, but also in Mexico in 1994–95 and in Russia and Brazil in 1998. The increasing size and volatility of capital flows has been associated with a change in the nature of crises that has both increased demands on IMF resources and increased uncertainty as to the role of these resources in resolving crises.

The scale of demands on IMF resources was clearly not anticipated before the 1997–98 crises. A series of bilateral arrangements were used to boost the resources available to help resolve these crises. These bilateral arrangements differed in both nature and membership across the affected economies (see Box 12.2).[3]

A key difference was whether supplementary financing was provided on a first line of defence or second line of defence basis. First line of defence financing was provided to Mexico, Thailand and Brazil. In these cases, 'hard money' was provided bilaterally by other countries in parallel with IMF resources. The second line of defence approach sees funds promised on an as-needed basis if IMF resources turn out to be inadequate. Second lines of defence were characteristic of bilateral support to both Korea and Indonesia. There is continuing dispute about the relative merits and effectiveness of these two approaches to the provision of complementary financing (see Box 12.3).

A crude taxonomy can be drawn between the crises of the late 1990s and those of earlier decades. 'Old style' current account crises tended to be driven by excessive current account deficits resulting from macroeconomic policy settings that were inconsistent with maintaining pegged exchange rates. Under conditions of lower capital mobility, such crises tended to unfold gradually as foreign exchange reserves steadily drained away. Resolution was (conceptually) a relatively straightforward matter of determining the adjustments to fiscal, monetary and exchange rate policies required to close the balance of payments 'gap' over some period, and providing sufficient financing to cover part of this gap in order to smooth the adjustment path and cushion the short-term contractionary impact.

More recent crises have tended to be in the capital account, characterised by large and rapid reversals in private capital flows.[4] Macroeconomic policy concerns may have played a role in some cases, but financial vulnerabilities seem to be the key to the nature and severity of most recent crises. They have tended to be the consequence of an interrelated set of factors: weak prudential arrangements; poor governance resulting in connected and/or directed lending; explicit or implicit government guarantees; inadequate risk assessments on the part of investors in the run-up to the crisis; and herding behaviour or panic by investors at the time of the crisis.

Dornbusch (2001) describes capital account crises as being triggered by emerging doubts about the balance sheets of a significant part of the economy

Box 12.2 Support arrangements for Thailand, Indonesia, South Korea and Brazil

Thailand, August 1997

The IMF standby arrangement for Thailand was announced on 20 August 1997, with direct IMF financing of US$3.9 billion. The World Bank and Asian Development Bank committed a total of US$2.7 billion. In addition, bilateral support amounting to US$10.5 billion was organised on a first line of defence basis and took the form of currency swaps between central banks. The financing was released *pari passu* with IMF tranches. Australia, Brunei Darussalam, China, Hong Kong, Indonesia, Japan, Korea, Malaysia and Singapore contributed to the package. Canada later assumed Indonesia's US$500 million contribution. The total credit from all sources made available to Thailand was US$17.1 billion.

Indonesia, November 1997

The IMF's standby arrangement for Indonesia was approved on 5 November 1997. The package comprised US$11 billion in direct financing from the IMF, US$8 billion from the multilateral development banks, and US$17 billion in second line of defence pledges from bilateral partners (Australia, China, Hong Kong, Japan, Malaysia, Singapore and the United States).

The second line of defence was never activated; in most cases negotiations did not commence. Australia entered into individual negotiations with Indonesia to release $300 million of its US$1 billion commitment, but these negotiations were never concluded. Had these Australian funds been provided, they would have been disbursed *pari passu* with IMF financing.

South Korea, December 1997

Direct IMF support to Korea amounted to US$20.9 billion, with a further US$14 billion from the multilateral development banks. The bilateral support for Korea was offered on a second line of defence basis. The bilateral support group comprised the G-10 members plus Australia and New Zealand, with pledges amounting to US$23.3 billion.

In the face of strong adverse market pressures, the support group announced in late December 1997 its willingness to activate one-third of the bilateral funds. European members of the support group envisaged providing their assistance through the Bank for International Settlements (BIS). The US took the lead in negotiations with Korea, but these were not concluded. Ultimately, the successful restructuring of Korea's international bank loans after January 1998, and a global bond placement by the Korean Government, reduced the need for the second line of support. Had the bilateral support been provided, it would have been disbursed *pari passu* with IMF funds.

Brazil, December 1998

On 2 December 1998, the IMF announced a US$18.1 billion package for Brazil under the Supplementary Reserve Facility. Of this, US$12.7 was provided through the NAB, which was activated for the first time. In addition, 19 European and North American central banks guaranteed BIS credits to Banco Central de Brazil. The financing made available by the BIS and its guarantors amounted to around US$13.2 billion. It was provided on a first line of defence basis and was disbursed *pari passu* with IMF funds. The Bank of Japan did not join this BIS facility, but made US$1.25 billion available to Brazil under a parallel facility. The World Bank and the Inter-American Development Bank committed a total of US$9 billion in financing for Brazil.

Box 12.3 First and second line of defence approaches to bilateral
supplemental financing

Perhaps the most important distinction between the cases described in Box
12.2 is whether bilateral financing is provided on a 'first line of defence'
(FLOD) basis or as part of a future 'second line of defence' (SLOD) if needed.
In the former case, bilateral financing is provided at the same time as the IMF
financing; in the latter it is announced in conjunction with the IMF program
but activated only if the original program proves insufficient. As noted above,
bilateral financing for Thailand and Brazil was mobilised on a FLOD basis,
while for Indonesia and Korea it was organised on a SLOD basis.

Advantages and disadvantages of first and second line of defence approaches

The main advantage of bilateral assistance committed on a FLOD basis is that
it can be relied upon both by the country facing a financing gap and by the
IMF when planning assistance, as it involves a definite commitment of
resources by the bilateral creditor. Because the assistance is relatively concrete, it may be more likely to assist confidence and positively affect the
behaviour of markets and investors. In contrast, commitments of assistance
made as part of a SLOD are essentially promises, which may or may not be
realised. Hard commitments are desirable if officials are to develop comprehensive strategies to address balance of payments 'gaps'.[1]

One argument advanced in favour of the SLOD approach is that it may
facilitate bringing together a larger number of potential donors than would
otherwise be the case (principally, it would seem, because no up-front
resources are needed to participate in the package). It is suggested that this
broad show of support may better help break the 'cycle of panic' in investor
confidence. However, investors can see through 'window dressing' and may
discount commitments that are not backed up by tangible resources. In
addition, second line commitments have generally required further negotiations or the fulfilment of conditions before the assistance can be activated. As
a result, there has been some uncertainty about whether the pledged second
line assistance will, in fact, materialise. In the case of both Korea and Indonesia it is likely that the failure to finalise the already announced SLOD added to
negative market sentiment in the midst of the crises. That no resources from
participating countries are required up-front appears to have contributed to
market scepticism about SLOD arrangements more generally.

One potential disadvantage of contributing assistance on a FLOD basis is that
definite commitments of resources from bilateral donors may incline the IMF
to reduce its own contribution. One way to address this prospect is to require
that supplementary financing be used only in exceptional circumstances,
when there is a shortage in the resources available to the IMF. The potential
bilateral creditors would retain their discretion not to lend if their assessment
was that the Fund had sufficient resources to deal with likely demands.

Another argument that has been made against supplementing IMF programs on
a FLOD basis is that it may encourage moral hazard on the part of private
creditors, or indeed on the part of national authorities. It is suggested that this
may occur because the certain commitments of assistance associated with a first
line approach may not involve sufficient 'constructive ambiguity'. Whether this
argument bears scrutiny is another matter. While ambiguity may be desirable

Continued on next page

Box 12.3 continued

ex ante, it is not likely to be helpful after the onset of a crisis when decisive measures are necessary.

In practice, bilateral financing advanced in support of IMF programs has been organised on an *ad hoc* basis and so is unlikely to give rise to the impression that it will always be available in every instance.[2] Moreover, so long as judgments about the appropriate balance of financing, adjustment and public sector investment are correct, it is hard to see how a bilateral contribution to the financing component would contribute to moral hazard.

[1] Blustein (2001: 178–179) provides an account of the difficulties the SLOD caused for the IMF's financial programming for Korea in 1997.

[2] There may be scope for arguing that the US Exchange Stabilisation Fund and its repeated use for certain countries may have created the expectation in those countries that its funds would always be available.

– whether due to solvency problems or mismatched exposures – and/or the exchange rate. There are differing views on the primary causes of particular crises, and whether investors have reacted to fundamental problems or have been caught up in a self-fulfilling panic. Either way, the interaction of vulnerable balance sheets, capital flight and a falling currency tends to produce a devastating combination of banking and currency crises that can shift the affected economy to a bad equilibrium.

Given these elements, resolving such crises once they get under way has proved extremely difficult. In the presence of multiple equilibria, investor confidence or psychology is pivotal, but impossible to predict with any certainty in the heat of the crisis. For instance, there has been a debate on whether extensive structural conditionality helps confidence (by reassuring investors that problems are being addressed) or damages it (by suggesting that problems may be even worse than first thought) – see Fischer (2001) and Feldstein (1998) for two contrasting views.[5] As Crockett (2000) has noted, the size of the balance of payments gap – and, hence, the official financing requirement under the old model – is virtually impossible to quantify in modern capital account crises.

This creates a dilemma as to the appropriate size of official financing packages. On the one hand, the classic 'lender of last resort' argument prescribes large-scale liquidity provision to arrest creditor panics. In this view, a crisis is analogous to a bank run, where a mismatch between short-term liabilities and assets can make it rational for individual investors to withdraw funds if they expect others to do so, even though borrowers may be able to service the debt over time. If the economy is fundamentally sound, then a sufficiently large up-front injection of international liquidity may restore creditor confidence and rule out the bad equilibrium. Fischer (2001) argues that the ratio of foreign exchange reserves to short-term external debt is a good crisis indicator, suggesting that external liquidity matters, at least for emerging market economies.[6] On the other hand, provision of even large amounts of liquidity may not be sufficient to prevent or resolve a crisis, given uncertainties about underlying causes and investor psychology.

Economists attempting to explain the Asian crisis have developed plausible models where expectations can be self-fulfilling in the presence of large exposure mismatches (for a survey, see Masson 1999), but these leave open the question of what triggers the change in expectations. In reality, creditor panics normally require the presence of some degree of weakness in fundamentals.

Discussion of the nature of crises often attempts to draw a distinction between 'illiquidity' and 'insolvency'. However, the concept of solvency is not readily applicable to sovereign countries, given the capacity of governments to tax future income streams in order to service debt (even if in practice this power is constrained by issues of political feasibility). Rather than debating whether a country is solvent, it may be more relevant to question the sustainability of its policies: whether existing policy settings (including the exchange rate regime) are compatible, on an ongoing basis, with servicing current levels of external borrowing. This corresponds broadly to the concept of economic 'fundamentals', a term which also tends to be somewhat loosely used in these discussions.

Fischer (2001) argues that a pure liquidity crisis is relatively rare, and that policy adjustments are generally required to restore external equilibrium. We find this argument appealing, particularly since there can be no certainty that liquidity alone will resolve a crisis if judgments about sustainability are not clear-cut. Kenen (2001) notes that, even if creditor panics reflect unfounded fears, these may take some time to subside and capital inflows may not resume immediately. In the meantime, some adjustment will be required, and financial support may be needed to mitigate the costs of adjustment. But if confidence is not re-established, this may be to little avail, as additional liquidity may end up financing further capital flight.

Even when no policy adjustment is required, the capacity of the IMF to respond may face practical constraints. The amounts required to ensure that external creditors have no reason to rush to the exits may be very large – probably larger than creditor countries would be willing to provide on a regular basis, particularly given moral hazard concerns. This suggests that time lags due to negotiating bilateral support may be inevitable, yet timely interventions are generally perceived to be critical in crisis resolution. Moreover, compared to national central banks, the IMF has two key limitations as a lender of last resort – it is constrained in the amount it can lend by its access to capital, and it cannot directly regulate its borrowers as an alternative to conditionality in order to safeguard its resources.

Future needs to supplement crisis resolution resources

What factors might impact on future demands on IMF resources and the need to marshal additional financing from outside the IMF? Since the Asian crisis, significant measures have been taken to increase the resources available to the IMF and to improve its ability to deal with capital account crises.

The Eleventh Review of General Quotas resulted in agreement on a 45 per cent increase in quotas to SDR212 billion (around US$260 billion at current exchange rates) from January 1999. The NAB were introduced with effect from November 1998, doubling to SDR34 billion (US$42 billion) the amount that could be borrowed under the existing GAB to supplement IMF resources in the event of a major threat to the international monetary system.

New financing facilities have also been introduced to better address the demands posed by capital account crises. The Supplemental Reserve Facility (SRF) was introduced in 1997 to meet a need for large-scale short-term financing. The SRF provides financing on something closer to lender of last resort terms than normal IMF lending, allowing borrowing in excess of normal quota-based access limits with a substantial interest surcharge.

The contingent credit line (CCL) was also established in 1999 to provide pre-committed financing for qualifying members with sound economic policies that find themselves threatened by a crisis through financial contagion. The effectiveness of the CCL remains an open question. Concerns over possible adverse signals to markets associated with being the 'first mover' mean that no country has formally applied for a CCL, despite numerous public statements from the IMF that discussions were under way. Potential applicants may be concerned that a crisis might be triggered by future exit from the facility, particularly where the country is deemed to be no longer meeting the qualifying criteria.

Emerging market economies and the international community are also taking steps to apply the lessons learnt from the crises of the past decade. While the 1990s experience cautions against confident predictions, there are grounds for optimism that these will help reduce the incidence of major crises and of large demands on IMF resources.

First, one generally accepted lesson from the Asian crisis has been the importance of prudential regulation of the financial sector, and the need to better manage exposures to short-term, foreign currency denominated external debt. In particular, countries that liberalise their capital accounts need to have strong prudential systems in place when they do so. Prudential enforcement is easier said than done, and many advanced economies have had financial sector problems over the past two decades. But we can be hopeful that emerging economies will now endeavour to avoid the large currency and maturity mismatches that made the recent crises so severe.

Second, since 1997 there has been a clear shift away from intermediate exchange rate regimes. It is now generally recognised that targeting a particular level or range of the exchange rate requires either an incredibly strong and sustained institutional commitment or capital controls. This reflects the 'impossible trinity': a country cannot simultaneously target the exchange rate, run an independent monetary policy and have an open capital account. Flexible exchange rates may not ensure immunity from crises for emerging markets, but flexibility should reduce the incidence of both sharp 'regime shifts' in the exchange rate and unhedged foreign currency exposures.

Third, there is a new emphasis on placing private sector involvement at the centre of international crisis resolution efforts. The size of shifts in private sector capital flows, relative to available official financing, as already noted, means that private sector involvement must be a critical part of future crisis prevention and resolution and this has been a major focus of the international community in recent times. An improved approach to private sector involvement would reduce the need for official financing, though appropriate balances will still have to be struck. It is critical that any future financing arrangements do not undercut the effectiveness of mechanisms for private sector involvement. We return to this issue later.

Even with effective private sector involvement mechanisms, there will be a need for official financing in crises. Debt restructuring may be able to avoid a disorderly 'rush to the exits' by creditors, but it will not ensure that pre-crisis levels of capital inflow will be resumed. The standard rationale for financing to cushion adjustment will still apply. There is also a rationale for official financing to help preclude or resolve a liquidity crisis, although, as noted earlier, pure liquidity crises may be rare and difficult to diagnose.

Charles Kindleberger's history of financial crises, *Manias, Panics and Crashes* (Kindleberger 2000), documents a long series of financial crises going back to the early seventeenth century. We leave to others the debate over whether financial systems are, by their nature, prone to crises. However, if there is a systemic tendency to crises, it may be impossible to eliminate them without a degree of financial repression that would make the cure worse than the complaint. A modern dynamic economy requires risk taking and financial interdependence. Information asymmetries – which may contribute to 'herding' as investors take their cues from the actions of other investors – are to some degree inherent in financial markets, as are maturity mismatches. Policymaking and regulatory supervision will never be perfect, and financial markets can be prone to bouts of excessive exuberance, disorderly corrections and overshooting. The critical thing is to keep a sharp eye on these issues; to paraphrase from another context, perhaps the price of efficient dynamic financial systems is eternal vigilance.

Emerging market economies – which, by definition, are experiencing a process of financial opening and institutional and market development and adaptation – are likely to be inherently more prone to crises than others. Over time, some current emerging markets will successfully 'graduate' through the process, but by then there will be a new group of economies emerging, opening to financial flows and confronting the same challenges.

These considerations suggest that it is impossible to be conclusive about future needs for official financing to supplement IMF resources. Unforeseen contingencies may arise from time to time, and it is sensible to consider how extra resources might be made available, if and when required.

Moreover, there are other reasons for packages that supplement IMF financing with funds from governments and other institutions, beyond just a need to boost the quantum of resources available. An important one is to assist credibility by demonstrating wider endorsement of the programs and associated policy measures being pursued by the crisis-affected economy (Costello 1999). In addition, individual governments may see it as being in their interests to provide bilateral assistance to particular countries, either because of concerns about spillovers from economic and financial linkages or contagion, or for broader foreign policy reasons. Irrespective of the motive for their involvement in crisis support, though, countries may, for a variety of reasons, want to retain discretion over some portion of the funding they are willing to provide, rather than putting all of their eggs in the IMF basket. This may be seen as analogous to the preference of countries to provide some portion of their development aid funding bilaterally and through regional development banks rather than solely through the World Bank and the United Nations.

REGIONAL FINANCING ARRANGEMENTS AND THE IMF

These considerations have a strong bearing on the issue of regional financing arrangements for the East Asian region. For a number of reasons, the crisis of 1997–98 has led to an upsurge in interest in regional financing facilities to operate in conjunction with the global role of IMF and to enhance the region's capacity for 'self-help'.

First, countries in the region have a greater sense of potential vulnerability to problems in other countries in the region. Contagion in the Mexican and East Asian crises was largely regional, and some studies have concluded that contagion has been predominantly a regional phenomenon (for example, Kaminsky and Reinhardt 1999). While there are clearly exceptions – witness the contagion to Brazil and other emerging markets associated with the Russian crisis of 1998 – the case for regional arrangements is typically argued in terms of the stronger spillover effects that prevail among neighbours.

Second, there has been criticism from within the region that the IMF failed to respond quickly enough during the Asian crisis of 1997–98;[7] that its disbursements were tranched over too long a period; and that particular policy conditions associated with the disbursements were not appropriate for the task (see, for example, Rajan 2002; de Brouwer 2003). Assessing the merits of these arguments is beyond the scope of this paper, but they have clearly provided an impetus for proposals for new architecture at the regional level. Discussions in the region have been driven by the belief that a regional facility may give regional decision-makers the capacity to react to and contain crises more quickly than the IMF, as well as the scope to provide policy conditionality that is better tailored to the circumstances of the crisis economy. A regional facility may also provide a means to encourage greater sensitivity in IMF responses to crises in the region, and to increase the region's leverage with respect to the ongoing international financial architecture reform agenda, including the reform of representational arrangements at the IMF. Furthermore, regional arrangements are seen as a means of improving surveillance and policy dialogue, and hence of improving policy in the region more generally.

These are all worthwhile reasons for thinking about a regional arrangement, but the challenge will be to ensure that any new regional facility actually delivers these benefits in practice. Accordingly, it is useful to canvass some operational issues that seem to be important for the success of a regional arrangement.

A regional facility and the IMF

The development of the CMI, and possible support for more elaborate arrangements, suggests that governments in the East Asian region see a rationale for having both regional and multilateral arrangements. They may see this as a way of reconciling their preferences for the allocation and modalities of official financing with their continuing need for strong institutions at the multilateral level.

What relationship should these regional financing sources have with the IMF, which presumably would remain as the primary provider of official financing at the global level? Several different possibilities come to mind, depending on whether an approach of complementary financing or concentric lines of defence is adopted. There are two essential choices, as presented in Figure 12.2. Complementary financing, on the one hand, involves both the IMF and a regional facility playing explicit roles in a coordinated approach to a crisis. Financing would be provided by the lead crisis manager, supplemented by funds from the other facility as either a first line of defence or a second line of defence. Concentric lines of defence, on the other hand, entail the lead manager initially acting alone. The implicit assumption would be that financing available from this source would be sufficient to resolve the crisis, although the lender of second resort might step in if this should fail.

Approach A1 in Figure 12.2 would see the IMF as the lead crisis manager, with complementary bilateral funding from various countries as part of either first or second lines of defence. This was the approach adopted when bilateral financing was committed to support programs for Thailand, Indonesia and South Korea in 1997, and Brazil in 1998 (see Box 12.2).

Approach A2 in Figure 12.2 would also see the IMF as lead manager, with a prearranged stock of funds – which could be vested in a stand-alone regional authority – that could be drawn upon to supplement IMF programs, in much the same way that bilateral financing was drawn on in the cases mentioned above. This would be a relatively *de minimus* approach to a regional financing

Figure 12.2 Complementary financing

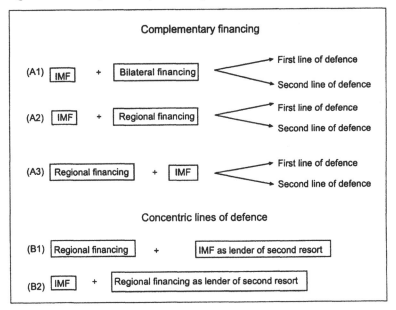

arrangement. It is worth noting that the same issues as to whether to provide the financing on a first or second line of defence basis that were discussed in Box 12.3 may also apply to regional funds intended to complement IMF programs.

The Manila Framework Group (MFG) – a regional grouping of 14 member economies plus the IMF, the World Bank and the Asian Development Bank (ADB) – recently considered the principles that might underlie arrangements for more rapidly marshalling complementary bilateral financing among its members; this might be seen as an attempt to move approach A1 somewhat towards that implicit in A2.

In contrast, approach A3 of Figure 12.2 would see a regional fund serving as the principal crisis manager, with the IMF providing complementary support. The possibility of an independent regional financing facility that might also have a capacity to function as lead manager raises further issues, including the IMF's capacity or willingness to provide supplementary funds without its own conditionality or the 'creditor of first right' status that it has under existing lending programs.

Turning to concentric lines of defence, approach B1 of Figure 12.2 would see the regional fund taking the initiative in extended financing as the 'first mover'. The essential distinction from approach A3 is that IMF financing would not form an explicit part of the initial crisis resolution program, although it may stand ready to take over management of the crisis if regional efforts were unsuccessful. In reality, the IMF's position as global crisis manager means that it is always a potential second line of defence, even if it is not explicitly identified as such.

In the schema envisaged by Kim et al. (2000: 39), regional funds would provide the 'first line of defence for countries faced with a temporary shortage of international liquidity before officially requesting emergency loans from the IMF'. In theory, if the liquidity problem was containable within the limits of resources available to the region it could be dealt with by the regional financing facility acting on its own without resort to the IMF. If, however, the crisis proved unmanageable at the regional level, perhaps due to the escalating intensity of spillovers throughout the region, then the IMF might be needed as a lender of second resort to back up the initial efforts made under the regional facility.

Approach B2 would involve the IMF serving as the 'first mover' to provide the initial attempt at resolving a crisis, supported by the regional fund as a lender of second resort if necessary. In practice, however, it is difficult to envisage a situation in which regional funds simply take over where the IMF leaves off. The IMF, with its relatively large resources and global responsibilities, is likely to have an ongoing role in coordinating attempts to resolve a crisis once it becomes involved. Hence, whenever the IMF serves as the primary crisis manager or first mover, regional funds are likely to be provided on a complementary basis (which is approach A2).

These different alternatives need not be regarded as mutually exclusive. The relationship of an independent regional facility to the IMF could conceivably shift between complementary financing (A2 or A3) and concentric lines of defence (B1) approaches, depending on the initial diagnosis of the nature of the crisis and whether it was considered manageable within the resources of the regional facility. One implication is that efforts to strengthen existing mechanisms for providing complementary financing (such as undertaken in the MFG recently) need not be incompatible with future moves toward developing concentric lines of defence.

Complementarity between a regional fund and the IMF

Under the current CMI arrangements, 90 per cent of available funds are to be tied to an IMF program or the expectation of one.[8] If a similar approach were adopted for a regional facility, the facility would, by and large, operate in a similar fashion to the past bilateral support packages discussed above (that is, it would be closest to approach A2 in Figure 12.2). The idea of a regional facility to provide supplementary financing in the context of an IMF-led program is relatively uncontroversial and it is hard to believe that most observers would not agree that arrangements of this sort could play a useful role.

Such an approach acknowledges that the IMF has a clear role as the primary global vehicle for addressing financial crises. It has at its disposal the tools necessary for a holistic approach to crisis resolution that takes into account the three key elements of financing, policy adjustment and PSI. It has relatively large resources – both staff and financial – and a capacity to conduct surveillance through Article IV consultations.

That said, the IMF does not have a monopoly on economic wisdom, nor is it immune from political pressures. Its knowledge of the economic and financial systems of crisis-affected countries may be less than that of regional officials. An arrangement to marshal resources from within the region for mutual support could bring greater regional knowledge and perspective into the crisis resolution process, and give countries in the region a greater sense of 'ownership' of the crisis prevention and resolution process.

While the huge scale of official reserve assets in the region suggests that any such facility could be well resourced, it is sometimes suggested that credible surveillance – which is central to both crisis prevention and crisis resolution – could be a weakness in any regional arrangements. Some critics point to the fact that the CMI is still developing a system of surveillance as 'evidence' that this is a fundamental flaw in proposals for regional arrangements. We reject this criticism: credible surveillance can be developed if there is sufficient political commitment and a willingness to engage in open dialogue. However, the experience of the European Union (EU) – even with the stimulus of monetary union – should caution against believing this can be done speedily.

All this suggests that there is potential for the IMF and a regional facility to play mutually supportive roles, although realising this potential would require careful consideration of the respective roles of the two institutions and their working arrangements in responding to a regional crisis.

A regional liquidity facility: a 'first line' in concentric lines of defence?

The notion that substantial regional financing might be provided independently of the IMF is more contentious, because such an approach throws up substantive coordination issues and raises concerns that IMF policy conditionality may be undermined. The extent of 'independent' financing may be re-considered when the CMI arrangements are reviewed in 2004, but in any event the issue needs to be considered more fully in the evolution of any more comprehensive regional facility.

Box 12.4 outlines a range of proposals from the region that envisage a regional facility that would have a capacity to act independently as the first line of defence, with assistance from the IMF if subsequently needed as a lender of second resort (that is, B1 in Figure 12.2). The remainder of the paper focuses on issues raised by this approach.

Some generalisations about the various proposals are possible. The most salient common feature is that a regional facility would aim to provide financing more quickly than the IMF. Another general characteristic is that a regional facility would have more limited policy conditionality than is the norm for IMF programs. Of course, no creditor is willing to lend unconditionally, but a regional facility may place more emphasis on the narrow conditions needed to safeguard donor resources and less on the sorts of broad policy requirements that tend to accompany IMF programs.

Indeed, the design of a regional fund may aim to avoid conditioning lending on a program of subsequent policy changes.[9] Instead, to draw from the facility, borrowers might simply need to have met prior criteria aimed at ensuring that their financial sectors and other aspects of their economies are

---

Box 12.4 Proposals for a regional liquidity facility

Framework for Regional Monetary Stability (FRMS)

This has been proposed by the Institute for International Monetary Affairs (IIMA), a Japanese think-tank. It would conduct two main activities: surveillance and emergency liquidity support. FRMS financing would depend on pre-qualification criteria devised on the basis of surveillance findings. The governance institutions of the FRMS would be very similar in structure to those of the IMF.

Regional Financing Arrangement (RFA)

In a report for the Asia Policy Forum, Yoshitomi and Shirai (2000) have outlined some design features for this type of arrangement. Like the FRMS proposal, the arrangement would aim to disburse financing quickly in the event of a capital account crisis, subject to the borrowing member's compliance with pre-qualification criteria. These criteria would focus on macroeconomic policies and the health of the domestic financial sector.

Network of Bilateral Swap Arrangements (NBSA)

Park (2000) has proposed a Network of Bilateral Swap Arrangements (NBSA) to provide liquidity support. The network would be supported by its own surveillance and decision-making institutions, giving it the capacity to act quickly as well as independently from the IMF. Park does, however, envisage some institutionalised links to the IMF, which would have representation in the NBSA's surveillance and decision-making bodies, at least at the observer level. Park served as a consultant to the ASEAN Secretariat, and the design of the CMI appears to have been influenced by his proposals.

Asian Arrangements to Borrow (AAB)

Kim et al. (2000) have proposed an Asian Arrangements to Borrow (AAB). Essentially the AAB would involve regional central banks standing by to provide credit as required. Credit allocations would determine the amount of financing each central bank could contribute and draw. Kim et al. envisage that the AAB could be drawn upon more or less automatically by the borrower subject to some simple preconditions. The AAB would be 'activated as a first line of defence for a country faced with a temporary shortage of international liquidity before officially requesting emergency loans from the IMF'.

in good order. The presumption is that countries that have met pre-qualification criteria are likely to be facing a liquidity problem rather than a solvency problem, so that substantial policy adjustments are not warranted.

In general, such a regional facility would be designed so as to minimise impediments to rapid lending, with the aim of reassuring investors that resources exist to meet their claims upon maturity and that there is no reason for them to cash out as a matter of urgency. In essence, a regional facility would be somewhat further along the spectrum than the IMF towards being an international lender of last resort, though without reaching that point.

An independent regional fund with a capacity to act as the first line of defence may be seen as providing 'insurance' against slow or inadequate responses by the IMF. Proponents of regional funds see the ability to provide liquidity quickly and without the need to negotiate extensive conditionality as a key advantage of a regional fund over the IMF in addressing creditor panic problems. Moreover, a regional facility may better be able to overcome the entry and exit problems associated with the IMF's CCL, as potential users would not need to go through a process of formally applying for access to the facility (see de Brouwer 2003).[10]

Difficulties of diagnosing a 'liquidity' crisis

Proponents of a regional first line defence appear to have in mind that the comparative advantage of such a facility would be to address liquidity crises. This would imply that the role of the IMF would be to address crises that have more fundamental causes – requiring debt rescheduling and adjustment – or involve wider contagion across regions.

Such an approach has logic. If the cause of a crisis is essentially creditor panic in a situation of balance sheet vulnerability due to mismatched exposures, the correct approach may be to extend funds quickly. If this were the diagnosis, there may be a case for a regional liquidity facility to handle the crisis, assuming it has sufficient resources to do so.

If the problem is more fundamental, in that a country's debt profile is unsustainable even if temporary liquidity resources are provided, the correct approach may be to seek systematic debt restructuring and make policy adjustments to ensure balance of payments sustainability in future. In this case, something more akin to an IMF program with policy conditionality may be needed to deal with the crisis.

The difficulty with attempting to separate crises into cases of creditor panic or fundamentals, however, is that they generally do not fall neatly into either category.[11] For instance, the Asian crisis might be characterised as having had elements of both. The underlying distortions to corporate and financial sector decision-making justified serious concerns that lending may have financed investments that were not economically viable, but there was also overshooting in efforts to safeguard assets. Radelet and Sachs (1998), while recognising the underlying problems, characterise the crises in the affected East Asian countries as displaying:

... elements of self-fulfilling crisis, in which capital withdrawals by creditors cascade into a financial panic and result in unnecessarily deep contraction. As we stress throughout, the panic itself may be 'rational' on the part of individual creditors, each of whom is trying to flee ahead of the other creditors, even though the collective result is disastrous and the panic itself unnecessary in the sense that the fundamentals could have supported a much more favourable outcome ....

Chang and Velasco (1998) also argue that the Asian crises were largely a result of international illiquidity. Other commentators (such as Corsetti et al. 1998; Goldstein 1998) place relatively greater emphasis on the fundamentals, but this room for different interpretations itself illustrates the difficulties of dividing crises neatly into cases of illiquidity or unsustainability.

These uncertainties pose challenges for a regional fund operating as a lender of first resort in the manner outlined above. These challenges, of course, apply to any crisis manager. Successful crisis resolution will always require judgments about the underlying causes of the crisis and about the appropriate balance between official financing, debt restructuring and national economic policy adjustment.

Failure to diagnose the problems correctly might be divided into type I and type II errors. Type I errors would involve diagnosing a crisis as being essentially fundamental in nature when in fact creditor panic that was largely unjustified by the fundamentals was the key to the problem. There may, as a result, be too much emphasis on policy adjustment and not enough weight on official financing, when designing the package of measures to resolve the crisis. If financing during a liquidity crisis is made conditional on expenditure-reducing policies, policy may also prove to be unnecessarily contractionary.

A type II error, on the other hand, would involve believing that the problem could be dealt with by providing liquidity, when in fact it was more fundamental. If this error resulted in the provision of extensive official finance – with minimal emphasis on conditionality and adjustment – the result could be to draw out the duration of the crisis; amplify the extent of the ultimate contraction; and give rise to moral hazard on the part of both the sovereign borrower and private creditors.

A central motive of many proponents of a regional approach is to insure against type I errors, which they believe the IMF was guilty of in the Asian crisis. However, any regional fund that is oriented toward providing contingent credit lines directed at dealing with problems of illiquidity will also need to be alert to risks of committing type II errors.

Compatibility with global efforts to develop effective PSI

A critical issue in this regard is how any regional facility would fit in with a future approach to international financial architecture that is likely to give increased emphasis to PSI. The recent proposals by Anne Krueger for a sovereign debt restructuring mechanism (SDRM) appear to have helped break the impasse over the use of collective action clauses. Both Krueger's proposals for an SDRM – a legislative basis for restructuring – and collective action clauses – a contractual basis – have strengths and weaknesses but both provide tools to deliver concerted PSI. Both also depend on changes to the policy approach that has governed access to the IMF's general resources (see IMF 2001: 11–12). Specifically, the IMF will need to give careful consideration to what are appropriate levels of financing if concerted PSI is to be achieved.

The issue of the appropriate response to a crisis is particularly important in the context of PSI. When the initial approach fails to stem the crisis, regional officials may seek to engage the IMF as a second line of defence, but any delay in instituting necessary adjustment may be costly. Private creditors may have used the initial injection of first-tier support from the regional fund as an opportunity to exit. Thus, the opportunity for a comprehensive approach to PSI at an early stage may have been missed. Moreover, the IMF's ability to manage problems may be strongest when comprehensive approaches are adopted at the outset.[12] The key to resolving this potential tension under any of the models discussed above would be close involvement with the IMF at all stages of the crisis management process.

The critical importance of credibility

Any regional arrangement will also need to address the criticism that the existence of alternative financing facilities may lead to 'facility shopping' or regulatory arbitrage. In this view, borrowers will naturally seek to secure official financing with the easiest terms and policy conditions. Hence, access to low conditionality funding may reduce incentives to adopt good policy by providing greater scope to defer difficult policy adjustments.

This may be an oversimplification, because far-sighted policymakers will also be concerned with the credibility of the response to the crisis.[13] Nor can one assume that tougher conditions are always necessarily better; the issue is whether conditions are appropriate. Nonetheless, this will be a real concern in the eyes of many. It will be critical that regional arrangements establish credibility with potential borrowers, the financial markets and outside governments and institutions.

In this regard, the failure of the CCL would need to be carefully examined before designing pre-qualification mechanisms. Members of the regional arrangement would also need to think carefully about how they could signal to markets their commitment to sound, even if very narrow, conditionality.

Coordination between a regional facility and the IMF

As noted above, the prospect of an independent regional facility that need not limit its lending to supplementing IMF-led programs raises important issues of coordination. Coordination problems and duplication sometimes emerge in the project activities of the World Bank and the ADB. But the consequences of coordination failure in the crisis resolution activities of the IMF and a regional facility could be much greater, given the lasting macroeconomic ramifications that crises – and problems with crisis mismanagement – can have.

Coordination would also be critical to ensuring there was no backlash from other IMF members against the regional facility. Any sense that a first mover regional arrangement had delayed policy action and left the rest of the international community to pick up the pieces would cause enormous resentment among non-regional members of the IMF.

Given this, there appear to be three key imperatives. The first is to ensure that, as far as possible, there is a comprehensive approach to addressing crises at the outset. The second is to avoid the possibility that competing lead managers adopt inconsistent approaches to a crisis. The third is to address concerns about 'burden shifting' and possible distorted incentives that inevitably arise when another institution is functioning as a lender of second resort.

This is not the place to canvass the question of how these issues may be addressed. However, we note that this would appear to require a close and cooperative working relationship between a regional facility and the IMF, and clear understandings between the two institutions as to how crises will be handled. This is achievable, but may not always prove an easy matter in practice, particularly if there are fundamental differences of view on the nature of a crisis.

CONCLUSION

Regional financing arrangements in East Asia have the potential to play a valuable role in the international financial architecture in complementing the global crisis management role of the IMF. They can contribute to the desirable goal of greater regional self-help in preventing and resolving crises, and provide a means of marshalling regional resources to complement those available from the IMF. They may encourage the IMF to have a greater focus on the region and a greater understanding of regional economic and financial systems and policy issues. They can also help give regional economies a greater sense of ownership in the international crisis management process.

Nonetheless, the relationship between any future East Asian financing facility and the IMF will need to be carefully considered. This will be critical if a future regional facility is to have a capacity to provide substantial financing independently of the IMF, especially if such a facility is explicitly intended to function as a first line of defence in rapidly providing liquidity to pre-qualifying countries. We appreciate that many in the region are interested in the idea of an independent source of liquidity – particularly in light of the experience of 1997–98 – but some difficult issues will need to be addressed if such a mechanism is to be effective.

In particular, it will be important to ensure that a comprehensive and rigorous approach to crisis management is taken at the outset, and that we do not have two competing crisis managers potentially operating at cross-purposes. Concerns about burden shifting and possible distorted incentives associated with having another institution functioning as lender of second resort will also need to be addressed. This will require close coordination and consultation between the IMF and any regional body. There will also need to be clear understandings as to the respective roles of the two institutions, and that the 'rules of the road' are clear in order to avoid inadvertently precluding the effective use of tools like PSI.

Notwithstanding the potential for a regional facility and the IMF to play mutually supportive roles in helping to prevent and resolve future crises in the region, there are also substantial risks if these aspects are not carefully thought through. Above all, it will be critical to ensure that the lending decisions and associated policy conditions gain credibility with financial markets. If a regional facility were seen as providing a soft option that reduces incentives for sound policy, the effect may be to increase the risk of crises.

NOTES

We thank Jack Boorman, Gordon de Brouwer, Peta Furnell, Veronique Ingram, Chris Legg, Stephen Miners and Maryanne Mrakovcic for helpful comments on earlier versions of the paper. All errors remain our own. The views expressed here are our own and do not necessarily reflect those of the Australian Treasury.

1   'Private sector involvement' can be interpreted to include any form of private sector response, including voluntary responses. In this paper, we define PSI to be a concerted approach to debt restructuring, involving some form of official coordination.
2   IMF World Economic Outlook Database, December 2001.
3   The US support for Mexico in 1995 could be seen as a forerunner of these arrangements.
4   'New style' crises in fact have similarities to crises that occurred in advanced economies during the gold standard era. The following description by Ben Bernanke (1994) of the process in the Great Depression is remarkably evocative of the Asian crisis.
    'A particularly destabilising aspect of this process was the tendency of fears about the soundness of banks and expectations of exchange rate devaluation to reinforce each other. An element that the two types of crises had in common was the so-called "hot money", short-term deposits held by foreigners in domestic banks. On the one hand, expectations of devaluation induced outflows of the hot money deposits (as well as flight by domestic depositors), which threatened to trigger general bank runs. On the other hand, a fall in confidence in a domestic banking system (arising, for example, from the failure of a major bank) often led to a flight of short-term capital from the country, draining international reserves and threatening convertibility. Other than abandoning the parity altogether, central banks could do little in the face of combined banking and exchange-rate crises, as the former seemed to demand easy money policies while the latter required monetary tightening'.
5   This debate is mainly about the relevance of structural measures to improve medium-term resource allocation; for instance, abolition of the clove monopoly and the national car program in the case of Indonesia. There is little dispute about the relevance of structural measures designed to improve prudential supervision, transparency, and so on.
6   This need not be the case for advanced economies that have strong policy credibility and well-developed institutional frameworks, and hence relatively assured access to financial markets.

7   It needs to be acknowledged also, though, that in 1997 some crisis-affected countries rejected warnings and refused repeated offers of assistance from the IMF until the crisis was in full flight.

8   In contrast to the current discussion in Asia of the relationship between a regional facility and the IMF, relatively little thought about coordination with the IMF appears to have gone into other plurilateral arrangements such as the short-term facilities under the European Monetary System; the G-10 swap network between 1962 and 1998; or the North American Framework Agreement between Canada, Mexico and the United States. On this issue, see Henning (2002).

9   In this regard, regional proposals are similar to some proposals for reform of the IMF, notably the Meltzer Commission Report to the US Congress (Meltzer Report 2000).

10 It is not clear, though, how this might occur unless membership of the facility itself is predicated on having already met criteria related to the pursuit of sound policies. Even then, it leaves unclear the issue of how to deal with a member that subsequently pursues lesser quality policies.

11 Argentina's problem is closer to this concept of 'insolvency'. The concept is, however, somewhat arbitrary when applied to sovereign states, where it is difficult to distinguish between inability to meet debt service commitments and unwillingness to make the difficult adjustments required to do so.

12 The IMF itself was criticised for not addressing PSI early enough in its programs for Asian countries in 1997.

13 That said, the experience of crises in both developed and emerging market economies in recent decades suggests that the capacity, or willingness, of policymakers to be 'far-sighted' can be over-estimated.

REFERENCES

Bernanke, B. (1994) 'The Macroeconomics of the Great Depression: A Comparative Approach', National Bureau of Economic Research Working Paper No. 4814.

Blustein, P. (2001) *The Chastening: Inside the Crisis that Rocked the Global Financial System and Humbled the IMF*, New York: Public Affairs.

Chang, R. and A. Velasco (1998) 'The Asian Liquidity Crisis', NBER Working Paper No. 6796.

Corsetti, G.; P. Pesenti and N. Roubini (1998) 'What caused the Asian currency and financial crisis?', mimeo, New York University.

Costello, P. (1999) *Australia and the IMF 1997–98*, Canberra: Commonwealth of Australia.

Crockett, A. (2000) 'Progress Towards Greater International Financial Stability', speech at the conference 'Reforming the Architecture of Global Economic Institutions', GEI Program, London, 5 May, available at <http://www.bis.org/speeches/index.htm>.

de Brouwer, G. (2003) 'The IMF and East Asia: A Changing Regional Financial Architecture', in Chris Gilbert and David Vines (eds), *The IMF and the International Financial Architecture*, Cambridge: Cambridge University Press.

Dornbusch, R. (2001) 'A Primer on Emerging Market Crises', Massachusetts Institute of Technology.

Feldstein, M. (1998) 'Refocusing the IMF', *Foreign Affairs* 77 (2) (April/May).

Fischer, S, (2001) 'Asia and the IMF', remarks at the Institute of Policy Studies, Singapore, 1 June.

GAO (General Accounting Office) (1996) 'Mexico's Financial Crisis: Origins, Awareness, Assistance, and Initial Efforts to Recover', Washington DC: GAO.

Goldstein, M. (1998) 'The Asian Financial Crisis: Causes, Cures and Systemic Implications', Policy Analyses in International Economics No. 55, Institute for International Economics.

Henning, R. (2002) 'East Asian Financial Cooperation After the Chiang Mai Initiative', *Policy Analyses in International Economics*, No. 68 (September), Institute for International Economics, Washington DC.

IMF (International Monetary Fund) (2001) 'A New Approach to Sovereign Debt Restructuring – Preliminary Considerations', paper presented to IMF Executive Board.

Kaminsky, G. and C. Reinhardt (1999) 'On crises, contagion and confusion', *Journal of International Economics* 51: 145–68.

Kenen, P. (2001) *The International Financial Architecture: What's New? What's Missing?*, Washington DC: Institute for International Economics, Policy Analyses in International Economics No. 68.

Kim T.-J., R. Jai-Won and W. Yunjong (2000) 'Regional Arrangements to Borrow: A Scheme for Preventing Future Asian Liquidity Crises', Seoul: Korea Institute for International Economic Policy.

Kindleberger, C. (2000) *Manias, Panics and Crashes*, Fourth edition, John Wiley and Sons.

Masson, P. (1999) 'Multiple Equilibria, Contagion and the Emerging Market Crises', Working Paper 99/164, Washington DC: International Monetary Fund.

Meltzer Report (2000) Report of the International Financial Institution Advisory Commission, Washington DC, March.

Park, Y.C. (2000) 'Beyond the Chiang Mai Initiative: Rationale and Need for Decision-Making Body and Extended Regional Surveillance under the ASEAN+3 Framework', paper prepared for ASEAN+3 Deputies Meeting, Bangkok.

Radelet, S. and J. Sachs (1998) *The East Asian Financial Crisis: Diagnosis, Remedies, Prospects*, Harvard Institute for International Development.

Rajan, R. (2002) 'Safeguarding against Capital Account Crises: Unilateral, Regional and Multilateral Options for East Asia', Discussion Paper No. 201, Adelaide University: Centre for International Economic Studies.

Yoshitomi, M. and S. Shirai (2000) 'Technical Background Paper for Policy Recommendations for Preventing another Capital Account Crisis', Tokyo: Asian Development Bank Institute.

13 The Basel Process and regional harmonisation in an Asian context

Shinichi Yoshikuni

INTRODUCTION

The globalisation of financial markets worldwide has produced seemingly conflicting results. On the one hand, central banks and regulatory authorities have cooperated to come up with a set of standards to be applied globally, with the so-called Basel Process, setting out requirements for the adequacy of bank capital, serving as one of the central vehicles. On the other hand, repeated episodes of financial crises with volatile market activities have led to calls for regional cooperation between such institutions. As a result, several questions arise. How can we reconcile global standards with regional interests? Is it possible to incorporate regional elements in the Basel Process? Do we need independent regional bodies?

In this paper I seek to address such issues from my own experience as a central bank practitioner.[1] First, I briefly review the recent move towards regionalisation and discuss the concept of globalisation and regionalisation. I then outline the Basel Process and its evolution, with special emphasis on the Basel Capital Accord. Finally, I attempt to answer the three questions posed in the first paragraph of this paper.

THE AGE OF REGIONALISM?

Even before the tragic events of 11 September in the United States, many economists and policy authorities had been talking about the end of globalism. The 1997 Asian crisis and the Russian and long-term capital management (LTCM) crises in 1998 were considered testimony to the failure of globalism. The introduction of capital controls in some countries, and their apparent success, as well as the active involvement of the US central bank on the occasion of the LTCM collapse, gave further proof of the need for public intervention in the global financial system.

At the same time, the role of regional cooperation was emphasised and actually enhanced. In Europe, economic and monetary union is now in its final stage, and the regulatory framework is being harmonised through uniform licensing. In the Asia Pacific region, we have seen a proliferation of economic forums. In addition to existing bodies such as ASEAN and APEC, the Asian financial crisis led to the establishment of the Manila Framework Group (MFG) and ASEAN+3.

The central banks of the Asia Pacific region have strengthened their cooperation through various channels, with the setting up of the South East Asia, New Zealand and Australia (SEANZA) Forum of Banking Supervisors, the South East Asian Central Banks' group (SEACEN) and the Executives Meeting of East Asia and Pacific Central Banks (EMEAP). In particular, the establishment of EMEAP in 1991, and its fundamental reform in 1996,[2] have provided the regional central banks with the opportunity to discuss the various financial issues in an informal and candid manner. The Reserve Bank of Australia (RBA) has played an important role in helping to strengthen central bank cooperation. The call for an Asian bank like the Bank for International Settlements (BIS) by former Governor Fraser of the RBA was an essential factor in the recent trend towards greater regional cooperation.

International financial institutions have also been involved in regional initiatives. Following the Japanese Ministry of Finance proposal to establish an Asian Monetary Fund, the International Monetary Fund (IMF) became deeply incorporated in the MFG and ASEAN+3. Also, the IMF has tried to modify its conditionality so as to more carefully accommodate the specific needs of regional economies, as evidenced by the recent change of attitude towards capital controls.

Meanwhile, the BIS has also strengthened its cooperation with regional central banking forums. The BIS started life as a European – and therefore regional – institution,[3] but its initiative in the context of regionalism took the form of globalising itself. Particularly in the 1990s, many non-European central banks became shareholders. In addition, various Basel-based forums for which the BIS provides the secretariat have given more emphasis to specific regional characteristics in their deliberations on initiatives aimed at the stability of the global financial system. The BIS opened its first representative office for Asia and the Pacific in Hong Kong in 1998 and opened the Hong Kong trading room in 2000. The Hong Kong office has hosted various meetings tailored to the needs of regional central banks. The BIS opened an office for the Americas in Mexico City in 2002.

ARE GLOBALISM AND REGIONALISM MUTUALLY EXCLUSIVE?

Is globalism really dead and has it succumbed to regionalism? My answer is clearly no. One source of confusion here is that there is no universal definition of globalism. It seems to me, however, that behind the notion of the end of globalism is a preoccupation that can be characterised along the following lines: 'globalism is essentially Anglo-Saxon capitalism, and Anglo-Saxon capitalism is based on the unrelenting pursuit of money and profit, which often leads to economic boom and bust or "irrational exuberance" in financial markets; also, it often ignores or even destroys specific social and cultural environments in the regions in which it operates.' If we look back on the history of modern capitalism, however, we can easily see that such an obsession is not always well grounded. In his well-known work on the spirit of capitalism, Max Weber (1904) provided a very thought-provoking picture of American capitalism:

> It is one of the fundamental characteristics of an individualistic capitalistic economy that it is rationalized on the basis of rigorous calculation, directed with foresight and caution toward the economic success which is sought in sharp contrast to the hand-to-mouth existence of the peasant, and to the privileged traditionalism of the guild craftsman and of the adventurers' capitalism, oriented to the exploitation of political opportunities and irrational speculation.

The words 'foresight and caution toward the economic success' are exactly what we today call 'prudence', which central banks and bank supervisors seek to maintain in the global financial system. Of course, the American economy has actually often deviated from this spirit of capitalism, giving way to 'brutal market forces'. Ever since the age of Weber, one of the most important tasks of economic policymakers has been to determine how to instil and maintain prudence or discipline in the economy.

In other words, if the term 'globalism' is defined as the mission to deliver the true spirit of capitalism, it should be accompanied by a mechanism to maintain and enhance the prudential aspect of the economy and financial markets. Also, given the complex and elusive nature of regional economic and financial systems, such a mechanism should be designed to take account of the social and cultural characteristics of economies if it is to be practicable.

On the other hand, if the purpose of regional cooperation is to enhance the economic welfare of the region, it should exploit the opportunity of free trade and the free flow of capital, although due consideration should be given to the sequence of liberalising and globalising the economy. The criticism of regionalism more often than not ignores the benefits of the free economy while at the same time concentrating on its costs.

In sum, I strongly believe that globalism and regionalism are not mutually exclusive concepts. Instead, they are complementary in the sense that, while globalism should be lenient enough to accommodate regional elements, regionalism should be open enough to avoid ending up as regional egoism.

With those general remarks, I would now like to move on to the more concrete issue of how to incorporate regional elements in the context of harmonising prudential regulation.

THE BASEL PROCESS

The current framework of regulatory harmonisation is known as the Basel Process, which is defined as 'groups of national officials coming together to discuss international issues of common interest with a view to reaching decisions about recommended forms of behaviour' (White 1999).

One of the most important products of the Basel Process is the 1988 Basel accord on capital adequacy. The Basel Capital Accord is undergoing fundamental revision, which was to have been completed by the end of 2002, with a view to implementation from 2005. The Capital Accord is often referred to as a symbol of the harmonisation of the regulatory framework of globalised financial markets.

More generally, the Basel Process itself can be seen as a sort of infrastructure to produce standards such as the Capital Accord. In each of the forums constituting the Basel Process – the Basel Committee on Banking Supervision (BCBS), which produced the Capital Accord; the Committee on the Global Financial System (CGFS); the Committee on Payment and Settlement Systems (CPSS); and the International Association of Insurance Supervisors (IAIS) – there is an established governing structure.

First, the BIS provides secretariat services with a high degree of expertise and an open-minded perspective. In particular, a large and complex project such as the Capital Accord requires the constant provision of highly sophisticated analyses to help members to identify problems and issues for discussion. It is important to have a clear division of labour between the secretariat and the committee itself, so that decisions are made by the committee based upon frank and high-quality discussions. It is often pointed out that meetings organised by international institutions tend to lack candid and informal discussions, since they are dominated by the conclusions prepared by the staff of the institution. In my view, most of the Basel-based meetings have avoided this bureaucratic syndrome, since the secretariats work to enhance open and high-quality discussions rather than trying to 'guide' the debate in a certain direction.[4]

Second, each committee is organised efficiently so as to ensure that every meeting lives up to the expectations of the members. In the case of banking supervision, the BCBS, at the time of writing chaired by William McDonough, President of the Federal Reserve Bank of New York, is made up of high-level experts from central banks and bank supervisors. In addition, permanent working groups have been formed to discuss particular issues. An example is the Models Task Force, which deals with internal ratings-based approaches to assessing credit risk, which is one of the key issues in the current revision of the Capital Accord (Basel II). The task force was already responsible for developing the 'market risk approach' (see below); it now also works out the proposals to be discussed by the BCBS.

Currently, more than 40 working groups, including many *ad hoc* and temporary groups, are active under the BCBS umbrella. People often criticise this arrangement for having too many working groups and for constituting an increasing burden on the member central banks and supervisors. To some extent, this is an inevitable consequence of the Basel Process, since the banking business has become more complex and sophisticated; the Capital Accord itself should reflect such new realities.

In a nutshell, the Basel Process is a mechanism which provides the international financial community with the opportunity to explore good governance in various regulatory and supervisory issues based on a frank exchange of views supported by highly sophisticated groundwork.

The influence of market participants

The Basel Process has evolved over time, reflecting the development of the global financial system. In particular, the rapid advances in financial products and in risk management at financial institutions have required all the Basel-based forums to take the process into account in their deliberations. The incorporation of market risk in the Capital Accord framework in 1996,[5] and the associated internal models approach, is a good example.

Even before the current fundamental review of the accord, the BCBS had made various changes to the original accord. The market risk proposal added a new element to the Basel Process, the internal models approach. In retrospect, this was a sort of revolution in the area of banking supervision and regulatory regimes in general. Contrary to the credit risk element, where the accord unilaterally specified the risk weight according to the regulatory category of the credit, the internal models approach allows commercial banks to use their internal risk management models to calculate the risk associated with their trading portfolios with certain provisos.

The introduction of the internal model approach was in response to a strong request from the private banking industry as part of the process of gathering public comments on the first proposal in 1993. This practice of public comment is one of the important characteristics of the Basel Process, aimed at rendering the supervisory process transparent and market-based.

I was closely involved in this market risk proposal at the Bank of Japan (BOJ), and I still recall the strong impact on us when the original proposal, not including internal models, was seen by some financial institution risk managers to be behind modern risk management practice. At that time, even within the BOJ, very few people knew such terms as 'value-at-risk' and 'stress testing'. The method presented in the original proposal for measuring market risk was essentially the same as the one adopted in credit risk measurement – based on the risk weights specified unilaterally by the Basel Committee.

Commercial banks, particularly US money centre banks that had already introduced a sophisticated risk management system based on value-at-risk models, strongly criticised the proposal. They stressed that the proposal would force them to maintain regulatory capital which was different from the 'economic capital' that they considered relevant based on their more sophisticated risk management models. Moreover, they would be forced to make quite a few information technology investments simply to comply with the new regulation.

The revised proposal offered two alternatives for measuring market risk: standardised and internal model methods. This practice of offering options is a very important element of the current Basel Process. On the one hand, it makes the standard applicable to a wide range of financial institutions by enabling them to use a simple method. On the other hand, its aim was to encourage banks to enhance their risk management skills so as to be able to avail themselves of internal models.

In the ongoing fundamental review of the Capital Accord, the lessons learned from past experiences, such as the market risk proposal, have been well taken into account. From the outset, the BCBS established close contact with major financial institutions with a view to incorporating the most advanced credit risk measurement models in the proposal. On the other hand, the proposal offers a variety of choices as to the measurement of both credit risk and operational risk, both of which include the use of internal models. This so-called 'evolutionary approach' enables banks to choose a methodology which fits their business practices and risk management skills.

Furthermore, the proposal added an important new element in the Capital Accord. In addition to the 'minimum capital requirements' (called Pillar I in the proposal), it includes 'supervisory reviews' (Pillar II) and 'market discipline' (Pillar III). They are expected to ensure and enhance the effectiveness of the accord through the constant dialogue between the supervisors and financial institutions (Pillar II) and high disclosure standards (Pillar III). This new element can also accommodate the regional elements that are difficult to incorporate in the minimum capital ratio.

Many people have criticised the details of the new accord, but most have supported its basic thrust as being consistent with market practice.[6]

Cooperation among Basel-based committees

An important development in the Basel Process is the strengthening of cooperation among the various committees. In addition to the main Basel-based committees – BCBS, CGFS, CPSS and IAIS – the International Organization of Securities Commissions (IOSCO) is now a broadly defined component of the Basel Process. The BCBS (commercial banks), IOSCO (securities houses) and IAIS (insurance companies) deal with the supervisory and regulatory issues of specific segments of financial institutions. The CGFS deals with macro-prudential issues and the CPSS with payment and settlement system issues; they aim to monitor the infrastructure of the international financial system in general.

The deregulation and globalisation of financial markets have necessitated cooperation among these committees on two grounds.

First, deregulation concerning the scope of business conducted by financial institutions has led to a blurring of the dividing line between banks, securities companies and insurance companies, if not their disappearance. It has resulted in a remarkable change in the regulatory framework, as evidenced by the establishment of independent supervisory agencies covering all types of financial institutions. It has also heightened the need for closer contact between the three committees dealing with banks, securities companies and insurance companies in order to maintain a level playing field among the various segments of financial institutions. A result has been the establishment of a joint forum of the three committees in 1996.

Second, the globalisation of financial markets has increased the need for interaction between the overall stability of the financial system (macro-prudence) and the soundness of the individual institutions (micro-prudence), particularly with respect to financial institutions with global networks. Hence, both the CGFS and the CPSS have strengthened ties with the other three committees in the Basel Process.[7]

The implementation and monitoring of various standards established by these meetings have increased in importance. For example, the Core Principles for Effective Banking Supervision developed by the BCBS have become the most significant global standard for banking supervision. The need for such standards was demonstrated by the Asian crisis, a major cause of which was lack of effective supervision. In this connection, the role of the Bretton Woods institutions is also essential and complementary. The IMF and the World Bank, for example, have introduced a Financial Sector Assessment Program (FSAP) and Reports on the Observance of Standards and Codes (ROSCs). In a similar vein, the Financial Stability Forum (FSF) was convened in 1999 as a comprehensive framework in which to coordinate the efforts of various international financial institutions and committees.

In sum, the infrastructure for setting standards for the global financial system and the infrastructure for implementing them are now more closely coordinated under the FSF umbrella. They can be broadly described as part of the Basel Process, given that the BIS provides the secretariat for both.

REGIONAL HARMONISATION IN THE CONTEXT OF THE BASEL PROCESS

How can we reconcile global standards with regional interests?

As I have pointed out, there is no real trade-off between global and regional interests. What is important is not whether a mechanism is globally or regionally oriented but whether it strikes a good balance between efficiency and prudence, or between dynamism and discipline.

It seems to me that the word 'globalisation' is usually associated with efficiency and dynamism. In fact, it is often used with such words as 'liberalisation' and 'deregulation', aimed at maximum exploitation of market forces. The regional character of the economy has generally been considered to complement such a market solution by providing a counterweight to serve as a moderating influence. In other words, maintaining a regional element in the economy could instil and maintain prudence and discipline in the economy.

There is, however, a strong caveat. A typical example of such a system is the long-term decision-making in East Asian countries represented by the

Japanese main bank system and the close relationship between the government and *chaebol* conglomerates in Korea. In the 1980s, East Asian countries and international financial institutions such as the World Bank credited such systems with bringing about the 'East Asian miracle' of high economic growth with low inflation (World Bank 1993; Aoki and Patrick 1994).

However, such 'Asian cronyism' was seen as the main cause of the Asian crisis in 1997 (Krugman 1998). There are still many schools of thought as to what really caused the Asian crisis, but it is now evident that some special characteristics of the Asian economies accelerated the excessive economic boom rather than acting as a brake. This provides an important lesson for regional economic cooperation: any rule or standard should be constantly reviewed in the light of its original purpose. The nature of regional rules evolves over time and rules can have quite a different impact from the one originally intended if other environments change. In particular, when the overall framework of an economy changes as a result of globalisation, it is sometimes counterproductive to artificially maintain regional rules. It is essential for policy authorities in any regional economy to have a clear understanding of the actual interaction between global and regional economic systems. Such understanding should be duly reflected in any global standards or rules.

Is it possible to incorporate regional elements in the Basel Process?

The Basel Process has already incorporated regional interests in its deliberations to some extent. Both the BIS and the Basel-based committees have modified their structures so as to better reflect the opinions of emerging market economies. An example is the Basel Committee's formation of the Core Principles Liaison Group, consisting of G-10 and non-G-10 senior supervisors, the IMF and the World Bank, and its strengthened ties with regional groups. In Asia, both the Basel Committee and the BIS regularly send experts to EMEAP, SEACEN and SEANZA meetings; the Financial Stability Institute and the BIS Hong Kong office are also active.

The evolution of the Basel Process should be viewed in the light of interaction with such regional bodies. A good example is the paper of the EMEAP Working Group on Banking Supervision on the second consultative paper of the New Basel Accord (May 2001); among 250 papers submitted to the Basel Committee, this was the only one to represent the collective views of regional central banks. The continued strengthening of such cooperative efforts can resolve conflicts between global standards and regional interests.

It is, however, easier said than done. There is a good example of how difficult it is to come up with truly relevant standards that duly take account of regional economic characteristics. In Japan, many economists have pointed out that the procyclical nature of the Capital Accord accelerated lending by Japanese commercial banks and helped create the financial asset bubble of the latter half of the 1980s. They also say that, after the bursting of the bubble, the accord accelerated deflation through the same mechanism. Under the current accord, 45 per cent of the latent profit in banks' equity portfolios is counted as tier 2 capital (up to the level of the narrowly defined core capital, tier 1). Hence, according to the critics of the accord, when the economy is booming, the rise in stock prices will increase the capital base and the capacity of banks to lend, resulting in excess lending. By the same token, the accord would lead to an excessive contraction of banking credit in a slump.

Such a criticism is not limited to Japan. In fact, the procyclical nature of the accord is still one of the controversial points in the ongoing revision of the accord. My personal view is that the main driving force behind the excess bank lending in Japan was the asset price bubble in the real estate sector. After the bubble burst, the decline in stock prices at some points in time served as a constraint on bank lending, in particular in 1997 and 1998, when Japan faced the real danger of a credit crunch.

I do not wish to say that the treatment of equity holdings in the Capital Accord was wrong. In fact, it was carefully designed to accommodate the special requests of the Japanese banking community, while at the same time preserving discipline by adding an appropriate haircut. What was wrong? In my view, what should have been addressed was the fact that Japanese banks had enormous equity portfolios as a result of cross-holdings with closely related companies under the main bank system. In the pre-bubble period, the system worked efficiently to ensure good corporate governance. Meanwhile, the unrealised gain cushioned bank profits, which in turn enabled banks to provide financial assistance if companies got into trouble.

In the bubble period, this system changed completely. The asset price bubble resulted in excessive bank lending, as I have mentioned. Furthermore, the rapid and persistent increase in the price of collateral (particularly real estate) discouraged banks from strengthening their risk management practices.[8]

Be that as it may, the treatment of the latent profit on equity portfolios was strongly requested by the Japanese authorities, backed by Japanese commercial banks, which at that time had enormous latent profits. This episode brings me to the fundamental challenge facing the Basel Process. Setting standards cannot replace good risk management on the part of individual banks in individual countries. What is important is ultimately the ability and willingness of individual supervisors and financial institutions to enforce discipline in the financial system. Any rules or standards – be they regional or global – should be assessed from the viewpoint of whether they can help to instil such discipline.

Do we need a regional regulatory institution?

Finally, I would like to touch upon the issue of whether we need a regional supervisory institution. My answer is yes and no.

First, as far as the Basel Process is concerned, the recent efforts aimed at incorporating the non-G-10 supervisors in the decision-making process should be further enhanced. The evolution of the Basel Process has already made its products flexible enough to be tailored to the needs of specific regions or countries, as evidenced by the variety of choices offered by the new Basel proposal. The pillar approach of the proposed new accord would further the efforts of regional supervisors in this connection. There have been some complaints about the complexity of the revised proposal, but the complexity reflects the efforts to incorporate as many views as possible.

I am somewhat sceptical about the possibility of establishing an independent supervisory body aimed at regional harmonisation in the Asia Pacific region. Even in Europe, where an EU-wide uniform regulatory framework is being put in place, there is no consensus about the integration of supervisory institutions. Furthermore, all the EU supervisors have committed to the Basel Process by enacting the Capital Accord and subscribing to the core principles.

On the other hand, I fully support the idea of strengthening cooperation between regional supervisors. As I mentioned at the outset, I welcome recent initiatives to enhance financial assistance, particularly in the context of ASEAN+3. As a result, it seems to me that, as far as financial support is concerned, regional cooperation in the Asian region has already reached a much higher level than at the time of the Asian crisis.[9] Such financial arrangements are aimed at helping each other; we also need a regional body for monitoring each other and for sharing experiences, to instil discipline in the regional economies. Helping each other can be viewed as crisis management and monitoring each other as crisis prevention.

I conclude by reflecting on the experience of Europe. I believe that two important factors led to the introduction of the euro. One is the fact that EMU stands for economic and monetary union, not European Monetary Union as some people mistakenly think. Without the convergence of the real economy through the long and unrelenting process starting from the European Coal and Steel Community, the Maastricht Treaty, which is the essential element of monetary union, could not have been brought to life. In thinking about possible future regional relations and institutions in East Asia, it is essential to keep focus on the real economic dimensions of integration.

The other is the existence of the German Bundesbank as the anchor of stability. The Bundesbank not only served as a virtual monetary policy board for Europe even before the establishment of the European Central Bank but also pursued stability for the overall financial system by consistently advocating prudent banking policies. While financial arrangements such as the European Monetary System and the exchange rate mechanism provided the crisis management mechanism, the basic discipline-oriented policies of EU countries at the national level served as the effective basis for crisis prevention. Regional institution building is no substitute for robust, stable economic management at the national level.

I reiterate that central banks and supervisory authorities in the Asia Pacific region should enhance cooperation, not only to actively participate in standard-setting processes such as that of the Basel Committee but also, more importantly, to maintain and enhance good governance of the financial systems in their own economies.

NOTES

1   As a staff member in the International Department of the Bank of Japan, I was involved in a series of discussions about financial derivatives and risk management at financial institutions, which involved two Basel-based committees – the Basel Committee on Bank Supervision (BCBS) and the Euro-currency Standing Committee (now the Committee on the Global Financial System). I was also closely involved in fostering cooperation between Asian central banks in the context of the Executive Meeting of East Asia and Pacific Central Banks. The opinions expressed in this paper are personal and not related to those of the BIS or Bank of Japan.

2   EMEAP is a group of 11 central banks in the region. It started as a regular meeting at deputy governor level. In 1996, the banks involved established regular governors meetings and three working groups.

3   The BIS was originally established to deal with the redemption of Germany's national debt after World War I, so its shareholdership and board membership have been centred on European central banks. Also, before the establishment of the European Monetary Institute (the precursor of the European Central Bank), the BIS served as a fulcrum of cooperation between European central banks.

4   An analogy is the decision-making process for monetary policy now used by a number of major central banks, in which decisions are taken through an independent monetary policy committee consisting at least partly, and often dominantly, of outside members. This new system should ensure independence not just from the political arena but also from the bureaucracy of central banking.

5   Amendment to the Capital Accord to incorporate market risks, BCBS, January 1996.

6   The Basel Committee has published the comments of both central banks and private institutions on the second version of the Basel II proposal.

7   One symbolic event was a joint meeting of three working group chairs dealing with the issue of financial derivatives. The meeting was held in Paris in 1995 between Danièle Nouy (representing the BCBS working group), Tim Sheperd-Walwyn (representing IOSCO) and me (representing the Euro-currency Standing Committee, now the Committee on the Global Financial System). In retrospect, derivatives made the financial markets more global and interdependent, making it necessary for such committees to strengthen cooperation.

8   In the context of the internal ratings-based approach in the new Capital Accord proposal, in the bubble period 'loss given default' of Japanese bank lending was always considered to be zero, so the banks did not have to worry about the probability of default.

9   In addition to the regional financing arrangement, the level of multilateral financial support has also increased as a result of the various arrangements in relation to IMF-supported programs such as the New Arrangements to Borrow, the contingent credit line and the Supplementary Reserve Facility.

REFERENCES

Aoki, M. and H. Patrick (eds) (1994) *The Japanese Main Bank System*, Oxford: Oxford University Press.

Krugman, P. (1998) 'What happened to Asia', available at <http://www.hartford-hwp.com/archives/50/010.html>.

Weber, M. (1904) *The Protestant Ethic and the Spirit of Capitalism*, translated by Talcott Parsons, London: Allen & Unwin (1930).

White, W. R. (1999) 'Mr White discusses the Asian crisis and the Bank for International Settlements', paper presented at the conference on 'Asia and the future of the world economic systems', Royal Institute of International Affairs, London, 17–18 March 1999. Available at <http://www.bis.org/review/r990331a.pdf>.

World Bank (1993) *The East Asian Miracle: Economic Growth and Public Policy*, Oxford: Oxford University Press.

Index

Printed and bound by CPI Group (UK) Ltd, Croydon, CR0 4YY

01/05/2025

01858362-0002